CHARTIST REVOLUTION

Rob Sewell

Wellred Books
London

Chartist Revolution
Rob Sewell

Wellred Books, October 2020

UK distribution: Wellred Books, wellredbooks.net
PO Box 50525
London
E14 6WG
books@wellredbooks.net

USA distribution: Marxist Books, marxistbooks.com
WR Books
250 44th Street #208
Brooklyn
New York
NY 11232
sales@marxistbooks.com

DK distribution: Forlaget Marx, forlagetmarx.dk
Degnestavnen 19, st. tv.
2400 København NV
forlag@forlagetmarx.dk

Cover design by Ben Curry

Cover image by Sergei Yakutovich with permission from Progress Publishers

Layout by Wellred Books

All images from public domain apart from 3, from Llyfrgell
Genedlaethol Cymru – The National Library of Wales.

ISBN: 978 1 913 026 18 9

To the memory of Phil Mitchinson (1968-2006)

"All men dream, but not equally. Those who dream by night in the dusty recesses of their minds, wake in the day to find that it was vanity: but the dreamers of the day are dangerous men, for they may act out their dream with open eyes, to make it possible."

– T.E. Lawrence, 'Seven Pillars of Wisdom'

CONTENTS

Preface   IX

Introduction   XXIII

1. "Dripping with Blood from Every Pore"   1

2. Sowing the Seeds   35

3. The Birth of Chartism   91

4. Masses on the Move   129

5. The Newport Uprising   175

6. The First Ever Working-Class Party   197

7. The 1842 General Strike   219

8. 1848: A Critical Year   273

9. Twilight and Legacy   317

10. Marxism and Chartism   363

Appendix: Internationalism   383

Chronology   387

Bibliography   395

PREFACE

The great cities are the birthplaces of labour movements; in them the workers first began to reflect upon their own condition, and to struggle against it; in them the opposition between proletariat and bourgeoisie first made itself manifest; from them proceeded the trades unions, Chartism, and Socialism.

– F. Engels, *The Condition of the Working Class in England,* 1844.

Some simpletons talk of knowledge making the working classes more obedient, more dutiful – better servants, better subjects and so on, which means making them more subservient slaves and more conducive to the wealth and gratification of idlers of all descriptions. But such knowledge is trash; the only knowledge which is of service to the working people is that which makes them more dissatisfied, and makes them worse slaves. This knowledge we shall give them.

– B. O'Brien, *Destructive,* June 1834.[1]

FIRST OF ITS KIND

"Why should one man be a slave to another? Why should the many starve, while the few roll in luxuries? Who'll join us, and be free?"

"I will," cried I, jumping up in the midst. "I will, and be the most zealous among you – give me a card and let me enrol."

"And so, Lord John, I became a Rebel – that is to say – Hungry in a land of plenty, I began seriously for the first time in my life to enquire WHY, WHY – a dangerous question, Lord John, isn't it, for a poor man to ask?"[2]

---

1 Quoted in S. Harrison, *Poor Men's Guardians,* p. 103.

2 *How I became a Rebel,* quoted in D. Thompson, *The Early Chartists,* p. 85.

Chartism was a revolutionary movement, the first of its kind, made up of millions of workers who asked similar questions. It was one of the greatest popular movements in British history. It represented a display of working-class consciousness and power that pushed Britain to the very brink of revolution. The British working class showed through Chartism that it was capable of revolutionary struggle. Such things may seem out of character with the seemingly mild-mannered British temperament, perhaps more in line with the French or Italian, but they form a crucial part of the experience of the working class of these islands. On this basis alone, the history of the Chartist movement deserves detailed study.

Engels remarked that the Chartist period displayed "the most advanced class struggle the world has seen".[3] In the decade from 1838 to 1848, the mass movement that swept the country threatened to topple the British establishment, its wealth, its power and its extensive empire. It would be no exaggeration to say that, in the last two hundred years, the working class has never come so close to taking power as then. This is certainly how contemporaries saw it. "A spark would ignite the combustible material and bring upon us all the horrors of servile [civil] war", complained Lieutenant Colonel Pringle Taylor.[4] "In living in it all, I always feel as if I were toasting muffins at a volcano", observed the colourful Lord Francis Egerton, a Lancashire landowner.[5]

Britain was in the grip of revolutionary upheavals, events which certainly resonate with us today. In the nineteenth century, Chartism was considered as dangerous as Bolshevism was in the twentieth century. The propertied classes reacted to this threat in the usual manner, with brutal class laws, treachery, imprisonment, chains, racks, gibbets, solitary confinement, transportation to penal colonies, as well as the spectre of public hangings. Ruthlessness was not a characteristic in which they were lacking.

The English judicial system still maintained on the statute books the medieval practice of perpetrators being hanged, drawn and quartered.[6] The majority of such executions were for offences against property. In February 1803, the executioner held up the head of his victim before a London crowd:

---

3   Marx and Engels Collected Works (Henceforth referred to as MECW), vol. 7, p. 297.

4   R. Brown & C. Daniels, *The Chartists, Documents & Debates*, p. 53.

5   M. Chase, *Chartism: A New History*, p. 192.

6   Some habits die hard. Although capital punishment was abolished in 1969 (1973 in Northern Ireland), you could still officially be hanged for treason up until 1998, when it was scrapped under the Crime and Disorder Act, only twenty-odd years ago.

"Behold the head of a traitor!" Edward Marcus Despard and six of his comrades had been found guilty of treason and died with fortitude. Despard, a member of the London Corresponding Society and the United Irishmen, declared he was innocent, but died because he was "a friend to the poor and the oppressed."[7]

In 1820, the Cato Street conspirators were also executed in full public view. After half an hour of being throttled by hanging, their bodies were lowered one at a time and decapitated with a carving knife. They were, I suppose, fortunate. Seven years earlier and their sentences could have included their heart and bowels being torn from their bodies while still alive. It was a savage and cruel reminder of what to expect for those – 'the lawless and furious rabble' – who dared challenge the power of the propertied classes. These defenders of private property and executors of state terror were the "bloodhounds" that Shelley talked of, which famously chewed on human hearts.

As the spectre of revolution cast its long shadow, the Chartist movement waged a courageous battle for democratic rights that was inextricably bound up with the fight for working-class emancipation. If a revolution can be defined as the direct interference of the masses in the destiny of a country, then Britain was certainly in the throes of such turmoil. Through their audacity, the common people – those who had no rights – sought to turn the world upside down so that those at the bottom would replace those at the top. Or, more accurately, they wanted to do away altogether with both top and bottom. They certainly did not lack courage, determination or self-sacrifice. They were prepared to "storm heaven", to quote the words of Marx in describing the Communards in Paris. Unfortunately, the Chartist leaders, who undoubtedly possessed a proletarian outlook, were nevertheless still feeling their way and were unsure as to what steps were needed to succeed.

I finished writing this book amid the greatest crisis that capitalism has ever experienced. The Bank of England announced it would be the deepest economic slump in 300 years, apparently since 1709, one which breaks all known records. The UK's Office for Budget Responsibility confirmed a likely economic crash on a scale not seen since the early eighteenth century. Even Karl Marx could not have envisaged a crisis of such magnitude.

For me, this makes the book more relevant than ever. Triggered by the effects of a virus, an organism no bigger than one-thousandth of the diameter of a human hair, all the accumulated contradictions of capitalism over the past decades have come to the surface with a vengeance. The apologists of the

---

7   E.P. Thompson, *The Making of the English Working Class*, p. 515.

'market economy,' the economic quacks, deny that it is a crisis of capitalism. But, in the words of Mandy Rice-Davies, 'they would say that wouldn't they?' The coronavirus was simply an accident that revealed a deeper necessity, as the German philosopher Hegel would have said. All the factors for a world slump were already present; in fact, the world economy was already dramatically slowing down. Now, dialectically, cause becomes effect, and effect becomes cause, as all factors interact upon one another, further intensifying and deepening the world crisis.

If there is a parallel with the Black Death of the Fourteenth century, it is that the COVID-19 pandemic is accelerating the demise of capitalism in the same way as the Black Death accelerated the breakdown of feudalism. Both were natural disasters that accentuated the economic, social and political collapse already taking place. "The Black Death … made the greatest single contribution to the disintegration of an age," wrote the historian Philip Ziegler.[8] The same could be said of this pandemic, which is intensifying the capitalist crisis.

Ominously, the former United States Secretary of State, Henry Kissinger, warned of global economic doom in the *Wall Street Journal*, issuing a dire proclamation that "failure could set the world on fire".[9] A new Great Depression is staring us in the face, on a scale like the 1930s or even worse. Growing mass unemployment, worsening austerity and falling living standards are symptoms of a social system in terminal decline, the features of a protracted death agony of capitalism.

APOLOGISTS FOR CAPITALISM

Only our grandparents or great-grandparents have experienced anything even approaching such a thing. The strategists of capitalism repeatedly told us that a crisis like this could never happen. According to Alan Greenspan, the former chairman of the Federal Reserve, the 2008 crisis was supposed to have been a "once-in-a-century event". Now it looks like a recurring crisis every decade. Of course, they assured us that they had learned the lessons of the past and that an 'invisible hand' would take care of us. Such assurances seem to confirm the view of Hegel that the only thing you learn from history is that nobody learns from history.

Of course, this poses the question: why study a workers' movement in Britain in the 1830s and 1840s, almost 200 years ago? I, for one, after studying

---

8 P. Zeigler, *The Black Death*, p. 288.
9 *Wall Street Journal*, 3 April 2020.

the subject, firmly believe that Chartism does have a special relevance for today. There are, of course, significant and obvious differences between the Chartist period and the present time. But I would argue there are also definite similarities or parallels. "'Life's a tumble-about thing of ups and downs', said Widow Carey, stirring her tea, 'but I have been down this time longer than I can ever remember.'" These lines, which have a modern ring to them, are from Disraeli's novel *Sybil*, published in 1845, when Chartism cast a long shadow across Britain.[10]

No doubt, many readers will be familiar with Charles Dickens' wonderful story, *A Christmas Carol*, written in the spring of 1843, again at the height of Chartism. In the beginning, Ebenezer Scrooge, the money-grabbing employer, is visited by two philanthropists. The scene is very revealing in its description of bourgeois morality. The lines on the page read as follows:

"At this festive season of the year, Mr Scrooge," said the gentlemen, taking up a pen, "it is more than usually desirable that we should make some slight provision for the poor and destitute, who suffer greatly at the present time. Many thousands are in want of common necessaries; hundreds of thousands are in want of common comforts, sir."

"Are there no prisons?" asked Scrooge.

"Plenty of prisons," said the gentleman, laying down the pen again.

"And the Union workhouses?" demanded Scrooge. "Are they still in operation?"

"They are. Still," returned the gentlemen, "I wish I could say they were not."

"The Treadmill and the Poor Law are in full vigour, then?" said Scrooge.

"Both very busy, sir."

"Oh! I was afraid, from what you said at first, that something had occurred to stop them in their useful course," said Scrooge. "I am very glad to hear it."

"Under the impression that they scarcely furnish Christian cheer of mind or body to the multitude," returned the gentlemen, "a few of us are endeavouring to raise a fund to buy the Poor some meat and drink, and means of warmth. We choose this time, because it is a time, of all others, when Want is keenly felt, and Abundance rejoices. What shall I put you down for?"

"Nothing!" Scrooge replied.

"You wish to be anonymous?"

"I wish to be left alone," said Scrooge. "Since you ask me what I wish, gentlemen, that is my answer. I don't make merry myself at Christmas, and I can't afford to make idle people merry. I help to support the establishments I have mentioned – they cost enough: and those who are badly off must go there."

---

10 B. Disraeli, *Sybil*, p. 325.

"Many can't go there; and many would rather die."

"If they would rather die," said Scrooge, "they had better do it, and decrease the surplus population."[11]

This is a vivid example, typical of Dickens, of the real morality of bourgeois society, and not only of the nineteenth century. It is a view presently held at the top of today's Conservative Party and government. A *Sunday Times* report claimed that at one private event at the end of February 2020 to discuss the pandemic, Dominic Cummings, the prime minister's chief advisor, outlined the government's strategy, which was summarised by some present as "herd immunity, protect the economy, and *if that means some pensioners die, too bad.*"

How different is this from the view held by Nassau Senior, the popular nineteenth century economist? He feared the famine in Ireland in the 1840s would 'only' kill a million people, which would 'scarcely be enough to do much good'.

Of course, Downing Street put out a statement denying the claim, but Cummings' views are notorious. He had suggested that the NHS should cover the cost of selecting babies to have higher IQs. At the beginning of 2020, Cummings called for "misfits and weirdos" to work in 10 Downing Street, which led to the appointment of Andrew Sabisky, who was soon forced to step down because of previously stated views: from claiming that black people have low IQs to asking whether benefit claimants should be encouraged to have fewer children.

These are today's vulgar Malthusians, alive and still kicking, who are dead set against the poor breeding, and are no different whatsoever from those of the 1840s, so vividly described by Dickens. The obscene wealth gap between rich and poor has never been greater than today. The 'Law of Increasing Misery,' as it became known, is clear for all to see. The Poor Law and the workhouses, the cruellest of imaginings, have been replaced with Universal Credit and the whip of benefit sanctions, where payments are withheld from the most vulnerable. It is no accident that Margaret Thatcher was fond of 'Victorian values' and presided over a vicious class war against the working class and the most vulnerable of society. "This country's getting Dickensian", stated Maxine Peake, the actor who starred in Mike Leigh's film *Peterloo*. A glance at the garment industry in Leicester, where workers in sweatshops earn £3.50 an hour, would confirm this view.

---

11 C. Dickens, 'A Christmas Carol', in *Christmas Books*, London 1876, pp. 9-10.

Many things have changed, we are told, and yet so much remains the same, including the vile, revolting hypocrisy of the political representatives of the ruling class. Today, British workers have already experienced the biggest fall in real wages for any decade since the Peterloo massacre of 1819. What we now face is a return to the 1930s, or probably worse. Austerity will be intensified. That will bring horror without end for millions. In other words, Britain is entering an unprecedented economic, social and political crisis. These are not the birth pains capitalism experienced in the first half of the nineteenth century, but the symptoms of its terminal decay. It has been a long time in the making, but now that it has finally arrived, it will be a thousand times worse.

This organic or endemic crisis was predicted well in advance by Marxists, who understood the contradictions of capitalism and the inherent crises that stem from them. This idea was ridiculed by the supporters of capitalism, including the reformists. Today, with the greatest slump in history, the downswing is plain for all to see, and confirms the absolute correctness of Marxism as opposed to the bragging of the bourgeois economists. As in Chartist times, the British ruling class are once again haunted by the prospect of revolutionary upheavals, at home and abroad. They are right to be alarmed. The working class is now a thousand times stronger and comprises the overwhelming majority of the population.

The relevance of this book is shown by the fact that this deep crisis poses the same fundamental questions that confronted the Chartist movement so long ago: how can the working class attain real political power? How can we put an end to this system of exploitation?

I have been politically active for more than half a century, arguing the case for Marxism and the revolutionary transformation of society. I personally have never seen such a situation as this, and neither has anyone else. The reformist way of gradual, incremental, piecemeal reforms has been tried for decades and has clearly failed. It is like using a leaky bucket to empty the ocean.

In this epoch of capitalist crisis, the idea of patching up the system or creating a 'nicer' capitalism is a dead end and the most utopian of dreams. The idea that tomorrow will be better than today and the day after tomorrow better still, which found its expression in reformism, has died a death. The capitalist crisis is producing terrible convulsions that threaten to push society towards barbarism. A horrendous period of austerity and attacks now confronts the working class, as faced by the working class in the first half of the nineteenth century. Everything has come full circle. Only a root and branch solution is now possible and that means the overthrow of capitalism and its replacement with a socialist planned economy. However, this is not an automatic process.

As Leon Trotsky explained:

> Marx did not imply that socialism would come about without man's volition and action: any such idea is simply an absurdity. Marx foretold that out of the economic collapse in which the development of capitalism must inevitably culminate – and this collapse is before our very eyes – there can be no other way out except socialisation of the means of production. The productive forces need a new organiser and a new master, and, since existence determines consciousness, Marx had no doubt that the working class, at the cost of errors and defeats, will come to understand the actual situation and, sooner or later, will draw the imperative practical conclusions.[12]

HISTORY IN THE MAKING

The glorious history of Chartism is therefore far from being an academic study, as is the case with so many history books. It is a history, a tradition, a case study for the here and now. "History", explained the celebrated historian, E.H. Carr, is "an unending dialogue between the present and the past". It is certainly not, in the words of Arnold Toynbee, "just one damn fact after another", bereft of meaning and incapable of interpretation. History would have zero value if it actually taught us nothing. Mark Twain, in emphasising the similarities between different historical periods, is reputed to have said that "history doesn't repeat itself, but it often rhymes." The task before us is to draw out the generalisations from past experience, so as to illuminate the way forward. To be forewarned is to be forearmed.

Lenin and Trotsky, the leaders of the Bolshevik Party, explained that without studying the lessons of the Great French Revolution, the revolutions of 1848, the Paris Commune, as well as the 'dress rehearsal' of 1905, there would have been no October Revolution in 1917. In other words, for them, a revolution cannot be improvised, but needs to be studied and prepared for seriously.

The driving force of history, as Marx explained, is the class struggle. It is made by and through men and women, but under conditions not of their own making. To fully understand history, we need to understand the struggle of different classes, parties, groupings and their leaders, and what actually motivated them. In this fashion we can truly dissect the anatomy of a movement; in our case, Chartism.

---

12 *The Age of Permanent Revolution: A Trotsky Anthology*, p. 224.

I write this book as a participant. My object is to shine a light on the remarkable experience of Chartism for today. However, I believe my political involvement in the labour movement over many years provides me with important insights into Chartism. Karl Kautsky, the German Marxist, made a similar point before the First World War, and quoted the words of the French philosopher Jean-Jacques Rousseau:

> "I think it is foolish to try to study society as a mere bystander. The man that wants only to observe, observes nothing; as he is useless in business and a dead weight in amusements, he is not drawn into anything. We see others' actions only to the extent that we act ourselves. In the school of the world, as in love's school, we have to start by practicing what we want to learn."[13]

He was correct. We are not simply bystanders, but stand unashamedly on the side of revolutionary Chartism and the movement to change society. In doing so, we become part of their struggle, feel their pain and excitement, but more importantly, we strive to learn from their experiences. Their struggle certainly resonates with today, and so does their audacity.

When he addressed the Labour Party conference on 26 September 2018, Jeremy Corbyn, its then-leader, quoted the following lines from 'The Song of the Low', written by the leading Chartist and socialist Ernest Jones:

> And what we get – and what we give
> We know – and we know our share.
> We're not too low the cloth to weave –
> But too low the cloth to wear.

He used these words to explain that in order to obtain economic justice it would be necessary to redistribute not only wealth, but also political power.

Ernest Jones, however, saw the questions of wealth and power as directly linked to the overthrow of capitalism, linked to the social and economic emancipation of the working class. Jones regarded himself as a revolutionary and ended his composition with the words:

> And yet when the trumpets ring,
> The thrust of a poor man's arm will go
> Through the heart of the proudest king!

The class struggle has coloured the whole of written history. The emergence of capitalism brought into being two new classes, defined by their relation to the

---

13 Quoted in K. Kautsky, *Foundations of Christianity*, p. xii.

means of production: a capitalist class and a working class, whose destinies are interlinked, but whose interests are irreconcilable.

The Chartist movement is part of an historic pageant that stretches back to before the birth of capitalism. For those looking to change society, it is essential to have a sense of history. The Chartists are our revolutionary predecessors: men and women who made Herculean sacrifices in the struggle for a better life. They speak to us down the ages, bequeathing to the new generation the banner of struggle. In that sense, Chartism is *our* history. We walk in the footsteps of the Chartists, not as disinterested observers, but as participants in the same struggle today to change society.

Tony Benn, who was once the standard bearer of the Labour Left, made frequent references in his speeches to labour history, especially the Levellers, the Chartists and the Suffragettes. He saw himself as part of this radical tradition, from which he drew inspiration and radical conclusions:

> Parliamentary democracy is, in truth, little more than a means of securing a periodical change in the management team, which is then allowed to preside over a system that remains in essence intact. If the British people were ever to ask themselves what power they truly enjoyed under our political system they would be amazed to discover how little it is, and some new Chartist agitation might be born and might quickly gather momentum.

Although not a Marxist, he came close here to the formulation in the *Communist Manifesto* that "the executive of the modern state is but a committee for managing the common affairs of the whole bourgeoisie." Again, this conception is also inherent in the writings of Chartism, as we shall see.

Marx and Engels, who spent most of their lives in London and Manchester, learned a tremendous amount from their experiences in Britain, which helped to enrich their understanding. The Chartist movement in particular had a significant impact on their political outlook. After all, Marxism is a theory of movement enriched by the class struggle. It may be defined as the generalised historical experience of the working class. Engels certainly developed and deepened his ideas when he came to live in England in late 1842, where he gathered material for his new book, much of which came from the Chatham Library in Manchester. It was here, in England, that he acquired a deep insight into the class struggle and the questions it raised.

Engels was only twenty-two years of age when in 1843 he visited the offices of the Chartist newspaper *The Northern Star* in Leeds and for the first time met Julian Harney, its acting editor. This first meeting developed into a lifelong friendship. Engels joined the Chartist movement, "openly aligned" himself, to use his expression, convinced that Britain was heading for a social revolution.

Based on his studies he wrote his *Sketch for a Critique of Political Economy*, an independent attack on the political economists of the day. He, along with thousands of others, was a frequent visitor to the Manchester Hall of Sciences, where Chartists and others spoke.

> I have often heard working men, whose fustian jackets[14] scarcely hold together, speak upon geology, astronomical, and other subjects, with more knowledge than most 'cultivated' bourgeois in Germany possess.[15]

He became a regular contributor to *The Northern Star*, and attended Chartist gatherings and meetings. As a result of this work, leading Chartists, especially Julian Harney and Ernest Jones, established close relations with Marx and Engels. "We kept in touch with the revolutionary section of the English Chartists through Julian Harney, the editor of the central organ of the movement, *The Northern Star*, to which I was a contributor", explained Engels in his essay 'On the History of the Communist League'.[16]

Both Marx and Engels lent their support to Chartism long before the appearance of the *Communist Manifesto*. They were keen to build up its revolutionary wing and imbue it with the ideas of scientific socialism. This was the approach they subsequently outlined in the *Manifesto*, explaining that they did not "set up any sectarian principles of their own, by which to shape and mould the [...] movement." They engaged with it as it existed and tried to influence it. Their advantage was that, theoretically, they had a clear understanding of the line of march, and the movement's ultimate general results.

REVOLUTIONARY AWAKENING

The Chartist movement was the first independent movement of the British working class, a proletarian revolutionary party, which was striving to conquer political power. "The stormy era of Chartism", explained Trotsky, witnessed "the revolutionary awakening of the British proletariat." Chartism stands out

---

14 Fustian jackets refers to heavy cotton cloth jackets commonly worn by workers at this time.

15 F. Engels, *Condition of the Working Class in England*, MECW, vol. 4, p. 528.

16 Marx and Engels Selected Works (Henceforth referred to as MECW), vol. 3, p. 197.

as the first of its kind. Above all, it reflected the belief that the emancipation of the working class could only be achieved by the working class itself. Moreover, for the first time in Britain, it *seriously* raised the prospect of social revolution.

However, given the way things turned out, the Chartist movement proved to be more of an *anticipation* of future developments. As Trotsky explained:

> The significance of Chartism lies in the fact that the whole subsequent history of the class struggle was as if summarised in advance, during that decade. Afterwards the movement turned backwards in many respects. It broadened its base and amassed experience.

He concluded: "On a new and higher basis it will inevitably return to many of the ideas and methods of Chartism."[17]

Chartism eventually died out, but, as Trotsky noted, it left behind a rich legacy. In the end, faced with the threat of revolution, at home and abroad, the British ruling class was forced to grant reforms and concessions, resulting in new laws to legalise the trade unions, the repeal of the Corn Laws, increased wages, successive extensions of the franchise in 1867 and later years, as well as the introduction of the ten-hour working day. This confirms the broad fact that reforms are a by-product of revolutionary struggle.

The decline of Chartism coincided with a new period of capitalist upswing, which was to push the working class away from independent politics and onto the path of skilled trade unionism and liberalism. By alternating the parliamentary struggle between Liberals and Conservatives, the ruling class found a vent for the opposition of the working class. Politically, the workers' movement was to trail behind the Liberal Party for the next fifty years, until the formation of the Labour Party. Politically, the Liberal careerists eventually jumped ship and their political offspring now infest the Parliamentary Labour Party.

Goethe said long ago that old truths have to be won afresh again and again. This also applies to our revolutionary traditions. That is why a real history of Chartism, which highlights its genuine meaning, is exceptionally important for the new generation of workers and youth. Engels attached great importance to such a history. He remained in touch with Julian Harney right up until his death and was keen for him to write his memoirs. As Engels wrote in October 1885:

---

17 L. Trotsky, *Writings on Britain*, vol. 2, p. 84.

What the bourgeois have written on the subject is for the most part false; nor have I ever concerned myself with such literature. It's unfortunate, for if Harney doesn't write his memoirs, the history of the first great worker's party will be lost forever.[18]

In February 1893, Engels had again urged Julian Harney to write a history of Chartism, but unfortunately Harney felt too old and sick to attempt such a task.

Engels collaborated with Herman Schluter when he wrote a work on Chartism entitled *Die Chartistenbewegung in England* (Zurich, 1887), but this is unfortunately unavailable in English.

Today the epoch of the rapid advance of capitalism, the so-called Golden Age, is long gone, and the system has come to a shuddering halt. British capitalism, together with world capitalism, is in the throes of the deepest of crises. It has exhausted itself and can no longer develop the productive forces. The system can no longer afford reforms, only devastating counter-reforms and blistering austerity. It is preparing new convulsions and dramatic changes in the consciousness of all classes. As Trotsky commented before the war, if you are looking for a comfortable and peaceful life, you have chosen the wrong time to be born.

In many ways, the working class today stands at a crossroads. Its destiny will be determined in the stormy years that lie ahead. Chartism, therefore, must not be viewed as some heirloom to be admired in a museum or from a great distance, but as an essential part of our working-class heritage. The Chartists showed colossal determination, courage and self-sacrifice, "mettle", as Marx described it. Above all, they were standard-bearers for a new society, who engaged in a whole spectrum of revolutionary struggle. In this present crisis, the real lessons of this history are vital. We should learn from them, from their strengths as well as their weaknesses, in preparation for the titanic events that confront us.

I would like to thank a number of people for helping to produce this book. The original idea for it came from Alan Woods, who gave me persistent encouragement to get it done, for which I am very grateful. Fred Weston has done a sterling job in going over the original draft, and his assistance has been much appreciated. Thanks also must go to Jack Halinski-Fitzpatrick, not only for the layout, but the marvellous work in seeing through the whole project from beginning to end. I am deeply indebted to a number of others for proofreading, Sue Norris, Darrall Cozens, Laurie O'Connel, Pascal

---

18 MECW, vol. 47, p. 337.

Salzbrenner and Josh Holroyd, all of whom have done an excellent job. I would also like to thank Ben Curry for his design of the cover, and Jesse Murray-Dean for assembling and editing the pictures.

We would like to express our thanks to Progress Publishers (www. progresspublishers.org) for their kind permission in allowing us to use the etching by Sergei Yakutovich for the front cover of this book.

Rob Sewell,
London,
August 2020

INTRODUCTION

"What hope, then, have you but in yourselves? Will your enemies help
you? From the time of the first murderer, they have been what they are.
They poisoned Socrates – they murdered Jesus – and would they help
you? No, no, you must help yourselves."
– Sheffield Chartist, *The Examiner*, 1838

What a row and a rumpus there is I declare,
Tens of thousands are flocking from everywhere,
To petition the parliament onward they steer,
The Chartists are coming, oh dear, oh dear…
Hurrah for old England and liberty sweet,
The land that we live in and plenty to eat;
We shall ever remember this wonderful day,
See the Chartists are coming, get out of the way.
– Anon

THREADS OF STRUGGLE

The subject of this book is clearly not about the lives of kings and queens,
generals or admirals – the so-called 'great and good' of society – which often
passed for history when I was at school. Of course, they play their part. But this
work is fundamentally about our class, the working class – weavers, spinners,
miners, carpenters, printers, labourers, engineers, toolmakers, builders, dockers,
operatives, and many others – ordinary folk who did everything in their power to
build the remarkable movement known as Chartism. It is a story of how, for the
first time, the workers in Britain developed a clear identity and class consciousness.

For the defenders of the old regime, such as Edmund Burke, they were the
"swinish multitude", who were beyond the pale. For Chartism's undisputed

leader, the fiery Feargus O'Connor, they were the salt of the earth, and therefore he always referred to them affectionately as "my fustianed, blistered, unshorn friends." It was a proletarian movement for the workers, by the workers, of the workers, 'warts and all'.

"Chartism was from the beginning in 1835 chiefly a movement among the working men", remarked Friedrich Engels, the companion-in-arms of Marx, and with him the founder of scientific socialism.[1] It was the heroic efforts alone of these proletarians that made the Chartist movement into the mass force it was destined to become. The working class placed an indelible stamp on this organisation that came to dominate their thoughts, lives and aspirations. For them, Chartism was not simply a struggle for six points, important as they were, but the fight for a totally new society, the means to secure their emancipation.

For far too long Chartism has been buried in obscurity, almost as a mere footnote in history. Most school students would remember the significance of 1066, or the many wives of Henry VIII, but very few, if any, would recall anything about Chartism. In fact, in the second half of the nineteenth century there was a concerted campaign to erase from public memory the very idea of Chartism. In this way, the Victorians foolishly hoped to banish the spectre of revolution. The eighth edition of the *Encyclopaedia Britannica* (1854), for example, made only a small passing reference to the movement: "An attempt, indeed, was made on the part of Chartism to avail itself of the universal commotion, but all that it could effect was a few monster meetings that evaporated in speeches, or paltry riots that were easily suppressed by the police."[2] Thus, this great movement was brushed aside as if of no consequence, like some dust swept under the carpet. "I know the heroic struggles the English working class have gone through since the middle of the last century," explained Marx in an anniversary speech of the Chartist *People's Paper,* "struggles less glorious, because they are shrouded in obscurity, and burked by the middle-class historian."[3] Such official histories of Chartism simply ridiculed its activities and poured scorn on its leaders, with Feargus O'Connor usually described as 'an empty braggart', an upstart of no importance.

This is a complete travesty, an utter distortion of working-class history. But we should not be surprised. In a society based on wage slavery and

1   MECW, vol. 4, p. 518.

2   Quoted in J. Saville, 1848, *The British State and the Chartist Movement,* p. 202.

3   MESW, vol. 1, p. 501.

exploitation, everything is done, especially the spreading of falsehoods, to defend such a class-based system. "To expect science to be impartial in a wage-slave society," explained Lenin, "is as foolishly naive as to expect impartiality from manufacturers on the question of whether workers' wages ought not to be increased by decreasing the profits of capital."[4] The same goes for history.

However, there has never been a more opportune time to raise the veil on this great working-class movement and put the record straight. In doing so, we hope that this extraordinary period will again be brought to life and its real significance made available for new generations.

Although we are an island nation, we have been greatly influenced by international events. The Great French Revolution of 1789-94 was one such earth-shattering event. While it attracted the hatred of the privileged classes, and brought back memories of the execution of Charles I, it provided a powerful impetus and inspiration – in the same way the Russian Revolution was to do later – to the development of democratic tendencies in Britain, especially in the emerging labour movement. On the other hand, the defeat of Napoleon at Waterloo in 1815, at the hands of the Duke of Wellington, had the effect of ushering in a period of triumphant reaction here and on the Continent. This served to strengthen the hand of the landowning clique that governed the United Kingdom and further tightened the noose of state repression around the neck of the working class.

England, of course, has its own peculiarities, as do all countries. The compromise of 1688, the so-called 'Glorious' Revolution, which was neither glorious nor a revolution, but a sordid coup that placed a Dutch nonentity on the English throne, ushered in an agreement between the landed aristocracy and a section of the rising bourgeoisie. It was a division of labour, whereby the bourgeoisie would rule all the decisive areas of economy and society, while the aristocracy would furnish the personnel of government and state. This nice little arrangement was consummated by the Great Reform Act of 1832, which nevertheless also confirmed the ascendancy of the bourgeois class. As Marx explained:

> The British Constitution is indeed nothing but an antiquated, obsolete, out-of-date compromise between the bourgeoisie, which *rules not officially* but in fact in all the decisive spheres of civil society, and the landed aristocracy, which *governs officially*. Originally, after the 'glorious' revolution of 1688, only a section of the bourgeoisie, the *aristocracy of finance*, was included in the compromise. The

---

4   Lenin Collected Works (Henceforth referred to as LCW), vol. 19, p. 23.

Reform Bill of 1831[5] admitted another section, the millocracy as the English call it, i.e. the high dignitaries of the industrial bourgeoisie.[6]

In 1819, the cold-blooded murder of unarmed demonstrators – contemptuously referred to as the 'great unwashed' – by privileged sabre-wielding yeomanry in St Peter's Fields, Manchester, became very much burned into the popular consciousness. 'Peterloo', as it became known, and the idea of universal suffrage, remained fixed in the minds of the working class. These were tumultuous times, which produced a intense class hatred and revolt, running from the naval mutinies at Nore and Spithead to the frame-breaking Luddites, from underground trade unions to the terrorising activities of the Scotch Cattle, from the hunger marches to the battles over the unstamped press and the Poor Law. The history of these times, wrote the Hammonds, "reads like a history of civil war."[7] Out of this civil war, Chartism was born, the first mass political movement of the British working class.

CLASS CONSCIOUSNESS

The Chartist epoch is characterised by unrivalled class consciousness, which took on an explicitly revolutionary character, and hatred for the ruling classes. "There is among the manufacturing poor a stern look of discontent, of hatred to all who are rich…" stated General Sir Charles James Napier, military commander in the North.[8] The birth of the working class in the fires of the Industrial Revolution was both shocking and violent – very far from the fairy-tale stories in school history books – and grounded in the politics of class struggle. The working class fought back not with good table manners and sweet words, but with every means it found necessary. As the movement grew, so did its confidence and its determination that no pampered aristocrat or penny-pinching capitalist would be allowed to stand in its way. The common battle cry of the workers at this time, reflected in Chartism, was 'Liberty or death', a measure of the degree of feeling among the 'lower orders', as they were contemptuously called. "Chartism means the bitter discontent grown fierce and mad", wrote Thomas Carlyle. "It is a new name for a thing which has many names, which will yet have many."[9]

---

5   The Reform Bill was introduced in 1831, but became the Reform Act in 1832, when it was finally approved in Parliament – ed.

6   MECW, vol. 14, pp. 53-54.

7   J.L. Hammond & B. Hammond, *The Skilled Labourer 1760-1832*, p. 1.

8   D. Thompson, *The Early Chartists*, p. 25.

9   T. Carlyle, *Chartism*, London 1840, p. 2.

"The agitation for the Charter has afforded one of the greatest examples in modern history of the real might of the labourers", wrote Peter Murray McDouall, one of the contemporary Chartist leaders. "In the conflict millions have appeared upon the stage and the mind of the masses has burst from its shell and begun to flourish and expand".[10] This 'bursting from the shell' reflected a transformation in consciousness, an expression of the molecular processes in the minds of the masses, in open revolt against a system that was oppressing them. Originally, the emerging working class was shell-shocked, brutalised and cowed. The rise of Chartism meant for the first time the working class as an independent force, standing squarely on its own two feet. In this fashion, the British working class entered onto the stage of history.

"True freedom is only possible when men lose every vestige of slavery", explained William Taunton, in a very perceptive comment. And it was precisely at this time that the working class began to cast off its shackles, mentally as well as physically. It was forced to learn the hard way from the harsh realities it experienced, from every blow, every setback, as well as every advance. The more the workers united together in struggle the more their confidence rose. To believe, as most do, that Chartism was simply a movement for reform, is to miss the point. "The Charter was only a means to an end", stated the Chartist James Leach, stressing its revolutionary intentions.[11] For the working class the demands of the Charter constituted much more. For them, it was a struggle for a new society – a society that would put an end to their misery and suffering. In a very real sense, Chartism was the first time ever that British workers fixed their eyes on the seizure of political power. Under its banner, the working class attempted to take power into its hands on three separate occasions: in 1839, 1842 and again in 1848. In this struggle, they conducted a class war that at different times involved general strikes, battles with the state, mass demonstrations and even armed insurrection. They forged weapons, illegally drilled their forces, and armed themselves in preparation for seizing the reins of power. Such were the early revolutionary traditions of the British working class, deliberately buried beneath a mountain of lies and distortions.

"But whoever knows the history of the British people and the British working class, the history of the English Revolution of the 17th century and then British Chartism of the 19th century," explained Trotsky, "will know

---

10 D. Jones, *Chartism and The Chartists*, p. 12.

11 D. Jones, pp. 34-35.

that the Englishman too has a 'devil inside him'."[12] Thomas Carlyle and Richard Oastler, figures of the time, warned about such a "devilish" mood in the people, who had become conscious of their strength. They claimed that "the avalanche is descending". The Reverend R.J. Stephens explained that "England stands on a mine – a volcano is beneath her…" These metaphors were a reflection of the impending social eruptions that threatened the existence of bourgeois rule.

"The movement is, in fact, an insurrection which is directed against the middle classes", noted the *Annual Register* of 1839 in a contemporary survey of Chartism.

> "A violent change in the system of government is demanded by the Chartists not for the purpose of receiving more power and privileges, but – as far as their aim permits any definition – for the purpose of producing a hitherto non-existent condition of society, in which wage labour and capital do not exist at all."[13]

Although these views were expressed by an opponent of Chartism, they certainly capture its general aims, and the cherished dreams of millions of workers. The principal enemy was not simply 'Old Corruption' as before, but, following the 'great betrayal' of 1832, it was a new powerful rich class, the slave-driving capitalist manufacturers who dominated their lives.

Through Chartism, the working class became collectively conscious of itself as a class, and more importantly, came to rely on its own strength. The old alliances with the middle classes, inevitable in the earliest stages of the movement, were now thrown aside. This provides a striking confirmation of the words of Marx that "the emancipation of the working class is the task of the working class itself." Marx and Engels therefore paid tribute to the Chartists and closely followed their development, seeking to influence the movement whenever possible.

It is often said that we stand on the shoulders of giants, the great pioneers of the trade union and labour movement. This is undoubtedly true. The Chartists contained some of these great figures. But we also stand on the accomplishments of the 'common' people, the real 'unsung heroes', whose role was erased by histories written by the other side. They are the "heroes of unwritten history", to quote the poet Percy Shelley. They make up the tens of thousands who faced imprisonment, transportation and the hangman's noose to fight for the six-point Charter and their liberation, but whose names are

---

12 L. Trotsky, *Writings on Britain*, vol. 1, p. 171.
13 Quoted in M. Beer, *A History of British Socialism*, Vol. 2, p. 45.

mostly forgotten or lost. They cry out to be heard. As Abraham Hanson, a local Methodist preacher who was expelled from the Church for his Chartist oratory said:

> Let not their children say "behold these vile chains are the legacy of our dastardly forefathers"; but let them have to say "behold these monuments erected to the men who broke our chains of slavery, and interested themselves in our welfare when we did not exist."[14]

OUR HISTORY

The Chartist movement, a mass movement of the oppressed and downtrodden, drew its strongest support from the proletarian heartlands of South Lancashire, the West Riding of Yorkshire, the East Midlands and East London, as well as parts of the Black Country, Wales and the West of Scotland. Its struggle constitutes an extremely important part of the history of the British working class. And yet, in truth, even within the labour and trade union movement, very little is known about it, perhaps save a few salient points.

It is true that the Chartists left behind a rich record of their activities, from journals, pamphlets and broadsheets, to the memoirs of participants, novels and more besides, including the reports of spies and informers. All this provides today's labour historians with a wealth of sources about this great working-class movement.

There have been numerous books on the subject of late, although many have been written *by* academics *for* academics. Most, of course, are works of non-revolutionaries writing about revolutions, divorced from any understanding of the subject. There are others deeply influenced by the 'narrative' of postmodernism, which are worse than useless. There are, of course, some very good works, even outstanding in their field, but even they only go so far. There are a number that contain interesting insights, such as local studies, or specific features, including studies about Temperance Chartism, Christian Chartism, Municipal Chartism, Complete Suffrage Chartism, Land Plan Chartism, Church Chartism, and so on. However, these tend to lack a broad understanding of the real processes and revolutionary motive force of the movement, that is, its very essence.

Such histories have mainly been written by scholars and academics, whose writings are for the most part dry and lifeless. Only a small handful of people has ever heard of them. Faced with the living processes of Chartism, they

14 D. Thompson, *The Early Chartists*, p. 68.

offer their own somewhat airless, dusty and sterile prejudices. They offer no dearth of factual material, mostly undigested knowledge about this and that. To read them is like chewing on cotton wool. In the main, their general aim is to promote a picture of the submissiveness or naivety of the British working class, which is part of the wider idea that a British revolution was futile in the second quarter of the nineteenth century and – by extension – remains equally futile today. These so-called 'educated' people sneer and scoff at the very notion of 'revolution', as something foolish and utopian, and only suitable, maybe, as a titillating subject for the seminar room. "Abandon all hope ye that enter here," is surely their motto, where revolutionary change is futile no matter what part of history they are dealing with. We should therefore take to heart the message of Bronterre O'Brien, the Chartist leader, when he said:

> Have no faith in history, look upon it as a mass of fabrications, concocted, like modern newspapers, not with regard to truth, or the interests of humanity, but to deceive the multitude, and thus bolster up all the frauds and villainous institutions of the rich.[15]

All 'official' history is coloured by the prejudices of the class society we live in, as O'Brien explained, the purpose of which is to justify the current system. Engels made the same point when he wrote his preparatory material for a history of Ireland:

> The bourgeoisie turns everything into a commodity, hence also the writing of history. It is part of its being, of its condition for existence, to falsify all goods: it falsified the writing of history. And the best-paid historiography is that which is best falsified for the purposes of the bourgeoisie.[16]

No doubt, there are many honest people, including historians. But this does not invalidate the point made by both O'Brien and Engels. There is no such thing as 'objective' historians, free from class prejudice. Bourgeois accounts of this period, in whatever guises, deliberately downplay and ridicule the revolutionary implications of Chartism. According to such historians, as soon as the workers 'came to their senses' and put aside their childlike illusions, bourgeois democracy saved the day. At bottom, the Chartists were regarded as naive, as most of their demands were eventually met. *Eventually* is the key word, as it would take another seventy years for all men to get the vote, and

---

15 The *Poor Man's Guardian*, 5 December 1835, Quoted in T. Rothstein, p. 93.
16 K. Marx and F. Engels, *On Ireland*, p. 211.

even longer for women. This outlook is the Whig or Liberal interpretation of history, viewed as a never-ending picture of historical progress, provided, of course, that we accept our chosen lot in life. According to this school, if only the Chartists had followed the advice of the London Working Men's Association under the 'moderate' William Lovett – the more educated and enlightened representatives of Chartism – then, they reason, a lot of pain would have been avoided, and an extended franchise would have been achieved much earlier. Unfortunately, the 'unruly mob', the 'physical force' Chartists, took over and ruined everything.

Sidney and Beatrice Webb, the leading Fabian historians, had this idea, which provided the cornerstone of their petty-bourgeois gradualist outlook. Their disdain for revolution led them to say that Chartism was:

> [D]isgraced by the fustian of its orators and the political and economic quackery of its pretentious and incompetent leaders whose jealousies and intrigues, by successfully excluding all the nobler elements, finally brought it to naught ... so typical of nineteenth century revolutionary movements.[17]

What a monstrous slander against the Chartists! But such slanders simply reflect the contempt of the middle-class intellectuals for revolutionary movements that threaten to upset their comfortable lives. Lenin correctly described such people as "obtuse eulogists of English philistinism", who "try to represent Chartism, the revolutionary epoch of the English labour movement, as mere childishness".

INSPIRATION

On the contrary, Chartism, far from being 'disgraced', is a heroic chapter from which we can draw great inspiration. As the historian R. H. Tawney correctly commented:

> It was, as Marx pointed out, the entry in politics, not merely of a new party, but of a new class... The essence of Chartism was, in fact, an attempt to make possible a social revolution by the overthrow of the political oligarchy.[18]

The fact that Chartism failed to carry this through must not be allowed to obscure its real significance. Being the first, it showed the rest of the world 'how things should be done', how the working class fights for its political independence.

---

17 S. Webb and B. Webb, *The History of Trade Unionism*, London, 1911, p. 158.

18 Quoted in H. Stanley Harrison, *Poor Men's Guardians*, p. 109.

This was not straightforward, however, as Chartism contained within it a struggle of political tendencies, which vied for dominance. Faced with colossal challenges, inevitable divisions opened up within the Chartist movement, reflecting different class forces. This revealed itself as a struggle between an opportunist right-wing tendency, the 'moral force' wing, and, broadly speaking, a revolutionary proletarian tendency, the 'physical force' wing. Some contemporaries referred to them as the 'stalwarts' and 'fair-weather birds'. This division was temporarily papered over by the adoption of a compromise solution, a motto, 'peaceably if we can, forcibly if we must'. This became the clarion call of all Chartist rallies and demonstrations.

"We are born again", ran the inscription on a radical banner, a declaration of faith in the classless society of the future. "We seek the most perfect of all revolutions, the revolving of the whole system", explained the Chartist newspaper *The Northern Star* of November 1840.[19] For the masses who followed Chartism, the six points of the Charter meant nothing less than a means to wrench power out of the hands of a corrupt ruling class, and the overthrow of the system. This hatred towards their exploiters inspired the Reverend Stephens, one of the most popular orators of the time, who, in addressing a meeting on Kersal Moor, cried out:

> Chartism, my friends, is no political movement where the main point is your getting the ballot ... This question of universal suffrage is a knife and fork question, a bread and cheese question, notwithstanding all that has been said against it; and if any man should ask me what I mean by universal suffrage I should reply: That every working man in the land has the right to have a good coat on his back, a comfortable abode in which to shelter himself and his family, a good dinner upon his table, and no more work than is necessary to keep him in good health, and so much wages for his work as should keep him in plenty and afford him the enjoyment of all the blessings of life, which a reasonable man could desire...[20]

This was what the Charter meant to millions of workers. It was this ordinary down-to-earth speaking that won the hearts and minds of the operatives of Lancashire and Manchester, and struck a chord with every worker throughout Britain. In Wiltshire, a Trowbridge Chartist put the matter even more plainly. According to him, the aim of Chartism was not simply a question of struggling for bread; instead he promised everyone "plenty of roast beef,

---

19 D. Jones, pp. 33-34.

20 M. Beer, *A History of British Socialism*, Vol. 2, pp. 47-48.

plum pudding and strong beer by working three hours a day."[21] In essence, the demands of the Charter represented a revolutionary social programme. It was the means to a better life, the details of which were certainly open to debate. However, all agreed that the first step to achieving this new life was to win the Charter.

UNBROKEN THREAD

Chartism is part of an unbroken thread we can trace back as far as the beginning of class society itself. The Chartists themselves shared this broad view of history, considering themselves an essential link in a long chain of struggle. In the words of Bronterre O'Brien, the intellectual leader of Chartism:

> "[T]he history of mankind shows that from the beginning of the world, the rich of all countries have been in a permanent state of conspiracy to keep down the poor of all countries, and for this plain reason – because the poverty of the poor man is essential to the riches of the rich man. No matter by what means they may disguise their operations, the rich are everlastingly plundering, debasing and brutalising the poor. All the crimes and superstitions of human nature have their origin in this cannibal warfare of riches against poverty. The desire of one man to live on the fruits of another's labour is the original sin of the world. It is this which fills the world with faction and hypocrisy and has made all past history to be what Gibbon so justly described it – 'a record of the crimes, absurdities, and calamities of mankind'. It is the parent injustice from which all injustice springs."[22]

We also encounter this view of a continual class struggle in the *Communist Manifesto*. "Freeman and slave, patrician and plebeian, lord and serf, guild-master and journeyman, in a word, oppressor and oppressed, stood in constant opposition to one another, carried on an uninterrupted, now hidden, now open fight", explained its opening pages.[23] As long as the class struggle exists so do the ideas of social emancipation and the abolition of classes.

Socialist or communist ideas have a long history in England. They were usually linked to the idea of creating a commonwealth where 'all things are held in common'. It is a tradition that was present centuries ago on the hillside outside Blackheath, to the south of London, when a priest called

---

21 A. Briggs, *Chartist Studies*, p. 10.

22 Quoted in J. Lindsay et al, *Spokesmen for Liberty*, p. 295.

23 MESW, vol. 1, pp. 108–109.

John Ball preached revolutionary ideas to rebellious peasants. According to his words:

> When Adam delved and Eve span
> Who was then the gentleman?[24]

According to Froissart, the Medieval chronicler, John Ball declared to great acclaim:

> "Ah, ye good people, the matters goeth not well to pass in England, nor shall not do till everything be common, and that there be no villeins nor gentlemen, but that we may be all united [equal], and that the lords be no greater masters than we be..."[25]

This was a call for social revolution at a time when, once again, the world was being turned upside down. These revolutionary ideas gained ground during the Peasants' Revolt, a class war in the fourteenth century, when the feudal system was in decline and capitalist relations were crystallising in the towns. It was the time of Wat Tyler, the revolutionary peasants' leader, who led a struggle against their oppressors. This was a world on the brink of a social and religious breakdown, where the old order was being challenged by the rise of new class forces. A new vision of communism is expressed in the writings of Thomas More and his *Utopia*. We find it even in Shakespeare:

> All things in common Nature should produce
> Without sweat or endeavour: treason, felony,
> Sword, pike, knife, gun, or need of any engine
> Would I not have: but Nature should bring forth
> Of its own king, all foison, all abundance
> To feed my innocent people.[26]

"The old world ... is running up like parchment in the fire", explained the Diggers' leader, Gerrard Winstanley of the True Levellers, some thirty odd years later.[27] This yearning for a classless society was expressed during the English Civil War, when the veil of censorship was temporarily raised and the activities of revolutionary sects flourished. It permeated Cromwell's New Model Army, a party in all but name, and was articulated by the Leveller

---

24 J. Lindsay et al, *Spokesmen for Liberty*, p. 28.

25 Ibid., p. 27.

26 W. Shakespeare, *The Tempest*.

27 C. Hill, *The World Turned Upside Down*, p. 14.

Colonel Rainsborough in the Putney Debates[28] of 1647: "I think that the poorest he that is in England hath a life to live, as the greatest he".[29] It is revealed when Colonel Edward Sexby argued that the common people have little property, "yet we have had a *birthright*". Gerrard Winstanley went further and argued that "the earth becomes a common treasury as it was in the beginning." In other words, the Levellers' principles of justice and equality must be extended from politics to economics, namely the abolition of private property, and the establishment of communism throughout the world.

From 'birthright' comes the *Rights of Man* (1791) of Thomas Paine, a 'subversive' work, eagerly read by workers awakened to the idea of a better life. "When the rich plunder the poor of his rights", explained Paine, "it becomes an example to the poor to plunder the rich of his property."[30] In attacking the conservative apologist Edmund Burke, he went on to draw revolutionary conclusions:

> "Why … does Mr Burke talk of this House of Peers, as the pillar of landed interest? Were that pillar to sink into the earth, the same landed property would continue, and the same ploughing, sowing, and reaping would go on. The Aristocracy are not the farmers who work the land … but are the mere consumers of the rent …"[31]

It was as if the Putney Debates had once again come to life. The legal sales of Paine's book by 1793 rose to around an astonishing 200,000 copies, mainly to artisans and journeymen. It was undoubtedly the most influential book of the time. Such subversive ideas were anathema to the ruling class, who in turn acted with brutal repression to safeguard their interests. Paine managed to escape by the skin of his teeth to France and, given his popularity there, was elected as a delegate to the French National Convention. This move to France saved his life, as Burke, along with others, wanted him hanged for treason. He was never again to step foot in England.

Even at Paine's trial *in absentia* the Attorney General complained that the *Rights of Man* was being widely spread and "thrust into the hands of subjects

---

28 The Putney Debates were the radical discussions over political liberty among Army Delegates from Cromwell's New Model Army, mostly under the influence of left-wing Levellers, that took place in Putney in October-November 1647. It had all the hallmarks of a Soviet.

29 A.S.P. Woodhouse [Ed.], *Puritanism and Liberty: Being the Army Debates 1647-49*, p. 53.

30 Quoted in E.P. Thompson, *The Making of the English Working Class*, p. 101

31 Ibid., p. 101.

of every description, even children's sweetmeats being wrapped in it".[32] Inspired by the American and French Revolutions, these revolutionary ideas of *our rights* fed the popular imagination of the dispossessed, regarded simply as the 'rabble' by the wealthy rulers of Britain. Such subversive notions were regarded as a serious threat to private property and the established norms, promoting anarchy and chaos. Therefore they needed to be ruthlessly rooted out. However, as a result of his ideas, Thomas Paine became the voice of the oppressed and the architect of radical political reform in England.

"If Mr Paine should be able to rouse up the lower classes, their interference will probably be marked by wild work, and all we now possess, whether in private property or public liberty, will be at the mercy of a lawless and furious rabble", stated Reverend Christopher Wyvill, the conservative Yorkshire reformer. He believed that the introduction of universal suffrage – the vote being granted to the men of no property – "could not be effected without a Civil War".[33] This was the authentic voice of the stone-faced British upper classes. For them, any concessions towards granting democratic rights could only lead in one direction: chaos, revolution and the abolition of private property.

However, the 'rabble', as such, did not need much rousing. The harsh conditions that the common people were forced to endure were enough in themselves to provoke anger and hatred. The cruelties of everyday life were sufficient to stir up bitterness and give birth to the yearnings for a better world.

EFFECTS OF REVOLUTION

It is therefore no wonder that these downtrodden masses were profoundly inspired by the American and French Revolutions of the late eighteenth century. These revolutions, with their calls for liberty and freedom, had immense popular appeal and propelled the masses to fight for their rights, if necessary, with cudgels in hand.

The American Declaration of Independence of 4 July 1776, born out of a revolutionary war, is permeated with a revolutionary and democratic spirit. "We hold these truths to be self-evident," states the Declaration, "that all men are created equal, that they are endowed by their Creator with certain inalienable Rights, that among these are Life, Liberty and the pursuit of Happiness. That, to secure these rights, Governments are instituted among

32 Ibid., p. 118.
33 Ibid., pp. 26-27.

Men, deriving their just powers from the consent of the governed, that whenever any form of Government becomes destructive of these ends, it is the Right of the People to alter or abolish it, and to institute new Government."

These are truly powerful revolutionary words, especially at that time. They justified the revolutionary overthrow of governments which had lost popular consensus by the population itself. Every single line of the Declaration was regarded as deeply seditious by the British administration at which it was aimed. The American colonists could only win a war of independence by revolutionary means and a direct challenge to the established authority. These rebel patriots required powerful arguments to use against the English Crown and its claims to continued sovereignty. Such ideas were supplied in good measure by Thomas Paine. "Of more worth is one honest man to society and in the sight of God," he declared, "than all the crowned ruffians that ever lived."

"I hold it, that a little rebellion, now and then, is a good thing, and as necessary in the political world as storms in the physical", wrote Thomas Jefferson, the spokesman for American revolutionary democracy. In those stirring times, ideas emerged or were rekindled that were based upon visions of equality, co-operation and socialism. Such ideas were put forward by Thomas Spence, William Godwin and Mary Wollstonecraft, who championed the equality of the sexes.

On the other hand, the ruling class became increasingly terrified at this rebellious state of affairs. While the American Revolution was far away, the fires of the French Revolution were close at hand. "The awakening of the labouring classes, after the first shocks of the French Revolution, made the upper classes tremble", wrote the contemporary, Frances Lady Shelley, in her diary.[34] The Revolution brought home to them the horrors of the guillotine and the fate that may have awaited them. "Everything rung and was connected with the Revolution in France", recalled Lord Cockburn. "Everything, not this thing or that thing, but literally everything, was soaked in this one event."[35] They knew full well that revolutions were very contagious things, and this virus was just across the channel. The British establishment therefore railed against the 'barbarism' of the Jacobin Terror, but punishments were just as barbaric under the English Crown, where men, women and children were publicly hanged, drawn and quartered; their insides removed and held up to public scrutiny.

---

34 Quoted in Ibid., p. 60.

35 Ibid., p. 61.

In revolutionary France, violence was used to cleanse the old order, while in England, it was used to uphold the old regime. In France, it was used to defend a revolution, in England it was used to defend privilege and private property.

The masses in England were told to accept their lot in life. Edmund Burke, who justified this servitude, explained: "Patience, labour, sobriety, frugality and religion, should be recommended to them." But this "swinish multitude", to quote his words, were prone to disturbance and riot in the face of increasing hardships, whether provoked by the rising cost of bread, turnpikes and tolls, enclosures, lockouts or unemployment. But such moral persuasion was backed up by state repression and the rule of law, such as it was. Trade unions (combinations) were outlawed and driven underground. Out of desperation, workers reverted to machine wrecking – the Luddites – for which they faced the hangman and transportation. At Peterloo, those who championed democratic rights for ordinary people were cut down and massacred in cold blood.

Robert Owen, the great Utopian Socialist and Welshman, was the first man in this country to articulate socialist ideas, although the first recorded use of the word 'socialist' only appeared in *The Co-operative Magazine* in November 1827. By the 1830s, socialism had become synonymous with 'Owenism'. Rather than dog-eat-dog competition under capitalism, Owen advocated co-operation for the common good. In the conditions of the time, where the working class was kept in an abysmal state and viciously exploited, these ideas touched a raw nerve and spread like wildfire. This socialism of the early nineteenth century was qualitatively different from the past and rested on a new class, an industrial proletariat, born out of the Industrial Revolution.

This proletariat began to gradually find its own identity. It began increasingly to become class conscious and aware that its labour was being exploited by others. The scales which covered its eyes were being ruthlessly torn away. As an anonymous contributor to the *Poor Man's Guardian* of March 1832 explained:

> "When I hear master manufacturers and tradesmen say – We must get large profits to enable us to pay you high wages, my blood curdles within me. I wish at once that I were a dog, or anything else, rather than a man… The manufacturer's profits, therefore, like the land-stealers' rent and the tithe-stealers' tithes, and all other profits, was obtained solely by keeping wages down… There is no common interest between working men and profit-makers."[36]

---

36 Quoted in A.L. Morton & G. Tate, *The British Labour Movement*, p. 57.

With the birth of the working class, together with the horrors of early capitalism, came a political awareness. We are dealing here with a fresh virgin working class, with little in the way of conservative fetters to hold it back. This growing politicisation in turn was fed by the hot embers of the American and French Revolutions. It is out of this ferment that we witness changes in the psychology of the masses and the emergence of the great Chartist movement. The aims of this movement centred around six democratic demands:

1. Universal suffrage for every man twenty-one and over, who is sound of mind and unconvicted of a crime;
2. Payment of members of Parliament, to enable poorer people to stand for election;
3. Voting by ballot to protect the elector in the exercise of their vote;
4. Equal electoral districts to secure equal representation;
5. Abolition of the property qualification for candidates to make every voter eligible;
6. Annual Parliaments, as a check to bribery and intimidation, and "since members, when elected for a year, would not be able to defy and betray their constituents as now".[37]

While on the surface these demands look less than revolutionary, given the context of the time, if enacted, such demands would challenge the very pillars of the establishment and lead on to greater things. The Charter, in the eyes of millions, meant nothing less than the assumption of political power by the working class in order to satisfy their social needs. In their hands, it was, in effect, a programme of class against class.

Friedrich Engels summed this idea up brilliantly in his book, *The Condition of the Working Class in England*:

> Since the workingmen do not respect the law, but simply submit to its power when they cannot change it, it is most natural that they should at least propose alterations in it, that they should wish to put a proletarian law in the place of the legal fabric of the bourgeoisie. This proposed law is the People's Charter, which in form is purely political, and demands a democratic basis for the House of Commons. Chartism is the compact form of their opposition to the bourgeoisie. In the Unions and turnouts opposition always remained isolated: it was single workingmen or sections who fought a single bourgeois. If the fight became general, this was scarcely by the intention of the workingmen; or, when it did

37 R. Brown and C. Daniels, p. 29.

happen intentionally, Chartism was at the bottom of it. But in Chartism it is the whole working class which arises against the bourgeoisie, and attacks, first of all, the political power, the legislative rampart with which the bourgeoisie has surrounded itself…

These six points, which are all limited to the reconstitution of the House of Commons, harmless as they seem, are sufficient to overthrow the whole English Constitution, Queen and Lords included.[38]

This view was reinforced by the Chartists themselves with their slogan, 'Political power, our means, social happiness, our end'. With the refusal of the ruling classes to accept their just demands, the people would rise up, arms in hand, and win them by force, as had their revolutionary cousins in America and France. In other words, if they were blocked on the Parliamentary front, the only road they could take was the road of insurrection. The Reverend Stephens underlined this point when he said: "If they will not reform this, aye uproot it all, they shall have the revolution they so much dread."[39]

The Charter was the battle cry of Chartism, but it also provided a radical learning curve for the working class. It proved to be the school of class struggle and social revolution. The campaign for the Charter involved mass petitioning on a scale never seen before in history. Rather than an activity in this or that locality, it was an unprecedented national campaign involving millions. In many ways, it became an article of faith for the working class. The campaign organised gigantic meetings, often torchlit and held in the pitch black of night, packed with fervour and blood-curdling speeches. The slightest suggestion that the Charter would be contemptuously rejected by a rotten and pampered Parliament only served to intensify the indignation of the working class against the upper classes. Given the opposition of the Whig/Tory Establishment, in all its guises, many people began to draw revolutionary conclusions.

SELF-SACRIFICE

In November 1839, the Chartists staged an uprising in Newport, South Wales. It was put down in blood by the authorities. George Shell, a seventeen-year-old carpenter, was shot dead by soldiers as he tried to enter the Westgate Hotel to free his comrades. He wrote a letter to his parents on the eve of the rising:

---

38 MECW, vol. 4, p. 517-8, emphasis added.

39 M. Beer, *A History of British Socialism*, Vol. 2, p. 57.

Pontypool, Sunday Night, 3 November 1839

Dear Parents,

I shall this night be engaged in a struggle for freedom, and should it please God to spare my life I shall see you soon; but if not, grieve not for me, I shall fall in a noble cause. My tools are at Mr Cecil's, and likewise my clothes. Farewell!

Yours truly,

George

Like so many others before him, this young unsung hero sacrificed his life for the cause of freedom and liberty. Our present liberties, very much taken for granted, were not given freely out of the kind-heartedness of the ruling class, but were wrenched from their hands. Without the courageous struggles of the Chartists and others, many of whom were prepared to face imprisonment, transportation and hanging, we would not have the democratic rights we enjoy today.

And yet, while we have gained certain democratic rights, which are constantly being eroded, the working class has certainly not gained its social emancipation. In spite of the progress, the working class still remains an exploited class, subservient to the will of the capitalists and their system. The liberation of the working class still lies ahead of us. Part of this struggle is to cleanse the labour and trade union movement of careerism and rearm it with a revolutionary programme that will do away with capitalism. If we are to make the labour movement and its organisations fit for purpose, we need to clean out the 'Augean stables' and replace the top layers with committed leaders that are prepared to fight to the end. The traditions of Chartism can serve us well in this regard.

Our task is to bring out the real significance of Chartism for today, despite its rudimentary and unfinished character. It was not simply an ordinary political party, but a movement striving to become a fully-fledged party of the British working class, revolutionary in its content, methods and slogans. "When Britain gave the world Chartism, [it was] the first broad, truly mass and politically organised proletarian revolutionary movement", Lenin explained.[40] Such a conclusion is far removed from the current histories of Chartism. According to Lenin, who paid close attention to the British labour movement, Chartism "in many respects was something preparatory to Marxism, the 'last word but one' before Marxism".[41] The working-class

---

40 *The Third International and its Place in History*, LCW, vol. 29, pp. 308-9.

41 *Lenin on Britain*, p. 449.

movement of that period certainly anticipated much that would later be contained in Marxism, as we will see.

ANTICIPATION

These appraisals, I believe, capture the essence of Chartism. It was an 'anticipation' in the sense of being the first independent revolutionary awakening of the British working class. It contained the pioneering spirit and demonstrated how quickly the working class could learn and become conscious of its historic role in the 'school of hard knocks'. Such experiences only served to drive them to revolutionary conclusions. A new class consciousness – and class hatred – was born, which permeated the whole of Chartism. These ideas were articulated in a popular tract at the time:

> *People* … What labour do you perform in the society?
> *Privileged Class*. None: we are not made to labour.
> *People*. How then have you acquired your wealth?
> *Privileged Class*. By taking the pains to govern you.
> *People*. To govern us! … We toil, and you enjoy; we produce and you dissipate; wealth flows from us, and you absorb it. Privileged men, class distinct from the people, form a nation apart and govern yourselves.[42]

The defeat of Chartism, which marked the end of an epoch, was to usher in a further period of heightened capitalist development. This, in turn, led to the strengthening of the ideas of reformism in the working class and a turn towards liberalism. This dead end would last until British capitalism's monopoly position in the world was finally broken.

OUR FUTURE

History has shown that the working class has gone through many battles, where significant victories are won, but many are lost. Despite the losses, the working class has always returned to the fray. Ted Grant, the great Marxist theoretician, whom I knew well and who had a great sense of history, frequently compared the working class to the Greek god Antaeus, who every time he was thrown to the ground drew strength from his mother, the Earth, and came back reinvigorated. The same is true of the working class, which, when thrown back, is always forced to resume the struggle with renewed energy. As Marx and Engels, with an eye on the British proletariat, explained in the *Communist Manifesto*:

---

42 E.P. Thompson, p. 108.

This organisation of the proletarians into a class, and consequently into a political party, is continually being upset again by the competition between the workers themselves. But it ever rises up again, stronger, firmer, mightier.[43]

In the year prior to the British General Strike of 1926, Leon Trotsky wrote that it was the duty of every class-conscious worker in Britain to study their history, especially the Chartist movement. "The clarification of the historical significance of... Chartism is one of the most important obligations for British Marxists", he stated.[44] Such was its vital importance, he explained that "without Chartism, however, there would have been no Paris Commune. Without both, there would have been no October."[45]

Trotsky's advice is doubly important at this time. Today, the capitalist world is experiencing a devastating crisis. This is going to prepare revolution in one country after another. In some quarters, revolution is regarded as very un-British – especially amongst liberal and reformist types – but revolution, like it or not, will be on the order of the day. The stark choice facing humankind is between socialism or barbarism, in a very real sense. "The crisis of our condition is at hand – close upon us", warned James Morrison, a self-taught building worker who edited a trade union paper in the 1830s. "The contest affects all alike; and woe unto the man who deserts his post."[46]

This crisis will be resolved in the years that lie ahead, either in the victory of the working class or in a new version of Jack London's *Iron Heel*. Following Trotsky's advice, we hope that this contribution on Chartism, an analysis based on historical materialism, the Marxist method applied to history, will help to illuminate some of the vital lessons from our past. Trotsky, as always, expressed the question most eloquently:

[T]he revolutionary slogans and methods of Chartism are even today, if critically dissected, infinitely higher than the sickly-sweet eclecticism of the MacDonalds and the economic obtuseness of the Webbs. To use a hazardous comparison then, it can be said that the Chartist movement resembles a prelude which contains in an undeveloped form the musical theme of the whole opera. In this sense the British working class can and must see in Chartism not only its past but also its future.[47]

---

43 MESW, p. 117.

44 L. Trotsky, 'Where is Britain Going?', *Writings on Britain*, vol. 2, p. 87.

45 L. Trotsky, *The Revolution Betrayed*, p. 303.

46 Quoted in A. Hutt, *This Final Crisis*, p. 31.

47 L. Trotsky, 'Where is Britain Going?', *Writings on Britain*, vol. 2, p. 94.

1. "DRIPPING WITH BLOOD FROM EVERY PORE"

"From the loom, the factory, and the mine, Good Lord deliver us."
— (Chartist prayer)

"The whistling of the birds is not for us — our melody is the deafening noise of the engine."
— *Pioneer or Trade Union Magazine*, 1833

"We demand universal suffrage because it is our right, and not only because it is our right, but because we believe it will bring freedom to our country and happiness to our homesteads, we believe it will give us bread and beef and beer."
— Julian Harney

THE MAKING OF THE WORKING CLASS

In the famous words of Dylan Thomas, let us begin at the beginning, at the very birth of the British working class. It was a birth-time, not full of sweetness and light, but of anguish, violence and pain on an industrial scale.

Before the Industrial Revolution, most people lived and died in or near the village in which they were born. Apart from overcrowded stench-ridden London, there was only one town of any importance, and that was Bristol. This had a population of between 80,000 and 100,000 inhabitants. Apart from Liverpool, which had itself grown from the proceeds of the slave trade, most other towns were in effect large villages. Then came the Industrial Revolution and the advent of power-driven machinery. Within a generation or so, Britain was transformed from a peripheral island to the 'workshop of the world', from an agricultural to an industrial society. It became the pathfinder of a new bourgeois civilisation and the centre of nineteenth-century expansionism.

Britain was the birthplace of modern capitalism, which bestowed on her great advantages over every other nation. The Industrial Revolution, a profound economic and social revolution, introduced the greatest changes experienced by any country in human history. It was the beginning of a Golden Age for British capitalism. "She was not under the yoke of other nations, but on the contrary held them more and more under her yoke", explained Trotsky. "She exploited the whole world."[1] This privileged position provided her with dazzling untold wealth and seemingly unlimited world power. This caused Thomas B. Macaulay, the 1st Baron of Macaulay, and Member of Parliament for the pocket borough of Calne, to become giddy with success:

> "Our houses are filled with conveniences which the kings of former times might have envied. Our bridges, our canals, our roads, our modes of communication fill every stranger with wonder. Nowhere are manufactures carried to such perfection. Nowhere does man exercise such a domination over matter."[2]

By 'man', Macaulay meant the capitalists and landlords who owned and ran the country. This, in turn, was reflected in the increased confidence of these classes, who, it has been remarked, began to think in terms, not of countries and years, but of continents and centuries. The Industrial Revolution was a revolution that not only changed the country, but the whole mode of life. It ushered in revolutions in science and industrial technique. Kay's flying shuttle, Hargreaves' spinning-jenny, Arkwright's water frame, Watt's steam-engine, Cort's puddling and rolling process, all contributed to the new revolution. "The steam-engine had no precedent, the spinning-jenny is without ancestry, the mule and the power-loom entered on no prepared heritage," stated Cooke Taylor, "they sprang into sudden existence like Minerva from the brain of Jupiter."[3]

"The age is running mad after innovation", stated the sarcastic Dr. Johnson. "All the business of the world is to be done in a new way; men are to be hanged in a new way; Tyburn [the place of public executions] itself is not safe from the fury of innovation."[4]

---

1   L. Trotsky, *The History of the Russian Revolution*, vol. 1, p. 107.

2   J.L. Hammond and B. Hammond, *The Town Labourer 1760-1832*, p. 1.

3   Quoted in E.P. Thompson, p. 208.

4   Quoted in P. Deane, *The First Industrial Revolution*, p. 119.

Above all, the social relationships between men and women were revolutionised. The victory of capitalism had introduced a new social order, characterised by two new antagonistic classes, the bourgeoisie and proletariat, both defined by their relationship to the means of production.

The first of these was a powerful class of capitalist manufacturers, which gathered into its hands a *monopoly of the means of production*, the factories, mills and mines. This class put its stamp on society, ruthlessly clearing the path for its own dominion. In the words of Marx and Engels:

> The bourgeoisie, wherever it has got the upper hand, has put an end to all feudal, patriarchal, idyllic relations. It has pitilessly torn asunder the motley feudal ties that bound man to his 'natural superiors', and has left remaining no other nexus between man and man than naked self-interest, than callous 'cash payment'.[5]

This bourgeoisie struck a compromise with the landed aristocracy to share power, while retaining the upper hand in the bargain. This was the so-called 'Glorious' Revolution of 1688, which laid the basis for expansion and empire. The country's new-found wealth and riches were extolled in the patriotic song, 'Rule, Britannia', which epitomised its dominant world position. Her economic power allowed her to 'rule the waves' and plunder her rivals. British shipping amounted to around half the world's tonnage. She commanded a divided Europe, by pitting one country against another, financed the struggle against the French Revolution, built a British Empire that covered a quarter of the world, and far more besides. This was the foundation upon which the dominance, prestige, and arrogance of the English ruling class was built. According to the fifth stanza of 'Rule, Britannia':

To thee belongs the rural reign;
Thy cities shall with commerce shine:
All thine shall be the subject main,
And every shore it circles thine.
Rule, Britannia! Britannia rules the waves:
Britons, never, shall be slaves.

The tune's refrain on the word 'never' was later often corrupted to 'never, never, never', a further indication of a growing national arrogance. However, while Britons would not be slaves, slavery was a profitable enterprise for English capitalists and merchants. It is estimated that only 10.7 million of the 12.5 million Africans who were shipped in English and other vessels to

---

5   MESW, vol. 1, p. 111.

the Americas during the period of the slave trade survived the two-month 'passage' on the disease-ridden slave ships. By 1783, the triangular route that took British-made goods to Africa to buy slaves, transported the enslaved to the West Indies, and then brought back slave-grown products such as sugar, tobacco, and cotton, represented about eighty per cent of the country's foreign income. The British government eventually banned the slave trade in 1807, but it was not until 1833 that slavery was abolished in most of the Empire. In 1837, the British government passed the Slave Compensation Act, which paid out £20m (£17bn at today's values) to slave owners, 3,000 of whom were in Britain, for the loss of their 'property'. Of course, the former slaves did not get a penny-farthing. Africa was then plundered for its land, raw materials and precious metals by companies such as the Royal Niger Company, the British East Africa Company and the British South Africa Company, which made large fortunes out of this lucrative business.

By the time of the last phase of Chartism in 1848, this island nation produced around two-thirds of the world's coal, around half of its iron, five sevenths of its supply of steel, and about half the cotton cloth produced on a commercial scale. In the seventy years up to 1840, the productive forces of industry, technique and science, increased by 2,700 per cent, or twenty-seven times. Britain's remarkable transformation from an agricultural to an industrial society within the space of one or two generations was both violent and bloody. "Today it is a country like *no* other", observed Engels in 1844.[6] Alongside this, Britain acquired colonies and great riches which put the empires of Rome and Egypt into the shade. In the words of the author William Thackeray:

> Look yonder where the engines toil;
> These England's arms of conquest are,
> The trophies of her bloodless war;
> Brave weapons these.
> Victorious over waves and soil,
> With these she sails, she weaves, she tills
> Pierces the everlasting hills,
> And spans the seas.

The reason why Britain, this tiny island off the coast of the European continent, became the first country to industrialise is a complex and puzzling question. The seeds of this process were planted in the bourgeois revolution of the 1640s. This brought to power a government that fostered industry and

6   MECW, vol. 4, p. 320.

commerce. England's insular position gave her colossal advantages as soon as national unity and internal peace were established.

By this time, she was already the largest free-trade area in Europe. She became the first country to make large-scale use of coal and iron, the very basis of machinery and industrial development. By using these important advantages, Britain's Industrial Revolution revolutionised the productive forces and destroyed the old way of life, transforming it from a rural one into an industrial one. It brought into being a society based upon capitalist methods, including brutal exploitation and toil, the likes of which had never been seen before. "The spirit of the age has broken with the world as it has hitherto existed", wrote G.W.F. Hegel.[7]

DRIPPING WITH BLOOD

"In the beginning was the Word", says the Bible. In fact, as far as the working class was concerned, it was the deed. Capitalism came into being, Marx famously wrote, "dripping from head to foot, from every pore, with blood and dirt."[8] This is an accurate description of England at this time, where the peasantry had long since been eradicated and replaced by agricultural labourers. This process of 'primitive accumulation', robbery, eviction, pillaging, piracy, and the like, was the foundation upon which capitalism was built, and which assured its future development.

The rise of capitalism also called into existence a propertyless proletariat, the mirror opposite of the bourgeoisie. This working class – the first-born sons and daughters of capitalism – emerged into this world fighting for their very survival. It was an exceptionally painful birth. "The working class did not rise like the sun at an appointed time", noted E. P. Thompson. "It was present at its own making."[9] From every corner of Britain, uprooted from the countryside and deprived of the means of production, it lost any semblance of independence, or what little it had. "Thus, an amazing number of people have been reduced from a comfortable state of partial independence to the precarious conditions of hirelings", wrote the Rev. D. Davies, who witnessed what was happening, in 1795.[10] The minister was certainly exaggerating the

---

7   G.W.F. Hegel, *The Phenomenology of Mind*, quoted in J. Loewenberg Ed., *Hegel Selections*, p. 9.

8   K. Marx, *Capital*, vol. 1, p. 926.

9   E.P. Thompson, *The Making of the English Working Class*, p. 9.

10 G.D.H. Cole and A.W. Filson, *British Working Class Movements: Selected Documents 1789-1975*, p. 4.

"comfortable state" of the rural population, as the countryside had its fair share of pain and squalor. Nevertheless, from 1797 to 1820, there were 1,727 Acts of Enclosure, which largely stripped the rural areas of their able-bodied population, creating a vast reserve army of landless labourers desperate for work.

From the moment it drew its first breath, this newborn class could only survive by throwing itself at the mercy of the capitalists and selling itself to the highest bidder. Herded into hellish factories, mines and mills, and lacking any organisation, the workers simply provided the industrialists with raw material for exploitation. For the manufacturers, the workers were merely so many 'hands', dehumanised, alienated and desperate for work. At first, they were completely impotent before the dictates of capital, the commands of the foremen and the speed of the machines. Their living conditions were atrocious, packed like animals in cramped and intolerable lodgings. Under the savage rigours of factory life, the working class was forced to endure continual humiliation, at the beck and call of the overseer's whip and the capitalist's greed for super profits.

The introduction of machinery by the capitalists only served to strengthen the power of capital over labour. Through higher productivity the machines would destroy the last vestiges of the home-based cottage industries. "History has no more pitiful spectacle to offer than that of the gradual decay of the English handloom weavers, a process which took several decades, and was finally completed by 1838", wrote Marx in *Capital*.[11] "It is questionable if all the mechanical inventions yet made have lightened the day's toil of any human being", noted John Stuart Mill in his *Principles of Political Economy*. In fact, the only purpose of the machines was to increase relative surplus value, to squeeze more unpaid labour out of the workers in a shorter space of time. The pace of the machines could be increased and could be employed continuously for twenty-four hours a day, further intensifying the process of exploitation. The introduction of the steam engine gave greater mobility to the capitalists and greater choice as to the location of their factories. The domination of the machines over the workers made them a prime target for their hatred, giving birth to the Luddite movement of machine-breakers.

Every socio-economic system is governed by its own laws, and the new capitalist mode of production was no different. These laws, epitomised by Adam Smith's *invisible hand*, operated in a contradictory fashion, behind the back of society. Unlike previous societies, the capitalist system was subject

---

11 K. Marx, *Capital*, vol. 1, p. 461.

to periodic crises of *overproduction*, a completely new phenomenon, where feverish economic activity was followed by economic collapse. At this time, the economic cycle appeared at five- or six-yearly intervals, then later ten-year cycles, reflecting the rhythm of investment and production, operating through the blind forces of the market. Slumps or depressions took place in 1819, 1826, 1829, 1832, 1837, 1842 and 1848, covering the entire period we are discussing. This had a devastating impact on the lives of ordinary people, causing widespread unemployment and destitution.

"What is to become of those destitute millions, who consume today what they earned yesterday," asked Engels, "who have created the greatness of England by their inventions and their toil; who become with every passing day more conscious of their might, and demand, with daily increasing urgency, their share of the advantages of society?" They were, of course, simply excess to requirements. As Engels went on to explain:

> The starving workmen whose employers could give them no work, stood in the streets in all directions, begged singly or in crowds, besieged the sidewalks in armies, and appealed to the passers-by for help; they begged, not cringing like ordinary beggars, but threatening by their numbers, their gestures, and their words. Such was the state of things in all the industrial districts, from Leicester to Leeds, and from Manchester to Birmingham.[12]

This description is taken from Engels' book, *The Condition of the Working Class in England*, which we have already quoted. It is a true masterpiece of social research and analysis that should be compulsory reading for all concerned. For anybody who wants to understand the conditions of this 'Bleak Age', there is nothing better.

BREED APART

While the emerging proletariat experienced nightmare conditions inside and outside the factories, the English bourgeoisie were truly a special breed apart. It was said the cotton masters were as grim as the stones that built the Satanic mills and "their souls bound up in gold ... as hardened as the bricks of their warehouses", to quote the words of a contemporary. These new lords of the mill had an insatiable thirst for the ready supply of cheap labour, like a vampire's craving for blood, a thirst only quenched by the torrent of men, women and children who flooded into overcrowded towns and who were herded into stinking rat-infested tenements. Half the workforce in the cotton

---

12 MECW, vol. 4, p. 387.

industry were children and a further sizeable proportion were women. Thus, the system was sucking up the labour of entire families.

The outlook of the English upper classes was described very well by Friedrich Engels, whose father was a capitalist in Manchester. Through his family connections, he was able to observe this bourgeois class at close quarters:

> I have never seen a class so deeply demoralised, so incurably debased by selfishness, so corroded within, so incapable of progress, as the English bourgeoisie, and I mean by this, especially the bourgeoisie proper, particularly the Liberal, Corn Law repealing bourgeoisie. For it nothing exists in this world, except for the sake of money, itself not excluded. It knows no bliss save that of rapid gain, no pain save that of losing gold. In the presence of this avarice and lust of gain, it is not possible for a single human sentiment or opinion to remain untainted. True, these English bourgeois are good husbands and family men, and have all sorts of other private virtues, and appear, in ordinary intercourse, as decent and respectable as all other bourgeois; even in business they are better to deal with than the Germans; they do not higgle and haggle so much as our own pettifogging merchants; but how does this help matters? Ultimately it is self-interest, and especially money gain, which alone determines them.

> I once went into Manchester with such a bourgeois, and spoke to him of the bad, unwholesome method of building, the frightful condition of the working-people's quarters, and asserted that I had never seen so ill-built a city. The man listened quietly to the end, and said at the corner where we parted: "And yet there is a great deal of money made here, good morning, sir."

> It is utterly indifferent to the English bourgeois whether his workingmen starve or not, if only he makes money. All the conditions of life are measured by money, and what brings no money is nonsense, unpractical, idealistic bosh... The relation of the manufacturer to his operatives has nothing human in it; it is purely economic. The manufacturer is Capital, the operative Labour. And if the operative will not be forced into this abstraction, if he insists that he is not Labour, but a man, who possesses, among other things, the attribute of labour-power, if he takes it into his head that he need not allow himself to be sold and bought in the market, as the commodity 'Labour', the bourgeois reason comes to a standstill. He cannot comprehend that he holds any other relation to the operatives than that of purchase and sale; he sees in them not human beings, but hands, as he constantly calls them to their faces; he insists, as Carlyle says, that "Cash Payment is the only nexus between man and man." Even the relation between himself and his wife is, in ninety-nine cases out of a hundred, mere 'Cash Payment'. Money

determines the worth of the man; he is 'worth ten thousand pounds'. He who has money is of 'the better sort of people', is 'influential', and what he does counts for something in his social circle. The huckstering spirit penetrates the whole language, all relations are expressed in business terms, in economic categories. Supply and demand are the formulas according to which the logic of the English bourgeois judges all human life.[13]

BOURGEOIS APOLOGISTS

The new breed of political economists, such as Nassau Senior, were simply apologists for capitalist exploitation and the new morality of the market. That is all they were good for. They were certainly not economists, but 'prizefighters' of the ruling class, to use the expression of Marx. Each of their pronouncements remain "the classical expression of the spirit of the factory," noted Marx, "not only because of its undisguised cynicism, but also because of the naivety with which it blurts out the thoughtless contradictions of the capitalist brain."[14]

The views of these creatures were graphically illustrated by the views of Dr. Andrew Ure from Glasgow. Although not an economist as such, he was an ardent apologist for business and the manufacturers. In 1834, Dr. Ure travelled around industrial Britain gathering information and looking at textile manufacture in the cotton, wool, linen and silk mills. His conclusions, *The Philosophy of Manufacturers,* was published as a book in 1835. In the preface he stated, as if butter wouldn't melt in his mouth, that he wrote the book so that "masters, managers, and operatives would follow the straight paths of improvement" and expressed his hope that it would help "prevent them from pursuing dangerous ideas." This appeared to be the most of noble causes, at least on paper.

Dr. Ure, however, was full of glowing praise for the notorious Quarry Bank Mill, near Wilmslow in Cheshire, owned by a certain Samuel Greg and Son, depicting idyllic scenes of blissful happiness. "At a little distance from the factory, on a sunny bank, stands a handsome house, two stories high, built for the accommodation of the female apprentices", stated Ure. "They are well fed, clothed and educated. The apprentices have milk-porridge for breakfast, potatoes and bacon for dinner, and meat on Sundays."

Compared to the 'normal' working conditions of the time, this sounded like a workers' paradise, while the exploitation of children sounded like the happy

---

13 MECW, vol. 4, pp. 562-564.
14 K. Marx, *Capital,* vol. 1, p. 564.

play of a kindergarten. "I have visited many factories, both in Manchester and the surrounding districts, during a period of several months and I never saw a single instance of corporal punishment inflicted on a child", he continued. "The children seemed to be always cheerful and alert, taking pleasure in using their muscles. The work of these lively elves seemed to resemble a sport. Conscious of their skill, they were delighted to show it off to any stranger. At the end of the day's work they showed no sign of being exhausted."

While hiding the real conditions that existed in the factories, Ure was scathing about the interference of Parliament, seeking to regulate conditions at work so as to prevent 'cheerful' children slaving their guts out non-stop for twelve hours or more in a factory. According to him, such interference was against nature and the workings of the economic system! Any such restrictions he considered anathema. This reflected his crude *laissez-faire* outlook.

Ure's book was condemned by factory reformers for its claims that children working in the factories and mills were treated well. The bourgeois economists of the day, while agreeing with their honourable friend, put their arguments in a more erudite fashion, so as to better pull the wool over everyone's eyes. All their economic theories were invented simply to justify the laws of capitalism and the workings of the market. While Adam Smith and David Ricardo had been genuine economists, seeking to understand the inner workings of capitalism, this new breed existed simply to justify the system of exploitation. Thus, they justified poverty wages, for instance, as a consequence of the 'Iron Law of Wages', which no one, including the employers, could contradict. Extension of the working day was justified by Nassau Senior with his 'last hour' theory, where profit supposedly came from the last hour of the working day, and therefore to reduce its length would eliminate profits. Trade unions were of course an extremely bad idea, which only served to prevent competition and distort the natural laws of supply and demand, thereby hurting masters and workers alike. This argument is still used to this very day!

Of course, not everyone was in agreement with wretched Malthusianism. As Benjamin Jewett wrote:

I have always felt a certain horror of political economists since I heard one of them [Nassau Senior] say that he feared the famine of 1848 in Ireland would not kill more than a million people, and that would scarcely be enough to do much good.[15]

---

15 J. Saville, *The British State and the Chartist Movement*, p. 199.

But these views were held by a minority. Far more typical were the likes of Lord Brougham, the chairman of the 'Society for the Diffusion of Useful Knowledge', who took to admonishing the working class:

> When there is too much labour in the market and wages are too low, do not combine to raise the wages; do not combine with the vain hope of compelling the employer to pay more for labour than there are funds for the maintenance of labour; *but go out of the market*. Leave the rotations between wages and labour to equalise themselves.[16]

This appeal to "go out of the market" was a demand to emigrate. However, this was not a solution to the problem, but simply a means of exporting it from one place to another. Such was the stern advice to the 'surplus population', a term popularised by the notorious Thomas Malthus, from the upper classes. If the poor insisted on breeding, then they should be forced to emigrate or enter the hell of the workhouse. Of course, such specimens were all united in their opposition to a minimum wage, which would only serve to ruin industry and undermine profits. This was at a time when handloom weavers were petitioning for a minimum wage, which was roundly condemned by the *Manchester Times* as "absolute folly".

This graphically illustrated how low these reactionaries were prepared to stoop in defence of rent, interest, and profit. They had little regard, if any, for human suffering, as long as it was not they who suffered. The working class only existed to serve as fodder for capitalism, a ready supply of cheap labour. Needless to say, our modern-day bankers and capitalists are little different from their counterparts of that era; they are still guided by their greed for surplus value and profit.

We can see how desperate things were becoming for the handloom workers in Table 1.1 overleaf, which showed the weekly wages of a Bolton handloom weaver from 1797 to 1830. It was like a never-ending descent into abject misery.

By 1837, things had hit rock bottom. A petition at the end of the year showed a weaver's family income had shrunk to only one-and-a-half pence a day. We have the words uttered by a handloom weaver in Benjamin Disraeli's novel *Sybil*. They are words of despair and of betrayal, but they also reveal a growing class consciousness and even rage:

> It is not a vice that has brought me to this, nor indolence, nor imprudence. I was born to labour, and I was ready to labour. I loved my loom, and the loom loved me. It gave me a cottage in my native village, surrounded by a garden, of whose

16 A. Hutt, *This Final Crisis*, p. 23.

claims on my solicitude it was not jealous. There was time for both. It gave me for a wife the maiden that I have ever loved; and it gathered my children round my hearth with plenteousness and peace. I was content: I sought no other lot. It is not adversity that makes me look back upon the past with tenderness.

Then why am I here? Why am I, and six hundred thousand subjects of the Queen, honest, loyal, and industrious, why are we, after manfully struggling for years, and each year sinking lower in the scale, why are we driven from our innocent and happy homes, our country cottages that we loved, first to bide in close towns without comforts, and gradually to crouch into cellars, or find a squalid lair like this, without even the common necessities of existence; first the ordinary conveniences of life, then raiment, and, at length, food, vanishing from us.

The capitalist flourishes, he amasses immense wealth; we sink, lower and lower; lower than the beasts of burden; for they are fed better than we are, cared for more. And it is just, for according to the present system they are more precious. And yet they tell us that the interests of Capital and Labour are identical.[17]

The weekly wages of a Bolton handloom weaver[18] (Table 1.1)

Year	Shillings[19]	Pence
1797	30	00
1800	25	00
1805	25	00
1810	19	00
1816	12	00
1820	9	00
1824	8	06
1830	5	06

(Source: G.R. Porter, *The Progress of the Nation*, 1847 edition.)

TWO NATIONS

In the first half of the nineteenth century, the working class, as compared with the bourgeoisie, lived in an entirely alien world. British society was based on "two nations", to quote Disraeli.

17 B. Disraeli, *Sybil*, pp. 99-100.

18 The purchasing power in today's currency of five shillings and six pence is £24.80.

19 In pre-decimal British currency there were 12 pence in one shilling and 20 shillings in one pound; therefore, 240 pence in each pound. The abbreviation for a shilling was 's' and for a penny 'd' (from the Latin *denarius*).

Two nations: between whom there is no intercourse and no sympathy, who are as ignorant of each other's habits, thoughts, and feelings, as if they were dwellers in different zones, or inhabitants of different planets; who are formed by different breeding, are fed by a different food, are ordered by different manners, and are not governed by the same laws.[20]

Disraeli, who was a young Tory politician, used this book to 'dish it to the Whigs', the party that represented the manufacturers.

Interestingly, Disraeli's novel, which created such a sensation at the time, was published in 1845, the same year as Engels' *Condition of the Working Class in England*, and was certainly coloured by the Chartist experience. In fact, Chartism forms the background story of *Sybil, or The Two Nations*, to give it its full title. Huge fortunes were being made by the capitalists, creating a massive gulf in society between the haves and the have-nots. Such was the degree of polarisation that, in 1843, Gladstone, a member of the Tory Cabinet, warned the House of Commons of the "most melancholy features in the social state of this country… increase of the pressure of privations and distress… at the same time a constant accumulation of wealth in the upper classes, an increase of the luxuriousness of their habits and their means of enjoyment."[21]

Gladstone's concerns were that such extreme polarisation would give rise to social upheavals that could endanger the capitalist system. Nevertheless, then, as today, the ruling class were impotent to prevent this polarisation, which was an integral consequence of capitalist accumulation. The gulf between the classes was ever-widening and the living conditions of the working class, especially in the industrial conurbations, were atrocious. Engels quoted the observations of Nassau Senior about Manchester:

"*Not one house in this street escaped the cholera.* In general, the streets of these suburbs are unpaved, with a dung-heap or ditch in the middle; the houses are built back to back, without ventilation or drainage, and whole families are limited to a corner of a cellar or a garret."[22]

Nassau, while expressing sorrow at the plight of workers, was a fervent supporter of *laissez-faire*, namely, leaving the 'market' to solve such problems. Nevertheless, William Dixon explained that it had nothing to do with

20 Ibid., p. 58.
21 A. Hutt, *This Final Crisis*, p. 19.
22 'Letters on the Factory Act to Rt. Hon., the President of the Board of Trade', London, 1837, quoted in MECW, vol. 4, p. 364, emphasis in original.

providence and everything to do with "the ruthless hand of the oppressor", which "has dragged our wives and little ones into the factory or loathsome mine... living upon the blood and vitals of those he loves."[23] Such loathing became commonplace, which would later feed into the Chartist movement.

Amid these festering social conditions in which the working class lived, disease and death were forever present, a constant ally. Diarrhoea was the greatest killer in terms of sheer numbers. Tuberculosis killed 59,000 in 1838 alone. Cholera killed 30,000 people in 1831. Whooping cough helped carry away 10,000 annually and measles 7,000 every year. Even minor injuries affecting the poor could lead to incapacity or even death. Life expectancy was extremely low, especially in children employed in the factories and mines. The startling figures reveal that the average lifespan for a labourer in Bolton was eighteen years, in Manchester seventeen and in Liverpool fifteen. The skilled trades fared little better. In Leeds their average life expectancy was twenty-seven years, in Bolton twenty-three and in Manchester twenty.

Into the mix were drawn the Irish immigrants, who served to swell the towns of the North and elsewhere, desperately searching for food and work. They crossed the Irish Sea in large numbers, settling in the manufacturing districts of Lancashire, Manchester, Glasgow and other towns. Between 1841 and 1851, at the time of the great Irish famine, half a million crossed the Irish Sea. An adult could cross to Liverpool for half a crown in fourteen hours; in 1827 fierce competition had driven the price down to four or five pence a ticket, as men, women and children were crammed into holds as human cargo. As a result, the Irish community made up ten per cent of the population of Manchester and seven per cent of Liverpool.

As the registrar of a Manchester district wrote:

> During the last two or three months large numbers of poor from Ireland have crowded themselves in this district, droves of them rambling about the streets seeking lodgings and no doubt being exposed to the severe and inclement weather. Many of the poor creatures have died from cold producing fevers and diseases.

In Liverpool there were "thousands of hungry and naked Irish perishing in our streets", and in South Wales, they were described as "bringing pestilence on their backs, famine in their stomachs".[24]

Shocked, brutalised and stripped of any ties with the countryside, they were introduced overnight to the system of grinding industrial exploitation.

---

23 D. Jones, p. 115.

24 J.L. Hammond and B. Hammond, *The Bleak Age*, p. 37.

The experience was unimaginable and soon taught them to rebel against such conditions. No wonder the Irish were commonly regarded as troublemakers. A Catholic priest said he noticed that the Irish were more prone than the English to take part in trade unions, which he attributed to the habits acquired under the bad laws of Ireland. Meanwhile, another employer complained: "The Irish are more disposed to turn out, to make unreasonable demands, to take offence at slight cause, and to enforce their demands by strikes or bad language."[25]

What is certainly true is that the Irish supplied many leaders for the British trade unions, the radical movements, and Chartism in particular. We will soon meet some of these outstanding figures.

CHILD LABOUR

Like moths drawn to a naked flame, desperate to earn a crust of bread, the dispossessed multitude rushed headlong into the factories and workplaces, referred to as 'bastilles'. Thrust into this cauldron of industrial life, dominated by the incessant, deafening noise of the machines, it resembled a scene from Dante's *Inferno*. Alongside the factories was the declining 'domestic' system, which relied on piece-work, the most degrading of all work. Children were sold to employers to clear a parent's debts, and worked in mills and even coal mines, where those as young as five, alongside women, were forced to drag along heavy carts on all fours. "Chained, belted, harnessed like dogs in a go-cart, black, saturated with wet, and more than half-naked – crawling, upon their hands and feet, and dragging their heavy loads behind them – they present an appearance indescribably disgusting and unnatural", read a report from the Children's Employment Commission of 1842.

The developing iron industry also soaked up labour like a sponge, as in Coalbrookdale, where iron ore was first smelted by Abraham Darby using easily mined 'coking coal'. In such dirty hell-holes, the heat was unbearable, forcing the workers to strip practically naked. Merthyr Tydfil became the new centre for iron smelting, which ushered in the dictatorship of the South Wales iron masters, eloquently captured in the novels of Alexander Cordell, such as *Rape of the Fair Country*.

When industry boomed and labour was in short supply, factory owners simply bought pauper children, at a cheap price, from the Poor Law Guardians. Women and children were transported from the workhouses in carts and barges, in a manner reminiscent of chattel slavery. They were

---

25 A.L. Morton and G. Tate, p. 82.

particularly valued for their nimble fingers, which could keep up with the power looms. Economic destitution often compelled families to give up their children into the greedy clutches of the mill owners. Before the committee of Parliament in 1816, John Moss, a former master of apprentices in a cotton mill, gave evidence about parish children forced into factory work:

> Were they parish apprentices? – All parish apprentices.
>
> At what age were they taken? – Those that came from London were from about seven to eleven. Those from Liverpool were from about eight or ten to fifteen.
>
> Up to what period were they apprenticed? – One and twenty.
>
> What were the hours of work? – From five o'clock in the morning till eight at night.
>
> Were fifteen hours in the day the regular hours of work? – Yes.
>
> When the works were stopped for the repair of the mill, or for any want of cotton, did the children afterwards make up for the loss of time? – Yes.
>
> Did the children sit or stand to work? – Stand.
>
> The whole of their time? – Yes.
>
> Were there any seats in the mill? - None … I have found them frequently upon the mill-floors, after the time they should have been in bed.
>
> Were any children injured by the machinery? – Very frequently.

Parliamentary reports give a comprehensive insight into horrific working conditions, such as the Factories' Inquiry Commission's Report on Children's Employment of 1833. The report provides evidence from the eleven-year old Thomas Clarke, who was earning four shillings a week piece-work (with the aid of his brother) in a mill:

> They always strapped us if we fell asleep … Castles used to get a rope about as thick as my thumb, and double it, and put knots in it … I used to go to the factory a little before six, sometimes at five, and work on till nine at night … I worked all night one night … We chose it ourselves. We wanted to have something to spend. We had been working from six in the morning the day before. We went on working till nine o'clock the next night … I am at the rope walk now … I can earn about four shillings … My brother turns for me. He is just seven. I don't give him anything … if it was not my brother, I must give him 1 shilling a week … I take him with me at six, and keep him till eight.[26]

Engels personally witnessed these conditions. "Women made unfit for child-bearing, children deformed, men enfeebled, limbs crushed, whole generations

---

26 L. Huberman, *Man's Worldly Goods*, p. 187.

wrecked, afflicted with disease and infirmity, purely to fill the purses of the bourgeoisie", he wrote.

And when one reads of the barbarism of single cases, how children are seized naked in bed by the overlooker, and driven with blows and kicks to the factory, their clothing over their arms, how their sleepiness is driven off with blows, how they fall asleep over their work nevertheless, how one poor child sprang up, still asleep, at the call of the overlooker, and mechanically went through the operations of its work after its machine was stopped; when one reads how children, too tired to go home, hide away in the wool in the drying-room to sleep there, and could only be driven out of the factory with straps; how many hundreds came home so tired every night, that they could eat no supper for sleepiness and want of appetite, that their parents found them kneeling by the bedside, where they had fallen asleep during their prayers; when one reads all this and a hundred other villainies and infamies in this one report, all testified to on oath, confirmed by several witnesses, deposited by men whom the commissioners themselves declare trustworthy; when one reflects that this is a Liberal report, a bourgeois report, made for the purpose of reversing the previous Tory report, and rehabilitating the purest of heart of the manufacturers, that the commissioners themselves are on the side of the bourgeoisie, and report all these things against their own will, how can one be otherwise than filled with wrath and resentment against a class which boasts of philanthropy and self-sacrifice, while its one object is to fill its purse *a tout pris*? (at any price – RS)[27]

An indication of how desperate and tragic things had become was seen from the evidence of a handloom weaver, Thomas Heath:

Question: Have you any children?
Answer: No, I had two but they are both dead, thanks be to God!
Question: Do you express satisfaction at the death of your children?
Answer: I do. I thank God for it. I am relieved from the burden of maintaining them, and they, poor dear creatures, are relieved from the troubles of this mortal life.[28]

The sheer agony and toil of factory work, where many young people became old before their time, cannot be exaggerated. Their life-forces were squeezed out of them. Within a generation, the handloom weavers were destroyed by the power looms, until, as one worker said to the factory campaigner, Richard

---

27 MECW, vol. 4, p. 457.
28 Quoted in L. Huberman, *Man's Worldly Goods*, p. 185.

Oastler, they were reduced to living on their children. They tried in vain to compete with the machines, which simply drove many into an early grave.

GROWTH OF TOWNS

The industrial towns, a product of the Industrial Revolution, were growing at an extremely rapid pace. At the beginning of the period, Manchester was a small town with a population of perhaps 45,000, including Salford and surrounding villages. It eventually grew to become the second largest conurbation in England. The census figures for three separate years, 1801, 1831 and 1851, for Lancashire and the West Riding, shown in Table 1.2, demonstrate this growth.

Table 1.2

	1801	1831	1851
Manchester and Salford	90,000	237,000	400,000
Leeds	53,000	123,000	172,000
Sheffield	46,000	92,000	135,000
Bradford	13,000	44,000	104,000
Oldham	22,000	51,000	72,000
Bolton	18,000	42,000	61,000
Blackburn	12,000	27,000	65,000
Halifax	12,000	22,000	34,000

This additional urban population was quickly swallowed up as the thirst for labour-power in the factories grew. In 1840, 380,000 were employed in the woollen industry alone (as compared with 40,000 in 1760) and some 420,000 were absorbed into the cotton industry, of which 242,000 were women and over 80,000 were children and juveniles.

The settlements that sprung up around the factories and mills were more like frontier barracks than towns, as described by Charles Dickens in his classic novel *Hard Times*:

> It was a town of red brick, or of brick that would have been red if the smoke and ashes had allowed it… It was a town of machinery and tall chimneys, out of which interminable serpents of smoke trailed themselves for ever and ever… It had a black canal in it, and a river that ran purple with ill-smelling dye, and vast piles of building full of windows where there was rattling and a trembling all day long, and where the piston of the steam-engine worked monotonously up and down, like the head of an elephant in a state of melancholy madness… all went in and out at

the same hours, with the same sound upon the pavements, to do the same work, and to whom every day was the same as yesterday and tomorrow...[29]

In *The Old Curiosity Shop* Dickens again described in vivid language the industrial landscape of the Black Country in 1840:

> On every side, and as far as the eye can see into the heavy distance, tall chimneys, crowding on each other, and presenting that endless repetition of the same dull ugly form, which is the horror of oppressive dreams, poured out their plague of smoke, obscured the light, and made foul the melancholy air... Men, women and children, wan in their looks and ragged in attire, tended the engines, fed their tributary fires, begged upon the road, or scowled half-naked from the floorless houses. Then came more of the wrathful monsters, whose like they almost seemed to be in their wildness and their untamed air, screeching and turning round and round again; and still, before, behind and to the right and left, was the same interminable perspective of brick towers, never ceasing in their black vomit, blasting all things living or inanimate, shutting out the face of day, and closing in on all these horrors with a dense black cloud.[30]

The rivers and drinking water in these towns soon became utterly polluted, stinking, filthy and disease-ridden. The *Leeds Intelligencer,* 21 August 1841, describes the putrid smells coming from the River Aire, running through the centre of Leeds, which was filled with:

> [T]he contents of about 200 water closets and similar places, a great number of common drains, the drainings from dung-hills, the Infirmary (dead leeches, poultices for patients etc.), slaughter houses, chemical soap, gas, dung, dyehouses and manufactures, spent blue and black dye, pig manure, old urine wash, with all sorts of decomposed animal and vegetable substances from an extent drainage ... amounting to about 30,000,000 gallons per annum of the mass of filth with which the river is charged.[31]

The permanent stench from these cesspits must have been overpowering, especially in the summer months. It permeated the cramped, disease-ridden dwellings and hovels that lined the river, and which had neither basic sanitation nor infrastructure. The streets teemed with all sorts of wretched elements looking to scrape a living, with all the dangers of crime and violence ever-present. Many of these workers' dwellings were built on sewage ditches,

---

29 C. Dickens, *Hard Times*, p. 65.
30 C. Dickens, *The Old Curiosity Shop*.
31 Quoted in R. Brown & C. Daniels, *The Chartists: Documents and Debates*, p. 18.

with damp rising up from the rotten foundations and sodden walls. They were utterly devoid of any basic human comfort. Tenement cellars, used as billets for new arrivals, lacked light or ventilation. It was reported that in Liverpool alone 50,000 lived in such underground hovels.

The horrific housing conditions in the industrial towns were vividly described by Engels in *Condition of the Working Class in England*:

> Such are the various working-people's quarters of Manchester as I had occasion to observe them personally during twenty months. If we briefly formulate the result of our wanderings, we must admit that 350,000 working-people of Manchester and its environs live, almost all of them, in wretched, damp, filthy cottages, that the streets which surround them are usually in the most miserable and filthy condition, laid out without the slightest reference to ventilation, with reference solely to profit secured by the contractor. In a word, we must confess that in the working-men's dwellings of Manchester, no cleanliness, no convenience, and consequently no comfortable family life is possible; that in such dwellings only a physically degenerate race, robbed of all humanity, degraded, reduced morally and physically to bestiality, could feel comfortable and at home.[32]

LOSS OF RURAL LIFE

For the Irish immigrants, this hell must have provided a ghastly experience, even compared to the hell they had left behind. This was the experience too of those escaping from rural areas of England. Although extremely harsh, rural life still had its own set rhythm dominated by the seasons. Of course, this was no *Paradise Lost*. It was far from idyllic, plagued by crop failures, bad weather, pestilence and other such natural disasters. Nevertheless, village life had its own customs, festivals and traditions, a leftover from the past. These allowed for certain holidays, some merriment and even a bout of relaxation. In the countryside, people might work very hard from dawn till dusk and then perhaps take days off. Monday, for instance, became a traditional day of rest, known as St Monday. Their lives had a daily routine, and, as such, few people possessed a clock to tell the time. This limited freedom was destroyed by factory discipline, regulated and regimented from the time they entered the factory gates until they left work. They wished their lives away, day-in and day-out, as they yearned for every passing hour until the end of their shift.

Of course, accounts varied. A picture of rural Leicestershire in the middle of the eighteenth century, quoted by the historian William Felkin, gave a rather colourful view of things. He described how:

32 MECW, vol. 4, p. 364.

[E]very village had its wake; the lower orders lived in comparative ease and plenty, having right of common for pig and poultry, and sometimes a cow. The stocking-makers each had a garden, a barrel of home-brewed ale, a week-day suit of clothes and one for Sundays, and plenty of leisure, seldom working more than three days a week. Moreover, music was much cultivated by them.[33]

At home, despite the long hours of labour, the domestic workers were still their own masters. The strict monotony of factory life dramatically changed all this. Their lives were now directed by the sound of the factory bell.

The idea of 'Merry England' was completely destroyed. Love, merriment and drink were driven beyond the oceans, explained the journalist W.E. Adams. In England, according to him, workers became no better than machines; their lives "a mere affair of cogs and wheels".[34] Under these circumstances, the artisans of pre-industrial England were all but driven to extinction. Cottage industry gave way to the factory. Old craft trades were squeezed and crushed by ruthless competition from the large manufactures, forcing artisans to seek employment elsewhere. However, a small section, especially handloom workers, refused to enter the mills, preferring instead to go hungry or even worse. This was particularly the case in the Manchester area, which was based on the cotton industry. By June 1837, 50,000 workers in this region were unemployed or working short-time. Members of weavers' families, explained a petition at the time, had only one-and-a-half pence a day each to live on.

The capitalist mode of production meant that the new discipline of mill and factory had to be hammered into the workers on a daily basis, until it became part of their nature. They had to be broken in, as with a fledgling horse; made to bend to the demands of the machine and the speed of production. Industrial life from dawn till dusk was shaped by the rhythm of the treadmill. Twelve, fourteen, sixteen hours or more of work became life's daily routine. Harsh factory rules and fines became a way of life. The workers very being was violently transformed, moulded to the needs of capitalism. They had to give themselves up whole, body and soul, to the factory system, which devoured them and offered nothing in return, save a paltry wage. As the Hammonds explained:

> The Industrial Revolution added discipline, and the discipline of a power driven by a competition that seemed as inhuman as the machines that thundered in factory

---

33 Quoted in J.L. Hammond and B. Hammond, *The Skilled Labourer 1760-1832*, p. 222.

34 Quoted in D. Jones, p. 21.

and shed. The workman was summoned by the factory bell; his daily life was arranged by factory hours; he worked under an overseer imposing a method and precision for which the overseer had in turn to answer to some higher authority; if he broke one of a long series of minute regulations he was fined, and behind all this scheme of supervision and control there loomed the great impersonal system.[35]

"We make a nation of helots", wrote Adam Ferguson in 1765, in his *Essay on the History of Civil Society*, but that was only the very beginning of the process.[36]

FACTORY DICTATORSHIP

The nightmare of the dark Satanic mills became a living reality for millions. The factory was dominated by a dictatorship, where the master was God. This was reinforced legally by the Master and Servants Law of 1823. This law demanded obedience from 'servants' to their contracted employer, with infringements before the courts punishable by prison sentences and hard labour. There were no meaningful Factory Acts until 1833, and even then, there was no adequate inspection or enforcement. In any case, the local magistrate, tasked with enforcing the law, tended to be the local mill owner.

Within the workplaces large signs were common, which read: "Any person leaving their work and found talking with any other work-people shall be fined two pence for each offence", and similarly for "talking with any one out of their own ally", or sixpence for "talking to another, whistling, or singing".[37]

Table 1.3 shows a list of heavy fines imposed on workers for misdemeanours at the Tyldesley works, near Manchester, where the temperatures in the workshops reached a sweltering 80-84 degrees (Fahrenheit, 27-29 degrees Celsius).

This may seem incredible to us today, but let us not forget that, even today, workers are penalised in a thousand-and-one different ways. Employed on zero-hour and short-term contracts, summoned to work by text message, these workers are also at the beck and call of their bosses.

The fines read more like prison regulations. They were reported by spinners during a strike, and later published in a separate pamphlet, which stated:

"At Tyldesley they work fourteen hours per day, including the normal hour for dinner; the door is locked in working hours, except half an hour at tea time; the

---

35 *The Town Labour*, p. 19.

36 Quoted in C. Hill, *Reformation to Industrial Revolution*, p. 214.

37 Quoted by D. Craig, 'Introduction' in C. Dickens' *Hard Times*.

workpeople are not allowed to send for water to drink in the hot factory; and even the rain water is locked up, by the master's order, otherwise they would be happy to drink even that…"[38]

These strict rules were not exceptional, but the norm in most places.

Table 1.3

Misdemeanour	Shillings	Pence
Any spinner found with his window open	1	0
Any spinner found dirty at his work	1	0
Any spinner found washing himself	1	0
Any spinner leaving his oil can out of place	1	0
Any spinner repairing his drum banding with his gas lighted	2	0
Any spinner slipping with his gas lighted	2	0
Any spinner putting his gas out too soon	1	0
Any spinner spinning with gaslight too long in the morning	2	0
Any spinner having his lights too large for each light	1	0
Any spinner heard whistling	1	0
Any spinner having hard ends hanging on his weights	0	6
Any spinner having hard ends on carriage band	1	0
Any spinner being five minutes after last bell rings	1	0
Any spinner having roller laps, no more two draws for each roller lap	0	6
Any spinner going further than the roving-room door when fetching rovings	1	0
Any spinner being sick and unable to find another spinner to give satisfaction must pay for steam per day	6	0
Any spinner found in another's wheel gate	1	0
Any spinner neglecting to send him sweepings three mornings in the week	1	0
Any spinner having a little waste on his spindles	1	0

Within the factories, the capitalists could do as they pleased. Workers were regarded simply as 'factors of production', shut away in factories, and did not see the daylight for large parts of the year. "Cut off from the light of heaven for sixteen or seventeen hours a day, they are obliged to undergo a drudgery

38 Quoted in J.L. Hammond and B. Hammond, *The Town Labourer*, pp. 19-20.

which the veriest slave in the plantations would think intolerable, for the mighty sum of fourteen pence", writes Richard Atkinson.[39] In the mines it was even worse. "We hardly see daylight for the best part of the year", reported Hughes, a collier, to the Midland Mining Commission.[40]

The working day seemed to be extended without limit, with the introduction of shift work, including for children. The machine worked non-stop; it never tired, never slept, and never took a break. When working, exhausted children had to be beaten to keep them awake and prevent them from falling into unguarded machinery and being mangled. Many were tragically crippled or died before their time. Age did not seem to matter as long as they could work. Incredibly, there were even cases reported of three-year-old children working a twelve-hour day. As the report, *Moral and Physical Conditions of the Operatives employed in the Cotton Manufacture in Manchester*, noted:

> Whilst the engine runs the people must work – men, women, and children are yoked together with iron and steam. The animal machine – breakable in the best case, subject to a thousand sources of suffering – is chained fast to the iron machine, which knows no suffering and no weariness…[41]

The mining industry was particularly brutal, employing women and children deep in the bowels of the earth. The working day in the pits varied; for men it was twelve hours, for women and children it was even longer. At the Felling Colliery near Gateshead, at the beginning of the nineteenth century, boys' hours were from eighteen to twenty a day. One collier described how he used to put his child in a cradle in the coal seam where he worked, out of reach from the rats. Children working in the mines were often brought to the pit on their fathers' backs. The Felling Colliery suffered four disasters in this period, in 1812, 1813, 1821 and 1847. The 1812 disaster alone claimed 92 lives, including women and children. The Select Committee on Accidents in 1835 reported that there were 447 deaths in the pits in Northumberland and Durham in the eighteen years before 1816, and 538 in the eighteen years following.

Such conditions were regarded as normal for the 'hewers of wood and carriers of water'. Working-class children were denied basic education, so

---

39 Quoted in Ibid., p. 18.
40 P. Hollis Ed., *Class and Class Conflict in Nineteenth Century England: 1815-1850*, p. 299.
41 Quoted in J.L. Hammond and B. Hammond, *The Town Labourer*, p. 21.

they would not get above their station. "Nothing is more favourable to morals than habits of early subordination, industry, and regularity", stated Mr. G. A. Lee, the owner of a cotton factory in which children worked from 6am until 8pm. Such views were widespread, including in the Royal Society, the president of which, a Mr. Giddy, explained:

> "Giving education to the labouring masses of the poor… would in effect be found to be prejudicial to their morals and happiness; it would teach them to despise their lot in life, instead of making them good servants in agriculture, and other laborious employments to which their rank in society had destined them… it would enable them to read seditious pamphlets… it would render them insolent to their superiors."[42]

As capitalist technique advanced so did the power and wealth of the employing class. "It makes an accumulation of misery a necessary condition, corresponding to the accumulation of wealth", wrote Marx. "Accumulation of wealth at one pole is, therefore, at the same time accumulation of misery, the torment of labour, slavery, ignorance, brutalisation and moral degradation at the opposite pole, i.e. on the side of the class that produces its own product as capital."[43] Likewise, an anonymous weaver in *The Poor Man's Guardian* explained:

> "There is no common interest between working men and profit-makers. This fact, like the sun, forever stares us in the face – that in exact proportion as these large capitals are obtained, so is the poverty of the working people most capitally increased."[44]

Under capitalism, the purpose of production is not the satisfaction of human need, but simply to increase surplus value, which means the quantity of unpaid labour-time.

These conditions of capitalist exploitation were vividly described by Marx in his striking phrase: "Capital is dead labour which, vampire-like, lives only by sucking living labour, and lives the more, the more labour it sucks."[45] He continued: "As a capitalist, he is only capital personified. His soul is the soul of capital. But capital has one sole driving force, the drive to valorise, to create surplus value, to make its constant part, the means of production, absorb the greatest possible amount of surplus labour." Through capitalist competition,

---

42 Quoted in L. Huberman, *Man's Worldly Goods*, p. 190.

43 K. Marx, *Capital*, vol. 1, p. 799.

44 J. Lindsay Ed., *Spokesmen for Liberty*, p. 279.

45 *Capital*, vol. 1, p. 342.

each capitalist is forced to plough the surplus value extracted from unpaid labour back into developing production, which in turn develops productive capacity. This leads to the gradual accumulation and concentration of capital in fewer and fewer hands. While surplus value is created in production, the realisation of profit takes place in the marketplace.

The lines above are taken from Marx's *Capital*, from the section dealing with the working day. They show that the law of capitalism is to squeeze out the maximum surplus value from the worker, either by increasing the intensity of work or by lengthening the working day. The former produces relative surplus value, while the latter produces absolute surplus value. Both are simply different ways of intensifying the exploitation of the working class. Marx's words provide an accurate description of working conditions at the time of Chartism. Basing himself on extensive research into Parliamentary reports, he reveals the bitter struggles in the factories and mines over the length of the working day.

The radical poet William Blake described the woes of the working class when he wrote:

> There souls of men are bought and sold,
> And milk-fed infancy for gold;
> And youth to slaughter houses led,
> And beauty for a bit of bread.[46]

THE 1834 NEW POOR LAW

As the Bible states, the poor will always be with us. But they still needed to be dealt with. The upper classes regarded poverty as an inevitable consequence of human nature, and a defect of the human character. The solution to pauperism, as they saw it, was hard work and thrift. In effect, the propertied classes declared war on the poor.

This was championed by the Rev. Thomas Malthus, whose 'theory' blamed pauperism on overpopulation. He theorised about the problem in his infamous book, *An Essay on the Principles of Population*, published in 1798, which was in part a reply to William Godwin, the father-in-law of Shelley. Godwin had claimed that all governments were evil, but that progress and happiness could be attained through reason. Malthus sought to challenge those 'subversive' ideas, which threatened England with its own version of the chaos and evils of the French Revolution.

---

46 'Gnomic Verses', *Blake's Poetical Works*, p. 193.

As Malthus wrote:

"The great error under which Mr. Godwin labours throughout his whole work is, the attributing almost all the vices and misery that are seen in civil society to human institutions. Political regulations, and the established administration of property, are with him the fruitful sources of all evil, the hotbeds of all crimes that degrade mankind. Were this really a true state of the case, it would not seem a hopeless task to remove evil completely from the world; and reason seems to be the proper and adequate instrument for effecting so great a purpose. But the truth is that, though human institutions appear to be the obvious and obtrusive causes of much mischief to mankind; yet, in reality, they are light and superficial, they are mere feathers that float on the surface, in comparison with those deeper-seated causes of impurity that corrupt the springs and render turbid the whole stream of human life."[47]

These "deep-seated causes", according to Malthus, were that population increases faster than the food needed to keep the population alive. It was therefore inevitable that there would come a point when there were more mouths to feed than food to feed them. "Population, when unchecked, increases in geometrical ratio. Subsistence increases only in an arithmetical ratio", he explained. Fortunately, the solution to this problem came from death, in the form of "epidemics, pestilence and plague ... and famine", which intervened to reduce the population, so that it came into balance with the food-supply.

Could anything, therefore, be done to relieve the suffering of the poor? "Nothing", said Malthus in the first edition of his book. However, in the second edition, published in 1803, he discovered a partial solution. Leaving aside vice and misery, a third check to population growth was "moral restraint". No amount of charity, government regulation, trade unions or other institution of that sort could help in any way to ease the plight of the poor. They had no one else to blame but themselves for breeding too fast. This, then, was the theoretical basis for the New Poor Law.

As Engels explained:

[T]he most open declaration of war of the bourgeoisie upon the proletariat is Malthus' Law of Population and the New Poor Law framed in accordance with it... Malthus declares in plain English that the right to live, a right previously asserted in favour of every man in the world, is nonsense.[48]

47 Quoted in L. Huberman, p. 207.
48 MECW, vol. 4, p. 570.

As you might expect, Malthus was hated among northern working-class radicals, who fought tooth and nail against the imposition of the New Poor Law.

Whilst hated by the workers, Malthus' ideas were very popular in ruling circles. Astonishingly, these Malthusian ideas are still highly prevalent today in the ruling class and their political representatives in the Conservative Party.

"Suffering and evil are nature's admonitions; they cannot be got rid of," explained *The Economist* of 1848, "and the impatient attempts of benevolence to banish them from the world by legislation before benevolence has learnt their object and their end, have always been productive of more evil than good."[49] Malthus also attracted the support of Francis Place, the social reformer, who promoted the idea of birth control as a solution to social ills. He wrote and published a book on the subject of abstinence. However, that did not prevent Place from personally fathering fifteen children. It was a case of do as I say, not as I do.

Poverty and pauperism were certainly on the increase, especially with the rise in the cost of bread, and the decline in real wages. A scheme of outdoor relief known as the Speenhamland system had been introduced in 1795 to mitigate rural poverty. This was used to do away with the Elizabethan Poor Law and to subsidise wages from the Poor Rates. It kept the poorest, who would otherwise have starved, barely alive, but it also kept wages down to subsistence levels to the benefit of employers. However, the cost fell on the ratepayers, the farmers and landowners in particular, to their dismay and anguish.

THE MALTHUSIAN COMMISSIONERS

The end of the Napoleonic Wars in 1815 saw the burden of the Poor Rate rise substantially, pushing many parishes to the verge of bankruptcy. It has been estimated that there were 1.5 million paupers in Britain by 1832, about twelve per cent of the population of 13 million. In the same year, the Reform Parliament was forced to set up a Commission of Enquiry to see what was to be done. The old prolific scheme, they concluded, was costing too much and was leading to the moral degeneration of the working class. Therefore, a good dose of discipline was required, which the authorities were keen to administer. The working class needed to stand on its own two feet and not be mollycoddled by subsidies from the public purse. They therefore introduced a new Bill. Not surprisingly, this proposal was supported by Reverend Malthus,

---

49 Quoted in J. Pratt & A. Eriksson, *Contrasts in Punishment.*

who believed that the Poor Law handouts simply encouraged 'idleness', early marriage and excessive procreation.

According to one correspondent in the *Poor Man's Guardian*, writing under the pseudonym 'One of the Oppressed':

> "The Bill is the most illiberal, the most tyrannical, the most abominable, the most infamous, the most hellish measure that ever could or can be proposed… I therefore conjure you to prepare your coffins if you have the means. You will be starved to death by thousands if this Bill pass, and thrown on to the dung hill, or on the ground, naked, like dogs."[50]

Encouraged by this new vision of 'welfare', a year later, in 1834, the Whig Parliament graciously passed the New Poor 'Amendment Act' which replaced the Speenhamland system. By doing away with parish relief the idlers would be forced to find work in the factories and thereby become more productive. Thus, the workhouses were revived in every parish and new ones built to "render the people industrious". The New Poor Law abolished outdoor relief and offered relief only *inside the workhouse*, where the idle could be employed on such 'worthy' tasks as breaking stones, crushing bones for fertiliser, or picking oakum. The administration of the Poor Law was taken out of the hands of the parish and placed under the central control of a nationally-appointed body of Commissioners, popularly known as the 'Three Bashaws (or "Kings") of Somerset House'. These, in turn, organised the country into 'Unions', which were supervised by a Board of Guardians. The secretary of the Commissioners was a man called Edwin Chadwick, a fanatical disciple of Bentham's utilitarianism and orthodox political economy. He set the necessary tone from the top. In the language of the Poor Law Commission, able-bodied inmates must be "subjected to such courses of labour and discipline as will repel the indolent and vicious". The main principle was that relief in the workhouse should be made more intolerable than the most unpleasant means of earning a living outside.

The Poor Law Commissioners did not go quite as far as the complete starvation of the poor, as Malthus had recommended. That was a trifle too excessive, even for them. They said:

> Good, we grant you poor a right to exist, but only to exist; the right to multiply you have not, nor the right to exist as befits human beings. You are a pest, and if we cannot get rid of you as we do of other pests, you shall feel, at least, that you are a pest, and you shall at least be held in check, kept from bringing into the world other 'surplus', either directly or through inducing in others laziness and want of

---

50 T. Rothstein, p. 95.

employment. Live you shall, but live as an awful warning to all those who might have inducements to become 'superfluous'.[51]

The old paternalistic system gave way to gruel and the lash. On entering the workhouse, families were broken up to 'prevent child-rearing' and inmates subjected to the utmost cruelty and misery. Of course, religion played an important part in workhouse life. Sermons were read to the paupers before breakfast and after supper each day, and each Poor Law Union was required to appoint a Church of England chaplain to look after the spiritual needs of their inmates.

As a result of the Act, expenditure on relief dramatically fell from £6.5 million in 1831 to only £500,000 in 1841. In Kent, for instance, the number of persons receiving indoor parish relief in twelve parishes fell from 3,512 persons in 1833 to five persons in 1836. The building of the required number of workhouses was completed by 1837, when the law came into full force, despite the mass protests and opposition.

The workhouse regime was so abominable that Charles Dickens based his second book, *Oliver Twist*, on an orphan brought up in such an institution, following the death of his mother during childbirth. It is no accident that *The Northern Star* in 1837 published long extracts from *Oliver Twist* for its working-class readership. The horrors of the workhouse system were brought to light in a national scandal that broke out over the treatment of inmates in the Andover workhouse in the south of England. The master of the workhouse was accused of starving the paupers to such an extent that the inmates fought among themselves for the gristle and marrow in the half-putrid bones they were supposed to crush.

The reason why the New Poor Law stirred up so much hatred and opposition was that many workers would be in likely need of relief at some point in their lives. It was therefore an issue of grave concern to every worker and their families. "Huge, prison-like workhouses had risen in various parts, serving to remind the poor of their coming doom", explained Gammage, a Chartist who wrote the earliest history of Chartism. "With scanty wages, in many instances insufficient to support life in a tolerable state of comfort, there was nothing before them but misery in the present, and the Bastille in the future, in which they were to be immured when the rich oppressor no longer required their services."[52]

---

51 Quoted by F. Engels, MECW, vol. 4, p. 572.
52 R.C. Gammage, *History of the Chartist Movement*, p. 54.

Nothing would whip up such intense feelings as this question, which came to a head as the trade union agitation of 1830-34 was petering out. In his final years, William Cobbett, who viewed the legislation as stealing the birthright of the poor, launched a campaign in the House of Commons against the 'Poor Law Bastilles'. But it was the campaign outside Parliament, especially in the industrial North, that mobilised mass opposition. It was led by Oastler and the Reverend Stephens, whose agitation caused workhouses to be stormed and burned to the ground.

Without exaggeration, the campaign against the New Poor Law reached insurrectionary proportions, and underscored an indelible hatred towards the Whig government. In 1839, the Ashton Female Chartist Association called on women "to do all that in you lies, to prevent the wholesale murder of your newborn babies, by Malthusian method of painless extinction".[53] In Lancashire, such was the militant agitation that it took more than fifteen years to implement the Poor Law even in a modified form.

As Bronterre O'Brien noted:

> In one respect, the New Poor Law has done good. It has helped to open the people's eyes as to who are the real enemies of the working classes. Previously to the passing of the Reform Bill, the middle orders were supposed to have some community of feeling with the labourers. That delusion has passed away. It barely survived the Irish Coercion Bill, it vanished completely with the enactment of the Starvation Law. No working man will ever again expect justice, morals or mercy at the hands of a profit-mongering legislature.[54]

This New Poor Law was seen as the 'reward' given by the Whig bourgeoisie to the working class for their help in achieving the Reform Act of 1832. It was to add insult to injury. The protests and incendiary actions against the Poor Law were subsequently channelled into Chartism, further reinforcing its proletarian mass character.

The formal abolition of workhouses would only finally come in 1930, a hundred years later. However, even then, many of these establishments continued to function as 'Public Assistance Institutions' under local municipal control. Remarkably, it was not until the National Assistance Act of 1948 that the last vestiges of the Poor Law, and with it the workhouses, disappeared. It nevertheless lived on in the consciousness of workers and their families. I

---

53 Quoted in J. Schwarzkopf, *Women in the Chartist Movement*, p. 93, *Northern Star*, 2 February 1839.

54 Quoted in T. Rothstein, p. 99.

can still remember quite vividly as a boy when I nagged my mother for things we could not afford, she would often reply with a frown that, because of my insistence, "you will put me in the workhouse". And would I put her through that? I knew it was a very bad place, which often decided the matter.

"WEALTHY BEWARE!"

The 1830s were a period of open class war. "Class against class", was how Ernest Jones often described it. The capitalist order had arrived, not like a thief in the night, but like an unstoppable juggernaut, crushing everything in its path. Money relations dominated everything, including life and the cost of a pauper's grave. As the Hammonds wrote:

> Thus, England asked for profits and received profits. Everything turned to profits. The towns had their profitable dirt, their profitable slums, their profitable smoke, their profitable disorder, their profitable ignorance, their profitable despair... For the new town was not a home where man could find beauty, happiness, leisure, learning, religion, the influences that civilized outlook and habit, but a bare and desolate place, without colour, air or laughter, where men, women and children worked, ate and slept... The new factories and the new furnaces were the Pyramids, telling of man's enslavement rather than of his power, casting their long shadow over the society that took such pride in them.[55]

It was the heyday of British capitalism. Free trade and free competition were on the order of the day. Everything was for the best in the best of all possible capitalist worlds. The discontent, in the context of things, appeared as a small cloud, no bigger than a person's hand, on the horizon. But these were changing times. In fact, this cloud was the harbinger of a violent storm of class warfare that was going to engulf British society. It was about this that the revolutionary poet Percy Shelley wrote in his address 'To the Men of England':

> Men of England, wherefore plough
> For the lords who lay ye low?
> Wherefore weave with toil and care
> The rich robes your tyrants wear?

> Wherefore feed and clothe and save
> From the cradle to the grave
> Those ungrateful drones who would
> Drain your sweat – nay, drink your blood?

---

55 *The Rise of Modern Industry: 1925*, p. 232.

Wherefore, Bees of England, forge
Many a weapon, chain, and scourge,
That these stingless drones may spoil
The forced produce of your toil?

Have ye leisure, comfort, calm,
Shelter, food, love's gentle balm?
Or what is it ye buy so dear
With your pain and with your fear?

The seed ye sow, another reaps;
The wealth ye find, another keeps;
The robes ye weave, another wears;
The arms ye forge, another bears.

Sow seed – but let no tyrant reap:
Find wealth – let no imposter heap:
Weave robes – let not the idle wear:
Forge arms – in your defence to bear...

At the time, this threat of class war was tellingly picked up in an editorial in *The Times*, which warned: "War to the mansion, peace to the cottage – is the watchword of terror which may yet ring through the land. Let the wealthy beware!"[56] However, despite this warning, the fat was already on the fire. As Engels commented, "it will be too late for the rich to beware."[57]

---

56 *The Times*, June 1844, quoted in F. Engels, *The Condition of the Working Class in England*, MECW, vol. 4, p. 579.

57 Ibid, p. 583.

2. SOWING THE SEEDS

"Property is nothing but human labour. The most inestimable of all property is the sweat of the poor man's brow; the property from which all other is derived, and without which grandeur must starve in the midst of supposed abundance. And shall those who possess this inestimable property be told that they had no rights because they have nothing to defend? ... No! Man and not movables is the object of just legislation."
– John Thelwall, 'The Natural & Constitutional Right of Britons to Annual Parliaments, Universal Suffrage, and the Freedom of Popular Association' (1795)

"Richard Carlile: "Choose ye, therefore, whom ye will serve; but as for me and my family, we will not serve either kings or priests or lords. *"Hetherington:* "We perfectly agree with Mr. Carlile on the propriety of abolishing Kings, Priests, and Lords, but he does not go far enough – he does not strike at the root of the evil which exists. It is in Property that the evil lies – were there no property, there would be no Kings, Priests or Lords. It is property which has made tyrants, and not tyrants' property – Mr Carlile points out the effects of monopoly – we grapple with the cause, and would at once destroy it. Down then with property, and Kings, Lords, and Priests will go down of themselves."
– *The Poor Man's Guardian*

FORERUNNERS OF CHARTISM

The celebrated labour historian G.D.H. Cole opened his book *Chartist Portraits* with the bold statement that "Hunger and hatred – these were the forces that made Chartism a mass movement of the British working class. Hunger gnawed at the hearts of the people, and seemed to gnaw the more fiercely..."[1] While hunger and hatred were certainly important factors in contributing to the rise of Chartism, others, especially those involved in the great political struggles for democracy, from Thomas Paine to William Cobbett, also made an essential contribution and added to the mix of radicalism. There were clearly a number of streams of radical thought and experience, including militant trade unionism, the revolt against factory conditions, and the fight against the Poor Law, to name a few that entered into the bloodstream of Chartism. To understand Chartism, we need to understand these separate sources and component parts, which combined to produce this astonishing development.

These collective struggles forced the working class, growing in class consciousness, onto the path of independent class politics. In doing so, the working class started to think and act for itself. This, in turn, horrified the propertied classes, who did everything possible to block its rise. Class consciousness, however, did not develop in a straight line. At the beginning of the Industrial Revolution, the emerging working class had no rights or independent existence, and faced a corrupt ruling class, represented in a corrupt Parliament. This privileged elite ruled unchallenged over the 'multitude', and considered themselves the country's 'natural rulers'.

The unwritten British Constitution, based on tradition and precedent, was simply a cloak for this class dictatorship. The 'Glorious Revolution' of 1688, which supposedly gave us 'liberty' and 'ordered' government, was simply a shift from one monarch to another that reinforced the power of the landed and moneyed profit-grubbers. The 'Revolution' was a victory of the propertied classes, nothing more. The Parliament of Commons and Lords was made up of the 'great and powerful', rich landowners, merchants and shire gentry.

Prior to the Reform Act of 1832, large towns such as Manchester, Sheffield and Birmingham had no representation in the House of Commons, while rural Cornwall, where the Crown's influence was greatest, had forty-four Members of Parliament. Gatton in Wiltshire, which had two houses and only a single voter, returned two Members of Parliament. The same was true of Old Sarum, the 'accursed hill', again in Wiltshire, which contained nothing but a thorn bush.

This parliamentary system, the 'Mother of Parliaments', was no more than a patchwork of corrupt 'rotten boroughs' dominated by a ruling elite and their hangers-on. Not surprisingly, given the high levels of corruption, such parliamentary seats were lucrative and often changed hands at an enormous

---

1   G.D.H. Cole, *Chartist Portraits*, p. 1.

price. Thomas Holcroft, a dramatist, was present at the sale of the seat of Gatton. He recorded the salesperson as explaining the virtues of the sale:

> "No tempestuous passions to allay, no tormenting claims of insolent electors to evade, no tinkers' wives to kiss, no impossible promises to make, none of the toilsome and not very clean paths of canvassing to drudge through; but, his mind at ease and his conscience clear, with this elegant contingency in his pocket, the honours of the State await is lucking and with its emoluments his purse will overflow."[2]

The working class, the majority of the country's growing population, were regarded as social and political outcasts, the great disenfranchised. "The tyranny of the multitude is but a multiplied tyranny", stated Burke, who had no time for the common rabble, and for whom the idea of universal suffrage was unthinkable. While the Leveller ideas of political democracy had been extinguished long ago, these were increasingly stirring times. At home and abroad, radical democratic ideas had begun to revive in a fertile ground ploughed by the emergence of a new working class. These ideas would soon blaze a trail.

WILKES AND LIBERTY!

It would be fair to say that the forerunners of Chartism came in many shapes and sizes. One of the strangest was the Wilkes movement of the 1760s and 1770s, which rekindled in its own fashion the battle for freedom of expression and universal suffrage. John Wilkes (1725-1797) was a Member of Parliament, a well-known politician of little principle, but great wit, who had been charged with seditious libel over attacks on King George III's speech on foreign policy. He was imprisoned, expelled from the Commons, then following his release was elected a further three times, but each time his election was declared void and he was banned from taking up his seat. This gained him fame and notoriety, especially among the emerging working classes, artisans and apprentices. From an individual cause it developed into a movement, known as the 'Wilkes and Liberty' agitation. In 1768, following the 'massacre of St. George's Field' in south London, where soldiers had opened fire on a large crowd and killed six people, Spitalfields weavers, in the course of a trade dispute, cheered Wilkes on his way to the hustings, and striking coal-heavers in East London raised the cry of 'Wilkes and coal-heavers for ever!' The procession was joined by merchant seamen, watermen,

---

2   Quoted in G.D.H. Cole and R. Postgate, *The Common People*, p. 88.

tailors, and other workers. Wilkes, given his growing popularity, was elected Lord Mayor of London, which further galvanised the London masses.

In many ways, Wilkes was an accidental figure, but he nevertheless came to encapsulate the mood of the masses. As a counterbalance to those who sought to exclude him, he turned to points of support outside of parliament. He was a man who appeared at the right place and the right time, and who became a catalyst for the movement. Although he was not from them, he leaned on the masses for help. Eventually Wilkes was returned to the House of Commons for Middlesex amid unprecedented demonstrations and strikes. The masses were being drawn into the process through this agitation, and Wilkes succeeded in conjuring up a movement that included the right of electors to select their members, reform of the Commons by the abolition of 'rotten' boroughs, and a wider, if not universal, suffrage. It could be said with justification that Wilkes' ideas became more radical with the ever-greater involvement of the masses, all of which fed upon one another. This movement had all the elements of the future Chartism: a radical programme and mass participation.

John Wilkes, now the leader of a mass popular agitation, was increasingly regarded by the ruling class as a dangerous radical whose actions were stirring up anarchy and chaos. As far as the privileged classes were concerned, one could raise such matters behind closed doors, but what was unforgivable was to raise them in front of the uneducated multitude, the 'great unwashed'. Wilkes simply gave vent to the discontent in society, which had previously been unheard or ignored. The masses had been generally passive ever since the days of the 'Great Rebellion' of the 1640s. Now, as the Industrial Revolution took hold, the growing discontent of the 'lower orders' was given an outlet in Wilkes, who became their tribune.

Wilkes and his supporters stood in the general election of 1774 on a democratic programme of reform, a prelude to the Chartists. Around twelve seats were won, which is remarkable given the limited franchise and restricted constituencies. In 1776, Wilkes went as far as to plead in the House of Commons for political rights of:

> "[T]he meanest mechanic, the poorest peasant and day labourer, who has important rights respecting his personal liberty, that of his wife and children, his property however inconsiderable, his wages… which are in many trades and manufactures regulated by the power of Parliament… Some share therefore in the power of making those laws which deeply interest them… should be reserved even to this inferior but most useful set of men…"[3]

---

3   Quoted in E.P. Thompson, *The Making of the English Working Class*, p. 91.

Here once again we have echoes of the Putney Debates and the rights of the 'poorest he'. This democratic rebellion stirred up the working classes, deliberately excluded from politics and Parliament. The agitation of Wilkes represented a new and dangerous departure: the entry of the 'dispossessed' into this once privileged domain. Such was the ferment that large crowds gathered daily outside the Commons, abusing and assaulting ministers, shouting and protesting, even pelting some with rubbish from the gutter. "No Wilkes, no King!", "Damn the King, damn the Government, damn the Justices!" went the cries. "This is the most glorious opportunity for a Revolution that ever offered!" shouted others.[4]

This reflected a most radical, even revolutionary, ferment in the 'lower orders'. The regular abuse of parliamentarians reached new levels. *The Annual Register* reported in the 1770s that the traditional merchants' cavalcades "were interrupted by a desperate mob, on passing through the city, who insulted, pelted and maltreated the principal conductors, so much so that several coaches were obliged to withdraw".[5] More importantly, these robust political expressions were mixed up with other questions: strikes, riots and protests over wages and conditions, including the high cost of bread, and growing economic distress. The activists involved coal-heavers, weavers, and even sailors, who occupied several ships in Deptford to force an increase in wages. London seemed to be, in the words of one critic, "a great Bedlam under the domination of a beggarly, idle and intoxicated mob without keepers, actuated solely by the word *Wilkes...*"[6]

A Bill of Rights Society was formed by Wilkes' supporters, in which the Radical Major John Cartwright played a prominent role. In 1776, Cartwright published a pamphlet entitled 'Take Your Choice', which argued for annual parliaments, equal electoral districts, payment of members and adult male suffrage. This constituted a forerunner of the demands of Radicals over the next seventy-five years, including the Chartists. Wilkes went so far as to champion the cause of the popular American Revolution and was in touch with the rebel leaders. He even organised London to petition the king. "This I know," he said, describing events in America, "a successful resistance is a *revolution*, not a *rebellion*."[7] In return, Wilkes received the enthusiastic support of the American colonists. This marked him out as a dangerous demagogue and put him beyond the pale as far as the ruling class was concerned.

---

4 Quoted in G. Rudé, *Paris and London in the Eighteenth Century*, p. 235.
5 Quoted in Ibid., p. 245.
6 E.P. Thompson, *The Making of the English Working Class*, p. 75.
7 J. Lindsay and E. Rickword, *Liberty*, p. 212.

Eventually, the decade-long Wilkeite movement, which had gripped the whole country, was cut across by the sectarian Gordon Riots ('No Popery') of 1780. Legislation to allow Catholics greater freedom sparked a sectarian Protestant backlash led by Lord George Gordon, who fanned the flames of religious intolerance. The most backward layers were incited and whipped up into a frenzy by the heads of the Church and dissenting communities. A mass demonstration degenerated into a week of rage, rioting and attacks on Catholics. This led to widespread looting, as well as attacks on Newgate Prison and the Bank of England, and was possibly the most destructive rioting in the history of London. Painted on the wall of Newgate prison was the proclamation that the inmates had been freed by the authority of 'His Majesty, King Mob'. The term 'King Mob' came to denote an unruly and fearsome lumpenproletariat.

"When the rude rabble's watchword was 'destroy'
And blazing London seem'd a second Troy."

Around 15,000 troops were rushed to London to quell the riots in which between 300 and 700 rioters were shot. Burke deplored the use of the military in suppressing the rioters, while Charles Fox, the leading Whig, declared that he would "much rather be governed by a mob than a standing army".[8] Following the French Revolution, no Whig politician would ever risk such dangerous suggestions. The riots put an end to Wilkes' career and succeeded in cutting across the democratic struggle for a whole period.

Nevertheless, the Wilkeite movement had sown the seeds. The democratic movement would eventually reignite, spurred on by the effects of the American and then the French Revolutions. The events in the Americas made a particular impact in Ireland. A force of 80,000 Irish Volunteers was raised to protect Ireland from invasion, but primarily regarded itself as an army for Irish independence. This movement, in turn, was betrayed by its middle-class and aristocratic leaders, who were denounced by Wolfe Tone, the Irish revolutionary. Arising from this betrayal, Wolfe Tone later went on to organise the United Irishmen and the 'men of no property', which united both Protestants and Catholics in the fight for Irish independence. This organisation stood broadly on the principles of Paine's *Rights of Man*, which Tone said had become the 'Koran' of Belfast. Interestingly, they adopted a programme of manhood suffrage, annual parliaments, no property qualification and other demands that anticipated the Chartists by half a century.

---

8   Quoted in E.P. Thompson, *The Making of the English Working Class*, p. 78.

IMPACT OF THE FRENCH REVOLUTION

'Radicalism' is by its very nature a broad term. It is a generic name given to various trends and tendencies involved in the 'reform' movement, which rested on different classes and different material interests. Radicalism, in the fight against the old aristocracy, 'Old Corruption', as it was called, gained support not only from the rising bourgeoisie, but from artisans, small masters and journeymen. It even drew the factory workers in its wake. The middle class provided the leadership for this Radical movement, drawing the other layers behind it. However, this alliance of different classes was soon to break down, not least under the impact of the French Revolution, a political earthquake that shook the whole of society. From then on, we have two divergent trends: a 'respectable' Radicalism, based on the middle-class liberals, and a far more militant one, based on the working class. This is further reinforced in the period under discussion.

The French Revolution came like a thunderbolt. Its impact provoked wild enthusiasm among the workers and downtrodden, and captured the popular imagination with its democratic and revolutionary principles of *Liberty, Equality and Fraternity.* These ideas were popularised by the writings of Thomas Paine, who had already been a protagonist of the American Revolution. Amid the mushrooming of capitalist industry, these ideas of hope and freedom became extremely attractive, and were expressed in Wordsworth's famous poem, 'The Prelude':

> Europe at that time was thrilled with joy,
> France standing at the top of golden hours,
> And human nature born again.
>
> [...]
>
> O pleasant exercise of hope and joy!
> For mighty were the auxiliars which then stood
> Upon our side, us who were strong in love!
> Bliss was it in that dawn to be alive,
> But to be young was very heaven!
>
> [...]
>
> Not in Utopia, subterranean fields,
> Or on some secret island, Heaven knows where!
> But in the very world, which is the world
> Of all of us, the place where in the end
> We find our happiness or not at all!

For many, the ideals of the French Revolution reflected the dawn of a new age of Reason and Enlightenment. Although Wordsworth's optimism withered, these revolutionary ideas penetrated the consciousness of nearly two generations of Radicals prior to the rise of Chartism. In Britain, well into the first half of the nineteenth century, the French tricolour was flown as a defiant symbol by Radicals. At demonstrations, they would publicly don the Red Cap of Liberty. It is not an accident that during the 1816 Spa Fields riots, the 1817 Pentrich rising, and the 1819 Peterloo Massacre, a tricolour green, white and red flag was displayed in defiance against the 'Old Order'.

These radical democratic ideas were fully expounded by individuals such as Robert Burns, Percy Shelley, William Blake, John Keats, Wolfe Tone, Thomas Paine, William Godwin, Mary Wollstonecraft, and many others. As revolutionary democrats, they championed the principles of the French Revolution and challenged the ruling classes with a passion. "May the last king be hanged in the entrails of the last priest," exclaimed the poet Robert Burns. "Lay bare with undaunted heart and steady hand that horrid mass of corruption called politics and statecraft."

In his poem 'Scots Wha Hae', written in 1793, when the English government declared war on the French Republic, Burns wrote:

By Oppression's woes and pains,
By your sons in servile chains,
We will drain our dearest veins
    But they shall be free!

Lay the proud usurpers low!
Tyrants fall in every foe!
Liberty's in every blow!
    Let us do, or die!

And again, in another, later, poem he speaks of sharing the earth together:

To-day 'tis theirs. Tomorrow we
Shall don the Cap of Libertie!
The Golden Age we'll then revive:
Each man will be a brother;
In harmony we all shall live,
And share the earth together;
In Virtue train'd, enlighten'd Youth
Will love each fellow-creature;

And future years shall prove the truth
That Man is good by nature:
Then let us toast with three times three
The reign of Peace and Libertie!

It is worthwhile noting that the Chartists looked back on Robert Burns and the others as cherished heroes. "Every Chartist mother should repeat his patriotic songs to her children, in the winter evenings, by the cottage hearth", wrote the *Chartist Circular* of February 1841. "His writings should be familiar to every young Chartist, and constitute part of his juvenile education."[9]

LONDON CORRESPONDING SOCIETY

In the middle of January 1792, when Louis XVI was being dispatched at the guillotine in the Place de la Revolution, eight workers, led by a man called Thomas Hardy, met at the Bell Tavern in London to establish the London Corresponding Society, a radical society inspired by the Jacobins. It represented once again the emergence of organised Radicalism in Britain. In a defiant manner, these democrats turned the insults of the ruling class back on themselves: "The SWINISH MULTITUDE are well aware that it matters very little who are the HOG DRIVERS," declared the Society, "while the present wretched system of corruption is in existence."

Within a year, the Corresponding Society's membership had climbed to 3,000 and similar groups sprang up in Sheffield, Norwich, Nottingham and elsewhere. The Sheffield Society boasted several thousand members, composed overwhelmingly of the working classes, mainly the 'lower orders' of artisans and labourers. The Society's main programme was universal manhood suffrage and equal representation, the aim of which was to bring justice to the common people. Members of such societies later took their radicalism into the Chartist movement. One example is George Brown of Leicester, the Secretary of a Corresponding Society in 1792, who, despite arrests and imprisonment, was still politically active and a supporter of 'physical force' Chartism in 1848.

One of the Society's active members was Thomas Spence, a bookseller and radical editor who argued for the social ownership of land and agrarian communism "capable of delivering us from the deadly mischief of great accumulations of wealth".[10]

In May 1792, a few months after the French King's execution, a Royal Proclamation from the British Crown, directed mainly at Thomas Paine,

---

9 S. Harrison, *Poor Men's Guardians*, p. 132.
10 G.D.H. Cole, *A Short History*, p. 4.

was issued against seditious publications in an attempt to stamp out such radicalism. However, in December of the same year, 160 delegates from eighty Scottish Jacobin societies gathered at a Convention in Edinburgh. The name 'Convention' was sufficiently provocative to the authorities given the events in France. Furthermore, during their proceedings they took an oath and read aloud an address from the United Irishmen, who were preparing their own uprising in Ireland, and promoted the writings of Paine. Robert Burns, fearing the worst, stayed away from the gathering, which prevented his arrest. In the course of the arrests that followed, the Scottish reformer Thomas Muir was taken into custody, then tried, found guilty and transported for fourteen years to Botany Bay for his part in the Convention.

At these treason trials, the Lord Justice, Lord Braxfield, outlined the case against Muir:

> "Two things the jury must attend to, which require no proof. First, that the British Constitution is the best that ever was since the creation of the world, and it is not possible to make it better. The next is that there was a spirit of sedition in the country last winter, which made every good man uneasy ... Yet Mr Muir had at that time gone among the ignorant country people making them forget their work, and told them that a Reform was absolutely necessary for preserving their liberty, which if it were not for him they would never have thought was in danger... Mr Muir might have known that no attention could be paid to such rabble. What right had they to representation? A government in every country should be just like a corporation and, in this country, it is made up of landed interests who alone have a right to be represented."[11]

When a juror passed behind him, Braxfield whispered to him in broad Scots: "Come awa', Maaster Horner, come awa' and help us hang ane o' thae damned scoundrels."[12] The result was a foregone conclusion. Although they were not hanged, all talk of reform was to be mercilessly crushed. A few weeks after Muir's sentence of fourteen years' transportation, Fyshe Palmer received seven years' transportation. But the Scottish reformers responded to the sentences by calling another Convention in October, which was angrier and 'Frenchified'. The authorities again acted and arrested the organiser, William Skirving, together with two London delegates, Joseph Gerrald and Maurice Margarot, and the Convention was dissolved. When the defendant,

---

11 Quoted in S. Harrison, *Poor Men's Guardians*, p. 26.
12 "Come master Horner and help us hang everyone of these damned scoundrels."

Gerrald, stated at the trial that Christ too had been a reformer, Braxfield simply replied, "Muckle he made o' that; *he* was hangit."[13]

The men were found guilty of sedition and transported. Skirving was so ill-treated on the voyage that he died. Gerrald perished soon afterwards. Only one man managed to survive, Margarot, who eventually returned home. But for many, transportation was a death sentence. Many months in a ship's hold, often in chains, without ventilation or sanitation, and existing on convict rations, meant the death rate for prisoners onboard the ships reached around twenty per cent. On arrival in Australia, they would be handed out to settlers as slave labour, to clear bush and perform menial tasks. Failure to perform such duties often meant they were flogged. Working in chain-gangs in unbearable heat, those who died would remain chained to the others until nightfall. "It is not surprising that in the popular imagination a sentence to transportation was only one degree less terrifying than a sentence to death", wrote Cole and Postgate.[14]

In July 1793, Thomas Hardy made a speech on behalf of the Corresponding Society, in which he argued:

> We conceive it necessary to direct the public eye, to the cause of our misfortunes, and to awaken the sleeping reason for our countrymen, to the pursuit of the only remedy which can ever prove effectual, namely; a thorough reform of Parliament, by the adoption of an equal representation obtained by annual elections and universal suffrage. To obtain a complete representation is our only aim – condemning all party distinctions, we seek no advantage [which] every individual of the community will not enjoy equally with ourselves.[15]

The government was growing extremely alarmed at the effects of the French Revolution in England. In response, Pitt the Younger suspended *Habeas Corpus* for twelve years in May 1794, which meant persons could be incarcerated without trial and all public meetings were banned. On this basis, a host of arrests took place and Thomas Paine was outlawed.

In the 1794 treason trial of Thomas Walker of Manchester, who had established a Reformation Society of mostly artisans, the Council for the prosecution summed up its activities:

> "[T]hey assembled, night after night, to an amount which you will hear from the witnesses. Sometimes, I believe the extended number of such assemblies amounting to more than a hundred persons... they assembled in greater multitudes, and read,

---

13 Quoted in E.P. Thompson, pp. 135 & 140; "A mess he made of that; he was hanged"

14 *The Common People*, p. 154.

15 https://spartacus-educational.com/PRhardy.htm

as in a school, and as it were to fashion and perfect themselves in everything that is seditious and mischievous... They read, amongst other works, particularly the works of an author whose name is on the mouth of everybody in this country; I mean the works of Thomas Paine."[16]

As a result of the 'subversive' activities of the London Corresponding Society in campaigning for democratic rights, Thomas Hardy and two others were committed to the Tower of London and charged with high treason. Hardy's trial began at the Old Bailey on 28 October 1794. The prosecution, led by Lord Eldon, who would later end up as an infamous government minister, argued that the leaders of the Society were guilty of treason by plotting to assassinate the King and Members of Parliament. However, the authorities blundered and the prosecution was unable to furnish any real or manufactured evidence against Hardy. The jury, to the horror of Lord Eldon, returned a verdict of 'Not Guilty' and acquitted the men. After delivering the verdict the Foreman of the Jury fainted, while the London crowd went wild with enthusiasm.

This slap in the face only served to anger the government, which, being increasingly fearful, rushed through the Treason Act and the Seditious Meetings Act of 1795. While this fell short of banning the reform societies outright, it made their functioning almost impossible. Finally, under the shadow of the naval mutinies at Spithead and Nore (on the Thames Estuary), the Unlawful Societies Act of 1799 banned all "societies established for seditious and treasonable purposes; and for better preventing treasonable and seditious practices," and mentioned the London Society specifically by name. It was the year they also started to bring in the Combination Acts that made trade union organisation unlawful.

Campaigning in favour of parliamentary reform was now a criminal act. In fact, the very terms 'reform' and 'revolution' were closely linked together, as to advocate reform in these years was itself a revolutionary and seditious act and was treated as such.

THOMAS PAINE

Under the impact of events, especially the revolutions in America and France, Thomas Paine became increasingly radicalised and began to link up political and economic demands. Christopher Wyvill, a Yorkshire gentleman and conservative Reformer, reacted with alarm at Paine's new-found radicalism. "It is unfortunate for the public cause," Wyvill wrote in May 1792, "that Mr Paine took such unconstitutional ground, and has formed a party for the

16 B. Simon, *The History of Education 1780-1870*, pp. 182-183.

Republic among the lower classes of the people, by holding out to them the prospect of plundering the rich."[17]

Thomas Paine (1737-1809) was a self-taught man from humble beginnings. Not only was he greatly inspired by the American and French Revolutions, he personally participated in them. He became an ardent revolutionary democrat and the main tribune for Radicalism. His pamphlet, *Common Sense*, which supported the call for American independence, sold nearly 100,000 copies in 1776. Following his active participation in the American Revolution, he rallied to the defence of the French Revolution, which was stirring the hearts and minds of democrats everywhere. Edmund Burke, on behalf of the *Ancient Régime*, attacked the French revolutionaries in his book *Reflections on the Revolution in France,* which was an all-out assault on the revolution as well as the whole concept of democracy.

In 1791, Paine replied with his own book, *The Rights of Man,* an open attack on Burke and his reactionary ideas. It was a defence not only of the French Revolution, but a clear call to the masses in Britain to follow the French example and do away with its own crown and aristocracy. It became a democrat's textbook, which was read everywhere. *The Rights of Man* sold around 200,000 copies and, given its popularity, was even translated into Welsh and Gaelic.

This clarion call of Thomas Paine stands head and shoulders above the spineless timidity of the hierarchy of today's labour movement, with their subservient deference towards the monarchy and all its miserable trappings. Sir Keir Starmer, in standing for the position of Labour Party leader, unsurprisingly stated that he would not support the abolition of the monarchy, but neither, it must be said, would his 'left-wing' challenger, Rebecca Long-Bailey. To their credit, Tony Benn was staunchly in favour of its abolition, as is Jeremy Corbyn.

It is true that it is a feudal relic. But the British monarchy is much more than this. It is not maintained for costly pomp and ceremony, but as a serious reserve weapon to be used against a genuine threat to capitalism. Its constitutional powers can be used to dismiss left-wing governments, as with the Gough Whitlam government in Australia in 1975. Of course, such powers would be used sparingly so as to maintain the fiction that the Crown was 'above' party politics.

Thomas Paine would have been aghast to see such snivelling servitude from a labour leader, who had accepted a knighthood for his services. No doubt, later, Sir Starmer will graciously accept a place in the House of Lords for services rendered, namely for his role in restoring the Labour Party into a 'safe

---

17 Quoted in E. P. Thompson, *The Making of the English Working Class*, p. 120.

pair of hands'. The staunch revolutionary and democrat Paine would have had none of it, and rightly so. His message was thoroughly egalitarian, bent on destroying the "quixotic age of chivalric nonsense". Kings and queens, being completely useless and unproductive, would be the first to be shown the door.

Paine asked why we should be beholden to such pampered upstarts, to their heirs and posterity, until the end of time. "The vanity and presumption of governing beyond the grave," wrote Paine, "is the most ridiculous and insolent of all tyrannies. Man has no property in man; neither has any generation a property in the generations which are to follow." Instead of lavishing praise on these privileged parasites, we should be calling for their abolition, including the House of Lords. Thomas Paine attacked the very idea of hereditary royalty, calling it "as absurd as an hereditary mathematician, or hereditary wise man; and as ridiculous as an hereditary poet-laureate". He continued: "France has not levelled; it has exalted, it has put down the dwarf, to set up the man. The punyism of a senseless word like *Duke*, or *Count*, or *Earl*, has ceased to please."

The privilege and power of the nobility are held by people of *no-ability*, to use Paine's play on words. It is a fitting description of the Royal Highnesses, the Dukes and Duchesses, the Princes and Princesses, and other such privileged bloodsuckers. Likewise with the so-called peers and knights of the realm, all of whom are incompatible with genuine democracy and accountability.

Thomas Paine was also reflecting the general disdain and even hatred towards the British monarchy throughout this period. This contempt for the Royal Family was graphically illustrated on the death of Frederick, the Prince of Wales, in 1751, which drew the pointed epigram from William Thackeray, 'Four Georges':

"Here lies poor Fred who was alive and is dead,
Had it been his father I had much rather,
Had it been his sister nobody would have missed her,
Had it been his brother, still better than another,
Had it been the whole generation, so much better for the nation,
But since it is Fred who was alive and is dead,
There is no more to be said!"

This incredible language graphically shows the ill-feeling towards this 'hallowed' institution. Frederick's father, the unpopular King George II, being German had returned to his beloved Hanover. On the gates of St James' Palace was pinned a satirical notice: "Lost or strayed out of his house, a man who has left a wife and six children on the parish."

As Walter Bagehot, the constitutionalist, wrote:

The two first Georges were men ignorant of English, and wholly unfit to guide and lead English society. They both preferred one or two German ladies of bad character to all else in London. George III had no social vices, but he had no social pleasures.[18]

According to *The Economist*:

Journalists and the public also showed little respect for monarchs themselves. On the death of George IV in 1830 *The Times* declared in an editorial that: "There never was an individual less regretted by his fellow creatures." Cartoonists such as Gillray, Rowlandson and Cruickshank attacked the monarch in a manner which would look savage even today.

Victoria was no more popular than her predecessors until her apotheosis near the end of her reign.[19]

Paine defined two classes – "there are two distinct classes of men in the nation, those who pay taxes, and those who receive and live upon taxes", and as for the Constitution, it is good for the likes of "courtiers, placemen, pensioners, borough-holders, and the leaders of Parties… but it is a bad Constitution for at least ninety-nine parts of the nation out of a hundred".

Compared to earlier radicals, Thomas Paine was clearly groping towards a revolutionary theory of the State and of class power, although this was still quite confused. For him, it was a conflict between the propertied and the propertyless.

"The revolutions of America and France have thrown a beam of light over the world", he stated, much in the same way the Russian Revolution inspired the world more than 100 years later. Paine therefore championed many radical and egalitarian ideas, including the nationalisation of the land and the abolition of the monarchy, aristocracy and the House of Lords. In Part Two of *The Rights of Man*, he advocated the redistribution of wealth to the poor. For this extreme radicalism, Paine was met with the bile and deep-felt hatred of the reactionaries of his day, who regarded him and his supporters as no better than foreign agents, intent on treason. According to one contemporary, the definition of a Radical was a "libellous, seditious, factious, levelling, revolutionary, republican, democratical, atheistical villain". In 1792, charges of seditious writings were lodged against Paine, and a trial was scheduled. Staged demonstrations were organised in different parts of the country to condemn him and his ideas.

18 W. Bagehot, *The Constitution*, p. 45.
19 *The Economist*, 22-28/10/94.

On 22 November 1792, a reactionary mob burned Paine's effigy at Chelmsford, Essex. According to the newspaper account:

On Wednesday last, the Effigy of that Infamous Incendiary, Tom Paine, was exhibited in this town, seated in a chair, and bourne on four men's shoulders; in one hand he held the *Rights of Man* and under the other arm he bore a pair of stays; upon his head a mock resemblance of the Cap of Liberty, and a halter round his neck.

On a banner carried before him, was written, 'Behold a Traitor! Who, for the base purposes of a Envy, Interest and Ambition, Would have deluged this Happy Country in BLOOD!'[20]

In December, according to the *Stamford Mercury*:

"The effigy of Thomas Paine was, with great solemnity, drawn on a sledge from Lincoln Castle to the gallows, and then hanged, amidst a vast multitude of spectators. After being suspended the usual time, it was taken to the Castle-hill and there hung on a gibbet post erected for the purpose. In the evening a large fire was made under the effigy, which... was consumed to ashes, amidst the acclamation of many hundreds of people, accompanied with a grand band of music playing 'God Save the King'..."[21]

Given the ugly mood, he was never going to receive a fair trial. Paine wisely escaped to France to avoid arrest, but was still tried in his absence, found guilty of high treason and outlawed by the government of William Pitt. According to Lady Hester Stanhope, Pitt "used to say that Tom Paine was quite right, but then he would add, 'What am I to do? As things are, if I were to encourage Tom Paine's opinions, we should have a bloody revolution'."[22] Whether Pitt agreed with Paine is doubtful, but there is no doubt he was vehemently opposed to revolution.

Following the trial, the government clamped down on the publication and sale of all 'seditious' literature. Despite this, Paine's democratic and radical ideas lived on. It is possible to ban a person, but you cannot ban an idea whose time has come. When the East London Democratic Association was formed by Julian Harney and other Chartist leaders in 1837, their manifesto declared that its object would be to liberate the working class "by disseminating the principles propagated by that great philosopher and redeemer of mankind, the Immortal Thomas Paine". Even in the early twentieth century, the great

---

20 *The Thomas Paine Reader*, p. 15.
21 Quoted in E.P. Thompson, *The Making of the English Working Class*, pp. 122-123.
22 R. Palme Dutt, *The Internationale*, London, 1964, p. 17.

American socialist Eugene V. Debs paid tribute to Paine as the founder of the American radical tradition.

Even much closer to our present time, Thomas Paine's democratic ideas have stirred up bitter class feelings. No statue to Paine's memory was to stand on English soil until more than 150 years after his death. In 1964, when a statue of Paine was erected in his birthplace of Thetford, Norfolk, protests were raised by a number of Conservative ratepayers and councillors. The Tory deputy mayor even tried to have the details of Paine's conviction as a traitor engraved on the plinth, but this spiteful attempt failed. Class hatred towards those who threaten private property certainly runs deep.

VICTORY AT WATERLOO

Britain under William Pitt was able to launch a war against the young French Republic in 1793. But this was not without opposition from Charles Fox and Richard Sheridan, who supported the French Revolution and spoke up in its defence in Parliament. "As to the question of war," stated Sheridan, "he should vote that English ministers be impeached who should enter into a war for the purpose of re-establishing the former despotism in France; who should dare in such a cause to spend one guinea, or shed one drop of blood."[23] Sheridan went on to ridicule Edmund Burke, who brandished a dagger in the Commons, apparently to act the part of a Jacobin. Sheridan is said to have shouted out "Where's the fork?", which led to much of the house collapsing in laughter. But war was declared which was to last, with a brief two-year interlude, until 1815, when Napoleon was finally defeated at Waterloo. This represented the triumph of Europe's reactionary monarchies over revolutionary France, with the restoration of the Bourbon monarchy. The aim of these Napoleonic Wars was to crush France and bury the ideals of the revolution, which still cast a long shadow over Europe.

In Ireland, the United Irishmen under Wolfe Tone, who succeeded in banding together the 'men of no property' in rebellion against Anglo-Irish rule, were suppressed in cold blood. This rebellion added to the government's growing alarm, leading them to rush through catch-all legislation banning "the societies of the United Englishmen, the United Scotsmen, United Irishmen and United Britons".

The fears of revolution among the upper classes at this time were evident everywhere. In 1801, Mr Ainsworth, a big manufacturer in Bolton, wrote to Sir Robert Peel warning that if the French invaded and the soldiers were

---

23 J. Lindsay and E. Rickword, *Spokesmen for Liberty*, p. 218.

withdrawn, the people would rise up. The mayor of Leicester also wrote to the Home Office:

"I think that if whilst the Enemy remains in force the people of this Town were to suffer from the want of Bread, a fourth of the population would join the French Standard if they had an opportunity."[24]

A series of corrupt Whig and Tory governments had kept the 'lower orders' firmly in place. Following the death of William Pitt in 1806, the government fell under the domination of a clique of reactionary upstarts: Sidmouth, Castlereagh, Eldon and Liverpool. Their policy was simple: smash all potential threats with open repression and the mailed fist. They were determined to secure the country, whatever the cost. Given the general state of unease, and concerns about revolution, the government thought it advisable to establish military barracks in different parts of the kingdom. A spirit of rebellion had appeared in many manufacturing towns, which made it necessary that troops should be stationed nearby. By 1814, the whole of England resembled a military camp: 155 barracks had been constructed to hold 17,000 cavalry and 138,000 infantry. The local militia supplemented these military forces, but they were considered largely unreliable in the face of popular outbursts of discontent.

As a result of this reign of terror, the workers – skilled and semi-skilled – were forced to organise underground illegal "combinations" and trade unions. This represented the flowering of revolutionary trade unionism, whose members were bound together by secret oaths and initiation ceremonies. Their illegal meetings were protected by doorkeepers, known as 'Inside' and 'Outside Tylers', who were usually armed with pistols. The government did everything in its power to crush these dangerous organisations, using a system of spies, the suspension of *Habeas Corpus* and other methods. Anyone found guilty of organising trade unions, usually on the evidence of these informers, was imprisoned or even publicly whipped. Despite this, such organisations and oath-taking increased. These oaths normally included a pledge to deal with strike-breakers: "I do swear that I will punish by death any traitor or traitors should there any arise up amongst us I will pursue with unceasing vengeance..."

The most immediate reaction of the workers was to engage in rioting and violence, even assassination, against any hated employers. In 1812-13, the Luddite movement terrorised the masters with their machine-breaking activities, under the banner of the fictitious 'General Ned Ludd'. Underground organisations, formed of committees and delegates, led the

---

24 Quoted in J.L. Hammond and B. Hammond, *Town Labourer*, p. 80.

struggle. In Lancashire and Cheshire, the main target was the power-looms, in Yorkshire, the shearing-machines. This rage against the machines was a blind but swift reaction to their introduction and the sacking of workers as a consequence. This resulted in extreme hardship for many.

> Around and around we all will stand
> And sternly swear we will.
> We'll break the shears and windows, too,
> And set fire to the dazzling mill.
>   (ANON)

Skilled clothing workers in Yorkshire issued an appeal to all 'croppers' (who finished the cloth) under the pseudonym of 'General Ludd':

> "Generous countrymen. You are requested to come forward with arms and help the Redressers to redress their Wrongs and shake off the hateful Yoke of a Silly Old Man, George III, and his Son more silly and their Roguish Ministers, all Nobles and Tyrants must be brought down. Come let us follow the Noble Example of the brave Citizens of Paris who in sight of 30,000 Tyrant Redcoats brought a Tyrant to the Ground..."[25]

Parliament quickly passed a law to make machine-breaking, already punishable by fourteen years' transportation, a capital offence. Hangings would quickly follow.

However, one honourable member of the House of Lords, Lord Byron, raised his objections:

> But whilst these outrages must be admitted to exist to an alarming extent, it cannot be denied that they have arisen from circumstances of the most unparalleled distress. The perseverance of these miserable men in their proceedings tends to prove that nothing but absolute want could have driven a large and once honest and industrious body of the people into the commission of excesses so hazardous to themselves, their families, and the community...
>
> You call these men a mob, desperate, dangerous, and ignorant... Are we aware of our obligations to the mob? It is the mob that labour in our fields, serve in our houses – that man your navy and recruit your army – that have enabled you to defy all the world, and can also defy you when neglect and calamity have driven them to despair... Setting aside the palpable injustice and the certain inefficiency of the Bill, are there not capital punishments sufficient in your statutes? Is there

---

25 Quoted in A.L. Morton & G. Tate, *The British Labour Movement*, p. 37.

not blood enough upon your penal code that more must be poured forth to ascend to Heaven and testify against you? ... Are these the remedies for a starving and desperate populace? Will the famished wretch who has braved your bayonets be appalled by your gibbets? When death is a relief, and the only relief it appears that you will afford him, will he be dragooned into tranquillity? Will that which could not be effected by your grenadiers, be accomplished by your executioners? If you proceed by the forms of law, where is your evidence? Those who have refused to impeach their accomplices when transportation only was the punishment, will hardly be tempted to witness against them when death is the penalty.[26]

These words, used by Byron in the parliamentary debate on frame-breaking on 27 February 1812, were all the more remarkable as England was still at war with the French. The law was nevertheless passed, troops despatched against the machine-breakers, and the death penalty imposed. In Yorkshire, six men were given seven years' transportation for taking illegal oaths. Seventeen others were hanged, and one transported for life. Others met a similar fate in Lancashire. Three men and a youth were sentenced to death for burning a mill. The boy, Abraham Charlson, had three soldier brothers, and he acted as a lookout. When he was brought to the scaffold, he pitifully "called on his mother for help, thinking she had the power to save him". Despite his pleas, he was unable to escape the hangman's rope, as with many others found guilty of Luddism.

The Luddites were not a revolutionary movement, but a protest movement against the hated machines. Such destruction was no solution, but a desperate reaction to the problems of unemployment, wage cuts and hunger. They represented those who tried to turn the clock back, hoping to return to the so-called 'good old days' without machines. By their actions, they posed a real threat to private property and employers alike, and were dealt with accordingly.

THE CORN LAWS

In 1813, the Tory government, under pressure from employers, repealed all Elizabethan legislation fixing the wages and conditions of apprentices; the following year the apprenticeship clauses were also abrogated. In 1808, the proposed Minimum Wage Bill had been unceremoniously thrown out. *Laissez-faire* economics became the new orthodoxy as wages were allowed to 'find their own levels' through competition, that is, to fall, without state interference.

The end of the war against France came in 1815. This victory strengthened the Tory government at home, which, faced with demobbed troops and a

---

26 http://www.luddites200.org.uk/LordByronspeech.html

trade depression, unleashed a clampdown throughout the country. The government under Lord Liverpool must be regarded as one of the most reactionary in British history and was to remain in office for some fifteen long years, the third longest tenure on record. Lord Liverpool, the Prime Minister, was served by ministers such as Viscount Sidmouth as Home Secretary, and Castlereagh as Foreign Secretary. Lord Eldon was made Lord Chancellor. Between 1812 and 1820, Liverpool's government was particularly repressive, fearing that the country was on the brink of revolutionary upheaval.

The economic slump, along with 300,000 jobless soldiers and sailors, meant a rapid growth of the reserve army of the unemployed. This depressed state of affairs served to push wheat prices down, which posed a threat to the profits of the landlords. This situation could not be tolerated. Under pressure, the government passed the Corn Laws, which kept the price of corn, and therefore bread, artificially high. As the historian A.L. Morton wrote:

> The Corn Laws of 1815 were the last clear-cut victory of the landowners as a class in England, but it was a suicidal victory because it inevitably isolated them from every other class and enabled the industrialists to pose, however hypocritically, as the champions of the whole people against a selfish and monopolising minority.[27]

The Corn Laws stipulated that only when the price of wheat rose above eighty shillings a quarter would wheat be allowed to be imported from abroad free of duty. This protected the interests of the big landowners, but decreased grain supplies and increased prices. Given the importance of bread as an essential part of a worker's diet, the Corn Laws led to increased hardship, especially in the textile towns, where wages also fell sharply. This provoked a series of riots in London, Newcastle, Glasgow, Birmingham, Merthyr and elsewhere. Amid this ferment, Hampden Clubs, named after the leader of the parliamentary opposition to Charles 1, sprang up in towns in the industrial North and London. These clubs were promoted by Major Cartwright to encourage debate and discussion about a programme for political reform. They had a far wider reach than the Corresponding Societies and were influenced by the radical writings of William Cobbett and his *Political Register*.

Manchester became the focal point of Radicalism in the North of England. By 1815, the town had become an industrial centre, the area around which was home to sixty factories alone. Over ninety per cent of those were spinning mills. They employed a considerable workforce of around 24,000 workers. As Thomas Carlyle asked:

---

27 *A People's History*, p. 391.

"Hast thou heard, with sound ears, the awakening of a Manchester, on a Monday morning, at half-past five by the clock; the rushing off its thousand mills, like the boom of an Atlantic tide, ten thousand times ten thousand spools and spindles all set humming there – it is perhaps, if thou knew it well, sublime as a Niagara, or more so."[28]

But these workers were suffering from long hours of work and falling real wages. With the introduction of the Corn Laws, factory wages fell to an average of twenty-four shillings a week, barely enough to live on. On top of this, there was a very poor harvest in 1816, again forcing wheat prices up. This mounting hardship was having a radicalising effect on workers' consciousness. "I shared the general distress of 1816," wrote the radical Richard Carlile later, "and it was this that opened my eyes… In the manufacturies nothing was talked of but revolution."[29] Workers and their families were at the end of their tether and became increasingly receptive to radical propaganda and meetings. One of these meetings was held in early December 1816 in Spar Fields, London, addressed by Henry 'Orator' Hunt and James Watson. The magistrates ordered the meeting to disperse, but there was an incident and a police officer was stabbed. As a result, four leaders of the meeting were arrested and charged with high treason.

This only added to working class anger. An appeal was issued on behalf of the workers, entitled 'Britons to Arms!':

"The whole Country waits the signal from London to fly to Arms! Haste, break open Gunsmiths and other likely places to find Arms! Run all constables through who touch a man of us; no rise of Bread; no Regent; no Castlereagh, off with their heads; no Placemen, Tythes, or Enclosures; no Taxes; no Bishops, only useless lumber! Stand true or be Slaves for ever."[30]

But this appeal to stage an uprising, with little organisation, came to nothing. Nevertheless, the flame of revolt was lit and could not be easily extinguished.

Attention, once again, turned to proletarian Manchester. It was said that if there was a single place in England where a revolution was possible, that place would be Manchester, seen as the most turbulent and most violent town in the kingdom. It could be regarded as England's nineteenth century equivalent to Russia's Petrograd. It was the year when the 'Blanketeers' organised a march

28 Quoted in A. Briggs, *Chartist Studies*, pp. 29-30.
29 B. Simon, *History of Education 1780-1870*, p. 185.
30 G.D.H. Cole & A.W. Filson, *British Working Class Movements: Selected Documents 1789-1875*, p. 130.

from Manchester to London, composed mostly of Lancashire weavers, to petition the Prince Regent over the desperate state of the textile industry, as well as to protest the suspension of *Habeas Corpus*. But the marchers, who carried blankets for the journey, were violently attacked and their leaders imprisoned. With this repression, many workers were drawing political conclusions and there were widespread demands for a democratic franchise.

In June 1817, an attempted insurrection in Derbyshire, provoked by government *agents provocateurs*, was put down by a score of dragoons. On 7 November, their leaders, Brandreth, Turner, and Ludlam, were captured, found guilty of treason, and sentenced to be hanged. On the allotted day, they "were drawn on hurdles to the place of execution, and were hanged and decapitated in the presence of an excited and horror-stricken crowd".[31] This was to provide an example. However, rather than dampening the mood, the executions provoked threats of insurrection, which became widespread in the industrial towns. The activities of many underground trade unions turned to drilling with pikes and staves in preparation, according to the authorities, for a likely rebellion. As the radical journal *Black Dwarf* wrote:

> "The public mind has already undergone a complete *revolution*. The ranks of reform have… been swelled beyond *all expectation*… It is satisfactory to see that *misery* has had one good effect – that of stimulating the mind to enquire into its causes."[32]

As a counter to this threat, Castlereagh and Sidmouth replied once again by suspending *Habeas Corpus* for twelve months. William Wilberforce, famous for his efforts to abolish the slave trade, supported Sidmouth's repressive measures, saying that he:

> "[C]ould readily conceive how the lower orders, that valuable portion of the community whose labour was so essential to the social system under which we live, might be tempted by the delusive and wicked principles instilled into their minds, to direct their strength to the destruction of the government, and the overthrow of every civil and religious establishment."[33]

This was followed by the introduction of the 'Gagging', a common name for the Treason Act (1817) and the Seditious Meetings Act (1817), used to curb the radicalised movement. As Cobbett wrote:

---

31 E.P. Thompson, *The Making of the English Working Class*, p. 306.
32 B. Simon, *History of Education 1780-1870*, p. 190.
33 *Hansard*, 23 June 1817, quoted in J.L. Hammond and B. Hammond, *The Town Labourer*, p. 243.

"The Bey of Algiers proceeds against his 'disaffected' by chopping off their heads, and our ministers proceed against their 'disaffected' by shutting them up in prison during their pleasure, in a gaol in the kingdom, and deprived of light, warmth, and all communication with relatives and friends, if they please. That is all the difference."[34]

PETERLOO MASSACRE

However, mass meetings were called in Birmingham, Leeds, and London between July and August 1819, culminating in a monster meeting in Manchester. This set the scene for a giant demonstration at St Peter's Fields. The crowds which gathered there on 16 August numbered, according to the speaker Henry Hunt, between 180,000 and 200,000 strong. The working people, who had marched from all around, carried huge banners inscribed with the slogans 'Suffrage Universal', 'Annual Parliaments', and 'Liberty and Fraternity'. The main speaker, 'Orator' Hunt, addressed the excited throng of workers and their families. In a clear orchestrated provocation, the magistrates ordered the arrest of Hunt and a drunken company of the 15th Hussars was sent in to clear the crowd. In the melee that ensued, the defenceless demonstrators were brutally attacked by sabre-wielding yeomanry, resulting in the cold-blooded murder of eleven unarmed demonstrators with a further 400 having been badly wounded. Samuel Bamford, who was present, wrote:

"Several mounds of human beings still remained where they had fallen, crushed down and smothered. Some of these still groaning, others with staring eyes, were gasping for breath, and others would never breathe more. All were silent save for those low sounds, and the occasional snorting and pawing of steeds."[35]

News of the massacre spread like wildfire across the country.

In Manchester itself, crowds gathered in the evening and there was talk of a 'thirst for revenge'. Missiles were thrown at the soldiers and the Riot Act was read. Finally, orders were given to open fire, which dispersed the crowd, with several injured and one man dead. This did not prevent rioting in the days that followed, including in Stockport and Macclesfield.

The immediate reaction of the Lord Liverpool government to the 'Peterloo Massacre' was to charge Hunt, Bamford and others with high treason, a charge that was subsequently reduced to seditious conspiracy. The authorities described the massacre as a 'riot', which was completely false, but it suited their plans. Hunt and the others received long prison sentences and the government

---

34 Quoted in J. Lindsay and E. Rickword, *Spokesmen for Liberty*, p. 251.
35 J. Lindsay and E. Rickword, *Spokesmen for Liberty*, p. 257.

rushed new repressive laws onto the statute books. Sidmouth showered praise on the gallant forces of law and order. His response to Peterloo was:

> "I am gratified equally by the deliberate, spirited manner in which the magistrates discharged their arduous and important duty on that occasion… I do not fail to appreciate most highly the merits of the two companies of Yeomanry, Cavalry and other troops employed on this service…"[36]

Henry Hunt was finally released on bail in September, whereupon he travelled to the capital. His triumphant entry into London was met with an enthusiastic crowd of not less than 300,000 people, according to *The Times*.

Later convicted, Hunt served a two-and-a-half-year sentence in Ilchester prison. Bamford, Johnson and Healey, the organisers of the event, were sentenced to one year in Lincoln. But the events at Peterloo, which had electrified the population, lived on in the consciousness of working people. Peterloo also served to fuel the growing resentment within the working class and was reflected in a popular toast of the time: 'May the Tree of Liberty be planted in Hell, and may the bloody Butchers of Manchester be the Fruit of it!'

Following the massacre at St Peter's Field, a wave of protest meetings swept the North of England, the Midlands and the Lowlands of Scotland, involving a total of seventeen counties. Alarmed, local magistrates appealed for help from the central government. In reply, within a few months, Sidmouth, the Home Secretary, had passed his draconian Six Acts. All criticism was to be crushed. Punishment for seditious libel was made more brutal and a stamp duty of four pence was imposed on any newspaper or pamphlet costing less than six pence. It was a blatant attempt to crush the radical press by driving them out of business, directed especially at Cobbett's two-penny *Register*. Seditious libel was construed as anything that "tended to bring hatred or contempt for King, the government, or Constitution, or, furthermore, to excite any attempt to alter any matter in Church or State established by law". The authorities clamped down on publishers, printers and sellers of radical literature. This provoked a wave of defiance in support of the great 'unstamped' press.

However, the repression introduced by the Six Acts succeeded in smashing the radicalism of 1819. Shelley reacted to Peterloo in his poem *The Masque of Anarchy*, in which Castlereagh, the Foreign Secretary, was his first target, followed by Lord Eldon, the main prosecutor for the government against the leaders of the London Corresponding Society:

---

36 Quoted by J. Marlow, p. 179.

I met Murder on the way –
He had a mask like Castlereagh –
Very smooth he looked, yet grim;
Seven bloodhounds followed him;

All were fat; and well they might
Be in admirable plight,
For one by one, and two by two,
He tossed them human hearts to chew,
Which from his wide cloak he drew,
Next came Fraud, and he had on,
Like Eldon, an ermine gown;
His big tears, for he wept well,
Turned to millstones as they fell;

And the little children, who
Round his feet played to and fro,
Thinking every tear a gem,
Had their brains knocked out by them,

In the next stanza, Lord Sidmouth, the Home Secretary, is dealt with:

Like Sidmouth next, Hypocrisy
On a crocodile came by.

Shelley had written this in protest soon after the massacre, although the
poem was not published until 1832, some ten years after his death, for fear
of government reprisals. The chorus bristled with defiance:

Rise like Lions after slumber
In unvanquishable number,
Shake your chains to earth like dew
Which in sleep had fallen on you –
Ye are many – they are few.

In response to the Peterloo Massacre and the government reprisals, a
plan was hatched in 1820 to provoke a revolutionary overthrow of the
government and Parliament, involving the assassination of the Cabinet and
the seizure of the armouries. The plot was foiled, however, and ended with
a violent showdown in Cato Street in London. Five conspirators, including
their leader, Arthur Thistlewood, were caught and executed, and five others
transported.

Lord Liverpool remained in office until February 1827, when he suffered a severe stroke. Castlereagh committed suicide by slitting his own throat with a knife in 1822, a just desert for the innocent blood he had shed. News of his death provoked an outburst of popular exultation. Byron composed a suitable epitaph:

Posterity will ne'er survey
A nobler grave than this,
Here lies the bones of Castlereagh,
Stop, traveller, and p**s

The Peterloo Massacre lived on in the hearts and minds of the working class. In 1829 the Duke of Wellington, who was so unpopular that guards had to be placed at his home, was greeted by hostile Mancunian crowds with placards on which were inscribed the words 'Remember Peterloo'. At the first great Chartist meeting in Manchester, Peterloo banners were carried in the procession. It was said that nothing excited the crowds more than the word Peterloo. Peterloo survivors, such as James Fenny, a shoe-maker from Wigan, were given a special place of honour in the Chartist movement. When, twenty years later, he set off as a delegate for the Chartist Convention, "he was escorted for miles by thousands, with bands and banners, each flag surmounted by a pike..."[37]

WILLIAM COBBETT

Following the death of Thomas Paine, the banner of radical reform passed to William Cobbett (1763-1835). Along with Henry Hunt, he became the outstanding champion of working-class radicalism. Cobbett was an English pamphleteer, farmer, journalist and Member of Parliament, who had to travel a long way politically to embrace radicalism. Born in Farnham, Surrey, he believed that reforming Parliament would ease the poverty and distress of farm labourers, who were very close to his heart.

To begin with, Cobbett was a conservative and a defender of the establishment, a critic of Paine, and a supporter of the British Crown against the American colonists. But events were to shake his conservative beliefs. Like others, he had fallen foul of the strict laws on censorship and had been imprisoned for publishing an article that criticised the government – an event which caused him financial ruin. On the basis of this experience, which made a life-long impression on him, he swung over to radicalism. This was to Cobbett's credit. Normally, people travel politically in the other direction,

---

37 D. Jones, p. 63.

corrupted or bribed by the establishment to change their views. Despite his financial difficulties, Cobbett managed to maintain and edit the *Political Register*, which became known to its detractors as Cobbett's 'Two-penny Trash'. In the paper he adopted a fierce defence of factory workers and mercilessly attacked the money-grabbing gentry and landowners. "I am pleased at the [French] Revolution, on this account, that it makes the working classes see their importance, and those who despise them see it too", stated Cobbett.[38]

Such bold language allowed him to build up a mass following. "There is in the men calling themselves 'English country gentlemen' something superlatively base", he wrote in *Rural Rides*, his most famous book about the English countryside. "They are, I sincerely believe, the most cruel, the most unfeeling, the most brutally insolent ... the most base of all creatures that God ever suffered to disgrace the human shape."[39]

He strenuously opposed the enclosures and their disastrous effects on the rural population. For him, the main enemy was 'Old Corruption', and his *Register* blazed the trail of parliamentary reform. According to a government spy: "Cobbett hath done more with his Two-penny papers than any Thousand beside him, as anyone can get them, the price being so low and contain so much matter as the Children can purchase and read them."[40]

In March 1817, under the government clampdown, Cobbett fled to America "in fear of the Government and his creditors", for which he was strongly criticised. Leaving England at this critical moment resulted in the loss of a great deal of his influence. However, on his return in November 1819, he was met with great acclaim. He nevertheless studiously avoided travelling to Manchester for fear of the consequences. Journeying back from the United States, he brought with him the bones of Thomas Paine, but bizarrely these remains were subsequently lost.

In later years, Cobbett spoke for the millions of disenfranchised workers and rural labourers, and against the landlords and employers. One of the few Radicals elected to the Reform Parliament, he pushed for greater reforms and sought to strengthen the Factory Act of 1833. He famously chastised the ruling class, whose wealth and glory depended, not on their shipping or credit, but, according to him, on "an eighth part of the labour of three hundred thousand little girls". He also attacked the "lords of the loom", who employed thousands of men, women and children to spin cotton for

38 J. Lindsay and E. Rickword, *Spokesmen for Liberty*, p. 235.

39 Ibid., p. 234.

40 Quoted in J. Marlow, *The Peterloo Massacre*, p. 35.

fourteen hours a day, locked in mills in stifling heat, and subject to rules "such as no negroes were ever subjected to…" He went on to attack the Poor Law Amendment, stating that the whole country had risen in opposition to it. "Here is the country disturbed; here are the jails filling; here are wives and children screaming after their fathers; here are the undeniable facts", he said.

However, Cobbett, although a tribune, was – in contrast to Paine – essentially a conservative backward-looking figure. Instead of seeking a bright new future, he wished for the return of 'Old England', a land "with room for us all, and plenty for us to eat and drink", a land fit for bees and not drones. In that sense, he wished to turn back time and do away with the industrial and commercial advance. Although a radical, he was perhaps the most conservative radical of the time.

ROBERT OWEN

Robert Owen (1771-1858) is regarded as the father of British socialism. He was a man who definitely had his eyes fixed on the future, and not on the past. He was certainly one of the giants in terms of the boldness of his thought. Engels credited him with all the real social progress made in Britain. "English Socialism arose with Owen", he explained.[41]

Robert Owen was born in the Welsh town of Newtown, Montgomery. His ideas – Owenism – over time became the most powerful tendency in the labour movement, built around conceptions of socialism and communism. The British working class was only just emerging onto the scene, and Owen's ideas corresponded to that early phase. Along with Fourier and Saint-Simon, his ideas can be described as Utopian socialism. In other words, they were based on schemes or models for a new society, which were not rooted in historical development or in the class struggle.

Nevertheless, Marx and Engels paid great tribute to Owen for his advanced thinking. As Engels pointed out:

> Banished from official society, with a conspiracy of silence against him in the press, ruined by his unsuccessful communist experiments in America, in which he sacrificed all his fortune, he turned directly to the working class and continued working in their midst for thirty years. Every social movement, every real advance in England on behalf of the workers links itself on to the name of Robert Owen.[42]

From humble beginnings, Robert Owen moved to London, then Manchester, in search of a livelihood. He eventually borrowed money from his brother

---

41 MECW, vol. 4, p. 525.
42 *Socialism: Utopian and Scientific*, MESW, vol. 3, p. 125.

and set up his own business. He travelled to Glasgow and saw the mills at New Lanark, and acclaimed at that point that he wanted to try a co-operative experiment, which would reject "man's inhumanity to man" and the brutality of the Industrial Revolution. He correctly believed that man's character was formed by his environment, and if the environment was planned on co-operative lines, this would result in harmony and universal well-being. In these ideas, which he expounded in a fascinating book titled *A New View of Society*, he was deeply influenced by the French philosophers.

For Robert Owen, good working and living conditions, together with decent education, could eliminate the terrible ills of capitalist society. He experimented with this revolutionary view in his factory in New Lanark, where his workers and their families were treated as human beings. Owen raised the demand for an eight-hour day in 1810 and set about implementing the policy at New Lanark. By 1817 he had formulated the goal of an eight-hour workday and the slogan 'eight hours labour, eight hours recreation, eight hours rest'. Through his actions, Owen transformed the lives of the ordinary workers he employed. He advocated that his methods should be universally adopted by society at large. "Let society be now based on the same principle, and all evil will soon disappear", he wrote. As Owen also explained, to stunning effect:

> The rapid accumulation of wealth, from the rapid increase in mechanical and chemical power, created capitalists who were among the most ignorant and injurious of the population. The wealth created by the industry of the people, now made abject slaves to these new artificial powers, accumulated in the hands of what are called the moneyed class, who created none of it, and who misused all they had acquired.[43]

This was a devastating criticism of capitalism. He believed that three things stood in the way of universal happiness: private property, religion, and marriage in its current form. "Private property", he said, "made men into devils, and the world into hell." This certainly corresponded to the direct experience of millions.

"Hand labour cannot compete with machinery", Owen wrote. "To denounce machinery would be a return to barbarism... machines must be placed in the service of human labour, instead of superseding it, which it does at present." These were revolutionary ideas that pointed to a new society.

In 1819, an early working-class newspaper, *The Black Dwarf*, outlined Owen's plans for a communist colony:

---

43 J. Lindsay and E. Rickword, *Spokesmen for Liberty*, p. 273.

"See what a pretty plan I have drawn out *on paper*. And at what equal distances I have placed such and such buildings. How imposing they are. There are all the offices, attached and detached, that could be wished. There are schools and lecture rooms, and Committee rooms and brew-houses and workhouses and granaries. There you will put the women, there the men and there the children. They will be called to dinner every day regularly, and they will be clothed and taught and not worked very much. Oh, how happy they must be! There is nothing to prevent it whatever. All the bad passions will be eradicated and I should like to live there myself. Nobody that *understands* it can for a moment object to it. Why, there is to be a chapel in which only the *truth* is to be taught; and schools where nothing but useful knowledge is to be inculcated."[44]

These were incredible ideas, amazingly advanced for their time, and written 200 years ago! Compare them to the feeble ideas that are expressed today, even on the left, despite all the advances since that time. Of course, Owen's ideas had their limits. Given that the working class was only emerging as a class, Owen looked first of all for support from the rich and powerful, such as the Archbishop of Canterbury, Sir Robert Peel, and even the Queen's father. If he wanted to gain influence, then those who held the power needed to be convinced. For a while, certain enlightened bourgeois toyed with these strange and exotic ideas of socialism, but soon lost interest and became hostile to his radical schemes. The more outspoken he was in his attacks on capitalism, the more they turned their backs on him. But Owen refused to tone down his ideas.

The upper classes naturally began to attack him and his notions. Eventually, this hostile reaction pushed Owen in a different direction altogether. As he explained in his autobiography:

"During this period, as I fully anticipated, I have been reviled, denounced as an infidel, and opposed in every one of my various attempts to liberate the human mind from slavery, and from all poverty or the fear of it…"[45]

COMMUNIST COLONIES

Owen had been influenced by the materialist philosophers of the French Revolution, who demanded that reason and justice should be the measure of all things, including society. Owen therefore embarked on setting up his own communist colonies or 'Villages of Co-operation', the first of which was New Harmony, Indiana, in the United States in 1825. It was followed

---

44 Quoted in J. Strachey, *The Theory and the Practice of Socialism*, pp. 341-2.
45 J. Lindsay and E. Rickword, *Spokesmen for Liberty*, p. 269.

by Harmony Hall in Hampshire, England. However, these experiments all failed for the same reason. They were bold attempts to change the economic system without changing the political system. These co-operatives attempted to operate within capitalism, and were therefore subject to competition with capitalist firms, which could drive down their costs by cutting wages. The co-operatives could not compete on such a basis, except by destroying their own support. As G.D.H. Cole explained:

> Even the 'good' employer was compelled to grind the faces of the poor for how else could he survive? The bad, ruthless employer was in a position to drive him out of business if he did not conform. And ruthless employers were many...[46]

This highlighted the flaw in Owen's plan.

The *Poor Man's Guardian* also challenged the Owenite illusions of co-operative enterprises:

> "Co-operation is of no use, unless the people would get the raw materials without going to the land-stealer, then dispense with the use of money, and live by bartering their manufactures with each other. No one could then get either rent, tax, or profit out of them, but as they cannot do this, Co-operation has little or no effect than of feeding the rich and starving those who can scarcely live... As soon as it becomes generally understood that Co-operators can live a shilling a week cheaper than before, their employers will reduce their wages to that amount; thus, will their employers reap all the advantages of their cooperation..."[47]

Co-operation could only work on a nation-wide basis when the economy was in the hands of the working class. Ernest Jones explained that it was necessary to take power "to reconstruct the bases of society". Addressing the members of the cooperatives, he explained: "Under the present system ... all your efforts must prove vain – have proved vain – towards the production of a *national* result."[48] In other words, it was not possible to do away with capitalism by simply establishing a chain of socialist or communist colonies which were, in the end, subject to the laws of capitalism.

Owenism gave rise to co-operative societies in the 1840s, which gave workers a 'dividend on purchases' in such ventures. Unlike Owen, their goods were sold at market prices and the profits redistributed to members according to how much they spent. From this developed the great Co-operative movement.

---

46 *Chartist Portraits*, p. 1.
47 Quoted in S. Harrison, *Poor Man's Guardians*, p. 80.
48 MECW, vol. 11, p. 577.

However, rather than distributing profits, explained its critics, workers should be struggling to abolish capitalist profit-making altogether. This was simply working within the capitalist system. The belief of the Co-operative movement, that the movement would peacefully put an end to the competitive system, was patently never going to happen. This was later proved by experience.

The attacks on Owen by the ruling class attracted huge support for him from the radicalised working class. In the 1820s and early 1830s, Owenism became a rallying cry for those who rebelled against the factory system. Marx said that Owen "not only set out from the factory system in his experiments, but declared this system to be, so far as theory was concerned, the starting-point of the social revolution".[49] This was the logical conclusion. The organisation and planning that applied to individual factories was also applicable to society as a whole.

On his return to England in 1828, Owen turned his back on the rich and powerful and instead turned his attention towards the working class. In 1833 he even established a national trade union, the Grand National Consolidated Trades Union, whose constitution envisaged a new classless society. It was a bold initiative, but as expected attracted the hatred of the employers, who resorted to lockouts to destroy the union. Within a few years, the union was unfortunately broken.

But Robert Owen made a deep impact on the working-class movement. "Owenism, as those who are aware who habitually watch the progress of opinion, is at present in one form or another, the actual creed of a great portion of the working classes", wrote the hostile *Westminster Review*.[50] However, his ideas remained rather utopian. With the collapse of the national trade unions in the mid-1830s, the working class turned to political activity, which reached new heights. But Owen remained aloof from all this. In fact, he refused to join the Chartists and criticised them for sowing discontent against the rich, thereby alienating them and in some way delaying the emergence of socialism. Had Owen become a Chartist, with his energies and prestige, new possibilities would have opened up. In doing so, he could also have learned from the likes of Bronterre O'Brien, Julian Harney, and others. Unfortunately, this was not to be and he remained isolated.

On his deathbed, a local priest came to visit Robert Owen to offer religious blessings, which he firmly declined. The priest then asked him if he had any regrets in wasting his life on fruitless endeavours. Owen replied: "My life was

---

49 *Capital*, Vol. 1, p. 54.
50 Quoted in M. Beer, *A History of Socialism*, p.45.

not useless; I gave important truths to the world, and it was only for want of understanding that they were disregarded. I have been ahead of my time."[51] In fact, rather than being ahead of his time, he was a product of his own time, especially of the early rebellion against capitalism. His ideas of socialism were based on schemas, which were doomed to fail. It was left to Marx and Engels to build upon the positive features of Owenism and develop the ideas of scientific socialism, ideas which were rooted in the real development of society and the struggle of the working class.

THE SOCIALIST ECONOMISTS

Long before the appearance of Marx's *Capital*, there emerged on the scene a group of British socialist economists, in particular Thomas Hodgskin, John Gray, John Francis Bray, and William Thompson, who based their ideas upon the labour theory of value. Of course, a labour theory of value had been put forward earlier by the classical economists Adam Smith and David Ricardo. In essence, this explained that the value of a commodity was determined by the amount of socially necessary labour contained within its production. However, the classical economists believed that capitalism was an eternal system, rather than a stage in human history. The socialist economists had a different perspective, and gave a revolutionary and class character to the theories of Ricardo and Smith. They used the labour theory of value to challenge capitalism and argue for a new society.

John Gray has the honour of being one of the first to pioneer this socialist and working-class approach. In his 'Lecture on Human Happiness' (1825), he explained that value is created exclusively by the working class, but they do not receive in wages the full value that they have produced. Gray calculated that workers at the time received in wages only one-fifth of the value they had created:

> "The rich man, who in point of fact pays nothing, receives everything, while the poor man, who in point of fact pays everything, receives nothing. We put it to the candour of every honest man whether such a state of society as this ought to be preserved! Whether it is not at variance with every principle of honesty!"[52]

As an Owenite, Gray had his limitations, but he was clear on one thing: "From human labour every description of wealth proceeds; the productive classes do now support, not only themselves but every unproductive member

---

51 Ibid., p.174.
52 Quoted in J. Lindsay and E. Rickword, *Spokesmen for Liberty*, p. 277.

of society." This was a truly revolutionary idea, which had been expressed before, but now received a theoretical explanation.

In the same year, Thomas Hodgskin, in his *Labour Defended against the Claims of Capital*, went a step further, equating profit to *surplus value* extracted from the working class:

"Before a labourer can have a loaf of bread he must give a quantity of labour more than the loaf costs, by all that quantity which pays the profit of the farmer, the corn-dealer, the miller and the baker, with profit on the buildings they use; and he must moreover pay with the produce of his labour the rent of the landlord... Whether there are Corn Laws or not, the capitalist must allow the labourer to subsist, and as long as his claims are granted and acted on he will never allow him to do more."[53]

He is not clear at what point surplus value is extracted, seeking the answer in "unequal exchanges", rather than in the actual process of production. This led Robert Owen and his supporters down the road of their ill-fated Labour Exchanges, a currency system based on labour notes. The scheme attempted to cut out the capitalist 'middleman', but the laws of the system soon prevailed. It lasted no more than two years before it collapsed.

As Hodgskin stated:

"Betwixt him who produces food and him who produces clothing, betwixt him who makes instruments and him who uses them, in steps the capitalist, who neither makes nor uses them, and appropriates to himself the produce of both. With as niggard a hand as possible he transfers to each a part of the produce of the other, keeping to himself the larger share. Gradually and successively he has insinuated himself betwixt them, expanding in bulk as he has been nourished by their increasingly productive labours, and separating them so widely from each other that neither can see whence that supply is drawn which each receives through the capitalist."[54]

William Thompson, an Irishman who had emigrated to England, gave lectures and also produced books that had a significant influence on working-class thought in this period. His *Inquiry into the Principles of the Distribution of Wealth most conducive to Human Happiness* (1824) was a direct attack on orthodox political economy and had a considerable effect. This was followed by his *Appeal of one half of the Human Race* (1825), a bold defence of women's rights. Then followed his book *Labour Rewarded* (1827), which was a reply to Hodgskin, and, although it based itself on co-operative production and

---

53 Quoted in A.L. Morton, *Socialism in Britain*, p. 28.
54 Quoted in Ibid., p. 29.

distribution, rejected the Owenite solution of exchanging products equally. However, he agreed that the origin of profit arose from "the value added to the raw material by the labour, guided by skill, expended upon it. The materials, the buildings, the machinery, the wages can add nothing to their own value."

This was an important advance. Both Gray and Thompson showed it was not the monopoly, or distribution, of property but the institution of private property itself that was responsible for the exploitation and misery of the working class. The conclusion drawn was that the workers had to take political power from the private property-owners if they were to establish a just society. As Thompson wrote in *Labour Rewarded*:

> "Labourers must become capitalists and must acquire knowledge to regulate their labour on a large united scale, before they will be able to do more than dream of enjoying the whole products of their labour. Added to knowledge, the Industrious Classes must also acquire *power*, the whole power of the social machine in their own hands, in order to render their knowledge available, on a national scale, and with an immediate effect, for promoting the impartial and equal happiness of all."[55]

Meanwhile, the publication of John Francis Bray's book, *Labour's Wrongs and Labour's Remedy* (1839), which built upon the ideas of the others, coincided with mass Chartist agitation throughout the country. The tone of this book was far sharper than the earlier economic writings. His criticisms of capitalism were far more uncompromising:

> "Every accumulation of the capitalist or employers, as a body, is derived from the unsurrendered earnings of the working class, or persons employed; and wherever one man thus becomes rich he does so only on condition that many men shall remain poor... The gain of the employer will never cease to be the loss of the employed – until the exchanges between the parties are equal; and exchanges can never be equal while society is divided into capitalists and producers – the last living upon their labour and the first bloating upon the profit of that labour."[56]

John Bray, who was active for a period in the Chartist movement, recognised that the workers themselves needed to fight for their emancipation: "The producers have but to make an effort – and by them must every effort for

55 Quoted in G.D.H. Cole & A.W. Filson, *British Working Class Movements: Selected Documents 1789-1875*, p. 203.
56 Quoted in A.L. Morton, *Socialism in Britain*, p. 31.

their own redemption be made – and their chains will be snapped asunder for ever." Again, in a vision of a new world, he remarked:

"[O]ne class shall not be allowed to ride through life on the backs of another… There can be no doubt that they will ultimately succeed, and the joys reserved for them in their futurity will amply repay them for whatever they suffer during their progress forwards; but this progress will depend upon their activity, stimulated by their sufferings under existing institutions."[57]

These ideas were an attempt to break through the veil of capitalist relations and appearances to its real laws, which operate behind the backs of society. They represented a search for the truth which is hidden and mystified under capitalism. Nevertheless, these economists, as yet, could not understand that capitalism was simply a stage in the development of history, simply a link in the chain. These early socialist thinkers must be congratulated for unearthing certain truths, as well as the contradictory tendencies that govern capitalist society. Although they did not have the clarity of Marx, they should still be considered pioneers in this field. Without doubt, they are giants compared with some of today's alleged 'socialists' who meekly talk of a 'mixed economy' or 'welfare capitalism'.

It is also worth recording John Bray's views about the rights of women and children, and how their subservient position could be completely transformed in a rational society. For instance, he stated:

Bad as are the social arrangements which leave children immediately dependent upon their parents for education and subsistence, a still worse feature in the present system, and one productive of the greater part of the demoralisation and vice which surround us, is that custom of society which leaves women dependent upon individual man for subsistence. Woman should be altogether as independent of man, in respect to her occupation and her maintenance, as man is independent of her or of his fellow-man. Woman is not naturally, and never can be legally, the slave or the property of man; but, in regard to every right appertaining to human existence, she stands with man on a footing of the most perfect equality. Under the present system, woman is dependent upon and is regarded as inferior to man – she is by turns his slave and his plaything – she has no equal social rights and no political existence. Spoiled by a pernicious and deficient education, half-despised for the apparent want of those mental powers which are not permitted to be called forth and exercised, and degraded by her dependent position – woman is now fixed in a labyrinth of tyranny and injustice from which she cannot be rescued

57 Quoted in Ibid., p. 31.

by any means which do not afford her entire independence of the control of her self-styled superior, in the same degree as he is independent of her.[58]

Marx also paid tribute to these thinkers, which provided important theoretical guidance to workers. Marx had in fact quoted extensively from John Bray in his reply to Proudhon, *The Poverty of Philosophy* (1847), in which he described Bray's contribution as a "remarkable work". Marx and Engels went out of their way to acknowledge their debt to him and the other socialist economists, who had begun to shed light on the nature of exploitation. Whatever their limitations, they are part of our socialist heritage, a heritage described by Engels as being of "such a sharpness and decisiveness that this literature, which has now almost disappeared, and which to a large extent was first rediscovered by Marx, remained unsurpassed until the appearance of *Capital*".[59]

The impact of these economists and their socialist ideas on Chartism, starting with thinkers such as Bronterre O'Brien, was certainly profound. As a poem published in the *Poor Man's Guardian* eloquently acknowledged:

Wages should form the price of goods;
Yes, wages should be all,
Then we who work to make the goods,
Should *justly have them all*;
But if their price be made of rent,
Tithes, taxes, profits all,
Then we who work to make the goods,
Shall have – *just none at all.*

One of the Know-Nothings

While the Chartist economists never achieved a comprehensive understanding of capitalist exploitation, it must be said that Hodgskin and Thompson came quite close. Their ideas were based upon Ricardo's analysis, which they extended and deepened. The labour theory of value provided the cornerstone for their advances. They asked the pertinent question: what is the function of the capitalist owners, who perform no labour at all? They believed the workers were being robbed in some way, but they were not able to go any further in uncovering the mechanism.

---

58 J. Bray, *Labour's Wrongs and Labour's Remedy: Or the Age of Might and the Age of Right*, p. 167.
59 Preface to Marx's *The Poverty of Philosophy*, p. 8.

Bronterre O'Brien, the Chartist thinker, correctly understood that the miseries imposed on the working class were not due to the malice of the individual capitalists, but were a product of the dictates and laws of the capitalist system. He vividly described the state of affairs in a piece about distributing the national income:

> "If God sent the rich into the world with combs on their heads like fighting cocks, if He sent the poor into the world with humps on their backs like camels, then I would say it was predestined that the rich should be born booted and spurred, ready to ride over the poor; but when I see that God has made no distinction between rich and poor – when I see that all men are sent into this working world without silver spoons in their mouths or shirts on their backs, I am satisfied that all must labour in order to get themselves fed and clothed.

> "You produce annually £450 millions of wealth, and the idlers take 4s. 6d. a pound of it. They take nearly one-fourth, though they are only one in two thousand of the people.

> "Next come the profit-mongers – those who make their fortune by grinding the poor and cheating the rich; that class who buy cheap and sell dear, who spoil the wholesome articles you have made, and distribute them to others – they take 7s. 6d. a pound of the wealth which you produce.

> "Thus 12s. is gone before you have a pick. They promise you a paradise hereafter. You pay 1s. a pound to the clergy for that, on condition they preach to you to be content with your lot and to be pleased with what divine provenance has done for you.

> "This shilling is not taken from the 12s. That would leave you without merit.

> "Then they take 2s. 6d. a pound for their military forces – to keep you down. This leaves 4s. 6d."[60]

These ideas have a modern ring to them, so the fact that they were written in the 1830s means they required considerable foresight and understanding. It was left to Marx, however, to discover the secret of surplus value, which arises from the unpaid labour of the working class, as well as the concept of labour power, which the workers sell for wages, as opposed to their labour. Labour power, Marx realised, is the only commodity that produces values greater than its own value. It is from this alone that surplus value arises. This solution to the question provided a revolution in our understanding.

---

60 Quoted in J. Lindsay and E. Rickword, *Spokesmen for Liberty*, p. 303.

Logically, the apologists of capitalism were deeply alarmed by such theories, which encouraged the workers to challenge the whole basis of the capitalist economy. As John Cazenove, an economist, wrote in 1832:

> "That Labour is the sole source of wealth seems to be a doctrine as dangerous as it is false, as it unhappily affords a handle to those who would represent all property as belonging to the working classes, and the share which is received by others as a robbery or fraud upon *them*."[61]

As a result, the labour theory of value was abandoned in favour of subjectivism, and bourgeois economics was reduced to mere apologetics.

WILLIAM BENBOW

Another influential individual at the time was William Benbow, a nonconformist preacher, pamphleteer, publisher, and a prominent figure within the Reform movement in Manchester and London. He became one of the most well-known and radical leaders of the working-class movement, and is credited as the father and advocate of the general strike, or 'Grand National Holiday'. Benbow toured the country, holding open-air meetings, giving lectures and hawking his pamphlets. He was closely involved with planning the attempted Blanketeers protest march by Lancashire weavers in March 1817 and was very active in 1831 in the National Union of the Working Classes. In April 1840, just as his ideas were becoming popular in Chartist circles, he was sentenced to sixteen months' imprisonment for sedition.

In January 1832, he had issued a pamphlet entitled the 'Grand National Holiday and Congress of the Productive Classes', which, among other things, argued for a general strike, or 'Sacred Month'. He also drew important lessons about the capitalist system, including the contradiction of overproduction, of idle hands and empty factories alongside unfulfilled needs. "We are oppressed, in the fullest sense of the word; we have been deprived of everything; we have no property, no wealth, and our labour is of no use to us, since what it produces goes into the hands of others..." explained Benbow.

> "One scoundrel, one sacrilegious blasphemous scoundrel, says 'that overproduction is the cause of our wretchedness.' Over-production, indeed! When we half-starving producers cannot, with all our toil, obtain anything like a sufficiency of produce. It is the first time that in any age or country, save our own, *abundance* was adduced as a cause of *want*. Good God! Where is this abundance? Abundance of food! Ask the labourer and mechanic where they find it. Their emaciated frame is the best answer.

---

61 R.L. Meek, *Studies in the Labour Theory of Value*, p. 124.

Abundance of clothing! The nakedness, the shivering, the asthma, the colds, and rheumatisms of the people, are proofs of the abundance of clothing! Our Lords and Masters tell us, we produce too much; very well then, we shall cease from producing for one month, and thus put into practice the theory of our Lords and Masters."[62]

However, Benbow envisaged the general strike of workers as a battle of "folded arms", believing an insurrection was unnecessary. He wrote:

"There will not be an insurrection. It will simply be passive resistance. The men may remain at leisure; there is, and can be, no law to compel them to work against their will… and what happens as a consequence? Bills are dishonoured, the Gazette teems with bankruptcies, capital is destroyed, the revenue falls, the system of government falls into confusion, and every link in the chain which binds society together is broken in a moment by this inert conspiracy of the poor against the rich."[63]

In this, Benbow was mistaken, but it was an honest mistake. It is not sufficient for the working class to strike and simply wait and hold its breath. Benbow nevertheless pointed to the potential power of the working class in such a strike and how it could be used. While these ideas may sound somewhat obvious today, and the concept of a 'Holy Month' perhaps sounds quaint, we must remember they were written at a time when the working class had never experienced a general strike. In other words, he was breaking new ground by exploring this question, as no other person had done before. In this way, he must be considered a real pioneer.

The general strike certainly poses the question of power, but does not resolve it. When production stops, who holds the power? Benbow did, however, point to the need for the working class during the strike to develop its own structures separate from the state. Accordingly, he called for the setting up of "committees of management" of strikers in every city, town and village. There should also be frequent meetings where those people could be held accountable, a pointer towards workers' control. In his plan, delegates should be sent from these local committees to a National Congress, like a Workers' Parliament, whose object was to:

"[R]eform society, for 'from the crown of our head to the sole of our foot there is no soundness in us'. We must cut out the rottenness in order to become sound. Let us see what is rotten. Every man that does not work is rotten; he must be made to work in order to cure the unsoundness. Not only is society rotten; but

---

62 Quoted in G.D.H. Cole and A.W. Filson, p. 231.
63 J.T. Murphy, *Preparing for Power*, p. 50.

the land, property, and capital is rotting. There is not only something, but a great deal rotten in the state of England. Everything, men, property, and money, must be put in a state of circulation."[64]

This concept of workers' committees shows that Benbow was clearly moving in the direction of the idea of workers' power.

As we shall see, the tactic of the general strike would become an important weapon in the arsenal of Chartism and was adopted as such by the Chartist Congress of 1839. The strike weapon was championed by the *Poor Man's Guardian*, and in 1838, Benbow held meetings all over Lancashire, the heartland of the labour movement, to propagate the idea. Unfortunately, he was imprisoned before the great general strike of 1842, the closest the Chartist movement got to his own vision.

THE 'GREAT BETRAYAL' OF 1832

Up until this point, namely prior to 1832, the industrialists had been excluded from the fruits of power, which was the preserve largely of the aristocracy. However, the economic power of the capitalists was growing exponentially and they now wanted the lion's share of political power. During the Napoleonic Wars, the alliance of the propertied classes was held together by their common opposition to Jacobinism. Now this unequal alliance began to fracture. The rising bourgeoisie were determined to take the helm of the state while, of course, still sharing some of the plunder with the landed class. After all, most Whig leaders, such as Lord Grey, Lord Grenville, Lord Althorp, Lord Melbourne and Lord John Russell, were themselves rich capitalist landowners.

This conflict within the ruling classes reflected itself in divisions within the Tory Party, which split into warring factions. The Whigs hardly fared better. These splits mirrored the shifting class alliances, with a layer of the Tories merging with the remnants of the Whigs. There was a constant shifting and jockeying between the political parties during this period. 'Parliamentary Reform' now became the battle-cry of the rising bourgeoisie, eager to get their hands on the reins of power. This meant upsetting the compromise of the 'Glorious' Revolution of 1688. To this end, they were prepared to lean for support on the working class, but, of course, only to later betray it.

1830 witnessed the formation of the Birmingham Political Union and similar reform groupings, which formed an ad hoc extra-parliamentary alliance of Radicals. By coincidence, it was also the same year that revolution broke out in France, which overthrew the Bourbon monarchy, and created

---

64 G.D.H. Cole & A.W. Filson, pp. 232-3.

a great stir within all classes of British society. It was at this point that the working class began once again to enter onto the scene. A year later, the National Union of the Working Classes was formed, the proletarian left wing of Radicalism, to campaign for universal suffrage as well as trade union rights. It held meetings in the Rotunda, a popular place for lectures on economics and politics, with speakers such as Robert Owen, Cobbett, Hunt, Daniel O'Connell and Feargus O'Connor. Once again, we have the elements of the future Chartist movement beginning to crystallise. Moreover, 1830 was the year in which Henry Hetherington established the weekly *Poor Man's Guardian,* a great addition to the working-class press.

Given the ferment, the Radical movement was beginning to build up a head of steam. The question of political reform, and with it the extension of the franchise, had long captured the popular imagination. Now, things began to stir in many towns and cities. In Merthyr Tydfil, in June 1831, following disturbances, the Red Flag was raised in Britain for the first time as a symbol of working-class revolt. A crowd of 10,000 confronted eighty soldiers of the Argyll and Sutherland Highlanders and twenty demonstrators were shot dead. As a result of the arrests that followed, two men were condemned to death: Lewis Lewis, whose sentence was commuted to exile for life, and Richard Lewis (alias Dic Penderyn), who was hanged.

The anger of this aroused working class was skilfully harnessed by the bourgeois Radicals, who used the movement to pursue their own particular agenda and gain political power for themselves. The working class was cynically used in this power struggle between the different sections of the ruling class. Those who blocked reform and defended the vested interests of the landowners were summarily threatened with the wrath of the crowd. The situation reached a fever pitch after the collapse of the Wellington government and its replacement in November 1830 by a Whig administration headed by Lord Grey. However, one of the first acts of the new government was to put down the revolt of the agricultural labourers, the 'Swing Riots'. Nineteen men were hanged (one for causing injury to a financier's hat), 481 were transported for machine-breaking and arson and a further 400 imprisoned. This demonstrated that Grey's administration was a government of property and was a clear warning of what was to come. Cobbett, who sympathised with the agricultural labourers, was charged with incitement, but the case collapsed. "Tranquillity being now restored", noted a contented Lord Suffield.[65]

---

65 J. Lindsay and E. Rickword, *Spokesmen for Liberty,* p. 286.

In early March 1831, Lord Grey turned his attention to reform and brought in a new Reform Bill, which proposed to abolish some rotten boroughs, grant representation to towns like Manchester, Leeds and Sheffield, and extend the franchise in boroughs to the £10 householder and better-off farmers in the counties. Under such plans, five out of six male adults, the overwhelming bulk of the working class, remained disenfranchised. Women were not even considered. Nevertheless, the Reform Bill still met with furious opposition within the Commons from those desperate to maintain the status quo. This opposition was reinforced by the Tory-dominated House of Lords. Lord Grey appealed to his opponents to be reasonable and assured them:

> "If any persons suppose that this Reform will lead to ulterior measures, they are mistaken; for there is no one more decided against annual parliaments, universal suffrage, and the ballot, than I am. My object is not to favour, but to put an end to such hopes and projects."[66]

A similarly reassuring argument was put forward by one of his allies, Lord Brougham, in the House of Lords, which was still stubbornly resisting the Bill:

> "You are now asked to pay a moderate price for restoring the old fabric of the representative system, and if you refuse it, the longer you delay, the more you will have to yield, till annual parliaments, elected by millions, and vote by ballot must be conceded... There are those who, even in this House, talk much of the Bills so adding to the strength of the democracy as to endanger all the other institutions of the country, and who therefore charge us as originators, as the promoters of spoliation and anarchy. Why, my Lords, have we ourselves nothing to fear from democratic spoliation? The fact is, that some of the members of the present Cabinet possess more property than any two administrations together within my recollection. I need not say I do not include myself, for I have little or no property, but what little I have depends upon the stability of existing institutions and is as dear to me as the much larger possessions of your lordships."[67]

This clearly revealed the intentions of the government. But the Lords, stubborn as a mule, stood firm and rejected the Bill. This provoked a mighty ruckus outside of Parliament, deliberately stirred up by the bourgeois Radicals such as Francis Place. Feelings ran so high that there were riots in London, Derby, Nottingham, Bristol, and talk of 100,000 pikes being made ready in Sheffield. Of course, unleashing the 'mob' was a dangerous strategy,

---

66 Quoted in T. Rothstein, *From Chartism to Labourism*, p. 95.
67 Ibid., p. 95.

as it stirred up unintentional thoughts of revolution. But the workers were considered 'small change', who could be cast aside when required. Francis Place was nevertheless alarmed by the danger, and warned that:

> "[T]he working people would see in the proceeding the old desire to use them for a purpose and then to abandon them… The gap between the working and middle classes would be widened, and the rancour that exists would be increased, and all chance of reconciliation put off for years…"[68]

Despite this concern, the bourgeois Radicals had no alternative but to exert extra-parliamentary pressure and lean on the workers to get what they wanted.

O'Brien attacked this cynical stirring up of the masses, with its pseudo-revolutionary talk by Place and company. In a manifesto demanding universal suffrage, O'Brien, pointing to the Lords, wrote:

> "Threats of a 'revolution' are employed by the middle class and 'petty masters' as arguments to induce your allowance of their measures; but be not intimidated by them: a violent revolution is not only beyond the means of those who threaten it, but it is to them their greatest object of harm; for they know that such a revolution can only be effected by the poor and despised millions, who if excited to the step, might use it for their own advantage, as well as for that of themselves, who would thus not only be placed in a less exclusive situation than at present, but would also have their rights of property endangered: be assured that a violent revolution is their greatest dread, and, should ever the poor millions be compelled to resort to such an alternative, they will be as firmly opposed to it as yourselves could possibly be: yes, alas! their assistance, in such event, is secured to you by the irresistible *sympathy of property*, without the necessity of any sacrifice on your part of your dear exclusiveness."[69]

The Reform Bill was rejected twice. Following its first defeat, Parliament was dissolved. During the following general election huge protests took place which demanded, "The Bill, the whole Bill, and nothing but the Bill!" The Whigs rode the popular wave and were returned to office triumphantly. Then the Lords were threatened with an ultimatum. Either they could allow this limited reform, or they could risk provoking the masses' struggle for complete universal suffrage, and much more besides. In a final throw of the dice, the House of Lords intended to support a military dictatorship headed by the Duke of Wellington. However, the threat of a run on the Bank of England

---

68 Ibid., p. 20.
69 Ibid., pp. 96-97.

soon brought the Lords and Crown back down to earth with a bang. The Great Reform Bill finally became law in June 1832.

When the smoke cleared, the Reform Act had succeeded in handing over effective political power from the landed aristocracy to the rising bourgeoisie. The domination of the bourgeoisie was fully consummated in 1846 when the hated Corn Laws were repealed, which represented a decisive defeat for the landlords. As expected, the working class, who had been mobilised for parliamentary reform under the leadership of the mealy-mouthed middle-class radicals, saw that their efforts had been betrayed. They had been cynically cheated. The House of Commons had been 'reformed', but not democratised in any shape or form. Wellington revealed the contempt of the aristocracy for the *nouveaux riches* when he reacted to the change with the words "I never saw so many shocking bad hats in my life".

As soon as the bourgeoisie was firmly in the saddle, they announced to the world that Britain's parliamentary system had now reached the highest degree of perfection possible. There would be no further reform or extension of the franchise. Lord Stanley assured the ruling classes "that it was to be a final measure".[70] The government therefore pledged to hold the line. That was to be the end of the matter.

This betrayal split the Radical cause along class lines. It taught the working class a hard lesson: the whole establishment was rotten, and the middle classes could not be trusted as far as they could be thrown. The experience served to raise the workers' class consciousness, not by reading books and pamphlets, but based on the harsh reality of events. It was a bitter pill to swallow, and some drew revolutionary parallels. "The French working people had gained a revolution, and the middle classes came in and deprived them of the fruits", stated James Ayr.[71] Many concluded that the working class needed to rely on its own strength and fight for its own class interests, including the franchise.

The *Poor Man's Guardian* of Hetherington declared that the Reform Bill was worse than the old franchise. It went much further than even Thomas Paine and exposed the Parliament as a parliament of the ruling classes, incapable of reform:

"People who live by plunder will always tell you to be submissive to thieves. To talk of representation, in any shape, being of any use to the people is sheer nonsense, unless the people have a House of working men, and represent themselves. Those

---

70 Ibid., p. 25.
71 Quoted in D. Jones, p. 68.

who make the laws now, and are intended, by the reform bill, to make them in the future all live by profits of some sort or another. They will, therefore, no matter who elect them, or how often they are elected, always make the laws to raise profits and keep down the price of labour. Representation, therefore, by a different body of people to those who are represented, or whose interests are opposed to theirs, is a mockery, and those who persuade the people to the contrary are either idiots or cheats..."[72]

As time passed, the lessons of betrayal were being learned.

'Tis twelve months past, just yesterday, since earth, and sky, and sea,
And rock, and glen, and horse, and man rang loud the jubilee;
The beacons blazed, the cannon fired, and war'd each plain and hill
With the Bill – the glorious Bill, and nothing but the Bill!

Our taxes, by the glorious Bill, were all to sink and fade,
Our shipping was to prosper, and think, oh! What a trade!
Our agriculture and our looms, our pockets were to fill,
By, ah! You rogues, the Bill, the Bill, and nought but the Bill!

But now each holds up his hands in horror and disgust
At this same document, once termed the people's trust,
That at last was to bring grist to all the nation's mill.
Ah! Curse the Bill, ye rogues, the Bill, and nothing but the Bill![73]

The above is an opening poem that was published in the *Poor Man's Guardian* and summed up the intense hatred felt towards the 'Great Betrayal', and especially the middle-class Radicals, who were regarded as a wretched crew. This feeling served to crush any illusions of harmonious class collaboration for a long time. This profound anger felt by the disenfranchised working class also extended to the whole charade of Parliament itself, which lacked any legitimacy in their eyes. A pamphlet appeared entitled 'The Rotten House of Commons', which pointed to this deep-seated hostility.

As Bronterre O'Brien wrote:

"What a farce the present system is! The present House of Commons does not represent the people, but only those fellows who live by profits and usury – a rascally crew who have no interest in the real welfare of the country. Pawnbrokers are enfranchised, and two thousand brothel-owners in London all have votes, but honest folk have none. Not a single stockbroker is without a vote, yet there

72 Quoted in S. Harrison, p. 80.
73 M. Beer, *A History of Socialism*, vol. 1, p. 248.

is not a man among them who does not deserve the gallows. Every lawyer in the country can vote – every thief of them – yet when did any one of this gang add a sliver to the wealth of the nation?... Votes have been given to parsons, who live by explaining those things which they tell us are inexplicable, who preach abnegation of the lusts of the flesh while losing no opportunities of greasing their own rosy gills... It is, indeed, disgusting to see how much of the honey is appropriated by the drones, and what a pittance is left to the bees of the hive; and how the parliamentary franchise is monopolised by one-tenth of the population – and that tenth the worst tenth."[74]

A liberal Whig politician was just as bad as a Tory one. The term Whig was originally short for *whiggamore*, a term meaning 'cattle driver'. Samuel Johnson, a Tory, often joked that "the first Whig was the Devil". But in reality they were all cut from the same cloth. As Ebenezer Elliott, the eloquent Sheffield Corn Law rhymer, said:

"The difference between them is your Whig is dressed in hen's feathers and has a sheep's heart in his bosom, with a serpent's cerebellum for a brain. Your Tory is a straight-forward robber and cut-throat, greedy as a shark, blind as a bolt."[75]

THE GREAT UNSTAMPED

Throughout this period, there was an upsurge in the 'battle for a cheap press', which sought to make ordinary newspapers accessible to the working class. Given the febrile atmosphere, there was a growing thirst for ideas, and radical papers began to emerge like mushrooms after a thunderstorm. This was very much tied to the struggle for the franchise, as well as the 1832 betrayal. This unbridled publishing was viewed with horror by the authorities, who saw it as a direct threat to stability and property. For them, the growth of seditious literature needed to be suppressed by whatever means necessary. The 'Six Acts' of 1819 stiffened up laws against blasphemous and seditious publications, and imposed a heavy tax on newspapers and periodicals. This was directed at the radical press, such as Cobbett's *Register*, Carlile's *Republican* and Wooler's *Black Dwarf*, which had not previously been taxed. In response, newspapers simply defied the law and published 'unstamped'. They refused to carry the red spot indicating that stamp duty had been paid on the paper's cover.

William Hone did a great job in satirising a speech from the Crown about censorship at the opening of Parliament:

74 R. Brown & C. Daniels, pp. 28-29.
75 D. Jones, p. 60.

'The body of the people, I do think,
    are loyal still,'
But pray, My L—ds and G—tl—n,
    don't shrink
From exercising all your care
    and skill,
Here, and at home,
TO CHECK THE CIRCULATION
OF LITTLE BOOKS
    Whose very looks—
Vile *two-p'nny trash,*
    bespeak abomination.
Oh! They are full of blasphemies
    and libels,
And people read them
    oftener than their bibles.[76]

The government took action against these 'vile and slanderous' papers, seemingly more popular than the Bible. Shopkeepers and news vendors who handled such material were harassed, imprisoned, fined and repeatedly closed down. Richard Carlile was sentenced to what amounted to six years' imprisonment for the crime of selling Paine's *Age of Reason*. This did not dampen the movement, but in fact served only to intensify it. Hetherington openly advertised for men ready to go to gaol for freedom's sake. Others showed their defiance in court, to which the following exchange between J. Swann, the defendant, and Captain Clarke, who sat on the Bench, testifies:

Bench: Hold your tongue a moment.

Defendant: I shall not! for I wish every man to read these publications (pointing to the *Poor Man's Guardian* and *Hunt's Address*, etc.)

Bench: You are insolent, therefore you are committed to three months' imprisonment in Knutsford House of Correction, to Hard Labour.

Defendant: I've nothing to thank you for; and whenever I come out, I'll hawk them again. And mind you, the first that I hawk shall be to your house (looking at Captain Clarke).

Bench: Sit down.

Defendant: No! I shall not stand down for you.

---

76 Quoted in B. Simon, p. 192.

He was then forcibly removed from the dock and back to the New Bailey.[77]

Radical papers like the *Black Dwarf* and the *Weekly Political Register* enjoyed circulations of tens of thousands, penetrating deep into the working class. Others also sprang up, among them *The Operative*, the *Northern Liberator*, *Tribune of the People*, the *London Democrat*, *The Poor Man's Advocate*, *The Extinguisher*, the *Plain Speaker*, *Friend of the People*, *Reynolds Political Instructor*, as well as one with an exceptionally long name, the *Unfettered Thinker and Plain Speaker for Truth, Freedom and Progress*, and many others. The 'unstamped' papers were passed from one person to another, read aloud in taverns, coffee shops and reading groups, a ready audience keen to discover the latest news and arguments against the powers that be. As one reader, in a letter to the Newcastle Weekly Chronicle in 1883, recalled:

> "I can very well remember reading aloud, week by week, when a boy, to groups of wool combers in the neighbourhood of Bradford, the fiery articles of Feargus O'Connor, G.J. Harney, Ernest Jones, Bronterre O'Brien, and others, which appeared in *The Star* when published at Leeds, and also at London..."[78]

"The 'great unstamped' was emphatically a working-class press", wrote E.P. Thompson.[79] As one letter published in the *Poor Man's Guardian* explained:

> "Of all the taxes levied (or attempted to be levied) upon the poor man, the most odious and the most inexcusable is the tax upon political knowledge ... But the *Poor Man's Guardian* ... if properly supported by the working classes will show them not only that 'knowledge is power' but that power in their hands shall produce knowledge."[80]

This paper first appeared under its original title of the *Penny Papers for the People*, published by Henry Hetherington on 1 October 1830. Its opening editorial proclaimed: "It is the cause of the rabble we advocate, the poor, the suffering, the industrious, the productive classes ... We will teach this rabble their power – we will teach them that they are your masters, instead of being your slaves." The stamp duty spot was replaced by the slogan 'Knowledge is Power'. Below this appeared the words "Published in Defiance of the Law, to try the Power of the Right against Might". It was sold for only 1 penny, whereas, with the addition of the stamp duty and paper tax, each paper would have costed 7 pence.

---

77 J. Lindsay and E. Rickword, p. 289.

78 Quoted in J. Saville, *The British state and the Chartist Movement*, p. 204.

79 *The Making of the English Working Class*, p. 800.

80 Quoted in S. Harrison, p. 75.

The *Poor Man's Guardian* boldly declared itself to be "established contrary to the law" and announced it would emphatically "contain (in the reproduced words of the Prohibitory Act, here in italics) *news, intelligence, occurrences and remarks and observations thereon tending* decidedly *to excite hatred and contempt of the government and constitution of* the tyranny *of this country as by law established, and also vilify the abuses of religion*".[81]

Hetherington wrote:

> "Defiance is our only remedy; we cannot be a slave in all; we submit to much – for it is impossible to be wholly consistent – but we will try the power of Right against Might; we will begin by protesting and upholding this grand bulwark of all our liberties – the Freedom of the Press – the Press, too, of the ignorant and the Poor. We have taken upon ourselves its protection, and we will never abandon our post: we will die rather."[82]

How very different from today, where the national press is dominated by the billionaire class and churns out a torrent of daily propaganda in defence of capitalism, the rich and the privileged. Today, so-called 'freedom of the press' has become the freedom of billionaires to spew out their lies. Today's newspapers are a monopoly of the rich for the rich, a dictatorship over the minds of the people by the likes of Murdoch and others. We should not be fooled by their hypocrisy and their slippery deceit, which is their stock-in-trade. They are on occasion, to quote the words of Dylan Thomas, as "sweet as a razor", but other times they are as blunt as an axe.

It was with exceptional difficulty that the *Poor Man's Guardian* was kept going, but for four whole years it heroically battled in complete defiance of the authorities. It provided a great example, despite all the real hardships, of the sacrifices that were undertaken to keep a workers' paper in existence. It stands as testimony to the courage and determination of these people. The 'unstamped' weeklies carried news of the trade unions, their strikes, lockouts, the protests over the Tolpuddle Martyrs, as well as the radical theories of Owen and many others. They provided propaganda for the struggle for a new world of co-operation and plenty. They went far beyond Cobbett's nostalgia for the past, and began raising socialist and communist ideas. A member of the Builders' Union, for instance, wrote to *The Man*:

> "The Trade Unions will not only strike for less work, and more wages, but they will ultimately ABOLISH WAGES, become their own masters, and work for each

81 J. Lindsay and E. Rickword, p. 287.
82 Quoted in S. Harrison, p. 78.

other; labour and capital will no longer be separated but they will be indissolubly joined together in the hands of the workmen and work-women."[83]

Between 1830 and 1836, an incredible 500 people - real working-class martyrs – were sent to prison for selling unstamped papers, a measure of the repression they faced. The struggle to defend the 'Great Unstamped' was a fight to preserve the *genuine* freedom of the press, of the underdog and the downtrodden, against tyranny in all its guises. These papers opposed the ruling class, and that is why it tried to crush them. This ideological battle of the 'Great Unstamped' served to prepare the ground for Chartism and the Chartist press, most notably *The Northern Star,* which pioneered the cause of the working class. It was further enhanced by Bronterre O'Brien, the Chartist theoretician, who took over from Hetherington as editor of the *Poor Man's Guardian.*

RE-EMERGENCE OF TRADE UNIONS

In 1824 came the repeal of the Combination Acts, which gave freedom to the shackled and illegal trade unions to organise. They took full advantage of this. There was a burst of trade union membership and strikes. Shocked by this militant upsurge, the government rushed through a new Act, which placed severe restrictions on picketing and other activities. 'Molesting' and 'obstructing' persons at work were outlawed. Nevertheless, despite this, unions were theoretically legal, which at least allowed them to operate.

In 1829, John Doherty founded the General Union of Operative Spinners. Six months later, in 1830, he launched a more ambitious organisation, the National Association for the Protection of Labour. Other trades followed suit, with the Operative Builders' Union, and eventually the formation of the Grand National Consolidated Trades Union, founded by Robert Owen. As the *Poor Man's Guardian* announced on 19 October 1833:

> "A grand national organisation, which promises to embody the physical power of the country is silently but rapidly progressing; and the object of it is the sublimest that can be conceived, namely – to establish for the productive classes complete domination over the fruits of their industry."[84]

The union embraced an estimated half-a-million workers or more, including agricultural labourers and women workers. It went so far as to advocate a general strike to secure the eight-hour day. More significantly, it emblazoned on its programme the revolutionary aim of bringing about:

83 Quoted in E.P. Thompson, *The Making of the English Working Class,* p. 912.
84 Quoted in A.L. Morton & G. Tate, p. 69.

An entire change in society – a change amounting to a complete subversion of the existing order of the world. The working classes aspire to be at the top instead of at the bottom of society – or rather that there should be no top or bottom at all.

Rule XLVI explicitly stated that:

> "The great and ultimate object of it must be to establish the paramount rights of Industry and Humanity, by ... bringing about A DIFFERENT ORDER OF THINGS, in which the really useful and intelligent part of society only shall have the direction of its affairs".[85]

This embodied the spirit of the earlier illegal trade unions, which could now be expressed openly. Furthermore, they were not local bodies, but national organisations.

The government could not tolerate this growth of industrial militancy, and under Melbourne, the Home Secretary, they set out to destroy it. Their opportunity came in March 1834. Melbourne struck the union movement at its most vulnerable point, among the agricultural workers at Tolpuddle in Dorset, who had formed a branch of the union in the hope of raising their wages. As part of the union's custom, they administered oaths of loyalty. But such oaths had been declared illegal under the 1797 Act against the Nore mutiny, and this statute remained in place. Under this pretext, six men were prosecuted and found guilty. They were transported to Australia for seven years for the crime of oath-taking, and became famous throughout the labour movement as the Tolpuddle Martyrs. Even to this day, an annual trade union march at Tolpuddle keeps the memory alive, despite the fact that the leaders of the British Trades Union Congress are far removed from the sacrifices and militancy of these early unions. In 1834, mass demonstrations took place to free the labourers, but the authorities were determined to hold the line. It took four years of campaigning before they were pardoned and brought home.

The government's actions gave the signal for a general employers' offensive: workers were now forced to sign a declaration renouncing the union or be sacked. The infamous 'Document' was used as a battering ram to smash the trade unions and institute a series of major lockouts. Faced with this situation, the Grand National Consolidated Trades Union unfortunately proved inadequate for such a struggle. By the summer, their funds were practically exhausted as numerous strikes were defeated. By the end of the year, with its fragile federal structure and emerging differences within the

85 A. Hutt, *British Trade Unionism: A Short History*, p. 18.

leadership, the national union finally broke apart. By this time, even Owen had become increasingly concerned at the class-war tone of many of the union's pronouncements. Consequently, he closed down its newspaper, *The Crisis*, and declared the organisation formally dissolved in August 1834.

From that point on, Owen's work took a different direction with the formation of a new association for co-operative and socialist propaganda. The demise of the Grand National proved an inglorious end for such a powerful beginning. The other national unions also broke up and disappeared. The only exception was the Miners' Association of Great Britain, which was founded in November 1842, and was said to have had 100,000 members. It was closely associated with Chartism and most of its leaders were in fact Chartists. The experience left an indelible mark on the consciousness of the working class, which was later to turn in a political direction.

The industrial situation was further overshadowed by the prosecution and transportation of the Glasgow cotton-spinners in 1837, which followed a strike over wage reductions. In the course of the struggle a blackleg was shot and later died. The strike leaders were arrested and charged on twelve counts, including murder and conspiracy to murder. The murder charges were finally dropped due to lack of evidence, but they were found guilty of engaging in illegal activities. All five leaders were sentenced to seven years' transportation in January 1838. The prosecuting Sheriff of Lanarkshire, Archibald Alison, referred to the trade unions as a "moral pestilence", and described Glasgow as being in the grip of an "insurrectionary fever". The brutal sentences imposed on the strikers ignited a national campaign against the Whig government. A broadsheet printed in Newcastle in 1838 put the case to rhyme:

> Ye working men of Britain come listen awhile,
> Concerning the cotton spinners who lately stood their trial
> Transported for seven years far, far awa'
> Because they were united in Caledonia.

> Success to our friends in Ireland, who boldly stood our cause,
> In spite of O'Connell and his supporters of whiggish laws,
> Away with his politics, they are not worth a straw
> He's no friend to the poor of Ireland or Caledonia.

> Success to O'Connor who did nobly plead our cause,
> Likewise to Mr Beaumont, who abhors oppressive laws,
> But after all their efforts, justice and law,
> We are banished from our country, sweet Caledonia.

Whigs and Tories are united, we see it very plain,
To crush the poor labourer, it is their daily aim,
The proverb now is verified, and that you can all knaw,
In the case of those poor spinners in Caledonia.[86]

A campaign was organised in support of the convicted men, which ended up being no less memorable than the campaign in defence of the Tolpuddle Martyrs. It brought disillusioned radicals streaming back into political activity, which was to provide leaders and organisers for the Chartist movement. It is often said that the unions were not interested in politics, but this was certainly not the case. The mining areas of the North East were one of the best-organised regions of Chartism, where the 'physical force' party was particularly strong. Augustus Beaumont published his *Northern Liberator* from Newcastle, which preached the cause of 'physical force' Chartism in the late 1830s. He wrote:

> Those men were well fed, and therefore they relied on moral force; but let them labour for one week, and be ill-fed and ill-clothed, and it would soon convert their moral force to physical force…[87]

As Raymond Challinor and Brian Ripley explained in their book, there was much cross-fertilisation of the movements:

> Many Chartists, from taking a sympathetic attitude to the colliers' struggles, found themselves drawn into the Miner's Association and eventually playing a leading role in it. Chartism placed a vast reservoir of talent at the union's disposal. It swelled its ranks with people who, but for Chartism acting as intermediary, would never have dreamt of going anywhere near a pit. Moreover, besides bringing in recruits from outside the pits, Chartism provided, through its own activities, a training-ground where most of those who were later to become miners' leaders gained their first knowledge and experience. As a result, it becomes difficult to find any prominent union member who did not have, at some time or other, Chartist connections.[88]

When the Miners' Association was founded, it was attacked by the *Newcastle Journal*, which, in its own vindictive style, attributed its actual formation to Chartism. "The agitation of Chartism," stated the paper, "brought to the surface of society a great deal of scum that usually putrefies in obscurity below." In this, we hear the authentic voice of the ruling class.

---

86 D. Thompson, *The Chartists*, p. 22.
87 *Northern Liberator*, 28 December 1838.
88 *The Miners' Association: A Trade Union in the Age of the Chartists*, p. 15.

The defeats on the trade union front, coupled with the betrayal over the Reform Bill, pushed the workers' movement in the direction of political struggle, which provided the basis for the rise of Chartism. As the Hammonds wrote:

> The working classes were brought to the revolutionary temper that broke out in 1816 and 1830, and found its most complete expression in the gospel of the Chartists, through a number of states...[89]

With every step forward, the working class grew in stature. In the process, it became increasingly conscious of its historic role in the struggle for its own self-emancipation.

---

89 *The Town Labourer 1760-1832*, p. 289.

3. THE BIRTH OF CHARTISM

"I shall part with my sabre only with my life, and my own hand shall
write the epitaph upon a tyrant's brow in characters of blood and with
a pen of steel."
– Dr. John Taylor

"France is on the eve of revolution, Belgium pants to be free, in
Germany liberty is awake, the patriots of Spain are ready to send
Isabella and Carlos to the devil together, the Italian lifts his head, and
the exiled Pole again dreams of the restoration of his fatherland; but
Englishmen all look to you – yes still 'England's the anchor and the
hope of the world'.
"Come, then, men of the North, from your snow-capped hills;
come, then, men of the South, from your sunlit valleys; come to the
gathering; unite, fraternise, arm, and you will be free!
"Let the one universal rallying cry, from Firth of Forth to the Land's
End be EQUALITY OR DEATH."
– Julian Harney

While during this period many looked to trade unionism and also Owenism,
their limitations and eventual failings caused the working class to swing
back in the direction of radical reform. The burning anger towards the New
Poor Law and the government's repressive actions also raised sharply the
question of political power. The streams of discontent so prevalent in the
working class were starting to merge and produce a qualitative change in
the situation.

In the year following the Reform Act, what Marx once referred to as
the "old mole" of revolution was beginning to burrow away, transforming
consciousness in its path. This was reflected in a flurry of Radical weekly

papers in London, which had a considerable circulation. These, together with their rough circulation figures, were: *The Gauntlet* by Richard Carlile (22,000), *Poor Man's Guardian* by Hetherington (16,000), *The Destructive and Poor Man's Conservative* by Bronterre O'Brien (8,000), *The Working Man's Friend* by Jas Watson (7,000), *The Man* by R.E. Lee (7,000), *The Crisis* by Robert Owen (5,000) and *The Reformer* (5,000). Cobbett's *Register* was also widely read in the capital. However, within two years, all but two of these papers had been driven out of business by the Whig government and the long arm of the law. But still the ferment continued. The idea of founding a Radical organisation based on the working class had firmly taken root.

By the mid-1830s, the revival, unlike in the pre-1832 period, was clearly on an independent class basis. 'Us alone', became the motto of the working class. With the death of both William Cobbett and Henry Hunt in 1835, a new generation was emerging to carry the flame of working-class radicalism. The scene had been well prepared for the rise of a new political movement – namely, Chartism.

BRONTERRE O'BRIEN

Chartism began not with an organisation but with a ferment of ideas. Probably the greatest contribution towards this came from a man christened by Chartists as the 'Schoolmaster', a name reflective of his considerable ideological input. This was James Bronterre O'Brien (1805-1864), a very advanced thinker for the time, who can be considered with justification as the theoretician of Chartism. "In the conditions prevailing at the time O'Brien could not be a Marxist," wrote Theodore Rothstein, "although we may admire the high level attained by his genius".[1] Some have correctly described him as the father of Chartism.

Educated at Trinity College, Dublin, he came to London in 1830 to complete his studies. However, deeply influenced by the French Revolution, he met Cobbett and Hunt and soon gave up his legal career to join the Radical movement. This demonstrates his real commitment to the cause. O'Brien was also deeply influenced by the ideas of Robert Owen, William Ogilvie and the socialist economist John Gray. He read with enthusiasm Thomas Hodgskin's *Labour Defended*, as well as John Francis Bray's work *Labour's Wrongs and Labour's Remedy*. John Bray, as we know, was himself for a time active in the Chartist movement. After moving to London, O'Brien

---

1   T. Rothstein, p. 106.

became involved with the National Union of the Working Classes, and he was soon championing the theories of class struggle.

The most able of all the Chartists intellectually, O'Brien was clearly attempting to create a theoretical foundation for the working-class movement, with a coherent social and economic programme. However, he was more a journalist and lecturer than an author of theoretical works. Influenced by Owenism and the communist ideas of Babeuf, he was certainly moving independently in the direction of scientific socialism. In 1836, he translated and published Buonarroti's *History of Babeuf's Conspiracy for Equality*, which proclaimed: "Nature has given to every man an equal right to the enjoyment of all goods." He was the first to stress social questions and exercised a revolutionary influence on the left wing of Chartism. He went on to publish a volume of the *Life of Robespierre*, which tried to defend Robespierre against his many detractors and flew in the face of established opinion. Moreover, he was an outstanding journalist for the *Poor Man's Guardian,* which he edited for Henry Hetherington, and then *The Northern Star.*

Bronterre O'Brien was a 'physical force' man. At Stockport, in July 1839, he countered government threats with his own threats: "Let the government dare to hang one Chartist – and for every one there would be ten of the other class hung up to their own doors [Applause]."[2] Commenting on O'Brien's speech, the *True Scotsman* wrote: "No man can doubt, on hearing O'Brien, that he has little faith in the efficacy of moral agitation; and that he looks to a revolution to overturn the present government..."[3] O'Brien certainly wanted to do away with capitalism as he saw it, but his conception of socialism was somewhat hazy and mixed up with 'labour money' and 'labour bazaars'. He nevertheless later wrote in the *National Reformer*:

"With the Charter, national ownership of land, currency, and credit, people would soon discover what wonders of production, distribution, and exchange might be achieved by associated labour, in comparison with the exertions of isolated individual labour. Thence would gradually arise the true social state, or the realities of socialism, in contradiction to the present dreams of it."[4]

It is easy to point out that, compared with the *Communist Manifesto* written a year later, O'Brien's ideas were still quite undeveloped. But he was largely isolated and did not have the advantage of a close collaboration with the

2   Quoted in R. Brown & C. Daniels, p. 67.
3   Ibid., p. 70.
4   M. Beer, p. 20.

likes of Marx and Engels. His ideas were nevertheless moving in a similar direction to Marx. Bronterre, and the more astute thinkers of his generation, were groping towards a real historical conception of society, and towards the understanding that the way forward depended upon the conquest of power by the working class. As with most revolutionaries at this time, his points of reference were the French revolutions of 1789 and 1830. That said, whatever their deficiencies, O'Brien's views were a million miles more advanced than those held by most of the labour and trade union leaders of today. The same can be said of the other proletarian leaders of Chartism, who possessed a burning determination and revolutionary spirit.

O'Brien understood that the English middle classes had achieved their own aims in 1832, and had become a bulwark against their former working-class allies. He had a clear understanding of the class character of society, realising that classes, and not simply governments, held political and economic power. He complained that people made the mistake:

> "[O]f imputing to *individuals* the glory and the guilt of these political acts and systems of governments, which are, in reality, the work of whole classes, and in the execution of which the individuals are but the chosen tools or instruments of these classes."

He was therefore firmly of the view that the workers' task was to destroy the power of this new class of bourgeois usurpers.

O'Brien applied this general understanding to society. Referring to the eighteen years' war against France, he said:

> "Fools, indeed, imagine that Pitt or Bonaparte caused it, or that it was the work of Cabinets or a few individuals in power. With such imbeciles we have nothing to do. Men capable of believing such stuff are not worth our notice. *Rulers and Cabinets have no power whatever beyond that society gives them.* The 'statesmen' who made war on France in 1793 did so because war was agreeable to the capitalists and profit-hunters... It was for the double purpose of crushing that revolution and of opening a new field for the 'enterprise of commerce' that our moneyed interests urged that war against France."[5]

Behind the role of individuals are parties and classes, with their own material interests. This certainly displayed a flash of political genius, of class understanding, which attempted to open the eyes of working people to the real state of affairs.

---

5   Quoted in J. Strachey, pp. 343-4.

MODEST BEGINNINGS

Organisationally, Chartism indeed had very modest beginnings. On 16 June 1836, a small group of skilled artisans, which included Henry Hetherington, John Gast and William Lovett, founded a society known as the London Working Men's Association (LWMA). This original group had a grand total of thirty-three members. This was of little concern to them; in fact, they scoffed at the idea of 'mere numbers'. You might say they represented the 'cream', an aristocracy of labour, as opposed to the unskilled proletarians of London.

To further their aims, these artisans had established links with about a dozen assorted bourgeois Radical members of the House of Commons, such as John Roebuck and Daniel O'Connell. The members of the Association were clearly influenced by the Radical intelligentsia, who had graciously offered their services. In that sense, it was not a truly politically independent labour organisation. They considered themselves to be radical democrats, and still looked to collaborate with the bourgeois Radicals to win an extended suffrage. In this, they displayed a deference towards their 'betters' from the 'educated' classes. Nevertheless, this modest, embryonic beginning was to have totally unexpected consequences. It was to provide the spark that would ignite a mass movement of the British working class that would strike terror into the hearts of the propertied classes. But this came later.

The newly-formed London Working Men's Association, as its name implied, attempted to formally stress its class independence. Working men were encouraged to take on responsibilities within the movement. However, this troubled the bourgeois Radicals such as Francis Place, who had generously lent their support. These bourgeois reformers were shocked to find that "the whole of the movement was calculated to alarm every man who did not... earn his living by the work of his hands and receive wages".[6] Much to their disgust, what was initially seen as a proletarian 'leaning' took on an overtly militant working-class character as soon as Chartism began to sink roots in the country. However, for the moment at least, this unstable alliance held together. The aims of the Association could not be described as revolutionary, after all. They simply wanted a parliamentary reform based upon the education and the enlightenment of the working classes. In fact, it was quite reformist in its character, as befitted its artisan composition. In the view of the Association, parliamentary reform would lead "to a gradual improvement in the condition of the working classes, without violence or

---

6   A. Briggs, *Chartist Studies*, p. 302.

commotion".[7] Heavy stress was laid on the 'without violence' and lack of 'commotion'.

As Chartism developed into a mass movement, the two tendencies of 'moral force' and 'physical force' battled for supremacy. These tendencies of reformism and revolution were represented by certain key individuals whose fates were linked to the political struggle.

WILLIAM LOVETT

The 'moral force' outlook was epitomised by the secretary of the London Working Men's Association, William Lovett (1800-1877). A self-educated man and skilled worker, he was deeply influenced by Owenism. He became the 'moderate' face of the Chartist movement, to whom revolution or violence were anathema. He was also responsible for drafting the original Charter in collaboration with Francis Place. A staunch advocate of sobriety, he put his trust in education as the path towards working-class emancipation. While no doubt a sincere man, he was a 'moderate' in politics as in life. A cautious man who very much fit the mould of a reformist leader, it would not be unfair to say that he possessed not an ounce of revolutionary zeal in his entire body.

Nevertheless, he was undoubtedly a committed activist. Born in Newlyn, Cornwall, Lovett later moved to London and became involved in a series of movements, including the anti-militia movement, the trade union struggle and the campaign over the 'Great Unstamped'. In 1831, during the Reform Act agitation, he helped form the National Union of the Working Classes with the like-minded Radicals Henry Hetherington and James Watson. In 1836, he was the central figure in founding the London Working Men's Association, the founding element of Chartism. "Without exaggeration," wrote his contemporary, R.C. Gammage, "it may be affirmed that he was the life and soul of that body."[8]

Lovett had pacifist leanings and frowned on the idea of violence and the working class arming itself. "Instead of spending a pound on a useless musket," he said, "I would like to see it spent in sending out delegates among the people."[9] Later, he stressed: "Muskets are not what are wanted, but education and schooling of the working people."[10] Of course, education has its place in the building of a workers' political movement. But Lovett's

---

7   D. Thompson, *The Early Chartists*, pp. 53-54.
8   R.C. Gammage, *History of the Chartist Movement*, p. 10.
9   D. Jones, p. 151.
10 R. Brown and C. Daniels, p. 61.

conception was entirely different and narrowly regarded education simply as the establishment of libraries and a process of working-class enlightenment. The vote for the male working class was simply part of this outlook.

Lovett, in practice, sought to limit the struggle of the working class to within the confines of capitalism. This was simply a reflection of his 'craft' mentality, which was very different to the class struggle experience of the mill and mine. As an alternative to social revolution, he advocated reform and 'moral force' persuasion.

This reformist approach was out of step with the growing anger and outlook of the working class, faced with unbearable conditions. In any case, the working class would attain class consciousness not through books, but through experience in the class struggle. In this way, they would learn, become aware of themselves as a class, and draw their own revolutionary conclusions. Having said that, the question of clear ideas and theory is vital for the workers' movement and its leadership. Theory, after all, is a guide to action. The role of Chartism, especially its left wing, was to provide the necessary tactics and strategy for success.

Given Lovett's outlook, he objected to the inflammatory language of Feargus O'Connor and Julian Harney. Their class struggle rhetoric both horrified Lovett and intoxicated the masses, who welcomed every strident attack on the ruling class and its system. These differences between 'moral force' Chartism and 'physical force' Chartism would eventually lead to a parting of the ways. At bottom, Lovett regarded Chartism, not as a class movement, but as a national movement, where the middle-class elements had the same weight as the working class. But the middle-class Radicals, where they participated, were little more than fair-weather friends. They tended to have one foot in the proletarian camp and one in the camp of the bourgeoisie. While the working class fought for the immediate implementation of the Charter, with revolutionary methods, the middle-class Radicals saw it in a far more limited, reformist fashion. For them, unity with the working class was regarded as a lever, like in 1832, and nothing more. However, events, namely the class struggle, would shatter this unity.

Even as a 'moral force' Chartist, Lovett, like most leading Chartists, was arrested and imprisoned for his views. Without doubt, he had gained a certain respect for the work that he had done, but the movement he helped to create was outgrowing him. *The Charter* of 17 March 1839 stated:

> "We know of few men who unite in themselves so much of the stern resolve of
> the Radical with the unobtrusiveness and courtesy of the gentleman. He is pre-

eminently a man of 'a meek and quiet spirit', and his earnestness and inflexibility of purpose are never evinced in an offensive or overbearing manner. He is essentially an honest man. He will never pander to the prejudices of any, for the sake of temporary popularity."

It concluded: "He is one of whom the working classes have reason to be proud; and we know of no man who enjoys a larger measure of their respect and confidence."[11]

As a result of the riots in Birmingham, he was sentenced to twelve months in Warwick prison and was finally released in July 1840. Following this, with the Chartist movement firmly in the grip of the 'physical force' party, Lovett graciously retired from politics. The character of the movement had become uncompromising and class conscious. For him, this meant that Chartism had lost its way. In 1841, he formed the 'National Association for Promoting the Political and Social Improvement of the People', a campaign for educational enlightenment. This marked the end of his political career. His autobiography, which deals comprehensively with Chartism's first stages, is influenced by his reformist outlook. In effect, he had become a casualty of the movement's success. Incapable of rising above his narrow outlook, he was destined to be left behind by events.

HENRY HETHERINGTON

Lovett was supported by such men as Henry Hetherington (1792-1849), who was also one of the founders of the London Working Men's Association. Hetherington was a printer by trade, and as stated earlier, he played an important role in the battle of the 'unstamped' press, which made him one of the government's main targets for prosecution. As a result, he was prosecuted, fined and imprisoned in 1833 and 1836. Such was the hatred of the authorities towards him that he had his printing presses seized and destroyed. He famously produced the *Poor Man's Guardian* between 1831 and 1835 and became a household name in working-class circles. Hetherington did not edit his own papers, but delegated the responsibility to James Bronterre O'Brien and other writers. In the words of his friend R.C. Gammage, he possessed:

[I]ndomitable courage and inflexible perseverance, defying persecution, and trampling on the Stamp Act as so much waste paper, he had earned for himself a reputation which caused the more advanced of the working class to gather round him in scores, sometimes in hundreds. His rough strong logic struck conviction

---

11 Quoted in R. Sewell, *In the Cause of Labour*, p. 69.

into every mind, while his dry and essentially English humour gave to it an agreeable zest.[12]

Hetherington was certainly a man of firm character. However, throughout his involvement he worked closely with Lovett and developed a personal and political bond with him. As a consequence, he was similarly highly critical of O'Connor and his robust language. As already noted, this led to a permanent rift in 1841 when he, Lovett, and others announced the formation of the 'National Association for Promoting the Political and Social Improvement of the People'. They were condemned as traitors by O'Connor and his supporters, and in spite of Hetherington's protestations of their innocence, became pariahs from mainstream Chartism.

Hetherington was a thinker and a follower of Owenism up until his death. Even in his last will and testament he explained:

"While the land, machines, tools, implements of production and the produce of man's toil are exclusively in possession of the do-nothings, and labour is the sole possession of the wealth-producers – a marketable commodity, brought up and directed by wealthy idlers – never-ending misery must be their inevitable lot. Robert Owen's system, if rightly understood and faithfully carried out, rectifies all these anomalies. It makes man proprietor of his own labour and of the elements of production – it places him in a condition to enjoy the entire fruits of his labour and surrounds him with circumstances that will make him intelligent, rational, and happy."[13]

Hetherington, like Lovett, was increasingly left behind by the growth of Chartism and the new militant leadership that emerged from it. He frequently suffered from illness and on 23 August 1849, he tragically died of cholera at his residence at 57 Judd Street, London.

THOMAS ATTWOOD

Figures such as Lovett and Hetherington were also generally backed by the 'moderates' in the Midlands, including Birmingham. Here the Radical movement was dominated by Thomas Attwood (1783-1856), a banker and Radical Member of Parliament. He led the predominantly middle-of-the-road Birmingham Political Union which had been re-established in 1837 from an earlier body. Although a banker, Attwood enjoyed the support of the Birmingham artisans and more well-to-do sections of the working

---

12 R.C. Gammage, p. 7.

13 M. Beer, *The History of British Socialism*, vol. 2, p. 7.

class. Given his background, he was infatuated with currency reform and the gold standard, arguing that gold should be replaced by paper money. But, to his disgust, this idea was rejected by the Chartist Convention. He managed to maintain his domination in the Midlands region up until 1840, but was clearly losing his grip. Overtaken by the situation, he retired from the movement, an early casualty of its increasing proletarianisation.

Attwood certainly had his flights of fancy. On one occasion, following a visit to Glasgow, he raised the idea of a general strike or 'Holy Month' to promote the Charter. However, he saw such a strike not in class war terms, but simply as a display of 'moral force', discipline and self-restraint. It was certainly not regarded as a means of taking power. Again, like Lovett, he despised violence and threats of this nature. He was alarmed by the language of the Chartist Convention and demanded the Convention withdraw any threats of violence before agreeing to present the Petition to Parliament. In presenting the Petition to the Commons in 1839, Attwood underlined the point: "I wash my hands of any talk of physical force or arms. I want no arms but the will of the people, legally, firmly, and constitutionally expressed..."[14]

At this early stage, the Chartist movement in Scotland was similar to London and Birmingham, where the 'moral force' party had the upper hand, although O'Connor, who was emerging as the national leader, also had his enthusiastic supporters in Scotland. Over time, several Scottish Chartist organisations rescinded their 'moral force' resolutions, as did a central meeting of the Scottish Radical Associations. By early 1841, support for Lovett in Scotland had evaporated and the movement there had turned to 'physical force'.

HENRY VINCENT

There were others who began as 'moral force' Chartists but abandoned this outlook on the basis of experience. This was the case with Henry Vincent (1813-1879). Born in London, he moved to Hull, where he served an apprenticeship for several years. He returned to London in 1833, getting involved in the Radical movement from the outset. Given his energy, he was soon dispatched by the London Working Men's Association as a speaker at meetings and demonstrations. He developed a great capacity for rousing the crowd, which was put to good use. "Vincent lived at this time in a whirlpool of pleasing excitement", explained Gammage. "His labours were confined

---

14 G.D.H. Cole, *Chartist Portraits*, p. 129.

principally to the Midlands and Western districts of England and South of Wales."[15]

In February 1839, he founded a weekly paper, *The Western Vindicator*, and concentrated his efforts as an agitator in the radicalised valleys of South Wales. He became increasingly intoxicated by the emerging mass movement. The more he was away from London and the influence of 'moral force' ideas, the more he came under the influence of more radical layers of the working class. As he toured South Wales, he became increasingly militant, ending one of his speeches with the words "Perish the privileged orders! Death to the aristocracy!"

As a result, on a scheduled trip to London in May 1839, he was arrested for taking part in a riotous assembly. He was forced to return to Wales for his trial and was sentenced in July at Monmouth Assizes to twelve month's imprisonment. This proved to be the catalyst for the revolutionary movement in South Wales, which was to culminate in the Newport Uprising in November. In March 1840, Vincent was again arrested and jailed for a further eight months. Under the impact of these events, he changed a great deal and abandoned his 'moral force' Chartism. Speaking in Bath on a platform that included Colonel William Napier, General Napier's brother, Vincent denounced a number of well-known people, including the duke of Wellington, as knaves. The Colonel jumped to his feet and objected, exclaiming: "I deny that. The Duke of Wellington is no knave; he fought for his country nobly, bravely, honourably, and he is no knave." Vincent calmly replied: "I say that any man, be he a Russell, a Wellington, or a Napier, who denies me the right to vote, is a knave."[16]

Henry Vincent was one of the most popular early leaders of Chartism. However, in 1842 he contributed to the setting up of the Complete Suffrage Union, which was regarded as a competitor to Chartism. This action was to lead to his break with the movement.

JULIAN HARNEY

The reformist London Working Men's Association was not the only working-class Radical organisation in London. Another important organisation entered the scene, which would eventually come to dominate the movement. This was the East London Democratic Association, a far more radical body than its moderate counterpart. It later dropped the 'East' from its name.

---

15 R.C. Gammage, p. 12.
16 Ibid., pp. 78-79.

It was founded on 29 January 1837 and was led by George Julian Harney (1817-1897), a young man who was to play a key role and was to be greatly influenced by Marx and Engels.

In contrast to the Working Men's Association, it attempted to organise the poorer, more downtrodden sections of the London proletariat. Founded on the revolutionary democratic principles of Thomas Paine, the London Democratic Association (LDA) argued from the start for the principles of radical working-class reform. They nevertheless differed from the LWMA by linking the political programme of the working class to its ultimate aim of economic emancipation. The LDA therefore drew far-reaching revolutionary conclusions compared to its rival. It also included in its programme complete opposition to the hated New Poor Law, which the London Working Men's Association refused to take a stand on for fear of alienating the bourgeois radicals. "There is only one remedy for the evils with which society is afflicted: equality of rights, equality of conditions", stated the Democratic Association. "But unless the 'People's Charter' is followed by measures to equalise the conditions of all, the producing classes will still be oppressed and the country will probably be involved in the most disastrous calamities."[17]

Julian Harney was the son of a seaman and born in Deptford in south-east London two years before the Peterloo Massacre. A shop boy, he was brought up in the struggle of the unstamped press, and was imprisoned three times for his troubles while he was still a teenager. He, like Bronterre O'Brien, joined the National Union of the Working Classes and learned about the class struggle. He became a devoted follower of O'Brien and was deeply influenced by the left wing of the French Revolution. Not surprisingly, he adopted the figure of Jean-Paul Marat, the leader of the extreme left of the *sans-culottes* as his model and took to wearing the Red Cap of Liberty at public meetings. He supported Marat's views on the role of the proletariat: "A revolution is accomplished and sustained only by the lowest classes of society," wrote Marat a month before the revolution of 10 August 1792, "by all the disinherited, whom the shameless rich treat as *canaille*, and whom the Romans with their usual cynicism once named proletarians."

In early 1837, after forming the left-wing London Democratic Association, Harney soon acquired a reputation as a key leader of left-wing Chartism. An insurrectionary 'physical force' Chartist, he was at sharp odds with the Lovett-Hetherington circle in London. Harney also joined the Polish Democratic Society, which placed him in touch with European revolutionaries and

17 T. Rothstein, p. 46.

pushed him further to the left. In 1843, the twenty-six-year-old Harney, when he was the acting editor of *The Northern Star*, met the young Friedrich Engels in Leeds. Engels, three years his junior, was collecting material for his book *The Condition of the Working Class in England*. Despite political ups and downs, they both developed a warm lifelong friendship. As Harney wrote years later:

> "I knew Engels, he was my friend and occasional correspondent over half a century. It was in 1843 that he came over from Bradford to Leeds and enquired for me at *The Northern Star* office. A tall, handsome young man, with a countenance of almost boyish youthfulness, whose English, in spite of his German birth and education, was even then remarkable for its accuracy. He told me he was a constant reader of *The Northern Star* and took a keen interest in the Chartist movement. There began our friendship over fifty years ago..."[18]

Harney's leftward evolution saw him organise the Fraternal Democrats in March 1846, an international grouping which was a forerunner of the International Working Men's Association, or First International. He met with Marx personally in 1847, while he was attending the conference of the Communist League. This led to a close political collaboration over a number of years. His political trajectory eventually led him to a split with O'Connor, who contemptuously regarded Harney, along with Ernest Jones, as "Socialists first and Chartists second". However, the two – Harney and Jones – were to form the bridge between Chartism, Marxism and the modern socialist movement.

As can be seen, the Chartist movement was a powerhouse for the development of extremely radical ideas, a school of revolution, if you like, and the precursor of the later socialist movement. The divisions in Chartism between 'moral force' and 'physical force' were a foretaste – a pale reflection in truth – of today's divisions between left and right wings in the labour and trade union movement. More correctly, they foreshadowed the split between reformism and revolution. But within the 'physical force' party there was a clearly defined revolutionary socialist current, which eventually became dominant.

RIVALRIES

The existence of two organisations in London – the Working Men's Association and the Democratic Association – was to eventually lead to a

---

18 G.D.H. Cole, *Chartist Portraits*, p. 283.

great rivalry between the two, which increasingly diverged. This certainly developed into a division between reformism and revolution. In the early stages, however, these groupings were only feeling their way forward.

As stated, the London Working Men's Association sought to extend its influence by respectable means. "By means of meetings, banquets, and printed addresses, the Association attempted to draw the attention of the country to the subject of parliamentary reform", observed R.C. Gammage.[19] This mild-mannered approach became their primary method of operation, which meant the struggle would be kept within legitimate bounds. They saw themselves as an elite propaganda society, and nothing more. They nevertheless believed they were the inheritors of the cause of John Wilkes, Thomas Paine, William Cobbett and Henry Hunt, as well as the virtues of Thomas Hardy and the London Corresponding Society, but without the mass movement. They had no inclination in the slightest that this small, respectable circle would become a mass movement. Ironically, this aloof approach led even Thomas Attwood to later describe them as "a little clique of people who had as much influence over the workers of London as over the workers of Constantinople".[20]

The idea that the Working Men's Association should regard itself as anything more than a pressure group horrified Francis Place and the parliamentarians. He had made it plain from the outset that his condition for helping to draft a People's Charter of demands was that there were to be no attacks on the Poor Law, or advocacy of socialism on their platforms. And he received this assurance from Lovett without a murmur of protest.

In early February 1837, however, the Working Men's Association sought to extend its influence and lay down a marker for the launch of a Charter. To this end, they organised a meeting at the Crown and Anchor public house on the Strand, the intention of which was to formulate a set of demands as the basis of a future petition to be presented to Parliament.

The idea of a petition, of course, was common practice and not considered too subversive. In fact, it was through such means that matters were brought to the attention of Parliament, serving as a starting point for most parliamentary debates. Manufacturers in particular would use petitions to press the Commons to impose or withdraw this or that duty on trade and generally support the aims of industry. Workers would also petition Parliament, especially to help with relief in times of hardship. The parliamentarians would sit and listen, then usually appoint some commission

---

19 R.C. Gammage, p. 6.
20 T. Rothstein, p. 45.

to investigate and report back at a later date. But in the hands of the Chartists, the simple petition was transformed into a successful rallying call in its class-struggle arsenal.

Although held in a public house, the leaders of the Working Men's Association were astonished to find that their public meeting attracted around 4,000 workers, who spilled out into the street and onto the Strand. It was at this packed meeting that five points of the famous 'Charter' were agreed upon. Later, a sixth point was added, namely the payment of Members of Parliament. Ominously for Lovett and his group, the size and enthusiasm of this meeting were a sign of things to come.

Bronterre O'Brien, who was present, gave a vivid account of the proceedings:

> "Lift up your democratic heads, my friends! Look proud and be merry. I was at a meeting on Tuesday night which does one's heart good to think on. I have been present at all sorts of political meetings, Whig, Tory and Radical, but never was it my good fortune to witness so brilliant a display of democracy as that which shone forth at the Crown and Anchor on Tuesday night. I often despaired of Radicalism before; I will never despair again after what I witnessed on that occasion.

> "Four thousand democrats, at least, were present at the meeting. The immense room of the Crown and Anchor was crowded to overflowing, several hundred stood outside on the corridor and the stairs, or went away for want of accommodation. The platform was equally crammed as the body of the room, and notwithstanding the great pressure and the great excitement that prevailed, the most perfect order characterised the whole of the proceedings from beginning to end.

"A working man was appointed to preside", explained O'Brien. This was very unusual at the time, as it was customary for meetings to be chaired by 'notable' people.

> "The resolutions and petitions were severally proposed and seconded by working men. The principal speakers who supported them were working men. In short, the whole proceedings were originated, conducted, and concluded by working men, and in a style that would have done credit to any assembly in the world."[21]

The meeting at the Crown and Anchor was an historic moment that gave birth to the demands of the Charter. Not only that, but it unknowingly set in train the great Chartist movement, which was to capture the enthusiasm of millions. As Marx once explained, an idea becomes a material force when

---

21 Quoted in R. Brown and C. Daniels, *The Chartists*, p. 27.

it grips the minds of the masses. Such an idea had been born at this unusual gathering.

CHARTER DEMANDS

The famous six final points of the People's Charter were as follows:

1. A vote for every man twenty-one years of age, of sound mind, and not undergoing punishment for crime.
2. The ballot – to protect the elector in the exercise of his vote.
3. No property qualification for members of Parliament – thus enabling the constituencies to return the man of their choice, be he rich or poor.
4. Payment of members, thus enabling an honest tradesman, working man, or other person, to serve a constituency, when taken from his business to attend to the interests of the country.
5. Equal constituencies, securing the same amount of representation for the same number of electors – instead of allowing small constituencies to swamp the votes of larger ones.
6. Annual parliaments, thus presenting the most effectual check to bribery and intimidation, since though a constituency might be bought once in seven years (even with the ballot), no purse could buy a constituency (under a system of universal suffrage) in each ensuing twelve months; and since members, when elected for a year only, would not be able to defy and betray their constituents as now.[22]

It is true that the six-point programme was deficient in many respects: it did not, for example, demand the vote for women; it did not demand a republic or the abolition of the House of Lords; it contained, at this point, no social or economic demands. Despite this, the programme represented a significant advance by a working-class based organisation, nominally independent of the bourgeoisie. To place it in its historical context, it was similar to the old Leveller programme of John Lilburne, now based upon a new revolutionary class, the industrial proletariat. While the Leveller programme collided with the limits of the bourgeois-democratic revolution, the new class forces created by capitalism opened up new possibilities for its advancement. If implemented, the Charter constituted a programme of fundamental political and social change, which, if carried to its logical conclusion, would open the road to working-class power. This was the view of Friedrich Engels, who famously said it was sufficient to "overthrow the whole English Constitution, Queen and Lords included."

---

22 G.D.H. Cole and A.W. Filson, p. 352.

As Bronterre O'Brien wrote:

"What the people want is a government of the whole people to protect the whole people, and this once acquired they will be in a position to establish Owenism, or St. Simonism, or any other ism that a majority may think best calculated to ensure the well-being of the whole. With a power over the laws, the people may do anything that is not naturally impossible; without it they will never be able to do anything."[23]

This opinion of O'Brien's hit the nail on the head.

The ever cautious William Lovett distanced himself from social demands. He had no time for Harney's Democratic Association and for what he thought were its outlandish ideas and language. When Lovett called a meeting to elect eight delegates to the new Chartist Convention, it was estimated that an astonishing 10,000 to 15,000 people were present. However, Lovett made sure that the leaders of the London Democratic Association were excluded from the platform. Only the forces of 'moderation' would be allowed to speak. This was, however, a Pyrrhic victory for Lovett, as we shall see.

The membership of the London Working Men's Association and the London Democratic Association often overlapped. However, Julian Harney was summarily expelled from the Working Men's Association after he denounced the MP Daniel O'Connell for his scandalous attacks on the Glasgow cotton spinners. Harney had been accused of taking the name of the Working Men's association in vain, thereby forfeiting his membership. But from the beginning, political differences were clearly evident, and these would only widen under the impact of events. The language of the Democratic Association, in comparison to Lovett's organisation, was always more militant and class conscious. An example of this was Harney's appeal, made in April 1839:

"Men of the East and West, men of the North and South, your success lies with yourselves, depend upon yourselves alone, and your cause will be triumphant. The SIXTH OF MAY is approaching. Prepare! Listen not to the men who would preach delay. The man who would now procrastinate is a traitor, and may your vengeance light upon his head. One word of advice. In the two or three weeks you have remaining, let me exhort you to ARM. I mean you that are yet unarmed; for oh, thank God, tens of thousands of you can now, hand to hand and foot to foot, assert your right to be free men. To you that are not so prepared I say again, ARM to protect your aged parents, ARM for your wives and children, ARM for your

---

23 *Poor Man's Guardian*, November 1833.

sweethearts and sisters, ARM to drive tyranny from the soil and oppression from the judgement-seat. Your country, your posterity, your God demands of you to ARM! ARM! ARM!"[24]

Such statements invariably ended with the fine words, 'Equality or Death', which stirred the blood and sent shivers down the spines of the ecstatic crowd. This was in marked contrast to the Association of Lovett and the advocates of 'moral force', who were horrified by such language. These differences were a reflection of class differences. Around the London Democratic Association quickly coalesced the revolutionary wing of the movement.

Within Chartism, it is possible to identify three separate trends: a right-wing openly bourgeois grouping of middle-class radicals, centred around the parliamentarians and the Birmingham Political Union; a reformist grouping of artisans, led by Lovett, Hetherington and Cleave, the core of which was the London Working Men's Association; and lastly a proletarian wing, led by Feargus O'Connor, John Taylor, Julian Harney and Ernest Jones. However, the proletarian wing itself would eventually split into a centrist and a socialist tendency.

While the 'exclusive' London Working Men's Association developed a membership of at most 400, based on the skilled sections of the working class, the London Democratic Association boasted a membership of three thousand, and drew its support from the more downtrodden workers, especially the distressed weavers of Spitalfields. Whereas the Working Men's Association did not admit women into membership, the Democratic Association welcomed them with open arms, out of which separate women's organisations were established. In fact, there was an attempt early on to include within the Charter a demand for votes for women. When the Lovett leadership circulated the Charter to local groups, a local proposal was made to include women's suffrage. This was turned down by the 'moderate' leadership, who feared it was a step too far. Despite this, many working-class women still got involved, especially in the mass movement between 1839 and 1842. "The Charter will never become the law of the land," argued Caroline Maria Williams, a Chartist woman, "until we women are fully resolved that it shall be so."[25]

FEARGUS O'CONNOR

Another very important figure was Feargus Edward O'Connor (1794-1855). He was known for his radical oratory and Lovett deliberately attempted to

24 Quoted in G.D.H. Cole and A.W. Filson, p. 356.
25 D. Jones, p. 182.

keep him isolated as far as possible. He was therefore excluded from speaking at the mass London meeting, where delegates for the Convention were chosen. However, some months later, in December 1837, Harney's Democratic Association took the initiative to organise another public meeting in London with its own speakers and speakers from the Working Men's Association. Feargus O'Connor, given his radical oratory, clearly carried the day, much to Lovett's horror.

Following this, O'Connor's reputation began to spread and he increasingly played a leading role. Eventually, he emerged as the undisputed popular leader of Chartism. Ireland has produced many radical figures for the British labour movement and Chartism was no exception. "I am a foreigner by language and blood", he told the operatives of Yorkshire. It is clear that his roots in Ireland, being from County Cork, and the wrongs inflicted on that country by the English ruling classes influenced O'Connor's temperament and outlook.

The 'Lion of the North', as Feargus O'Connor became known, came from a revolutionary background. His uncle, Arthur O'Connor, was one of the leaders of a secret Irish revolutionary organisation known as the *Whiteboys*, which fought against enclosures, rack-renters and land-grabbers. They employed terrorist methods against the landlords, but were hunted down, and scores of them were hanged. As a young man Feargus belonged to this organisation, which hardened him as a man, and then as a leader who had a natural hatred of oligarchy and the English absentee landlords. He developed a strong bond with the underdog and pity for the Irish peasants, crushed by the rack-renters and foreign exploiters.

He became a Member of Parliament for Daniel O'Connell's National Party, but fell out with him and was excluded from Parliament in 1835. The following year, he went on to establish his own Radical movement, having moved from London to the North of England. He also provided assistance in setting up the London Democratic Association. While O'Connor had an affinity with the radical movement of the British working class, he was not a socialist. "I am no socialist or communist", he declared. He was neither a theoretician nor a very deep thinker, and tended to look backwards and to favour smallholdings in land as a way out of the oppression under capitalism. This was to later evolve into his famous Land Plan.

Nevertheless, Feargus O'Connor had other qualities. He had put himself at the head of the revolt against the Poor Law in the North. Using a fiery oratory, he was able to connect with the radicalised mass movement of the working class. A brilliant platform speaker, his speeches were always direct, thunderous, and at times even vulgar. He had an engaging turn of phrase and manner, attacking the capitalists as "traffickers in human blood and in infant gristle". According to W.E. Adams, a Chartist: "The people of that period seemed to relish denunciation, and O'Connor gave them plenty of it. Blatant in print, he was equally blatant on the platform."[26] The crowds loved him and could identify with him, and he with them. He spoke their language and he articulated their aspirations, with "lungs of brass and a voice like a trumpet". O'Connor radiated hope and offered a bold vision to worker audiences who were thrilled when he addressed them as 'Fustian Jackets', the 'Old Guards' and 'Imperial Chartists'. For him, speaking to them was instinctive and, for that very reason, the London artisans saw O'Connor as a dangerous demagogue and rabble-rouser. Georg Weerth, a young German exile, wrote an interesting description of his performance before a crowd:

> "After listening attentively for half an hour there gradually arose a visible restlessness among the whole mass… He had already several times audibly slammed the edge of the rostrum with his right hand, several times he had stamped his foot more and more angrily and shaken his head more wildly. He made preparation to attack the enemy – the meeting noticed this and spurred him on by loud clapping – it was as a red rag to a bull. Then the Titan had gripped his victim! The voice took on a fuller sound, the sentences became shorter, they were wrung in spasms from his seething breast, the fist drummed more wildly against the edge of the rostrum, the face of the orator became pale, his limbs trembled, the cataract of his rage had flooded over the last barrier, and onwards thundered the floodtide of his eloquence, throwing down all before it, breaking up and smashing everything in its way – and I do believe that the man would have talked himself to death if he had not been interrupted by an applause which shook the whole house and set it vibrating."[27]

This gives you a flavour of the Chartist meetings: exciting, radical, colourful, full of enthusiasm, hope and zeal. They had all the characteristics of a religious revival.

O'Connor soon came into conflict with the more conservative artisans, along with their leaders. Such was his contempt for them that he did not even consider them part of the working class. Instead, he travelled around the country, inspiring thousands of workers with his uncompromising

26 R. Brown and C. Daniels, p. 36.
27 D. Jones, p. 104.

message. Francis Place called him, with justification, "the constant, travelling, dominant leader of the movement".[28]

NORTHERN STAR

Alienated by the London Radicals, O'Connor concentrated his efforts in Yorkshire, where workers were preparing to launch a newspaper in the autumn of 1837. He was appointed the editor-in-chief of the first issue of *The Northern Star* on 18 November, and through it he spoke to his working-class audience by sprinkling the articles with words and sentences in capital letters. Later Julian Harney joined the newspaper. At its height, its circulation reached 45,000, but each paper was read by at least ten other people, and many copies were read aloud in coffee shops and workplaces. *The Northern Star* served as the official organ of Chartism, although this title was never openly proclaimed. The great attraction of the paper was that it was alive with regular reports of meetings, large and small, as well as letters and speeches printed in column after column. It reflected all the controversies and quarrels of the movement. It was full of appeals about campaigns and those imprisoned or transported. It can be considered one of the finest working-class newspapers ever produced. It was a genuine tribune of the workers. As expected, the ruling class hated it with a vengeance. Lord John Russell, the Home Secretary, wrote to the Law Officers of the Crown, urging them to consider the criminality of the paper, with a view to shutting it down.

O'Connor never held anything back in the paper. In its pages, he frequently clashed with his opponents and adversaries, inside and outside the movement. He based himself on the proletarians, with whom he had a proud and close affinity. "He began his career by ridiculing our 'moral force humbuggery'!" explained Gammage. He attacked Lovett mercilessly, saying "knowledge without power is useless" and that "only a great political movement can obtain the new moral world".[29] There was no love lost between the men.

In the spring of 1838, O'Connor set up the Great Northern Union, based on a radical programme of democratic reform and trade unionism. It swallowed up the existing Leeds Working Men's Association, and he inserted a clause in its constitution that pledged in the event of the failure of the 'moral force' strategy, it would resolve "that physical force shall be resorted to, if necessary, in order to ensure the equality of the law and the blessing of those

---

28 S. Harrison, p. 107.

29 D. Jones, p. 39.

institutions which are the birth right of free men".[30] This policy of 'physical force' was intended to be a last resort, but this did not prevent O'Connor's insurrectionary speeches or his references to the Whiteboys. This policy was adopted with acclaim by the mass of factory workers of the North, who were determined to finally win their emancipation.

However, O'Connor's weakness was to see a solution in a return to the past of peasant ownership and land redistribution. This policy was later contained in his Land Plan. This contrasted with the forward-looking views of Bronterre O'Brien, who argued for the socialisation of the land and the means of production (at least in agriculture) as a guarantee against "wage slavery for middle-class demons". The weaknesses of leaders like O'Connor were a reflection of the weaknesses of the movement generally, of its first independent steps, which unfortunately lacked the clarity of scientific socialism – an ideology that had yet to emerge.

SUPPORT FOR THE CHARTER

In 1837, both the London Working Men's Association and the London Democratic Association pooled their forces in an effort to build support for the Charter. Soon after the Crown and Anchor meeting, 'missionaries' for the Charter were sent out to agitate for the six demands and gather support. The word of a new People's Charter spread like wildfire in the industrial heartlands of Lancashire and Yorkshire, which were reeling under the impact of the New Poor Law. "Your success lies with yourselves, depends upon yourselves alone…" stated the *London Democrat*, Henry Hetherington's paper. Giant meetings sprung up almost everywhere, but especially in the factory districts, such as the meeting in Peep Green in the West Riding of Yorkshire in May 1837, which was attended by 250,000 people to hear Richard Oastler and the fiery Reverend Stephens speak. Stephens proclaimed to the eager crowd that the ownership deeds of every mill were "written in letters of blood on every brick and stone in the factory". For this speech, Stephens was dismissed from the ministry, but this elevated him far higher in the eyes of ordinary workers.

As we can see, the ground was being repeatedly ploughed for the emergence of working-class Radicalism. Local Chartist associations sprang up throughout the country and became the foundation stones upon which this epic movement was constructed. Within a short space of time, it was reported that over a hundred societies had been founded or had sought affiliation. In

---

30 M. Beer, p. 13.

the North of England, the Great Northern Union led by Feargus O'Connor had been formed. This was another high point in the movement. It was clear that Chartism had become the catalyst for the mass discontent that existed in the working-class towns. Furthermore, the class composition of the movement was to radically change with an influx of industrial proletarians from the factory regions, miners and iron workers from Wales, and the low-paid of London. Over time, a whole range of worker leaders began to emerge, especially at a local level, keen to articulate the feelings of the working class. In addition, with the break-up of the national trade unions, a layer of union activists was attracted to Chartism. Men like Thomas Hepburn, the miners' leader, took their talents into the movement, as did many others.

There was also a flourishing of socialist ideas at this time. These were absorbed by Chartism and promoted especially by Joshua Hobson, who published a series of lectures under the title *Socialism as it is! Lectures in reply to the Fallacies and Misrepresentations of the Rev. John Eustace Giles, Baptist Minister*. Hobson was also the publisher of *The Northern Star* and Owen's *New Moral World* from 1839 to 1841. He was joined by another Leeds Radical and socialist economist, John Bray, who played a leading role in founding the Leeds Working Men's Association. At the first meeting of the Association, he stressed the need to not only make political reforms, but to change the whole social system. He went on to publish his book *Labour's Wrongs and Labour's Remedy*, which broadcast the socialist cause.

STRANGE BEDFELLOWS

The Chartist movement did, however, also attract a strange mix of people. This was inevitable given its mass following. In terms of the fire-and-brimstone delivery of his speeches, the Reverend Joseph Raynor Stephens (1805-1879) stood head and shoulders above the rest. Although Stephens was closely associated with the movement and certainly played his part, he refused to call himself a Chartist. Both he and Oastler were strange bedfellows. Politically, they can be described as Tories, but they were men who wholly identified themselves with the struggle of the working class, especially in opposition to the New Poor Law and the conditions in the factories.

In 1836, Stephens was agitating against the capitalists and their breaches of the Factory Act, declaring to meetings:

> "We will have every one of them that dares break the law sent to the treadmill; and
> if that will not do, we will have them sent to Botany Bay; and if ever they come
> back, and should be bold enough to break the law again, we will have them sent to

Lancashire Castle and there hung by the neck. (Cheers). No more drivelling mill owners: no more of your big words, and scowling looks, and frightening speeches; we don't care for you..."[31]

During 1837 and 1838, Stephens displayed extraordinary energy in fighting injustice and the crimes of the rich. In his arguments he naturally appealed to the laws of nature and especially the Bible, calling upon the wrath of God to smite his enemies. He was certainly no pacifist and his speeches were both inflammatory and prone to incite violence. Stephens' oratory was utterly captivating when speaking to a spell-bound mass audience of the poor and the 'wretched of the earth'. Both he and his audience worked themselves up into a frenzy as he preached hellfire against the powers that be. It was a veritable tempest of hatred against the rich and privileged. In January 1838, he addressed a meeting in Glasgow, in which he threatened revolution and concluded:

"We shall destroy there abodes of guilt, which they have reared to violate all the law and God's book... we have sworn by our God, by heaven, earth, and hell, that from the East, the West, the North, and the South, we shall wrap in one awful sheet of devouring flame, which no arm can resist, the manufactories of the cotton tyrants, and the places of those who raised them by rapine and murder, and founded them upon the wretchedness of millions whom God, our God, Scotland's God, created to be happy."[32]

From the battles over the Poor Law, then to Chartism when it arose, Stephens put his body and soul into it. As the historian Max Beer wrote:

Towards the end of the year 1838, his agitating reached boiling point. The nocturnal gatherings must have presented a solemn and fantastic scene, held as they were in the open air, attended by thousands of working men, many of them with flaming torches in their hands, others armed with muskets, all of them eagerly listening to Stephen's violent oratory. The propertied classes became alarmed, and on 12 December 1838, the torchlight meetings were declared illegal by royal proclamation.[33]

As a result of his hyperbole, historians tend to dismiss him as a ranting preacher. But Stephens simply articulated the horrors and suffering of the working class as he saw it. Driven out of the Church, he gathered his own

---

31 Quoted in J.L. Hammond and B. Hammond, *Lord Shaftesbury*, p. 50.
32 Quoted in R.C. Gammage, p. 57.
33 M. Beer, p. 16.

congregation amongst the distressed miners and factory workers. It is a paradox that, while Stephens was extremely militant in his language, he did not support all six points of the Charter. Ultimately, following his arrest and imprisonment, he broke from the movement and disavowed its aims. As the Chartist movement became an openly political party, his Tory upbringing eventually got the better of him.

The other strange figure was Richard Oastler (1789-1861), regarded as the 'factory king' for his energetic campaigning on behalf of poor workers and factory children. Once again, although a Tory, he vividly exposed the hypocrisy of the employers and their system of exploitation.

> "The very streets which receive the droppings of an 'Anti-Slavery Society' are every morning wet with the tears of innocent victims at the accursed shrine of avarice, who are compelled (not by the cart-whip of the negro slave-driver) but by dread of the equally appalling throng or strap of the overlooker, to hasten half-dressed, but not half-fed, to those magazines of British Infantile Slavery – the Worsted Mills in the town and neighbourhood of Bradford!

> "Thousands of little children, both male and female, but principally female, from seven to fourteen years, are daily compelled to labour from six o'clock to seven in the evening with only – Britons, blush whilst you read it! – with only thirty minutes allowed for eating and recreation."[34]

In particular, Oastler threw his weight behind opposition to the Poor Law. Again, he did not mince his words:

> "Arm then, arm, my fellow-countrymen, against this most execrable law of tyrants! Arm ye, sons of Britain, whose souls are in the Ark of the Constitution! Arm, and make the traitors pause and tremble… Let no other ornaments be cared for in your houses but bright and well-made arms. Arm then, arm for peace and justice. If the tyrants know that you possess arms, there will be no need for you to use them… Be sober, be vigilant, be *men*!"[35]

Again, Oastler was not a Chartist as such, but was certainly bound up with the movement through the massive anti-Poor Law protests. His views were more like those of a paternalistic landowner than a militant Chartist. However, it was inevitable that such a broad mass movement would throw up such accidental figures. "I am a loyal subject of the Queen", he said. "I am a friend of the aristocracy and have sacrificed much on their account. I

---

34 J. Lindsay and E. Rickword, *Spokesmen for Liberty*, p. 278.
35 Quoted in M. Beer, p. 17.

revere the National Church and have always told the people so." However, he went on to threaten:

> "[B]ut if the Church, the Throne, and the aristocracy are determined to rob the poor man of his liberty, of his wife and of his children, then is the Church no longer that of Christ; then is the Throne no longer that of England; then are the nobles no longer safeguards of the people; then are they worse than useless; then with their bitterest foes, would cry, Down with them, Down with them all to the ground! Let no trace of them remain."[36]

This is quite remarkable language, but his outlook was certainly coloured by his deep-seated prejudices and his hatred of Liberal philosophy. Therefore, despite his great efforts, he never considered himself a Radical and was opposed to universal suffrage. However, he genuinely identified with the oppressed. In his deeds, in practice, he was bound closely to Radicalism and became an advocate for change. As a result, he stood close to O'Connor and Bronterre O'Brien. Both men, Oastler and Stephens, were also on friendly terms with Robert Owen, which shows how movements and tendencies criss-crossed each other in the turmoil of the period.

DIFFERENCES WIDEN

By this time, the Chartist movement was making progress by leaps and bounds. London, Birmingham, Leeds and Glasgow became its main centres, which drew in all the surrounding areas and regions. However, no sooner had the movement made headway than serious differences began to emerge regarding the means of achieving the Charter. Thomas Attwood described these as "unhappy discords", but it was much more than this.

Everyone agreed upon the necessity of the Charter, but how were its aims to be obtained? If Parliament was to reject the Charter, which seemed entirely likely, what should be done? It was on this fundamental issue that the Chartist movement split into the 'moral force' party and the 'physical force' party. The 'moral force' grouping wanted to convince members of the House of Commons simply by the force of argument and gentle persuasion. While this may have sounded reasonable, it had no guarantee of success, and what then?

In contrast, the 'physical force' party wanted to force through the aims of the Charter, if necessary by revolutionary means. This represented the realisation that no ruling class has ever given up its power or privileges

---

36 Quoted in T. Rothstein, p. 54.

without a no-holds-barred struggle. As O'Brien wrote in the *Poor Man's Guardian* of June 1834:

"The rich have never cared one straw for justice or humanity, since the beginning of the world. We defy the historian to point out one single instance of the rich of any age or country having ever renounced their power from love of justice, or from mere appeals to their hearts and consciences – there is no such instance! Force and force alone has ever subdued them into humanity."[37]

To most workers, already blooded in the fight over the New Poor Law, 'moral force' Chartism seemed impractical in the face of Tory and Whig intransigence. Joshua Barnard, a veteran of seventy years, compared 'moral force' to "striving to drive a nail with a feather". This difference also took the form of a geographical division. At this stage, London and Birmingham were the chief strongholds of the 'moral force' group, with Scotland bringing up the rear, although support for 'physical force' still resided in Spitalfields and Lincoln's Inn Fields. Meanwhile, 'physical force' Chartism drew its main strength from the industrial districts of the North and Wales.

In October 1837, the *Northern Liberator* was launched, followed a month later by *The Northern Star*, under the direction of Feargus O'Connor. In December, the Birmingham Political Union declared for universal male suffrage, and joined forces with the London Associations.

However, as the movement expanded, the centre of gravity of Chartism shifted to the industrial areas of Yorkshire, Lancashire and South Wales. As explained, the North was completely solid behind the advocates of 'physical force' Chartism, under the leadership of figures such as Feargus O'Connor, Dr. John Taylor, Reverend Stephens and Robert Lowery. William Rider from Yorkshire summed up the mood on the ground:

"…the citadel of corruption cannot be taken by paper bullets (hear, hear). There is a crew of some sort – I don't know whether I am one or not – called physical force men, who are for trying something more than argument. It is this that makes the Whigs and Tories tremble."[38]

Only with the threat of 'physical force' Chartism would anything be achieved. This was the language of the battle against the Poor Law, used by those who now had considerable influence in the Chartist movement.

---

37 A.L. Morton, *Socialism in Britain*, p. 37.
38 A. Briggs, *Chartist Studies*, p. 77.

The left wing clearly saw the Charter as the road to a genuine people's government and the transformation of society. They in turn expressed support for more revolutionary tactics and a political struggle on a strictly class basis. As Bronterre O'Brien stated:

> "Don't believe those who tell you that the middle and working classes have one and the same interest. It is a damnable delusion. Hell is not more remote from Heaven, nor fire more averse to water, than are the interests of the middle to those of the productive classes."[39]

The reformist wing, while interested in gaining the Charter, epitomised the approach of gradualism, changing things piecemeal and by consent. But the unskilled workers and operatives were more militant and prepared to go to the very end. As G.D.H. Cole and Raymond Postage noted:

> The 'moral force' men were middle-class supporters and skilled artisans, who had leisure and security enough to reflect. The 'physical force' men, except for a handful of leaders, were the more miserable masses of the North and Wales, whose sufferings made them impatient and who were unable to judge the forces against them.[40]

Whether they could 'judge' or not is a matter of opinion, but they were understandably impatient for change. The 'moral force' outlook tended to dominate among the initial leaders of the movement, but was eventually supplanted as the dominant ideology by 'physical force', which leant on the new-found mass base of industrial workers.

Such divisions within the workers' movement have always arisen when the question of political power has been posed: divisions between those who want to change society and those who are fearful of the consequences. How is the power of the ruling class to be overcome? By stealth or direct action? This conundrum runs like a red thread throughout the history of the British working class, dividing the movement between reformism, in all its varieties, and a revolutionary perspective. When push comes to shove, the reformists tend to capitulate, as they have no perspective or faith in the working class to change society. This has nothing to do with sincerity, as such, and everything to do with the logic of accepting the capitalist system.

For a while, the Chartist movement was able to paper over the differences between 'moral' and 'physical' force Chartism. Instead, they all rallied around

---

39 *The Poor Man's Guardian*, 17 August 1833.
40 G.D.H. Cole and R. Postage, *The Common People*, p. 276.

the motto 'peaceably if we may, forcibly if we must'. This formula served to satisfy both wings, as each could read into it whatever they wanted. This led Feargus O'Connor to comment: "If peace gives law, then I am for order; but if peace giveth not law, then I am for war to the knife."

RALLYING FOR THE CHARTER

In the summer of 1837, attempts were made to raise the Charter in the House of Commons, involving a layer of Radical MPs who pledged their support. William Lovett published an important address in the Radical press, which contained the following appeal:

> "In the course of a few weeks these Bills will be prepared and printed for circulation under the title of 'The People's Charter', and will form a rallying point for Radical reformers, a standard by which to test all those who call themselves the friends of the people... Working men's associations should be established in every town and village throughout the country, and the wise and good of every class should be enrolled among them. We caution you not to branch your associations, because the Correspondence Act is still in power, not to correspond privately, but through the press."[41]

The 'Correspondence with Enemies Act' of 1793 had made it illegal to communicate between the associations in London and the provinces. Instead, agitators, notably Hetherington, Vincent and others, were dispatched throughout the country to carry the message and garner support. In this fashion, largely by word of mouth, they made a big impact, especially in the northern towns.

However, the dissolution of Parliament cut across their plans. With a new general election being called, the publication of the Charter was severely delayed. When Parliament finally reassembled, Lord John Russell made it clear that the government had no intention of extending the franchise, which earned him the nickname 'Finality Jack'. This simply reinforced the sense of betrayal, as Radical working-class opinion only hardened and class feelings among the workers were stirred up to a new pitch.

It was seemingly due to the diligence of Lovett that the Chartist Bill finally saw the light of day. On 8 May 1838, the People's Charter, including the famous six points, was at last published with a preamble by John A. Roebuck MP, a friend and collaborator of Francis Place, all wrapped up in suitable legal parliamentary language. Lovett then wrote a manifesto from "The Working

---

41 M. Beer, p. 28.

Men's Association of London to the Radical Reformers of Great Britain and Ireland", announcing the Charter's publication. On 14 May, a National Petition was drafted and published by the Birmingham Political Union in support of the demands of the Charter, which became the starting point for a national campaign of mass agitation. Part of this Petition reads as follows:

> "We have looked on every side; we have searched diligently in order to find out the causes of distress so sore and so long continued. We can discover none in nature, or in Providence. Heaven has dealt graciously by the people; but the foolishness of our rulers has made the goodness of God of none effect. The energies of a mighty kingdom have been wasted in building up the power of selfish and ignorant men, and its resources squandered for their aggrandisement. The good of a party has been advanced to the sacrifice of the good of the nation; the few have governed for the interest of the few, while the interest of the many has been neglected, or insolently and tyrannously trampled upon. It was the fond expectation of the people that a remedy for the greater part, if not for the whole, of their grievances, would be found in the Reform Act of 1832. They were taught to regard that Act as a wise means to a worthy end; as the machinery of an improved legislation, when the will of the masses would be at length potential. They have been bitterly and basely deceived. The fruit which looked so fair to the eye has turned to dust and ashes when gathered. The Reform Act effected a transfer of power from one domineering faction to another, and left the people as helpless as before. Our slavery has been exchanged for an apprenticeship to liberty, which has aggravated the painful feeling of our social degradation, by adding to it the sickening of still deferred hope."[42]

This public declaration and launch became the catalyst for the further growth of the Chartist movement. Large sections of the working class were for the first time stirred into political life and political action. It became, in the words of Thomas Carlyle, "the cry of pent-up millions".

FIRING UP THE MOVEMENT

The seeds of the Charter fell on very fertile ground, in a country already in the grip of political ferment. The prosecution and transportation of the Glasgow cotton-spinners in 1837-1838 had unleashed a nationwide campaign against the Whig government. The hatred generated by the New Poor Law, the suppression of the trade unions, the campaigns around Tolpuddle and other causes, combined with the general hostility towards an arrogant ruling class, all served to fire up the movement. The Charter served as the catalyst to bring

---

42 J. Lindsay and E. Rickword, *Spokesmen for Liberty*, pp. 300-301.

everything together. The demonstrations in favour of the six points suddenly took on a semi-military mass character, made up of serried columns of proletarians, bands and standard bearers. Mass meetings, without exception, were held in the industrial areas. Night-time meetings became more frequent, illuminated by burning torches and addressed by the likes of Reverend Stephens and O'Connor. Their militant speeches, totally uncompromising, served to capture the angry mood. To Lovett and the 'moderates' such developments were distressing. To the authorities they were horrifying.

Such was the atmosphere that the year of 1838 appeared to Bronterre O'Brien as the beginning of a social revolution. Francis Place, who began as a worker, but moved up in the world to become a bourgeois Radical, was shocked by the sweep of the movement:

> "The great excitement, which had already become noticeable at the commencement of 1838, swept over the southern and eastern counties of England and over South Wales. Birmingham was the centre of the Midlands; Manchester and Newcastle were the hotbeds of the northern counties; Edinburgh and Glasgow the foci of Scotland. The excitement spread rapidly in all directions."[43]

Those who had been battle-hardened by the struggle over the New Poor Law and encouraged by the violent language began to employ direct action to further their cause. The trade unions also lent their support. The mood began to crystallise as the campaign around the Charter increasingly struck home. As a rank-and-file Chartist stated:

> "How can we emancipate ourselves from this state of political bondage? Not by pandering to the fears of that timid and irresolute class of politicians who have lately appeared among the Radical ranks, not by relying on the dastardly Whigs, not by placing faith in the tyrannical Tories, but by full reliance on our own strength, upon the inherent justice of our claims."

The cause of the Charter became the cause of the working class.

The Chartist leader Peter Bussey from Bradford urged in January 1839, that:

> "[E]very man before him should be in possession of a musket, which was a necessary article that ought to provide part of the furniture of every man's house. And every man ought to know well the use of it, that he may use it effectively when the time arrives that requires him to put it into operation…"[44]

---

43 M. Beer, pp. 38-39.

44 D. Thompson, *The Early Chartists*, p. 19.

The question of the use of force flowed naturally from the continual repression meted out by the magistrates, state and government. The whole experience of the previous fifty years had demonstrated this fact. The Chartists were not going to tolerate another Peterloo, where unarmed defenceless workers and their families were attacked and bludgeoned by the yeomanry.

There is scarcely a single leader from 1838 and 1839 who did not adopt this 'physical force' line. Even those of a moderate temperament, such as William Lovett or the Scottish delegate Bailie Hugh Craig, felt obliged to put their signatures to the May Manifesto of the 1839 Convention, which talked of needing to prepare "themselves with the arms of freemen to defend the laws and constitutional privileges their ancestors bequeathed to them". Not long afterwards, following the authorities' attack on workers in the Birmingham Bull Ring, Lovett and Collins were arrested for seditious libel in verbally attacking the magistrates and police. Henry Hetherington, also a 'moral force' Chartist, stated that henceforth he would urge working people to go armed to meetings.

According to Gammage, *The Northern Star* accurately reflected the movement and the spirit of the times:

> Its pages were read every week with surprising eagerness, and at every draught the fever increased; to appease their thirst its readers drank deeper than before, until they were seized with a kind of delirium, and nothing that did not savour of physical force stood the slightest chance of being swallowed by the vast majority.[45]

One writer reported that at Todmorden, on the day that *The Northern Star* was due to arrive, people used to line the roadside waiting for its arrival. The readership of radical papers, especially the *Star*, ran into tens of thousands, as they were passed from one person to another. Again, this speaks volumes of the enormous excitement generated by the Chartist movement. The language was uncompromising, direct, filled with passion and class hatred against the rich. It was the language of 'class against class'. It spoke directly to the working class, in proletarian language and in terms of political and social emancipation, for which there was an increasing thirst.

This proletarianisation of the Chartist movement and its lurch to revolutionary language and fervour alarmed the middle-class Radicals who had attached themselves to the cause. Now, frightened by its scope and anti-establishment character, they began to abandon the movement in Birmingham, Scotland and elsewhere.

---

45 R.C. Gammage, p. 18.

"I AM A REVOLUTIONIST"

Chartism served to breathe new life and energy into the working-class areas of Britain. The mass demonstrations and rallies, coupled with the enrolment of workers into its ranks, were ubiquitous. The 'missionary' speakers scoured the country with their message of liberation and fundamental change. In Newcastle, on 1 January 1838, the Reverend Stephens addressed a mass meeting against the Poor Law Commissioners:

> "The people were not going to stand this, and would say, that sooner than wife and husband, and father and son, should be sundered and dungeoned, and fed on 'skillee' – sooner than wife or daughter should wear the prison dress – sooner than that – Newcastle ought to be, and should be – one blaze of fire, with only one way to put it out, and that with the blood of all who supported this abominable measure."

Stephens refused to hold back and continued in a similar vein:

> "I am a revolutionist by fire, was a revolutionist by blood, to the knife, to the death… [I urged] every man to have his firelock, his cutlass, his sword, his pair of pistols, or his pike, and for every woman to have her pair of scissors, and for every child to have its paper and pins and its box of needles, (here the orator's voice was drowned in the cheers of the meeting) and let the men with a torch in one hand and a dagger in the other, put to death any and all who attempted to sever man and wife."[46]

In the summer of 1838, tens of thousands gathered on Glasgow Green to hear a number of Chartist speakers, including Attwood, with some putting the attendance figure at 200,000. Workers had marched onto the Green with bands and banners flying. Murphy and Wade led a delegation from the London Working Men's Association, who delivered cautious speeches. "We have," they exclaimed, "sufficient physical power, but that is not necessary, for we have sufficient moral power to gain all we ask."[47] How they were received is not recorded.

A rally in Newcastle was estimated at 80,000 in attendance, again with bands and banners. Many had radical inscriptions on them such as this from Lord Byron:

> "I've seen some nations, like o'er-loaded asses,
> Kick off their burdens, meaning the high classes."

---

46 Ibid., pp. 56-57.
47 Ibid., p. 21.

Or a flag with the quotation from Robert Burns:

"Man's inhumanity to man
Makes countless thousands mourn."

Speeches were made by many, including Feargus O'Connor and James Ayre, a worker and leading local figure of Chartism. "The interests of working men were everywhere the same," stated Ayre, "and oppressors would find that working men were about to be everywhere united. Knowledge was power, and the union was strength." O'Connor addressed the crowd with the promise to lead them on to death or glory. He was followed by Robert Lowery, who welcomed the crowd, who had come despite government threats for them to stay away:

"Every means has been tried to keep the people at home on this momentous occasion, but they have been tried in vain. At Cookson's Alkali Works in South Shields both persuasion and threats have been resorted to, and even the military, whom the people feed and clothe, had had the audacity to march past them with their fixed bayonets; but let them be told that Englishmen too could arm, that there was a sufficiency of muskets and of men that could handle them on the banks of the Tyne, to put to flight all the men that ever entered yonder barracks."[48]

After he had spoken, a body of dragoons arrived, marching from their barracks. This drew deafening cries of defiance from the unarmed crowd. O'Connor again addressed the soldiers directly so as to warn them and persuade them to retreat, for the demonstrators too could bring arms. In the end, bloodshed was averted.

Other mass meetings followed. A demonstration in Birmingham was called by the Birmingham Union and gathered 200,000, with Chartist divisions from Wolverhampton, Walsall, Dudley and other areas. Banners and drummers accompanied the marching throng. Attwood, as chairman, delivered the first speech. He swore that he was a peaceful man who would not sanction violence to gain the Charter. He talked instead of the support of millions which would force Parliament to act. However, he warned that if this failed, he proposed a peaceful week-long general strike. This proved to be an empty threat. Under pressure from the crowd, however, it was clear that Attwood, a 'moral force' individual, had been forced to go much further, at least in words, than he intended.

---

48 Ibid., p. 26.

Others spoke, but Feargus O'Connor, six-foot-tall and stout, made his presence felt. He was determined on this occasion to make his mark. As bold as brass, O'Connor stated that 500,000 men would assemble in London to await Parliament's decision about the Charter. As he proceeded, his language became more militant, quoting the words of Thomas Moore:

"Then onward, our green standard rearing;
Go flesh every sword to the hilt.
On our side is Virtue and Erin,
On theirs is the Parson and Guilt."

The Birmingham leaders, clearly distressed, frowned as he spoke, but his strong language proved the most popular. O'Connor's intervention served to drive a wedge into the Birmingham Radicals that was to undermine and eventually displace the advocates of 'moral force' Chartism. Even at this early stage, the 'physical force' party was gaining ground. The more the Chartist movement grew, the more the balance shifted towards the side of 'physical force'. The more Attwood warned his supporters of the machinations of 'impudent and dangerous men', the stronger the O'Connorite faction became.

APOSTLE OF TERRORISM

In fact, it was not O'Connor who first shocked the Birmingham Chartists, but the Reverend Stephens, "the apostle of terrorism", to quote Gammage. A speech by Stephens given in nearby Saddleworth, where he said that the only question was "when should they commence burning and destroying the Mills, and other Property", was reported to the Birmingham Political Union. Apparently, he also urged the crowd to murder any particularly obnoxious member of the constabulary. As soon as they heard such language, the Birmingham men demanded his expulsion from the movement. But O'Connor stood solidly behind Stephens. Even more incensed, the Union passed the following motion: "This Union expressly and in the strongest manner condemns all exhortations to physical force for the purpose of procuring Universal Suffrage and the other objects of the National Petition." The Scottish organisations took a similar stand. At an Edinburgh gathering a resolution was passed, which denounced "in the strongest terms any appeals to physical force, any exhortations to buy arms…"

Stephens, however, was not at all intimidated and brushed these protests aside, determined to adopt even more bloodthirsty rhetoric. In a public meeting of 6,000 operatives in Norwich, he let fly:

"I tell the rich to make their will. The people are with us, the soldiers are not against us. The working men have produced all the wealth and they are miserable. They want no more than a fair day's wage for a fair day's work. There is one pin on which the title of toil of all property is hung, and that is the unchangeable right of the working men to a comfortable subsistence... The working man is the ground landlord of all property in the kingdom. If he has it not, he has a right to come down on the rich until he gets it."[49]

These speeches were faithfully reported each week in the Chartist press, which excited their readers and spurred them on.

The meeting in Birmingham was followed by one in London, which attracted a smaller, but still significant, crowd of 30,000. Again, O'Connor used the opportunity to show his ability to rally the crowd. He said his desire was to try 'moral force' as long as possible, but reminded his audience that it was better to die a free man than to live as a slave. In an instant and to great acclaim, he had captured the mood of those present, who were anxious for action. But R.J. Richardson from Manchester managed to outshine even O'Connor in his references to 'physical force' and the need for weapons:

"The people of Lancashire had last session laid on the table of Parliament, a petition bearing a quarter of a million signatures, and praying for a repeal of the Poor Law Amendment Act. How was the petition treated? Why it was carried away by two gentlemen in long robes and grey wigs, and never heard of more. The people of Lancashire had therefore determined to petition no more, but would remonstrate, some said they would not remonstrate but would arm; the people began to arm, the people were armed, I have seen the arms hanging over the mantle pieces of the poor with his own eyes."

He went on:

"But the National Petition came in most opportunely, though the people could not have been persuaded to sign it if it had not demanded Universal Suffrage. If that petition should fail, I could not attempt to say what would be the consequences. Rifles would be loaded, that would be the next step no doubt, and I would defy the power of any government, or any armed Bourbon police to put them down."[50]

There was no avoiding the meaning. And it was a recurring theme everywhere, as the open clash between the two wings of the Chartist movement became more intense. They were two distinct tendencies fighting for supremacy.

---

49 M. Beer, p. 41.

50 R.C. Gammage, pp. 52-53.

O'Connor's message of 'physical force' was taken to London. But Lovett, desperate to hold on, strenuously opposed him, saying:

> "The whole physical force agitation is harmful and injurious to the movement. Muskets are not what are wanted… Stephens and O'Connor are shattering the movement, in setting secondary demands in the foreground. Violent words do not slay the enemies but the friends of our movement. O'Connor wants to take everything by storm and to pass the Charter into law within a year. All this hurry and haste, this bluster and menace of armed opposition can only lead to premature outbreaks and to the destruction of Chartism."[51]

Things were now coming to a head. Questions of force or peaceful persuasion were now posed extremely sharply, not behind closed doors, but in mass meetings. Lovett certainly had support for his views, as was shown by the resolutions passed in Birmingham and Edinburgh. But despite this, he was increasingly out of step with the mood and language of the mass movement. The organisation he had once controlled was slipping from his grasp.

The pent-up anger of the masses was looking for an expression, which it now found in the likes of O'Connor and Stephens. The bigger the meetings, the more militant and violent the language became. There was certainly no going back, as Chartism grew from strength to strength. The genie was out of the bottle and the masses were on the move. However, both wings of the movement – as we saw earlier – were still held together, despite the bitter controversy, by the watchword 'peaceably if we may, forcibly if we must'. But this served only to paper over the cracks. In the mass meetings, there was far more emphasis placed on the 'must', and far less on the 'may'. In reality, they had reached the point of no return.

---

51 M. Beer, pp. 42-43.

4. MASSES ON THE MOVE

"Let not a spade be used unless to dig some tyrant's grave."
– Bronterre O'Brien, *The Charter*

"Men of Ashton, Universal Bread or Universal Blood, prepare your Dagger Torch and Guns, your Pikes and congreve matches and all march on for Bread or blood, for life or death. Remember the cry for bread of 1,280,000 was called a ridiculous piece of machinery. O ye tyrants, think you that your Mills will stand?"
– Placard pinned to church door in Ashton-under-Lyne

"Every proletarian who does not see and feel that he belongs to an enslaved and degraded class is a fool."
–Julian Harney

ANTI-CORN LAW THREAT

There was a serious competitor that emerged to challenge Chartism, namely the Anti-Corn Law League. In 1836, its forerunner, the Anti-Corn Law Association, was founded by some Radicals in Parliament, representing liberal manufacturers. But up until this point, the organisation had made little progress.

The issue of free trade was not a controversial issue among the working class. Opposition to the Corn Laws had been a part of the Radical programme ever since their introduction in 1815.

But following the 1832 betrayal, the attention of the working class was directed towards the question of universal suffrage. The leaders of the Anti-Corn Law Association, later to become the League, argued that the working class should join with the middle class and fight in the first place to repeal the Corn Laws. Afterwards, the demands of the Charter could be considered.

Francis Place, now alienated by the 'physical force' rhetoric of Chartism and the proletarianisation of the movement, deplored "the complete estrangement of the working men from the middle classes".[1] He therefore unceremoniously abandoned the Charter and joined the Anti-Corn Law League.

As a result of the false promises made between 1830 and 1832, there was naturally colossal mistrust among the Chartists towards the middle classes, as in the working class generally. But the distrust was mutual. The Anti-Corn Law campaigners, while not opposed 'in principle' to universal suffrage in the dim and distant future, argued that the time was not right and, in reality, the workers could not be trusted with such responsibilities. For the middle classes, in practice, the time would never be right.

John Mason expressed the position of the Chartist movement very clearly at the time:

"Not that Corn Law Repeal is wrong; when we get the Charter, we will repeal the Corn Laws and all other bad laws. But if you give up your agitation for the Charter to help the Free Traders, they will not help you get the Charter. Don't be deceived by the middle classes again. You helped them to get their votes – you swelled their cry of 'The bill, the whole bill, and nothing but the bill!' But where are the fine promises they made you? Gone to the winds! They said when they had gotten their votes, they would help you to get yours. But they and the rotten Whigs have never remembered you. Municipal Reform has been for their benefit – not for yours. All other reforms the Whigs boast to have effected have been for the benefit of the middle classes – not for yours. And now they want to get the Corn Laws repealed – not for your benefit – but for their own. 'Cheap Bread!' they cry. But they mean 'Low Wages'. Do not listen to their cant and humbug. Stick to your Charter. You are veritable slaves without your votes!"[2]

In 1839 the Anti-Corn Law League was officially established in Manchester, and immediately came into conflict with the Chartists. The League and the Chartists, as competitors, found it almost impossible to co-exist. The Leaguers, keen to win support from the working class, were brought into direct collision with the Chartists. In an effort to appeal to the workers, Richard Cobden, the League's spokesman, in true opportunist fashion, increasingly adopted class war language directed against their common enemy, the landlords. Eventually, the League launched its own petition on free trade to be presented to Parliament, but it was rejected out of hand by the landed interests.

---

1   M. Beer, p. 23.

2   A. Briggs, *Chartist Studies*, p. 137.

Relations between the League and the Chartists became extremely embittered. Cobden could not hold public meetings of the League without the Chartists turning up to cause disruption. From then on, until 1846, Chartists intervened in every free trade meeting, moving resolutions and amendments that called on the audience to work firstly for the Charter, to the acrimony of the League leadership. Demands for cheap bread from League speakers were drowned out from Chartists with shouts of 'Cabbage! Cabbage!' With jeers at the 'respectables', the 'millocrats' and the 'shopocrats', O'Connor and O'Brien had little trouble in convincing the Chartist ranks to reject the appeals of the free traders, who only wanted to increase their profits. "Why do the liberal manufacturers howl so lustily for a repeal of the corn laws? – Because with the reduced price of corn, they will be enabled to reduce the wages of the working man, in order that they may compete with foreigners who live upon potatoes", reported a speech in the *Manchester and Salford Advertiser*. This was the real purpose, explained the Chartists, of the "hollow-hearted scheming of the mill owners".[3] As one worker heckled at a public meeting: "If the landlords were to sell our bones, you manufacturers would be the first to buy them, and to put them through the mill and make flour of them!"[4]

Engels had the good fortune to personally witness one of these astonishing meetings. "The writer had the 'satisfaction' of being present, in 1843, at the last attempt of the League to hold such a meeting in Salford Town Hall," he explained, "and of seeing it very nearly broken up by the mere putting of an amendment in favour of the People's Charter." Since then, noted Engels, the rule at all League meetings was "admission by ticket" only.[5]

The priority of Chartism was to obtain universal suffrage and the demands of the Charter. Following that, of course, other reforms could be considered, including the abolition of high taxes on food and drink, including the Corn Laws, but not before. The Anti-Corn Law League supporters, however, were opposed to such sweeping reforms, which for them went much too far. The war of words between the two organisations grew to a crescendo. The middle-class Leaguers were in reality against working-class organisations and Cobden did not disguise his hatred for trade unions and organised labour, which he described as "founded upon the principles of brutal tyranny and monopoly". Similarly, John Bright, the Quaker and a factory owner in Rochdale, was a

---

3   D. Read, *Chartism in Manchester*, in A. Briggs, *Chartist Studies*, pp. 35-36.
4   J. Lindsay and E. Rickword, *Spokesmen for Liberty*, p. 320.
5   MECW, vol. 24, p. 402.

bitter opponent of pro-worker legislation, especially the Ten-Hour Bill. The League, in fact, prided itself greatly on being a *middle-class* organisation, as opposed to one based on the working class. "We have obtained the co-operation of the ladies; we have resorted to tea parties and have taken those specific means for carrying out our views, which mark us as rather a middle-class set of agitators", explained Cobden.[6]

O'Connor took the gloves off when dealing with the representatives of the Anti-Corn Law League. He accused them of being:

> "[C]omposed principally of master manufacturers, whose interest is to buy labour at the cheapest market and sell the produce of labour at the dearest market. Machinery will always help the employer to buy labour cheap... The League is composed of the owners of machinery, and machinery is the great, the monster enemy of an unrepresented people. It is the new-born influence of the master manufacturers, which forced the Reform Bill from the Tory Party. And for the last ten years they have gone on establishing the details by which the Bill should be made beneficial to their order. Poor Law, Corporation Reform Bill, Rural Police Bill, appointment of Whig magistrates, and now they require the abolition of the Corn Laws. Since machinery and capital became represented in the House of Commons the hostility between master and man has become greater every year, and this has arisen from the discovery made by the working classes that capital thinks of nothing else but of the subjugation of labour."[7]

This frank assessment pretty well summed things up. Relations had sunk to rock bottom between the Chartists and these "stock jobbers and tricksters", as O'Brien called them. In rebuttal, the Leaguers accused the Chartists of being in the pay of the landowners. Clearly, there was no love lost between them, and never would be.

MONSTER PETITIONS

The question of the 'Humble' Petition has a long history. Chartism had three of them: 1839, 1842 and 1848. The difference with these and previous ones was that they were truly *national* in character. Not only that, they were monster petitions, attracting the support of *millions*. The first National Chartist Petition in 1839 was presented to the Commons on 12 July by Thomas Attwood MP and supported by a handful of Radical parliamentarians. In his speech, as reported in Hansard, he referred to its background:

6   A. Briggs, *Chartist Studies*, p. 298.
7   M. Beer, p. 59.

"That great petition, unequalled in the Parliamentary History of England, was produced by the long sufferings, the injuries, the wrongs, the distress of the working classes of the people... For the last twenty years his opinion had been rooted and fixed that the Commons of England had not been treated with common justice and humanity. Many petitions had been presented to that House from Birmingham, complaining of the state of suffering in which the people were, but their petitions had been altogether disregarded, and that hon. House had refused, in several instances, not only to grant the prayers, but even to receive the petitions of the industrious classes, and relied on the representations of lawyers and gentlemen and the public press, instead of attending to the entreaties and statements of their honest tradesmen and artisans. These petitions had been refused in 1815, 1816, 1819, and 1825, and on subsequent occasions, when they complained of distress, and desired that House to take such steps as would mitigate their sufferings."[8]

But, despite being signed by over one-and-a-quarter million people, an unprecedented number, Attwood may as well have been talking to a brick wall. The politicians of the propertied classes were not interested in such demands and were indeed contemptuous of the Chartist petition and Chartism itself. The track record of the Commons in dealing with distress and the 'humble' petition was plain for all to see. But its presentation was certainly not a waste, as the campaigning around the National Petition was a valuable and effective means by which the Chartist movement and its ideas reached every corner of the British Isles, every town and every hamlet.

Nevertheless, there were not a few genuine voices within the Chartist movement who were against the idea of submitting such petitions, describing them as "the most abject of things – the prostration of manhood". The 'humble' petition, by its very nature, was a plea on behalf of the powerless to those considered most powerful, beginning with the Crown. Such deference grated with those who believed it wrong to grovel for rights which were theirs by birth. This was a minority, though a sizeable one. The majority regarded the Chartist demands as legitimate, demands to which Parliament must surely give its assent. They were to learn important but hard lessons from this bitter experience.

The Chartists not only created a National Petition, but, as we have seen, they also took steps to organise a National Convention, a name with

---

8   Hansard, https://api.parliament.uk/historic-hansard/commons/1839/jul/12/the-national-petition

overtones associated with the French Convention of 1792 and the rule of the Jacobins. This was not the first time the name 'Convention' had been used. The Corresponding Societies had their 'Conventions' in the years following the French Revolution. The Hampden Clubs also held a Convention in 1817. In a similar fashion, delegates were to be elected to a Chartist Convention by mass meetings up and down the country, which gave a further national focus to Chartism. "Parliament does not represent me, and I will not obey its laws," said Edward Charlton at Newcastle, "but I second this resolution to support my own Parliament, as the most likely means of securing justice to my family."[9]

The place and date set for the first National Convention was in London on 4 February 1839. The Convention was proclaimed as a real parliament of the working classes. Nevertheless, before this could take place, mass meetings needed to be organised where delegates to the Convention could be democratically elected. In the North of England – Lancashire, Manchester, Yorkshire and elsewhere – the most downtrodden sections of the working class were on the move, fired up with enthusiasm for the Charter. They poured into the meetings, attracted by the uncompromising language of Stephens, O'Connor and the other leaders, to listen and be inspired by their attacks on the Whigs, Tories, manufacturers and exploiters, and to hear what the Charter could achieve for them. As far as they were concerned, the Charter was a 'bread and butter' question that opened up the vision of a new world, where they could finally attain the full fruits of their labour. "The people were those who had built our towns, who made England what it is", wrote the *Manchester and Salford Advertiser*.[10] The workers knew it and now demanded what was theirs by right.

This was not cap-in-hand politics, but the politics of class war. Workers knew there was an unbridgeable gulf between their interests and those of the masters, the same gulf that existed in the bitter trade union struggles and in the battle over the Poor Law. Even Disraeli recognised there were 'two nations'. The same capitalists who robbed them of their wages now robbed them of their vote. All this added to a growing polarisation between the classes throughout this period.

Very quickly, under such conditions, Chartism became a mass movement that inspired millions. As more and more turned to its cause, venues became too small to hold the vast numbers wanting to attend its indoor events. To

9   D. Jones, p. 88.
10 A. Briggs, *Chartist Studies*, p. 34.

make matters worse, town halls and official buildings were banned from holding Chartist meetings. Consequently, outside assemblies became more frequent, taking place on the outskirts of towns and on hillsides, as with the ones held at Kersal Moor, Hartshead Moor, Blackstone Edge or Druid's Altar, which attracted tens of thousands of people. On one occasion, 24 September 1838, Salford's biggest ever demonstration took place on Kersal Moor. 300,000 people gathered from Manchester, the towns of Lancashire and all over the North West to demand the vote. It was the biggest assembly held at any time since Peterloo. Many of the factories and workshops were forced to close as workers turned out, walking miles to attend the meeting. They were joined by many trade unions, with banners present from numerous trades: The United Trades, Tailors, Smiths and Wheelwrights, Dyers, Joiners, Fuysian Shearers, Calenderers, Painters, Men's Boot and Shoemakers, Marble and Sawyers, Spinners, and Farriers. You name it, they came in vast numbers.

As Engels noted:

> The factory operatives, and especially those of the cotton districts, form the nucleus of the labour movement. Lancashire, and especially Manchester, is the seat of the most powerful unions, the central point of Chartism, the place which numbers most Socialists.[11]

At these giant rallies, bands played and hundreds of flags and banners fluttered in the breeze, well before the allotted time of the afternoon speeches. The slogans were overtly radical, such as 'Murder demands justice!', while others were on the humorous side: 'More pigs and less parsons!' On the other hand, there were some more menacing, depicting a Skull and Cross Bones along with the inscription 'Oh tyrants! Will you force us to this?'

> Then every eye grew keen and bright,
> And every pulse was dancing light,
> For every heart had felt its might
> The might of labour's chivalry.
>
>   (Ernest Jones)

At such great mass meetings, attended by hundreds of thousands, several speakers, mounted on carts, would simultaneously address different sections of the assembled multitude. Then the speakers would rotate to an eager crowd, attentively listening to every word. As Gammage noted:

---

11 MECW, vol. 4, p. 528.

Stern were the countenances of the men in that vast assemblage. Their haggard emaciated features bore evidence of suffering, and were more than sufficient to excuse wrath at the conduct of their oppressors. The pale wrinkled cheek, the sunken eye, and the stooping attenuated frame, were standing witnesses against a system which forced the many to labour in order that the few might enjoy.[12]

This was a staunchly proletarian assembly. Despite the heavy rain, Stephens and O'Connor arrived on the Moor by coach and were greeted with great enthusiasm by the crowds. Loud cheering and applause accompanied every speaker who was introduced: O'Connor, Stephens, Lowery, Duffy, Halliday, and many other local speakers. Then the proposed delegates to the Convention were presented for the approval of the attendees and, with a forest of hands as far as the eyes could see, they were elected.

Other mass meetings took place to elect their delegates in Glasgow, Newcastle, Birmingham, London, Manchester and many other places. Bolton elected Carpenter and Warden; Preston, a working man by the name of Richard Marsden, a hard-line supporter of 'physical force'; Bradford elected Peter Bussey, again a 'physical force' man; Ashton-under-Lyne chose Peter Murray McDouall; Sheffield elected William Gill, a worker; Deegan was chosen for New Mills; Marylebone elected William Cardo; Wales elected John Frost and Henry Vincent. Many others, in the same way, were chosen from other parts of the country and sent to the Convention.

MASS MEETINGS AT NIGHT

Given the long working day, with winter nights drawing in, and with the sheer size of the gatherings, it became increasingly popular to hold meetings outdoors by torchlight. These events, the likes of which had never been seen before, were truly spectacular. Thousands of people thronged to meetings on isolated dark hillsides with banners, pikes and blazing torches, which lit up the faces of the assembled crowds. "The psychological effects of large crowds and excited speakers were emphasised by the eerie surroundings; it was but a short step from torchlight meetings to factory burnings", explained the historian Mark Hovell.[13] It seemed the whole country was ablaze with such torch-lit processions, the smoke and the smell of the multitude straight from the factories.

As Disraeli portrayed it in *Sybil*:

---

12 R.C. Gammage, p. 60.
13 Quoted in A. Briggs, *Chartist Studies*, pp. 44-45.

The shadowy concourse increased, the dim circle of the nocturnal assemblage each moment spread and widened; there was a hum and stir of many thousands. Suddenly in the distance the sound of martial music: and instantly, quick as the lightning, and far more wild, each person present brandished a flaming torch, amid a chorus of cheers, that, renewed and resounding, floated far away over the broad bosom of the dusk wilderness.

These were indeed stirring times.

The Chartist R.C. Gammage attended such events in the North, where most of the torchlit meetings were held, and described the incredible atmosphere:

Bolton, Stockport, Ashton, Hyde, Stalybridge, Leigh, and various other places, large and small, were the scenes of these magnificent gatherings. At the whole of them the working people met in their thousands and tens of thousands to swear devotion to the common cause. It is almost impossible to imagine the excitement caused by these manifestations. To form an adequate idea of the public feeling, it was necessary to be an eye witness of the proceedings. The people did not go singly to the place of meeting, but met in a body at a starting point, from whence, at a given time, they issued in huge numbers, formed into procession, traversing the principal streets, making the heavens echo with the thunder of their cheers on recognising the idols of their worship in the men who were to address them, and sending forth volleys of the most hideous groans on passing the office of some hostile newspaper, or the house of some obnoxious magistrate or employer.

He continued:

The banners containing the more formidable devices, viewed by the red light of the glaring torches, presented a scene of awful grandeur. The death's heads represented on some of them grinned like ghostly spectres, and served to remind many a mammon-worshiper of his expected doom. The uncouth appearance of thousands of artisans who had not time from leaving the factory to go home and attend to the ordinary duties of cleanliness, and whose faces were therefore begrimed with sweat and dirt, added to the strange aspect of the scene. The processions were frequently of immense length, sometimes containing as many as fifty thousand people; and along the whole line there blazed a stream of light, illuminating the lofty sky, like the reflection from a large city in a general conflagration. The meetings themselves were of a still more terrific character. The very appearance of such a vast number of blazing torches only seemed more effectually to inflame the minds alike of speaker and hearers. O'Connor, Stephens, and McDouall were frequent attendants at such torchlit meetings, and their language was almost unrestrained by any motives of prudence. Incitements to the use of arms formed the staple of the speeches of the two latter gentlemen. O'Connor, in nearly every speech, went so far as to name the day when the Charter was to become law, and usually finished up by a declaration that if it were not granted by 29 September, the Legislature should have Michaelmas goose on the 30th. Stephens did not hesitate to declare that the ruling class were nothing better than a gang of murderers, whose blood was required to satisfy the demands of public justice.[14]

Banners displayed defiant slogans, such as 'Remember the bloody deeds of Peterloo!', while another read, 'Tyrants, believe and tremble!'. In addition, there were a large number of Red Caps of Liberty carried on poles and, not infrequently, pistol shots to remind people that the audience was armed. This only served to raise the meeting to fever pitch. "One of those torches (pointing at one near at hand) was worth a thousand speeches," said O'Connor, "it spoke a language so intelligible that no one could misunderstand."[15]

At one meeting at which the Reverend Stephens was speaking, dressed in Bible black, his expression contorted, he alluded to the factory system, and stated that the title to a certain Mr Howard's mill was written in the letters of blood on every brick in the factory. You could hear a pin drop as he advised the crowd to obtain a large carving knife, which would do well to cut a rasher of bacon, or run through any man who opposed them. The crowd was enthused and fired up, eager for more. In conclusion, the speaker asked if they were armed, when two or three shots were fired. Then, raising his voice he replied, "Is that all?" This was then immediately replied to with several volleys of shots from different parts of the crowd. Stephens then asked all those present to raise their hands if they intended to buy weapons. As if commanded, a mass of hands shot up and again there was firing of guns. Afterwards, he told them to get arms, pistols, swords, pikes, or anything that would tell sharper tales than their tongues. He then concluded: "I see it is all right, and I wish you good night", whereupon he left the platform and vanished from sight. The crowd was ecstatic.

In such an atmosphere, any recommendation to pursue a 'moral force' road would have been treated with utter derision and ridicule, if not worse. More moderate speakers, fearing the scorn of the crowd, never dared to show their faces. A burning class hatred was deeply imbued in this mass of over-worked, ill-fed sons and daughters of toil. That is why meetings would invariably begin

---

14 R.C. Gammage, pp. 94-95.
15 Quoted in A. Briggs, p. 45.

with the chairman pleading for all those attending to be of good conduct, only then for speakers to launch into a vitriolic attack, in the most savage language, on tyrants and despots, including Whigs and Tories alike.

MEETINGS BANNED

The menacing mass character of these meetings, so attractive to the masses, naturally caused alarm in the middle and upper classes, and especially among the local magistrates. They believed it was a small step from burning torches to burning factories and incendiarism. They therefore constantly urged the government to suppress such gatherings. The government was swift to respond. The Home Secretary issued immediate instructions to magistrates to clamp down on such rallies, but this had little effect. In the end, a more strenuous approach was needed, pushing the government of Lord Melbourne to issue a Royal Proclamation that banned them outright. As the man responsible for crushing the 'Swing Riots', Melbourne had no hesitation in suppressing these 'heinous' gatherings.

In doing so, Notices of Royal Proclamation were posted everywhere announcing the ban and threatening that those defying the instruction would be imprisoned. Yet the mood was such that thousands openly expressed their determination to defy the Proclamation. O'Connor, however, preached caution in the pages of *The Northern Star*. Stephens, on the other hand, was in a state of defiant rage. He declared that the ban was unconstitutional and an insult to the people. O'Connor's arguments nevertheless carried the day and the nocturnal meetings ceased.

As is known, weakness invites aggression. The retreat by the Chartist leadership was followed by a warrant for the arrest of the Reverend J.R. Stephens on three separate counts of attending illegal meetings and using seditious language. He was arrested and committed for trial amid public protests. O'Connor then declared publicly that if Stephens was sentenced to transportation, it would be over his dead body. Protest committees immediately sprang up in every town and village. Nevertheless, despite the threats, Stephens was convicted and sentenced, not to transportation, but to eighteen months' imprisonment, serving his sentence in Chester Castle under extremely difficult conditions.

The law not only banned torchlit meetings, but also declared any national organisation illegal, a measure aimed specifically at the Chartists. Despite this ban, the workers were not deterred and remained defiant. Harney regarded the atmosphere during this winter period as exhilarating:

"In small villages lying out from Newcastle the exhortation to arms was being taken quite literally, a strong tradition of owner-paternalism had been replaced by an extremely class-conscious Chartism, and fowling pieces, small cannon, stoneware grenades, pikes and crow's feet or caltrops – four-spiked irons, which could be strewn in a road to disable cavalry horses – were being turned out in quantities. It was localities like this which, on hearing rumours that troops would be present at the great meeting in Newcastle on Christmas Day, sent couriers to find out if they were to bring arms with them."[16]

While torchlit rallies ceased, other mass meetings continued to hear speeches and elect delegates to the National Convention. This went hand in hand with the collection of signatures for the National Petition which was to be presented to the House of Commons. "There is now more of a political feeling in this country than ever existed, perhaps, in any nation in the world," declared the *Western Vindicator*, and "it would seem that every man has become a politician."[17] This growing political class consciousness, a burning anger towards the ruling classes, was the background to the first Chartist Convention.

THE FIRST CONVENTION

On 4 February 1839, delegates began to arrive for the opening session of the Convention, meeting in the British Coffee House, Cockspur Street, in Charing Cross. The opening proceedings took place amid great excitement. The year 1839 was an important anniversary year which had its own revolutionary connotations. To begin with, it marked fifty years since the great French Revolution of 1789, a fact not lost on the delegates. It was not lost either on a jittery Whig government. The year also marked the twentieth anniversary of the Peterloo Massacre, an event burned into the consciousness of workers, which mercilessly provoked a desire for revenge. This was therefore not an ordinary gathering, but a truly historic occasion. Such was the enthusiasm for the Chartist Convention that some 8,000 Londoners turned out to welcome the delegates at a rally at Clerkenwell Green. It was regarded by many as a real turning point, the beginning of the end of tyranny.

However, the Chartist leaders were forced to tread a legal tightrope. 'Corresponding Societies' were still illegal. The strict law of the land under the Seditious Meetings Act technically forbade a body such as a National Convention of mandated delegates. Therefore, the title 'National Convention' was avoided in favour of another title, namely the 'General Convention

16 Quoted in Challinor and Ripley, p. 12.
17 M. Chase, *Chartism: A New History*, p. 65.

of the Industrious Classes'. Everything was done to avoid the appearance, while maintaining the reality, of the Convention. Furthermore, in order to circumvent the law, rather than delegates chosen by local Chartist societies, they were chosen by a show of hands at public meetings. Of course, lists had been prepared beforehand by the branches for endorsement. The law additionally limited the numbers attending a representative gathering to a maximum of fifty persons. Convention numbers were therefore limited to forty-nine, hoping to avoid unnecessary prosecution. Despite these precautions, remaining 'within the letter of the law', the Convention was continually under threat from the authorities, who were simply biding their time.

The Chartists themselves considered the Convention a Labour Parliament, the first of its kind, which was to take all the legal steps needed to force the Commons to concede to the people's demands. However, the Convention was far from united in its approach. It reflected a number of political tendencies made up of the right, centre and left wing. What was the function of the Convention? This posed things sharply. The right wing insisted that the Convention should act strictly within the law and saw its role as merely to present the Petition to the Commons and then disband. The right included such people as James Paul Cobbett (the son of William Cobbett) and the Reverend Arthur Wade. The 'centre', which made up the majority at this stage, were in favour of something more, but were unclear as to what should be done. The left wing wanted the Convention to become an alternative government in waiting. Such views were an anticipation of those expressed in 1917 in Russia, when the Congress of Soviets needed to define its role, either simply as a political cover for the Provisional government, which the Mensheviks and Social Revolutionaries favoured, or to become an organ of workers' power, the option supported by the Bolsheviks.

The Convention also contained a certain flavour of the discussions that had taken place during the Putney Debates of the mid-seventeenth century. The opening words of Henry Vincent's paper, *The Western Vindicator*, proclaimed the great hopes for the Convention:

"Where are the statesmen with minds sufficient to comprehend the present alarming state of affairs? Most assuredly not in the present administration … BRITAIN IS WITHOUT A GOVERNMENT! … there must be a Conventional Delegation of the people's will; and that conventional delegation is to be found in the 'National Convention' now assembled in London."[18]

---

18 Quoted in M. Chase, p. 59.

The costs of the Convention were borne by the National Rent, a fund raised from local collections. This covered the expenses of the delegates' upkeep when the Convention was meeting. Given that the Convention met for long periods at a time, this put a considerable strain on those delegates who had to earn a living and had to rely mostly on their own resources. George Loveless, for instance, the Tolpuddle Martyr who was elected as a delegate from the South West of England, was forced to give up the position because he could not afford to be away from his family. Others had to rely on the goodwill of local Chartists who could provide lodgings. The families of delegates had to make do in their absence, but were generally aided by local supporters. Given the hopes raised by Chartism, these were small sacrifices to make for the good of the cause.

Such debates in the Chartist Convention, combined with the strong language from 'physical force' quarters, provoked three right-wing delegates to resign from the Convention within days. According to Oastler, the Birmingham delegates had come to the Convention with the express purpose of weakening its revolutionary policy, but were frustrated. Following the resignations, the right faction became rather isolated and from then on featured little in the proceedings. Remarkably, it took a mere six weeks for the Convention to be purged of its openly bourgeois elements.

Nevertheless, the Convention was still attempting to clarify its role. The decisive majority was made up of an uneasy broad alliance, composed of those around Feargus O'Connor and Bronterre O'Brien, but still embracing the likes of William Lovett, who clung to the coattails of the 'centre'. They tended to stress legal and constitutional means, which served to blur over their differences. While O'Connor regarded street fighting as legitimate resistance, Lovett leaned towards *peaceful* demonstrations and protests, which would defend themselves only as a last resort.

The Democratic Association of Harney represented the left wing of Chartism, which attempted to replicate the role of the Jacobin Clubs of the French Revolution. They saw themselves in the mould of Robespierre, Danton, Saint-Just and Marat. The Convention's far left was made up of people like Julian Harney, John Taylor, Richard Marsden, Peter Bussey, and Robert Lowery, who firmly believed in insurrection as a response to government obstruction. They took their seats on the 'Mountain', in the same fashion as the Jacobins, the *Montagnards*, who occupied the higher seats in the French Convention. From this standpoint, Harney and his collaborators accused the majority of the Convention of cowardice for turning their backs on such insurrectionary methods. To promote their views, the left established a Jacobin newspaper, the *London Democrat*, with Harney as the main propagandist. Beniowski also contributed articles on the Polish Revolution as well as tactics and strategy.

Nonetheless, the dominant personality of the Chartist Convention was Feargus O'Connor, who favoured the use of 'physical force' when necessary, but was not at all clear as to the steps that needed to be taken. Like others, he had illusions that the government would capitulate in the face of mass pressure and hoped to gain a quick victory. Initially, the overwhelming mood at the Convention was for unity, which was reflected in the election of William Lovett as its secretary. In the words of the hardliner John Taylor:

> "While I am bound to confess that I came to London much prejudiced against Lovett and all who belong to the Working Men's Association, looking upon them as no better than tools of the Whigs... I will unhesitatingly affirm now that no appointment could have given more satisfaction to the Convention or to the country, nor could any man have surpassed William Lovett in talent, in energy, and in honesty."[19]

This new-found unity however was not to last. The next item of business was the election of a committee to liaise with the parliamentarians about the formal presentation of the National Petition to Parliament. Harney announced that he would not take part in such a committee, saying he was not in favour of petitioning nor lobbying a corrupt parliament. Instead, the left wing proposed the establishment of a parallel commission to discuss "ulterior measures" in the likelihood of the Petition's rejection. These 'measures' were to include a host of things up to and including a general strike or 'Holy Month', as it was called. Bronterre O'Brien thought the proposal premature, while the Birmingham people objected to it on principle. In the vote, the 'centre' carried the day, forcing Harney and the *Montagnards* to take to the streets to agitate for the adoption of more revolutionary measures.

In the end, under pressure, the Convention did establish a commission to look at possible proposals for "ulterior measures". This defiant attitude, although couched in defensive terms, was not only the feeling of the Convention, but also reflected the real mood among the Chartist ranks throughout the country.

Julian Harney and Thomas Ainge Devyr recalled that the atmosphere in 1839 was so intense that everyone expected an immediate recourse to arms. As Henry Vincent, following a previous tour, explained:

---

19 M. Beer, p. 50.

"One feeling prevails in every town – or rather I should say *two* feelings – the first a general and almost universal radical opinion – resolved to aid *one more attempt* to obtain by peaceful means a full recognition of the universal rights of the people – and *second* an apparent fixed resolution to appeal to arms should this last moral effort fail..."[20]

Those assembled at the Convention felt that more time and work was needed to collect additional signatories and chose to appoint a number of 'missionaries' to tour the country and urgently gather more support for the Petition. Robert Lowery and Abram Duncan, for instance, were sent to build up the movement in Cornwall, a region somewhat isolated from radical politics. As a result, the delegates decided to defer the presentation of the Petition to Parliament for a number of weeks, although that proved ambitious. On the basis of report backs, mass meetings were planned for Whitsun, Sunday 19 May, to get a clearer picture of the mood and see how far people were prepared to go in these "ulterior measures".

Given the options, the Convention had clearly shifted to the left since its opening session in February. However, in the country, things were becoming more serious. Revolutionary ideas were circulating and gaining support. A handbill from May 1839 illustrates the point:

"Dear brothers! Now are the times to try men's souls! Are your arms ready? Have you plenty of powder and shot? Have you screwed up your courage to the sticking place? Do you intend to be freemen or slaves? Are you inclined to hope for a fair day's wages for a fair day's work? Ask yourselves these questions and remember that your safety depends on the strength of your own right arms. How long are you going to allow your mothers, your wives, your children and your sweethearts, to be ever toiling for other people's benefit? Nothing can convince tyrants of their folly but gunpowder and steel: so, put your trust in God my boys and keep your powder dry. Be patient a day or two, but be ready at a minute's warning; no man knows today what tomorrow may bring forth: be ready then to nourish the tree of liberty, WITH BLOOD OF TYRANTS.

"You can get nothing by cowardice, or petitioning. France is in arms; Poland groans beneath the bloody Russian yoke; and Irishmen pant to enjoy the sweets of liberty. Aye dear brethren, the whole world depends on you for your support; if you fail the working man's sun is set for ever! The operatives of Paris have again taken possession of the city. Can you remain passive when all the world is in arms? No, my friends! Up with the cap of liberty, down with all oppression

---

20 D. Thompson, *The Chartists*, p. 66.

and enjoy the benefits of your toil. Now or never is the time: be sure you do not neglect your arms, but let the blood of all you suspect moisten the soil of your native land, that you may forever destroy even the remembrance of your poverty and shame.

"Let England's sons then prime her guns
And save each good man's daughter,
In tyrants' blood baptise your sons
And every villain slaughter.
By pike and sword, your freedom strive to gain,
Or make one bloody Moscow of old England's plain."[21]

This was no tea party but a serious call to arms. The question of an insurrection was being raised seriously and widely in Britain. The Chartists had no alternative but to put themselves at the head of this movement. But this provoked differences in the Convention.

GOVERNMENT THREATS

The government increasingly regarded the National Convention as a threat and a challenge to its authority. In response, ministers began to beat the drum about the dangers of disorder and anarchy. The Queen's Speech at the new Parliament's swearing-in also included a direct warning about subversion:

"I have observed with pain the persevering efforts which have been made in some parts of the country to excite my subjects to disobedience and resistance to the law, and to recommend dangerous and illegal practices."[22]

This gave the green light to Lord Melbourne to issue a proclamation, clearly aimed at the Chartists, warning people against seditious speeches and actions.

It was obvious that the capitalist state was preparing to use force at some point against the Chartists. As a result, the government's threats were taken seriously by the Chartist Convention. But while Lovett demanded that all "physical measures" be repudiated, Harney and the left wing demanded that they simply ignore the government. Eventually, a compromise was reached where the Convention urged that meetings be conducted peacefully and provocations should be avoided. But this was neither fish nor fowl, for while the Convention was urging caution, it also maintained that arms should be kept at the ready in case of trouble. The Convention stated:

---

21 P. Hollis, *Class & Class Conflict in Nineteenth Century England: 1815-1850* p. 231.
22 Quoted in *The Times*, 6 February 1839.

"If forced to resort to self-defence, even to that last tribunal we are prepared to appeal rather than continue in bondage, and rather to lay our heads upon the block as freemen than to rest them on the pillow as slaves. Interference by force, however, depends not upon us; and if the infatuation of those in power prompted them to have recourse to it, so surely as in the exercise of it they dare to trench upon the liberties of Britons, so surely shall they be met with that stern resolve which promotes men either to conquer or die."[23]

As far as the government was concerned, this was nothing less than a show of defiance. Given the intransigence of the government, violence was a very real possibility. Throughout the country the situation had become increasingly polarised and extremely tense. It could be compared to a tinder box ready to explode into flames. An outbreak in one area could quickly spread to other parts of the country. Even government troops were considered unreliable.

In face of the growing trouble, the government appointed General Sir Charles J. Napier to the position of commander-in-chief of the troops in Northern England in April 1839. He belonged to a family that had supplied Britain with gifted generals, admirals, and writers on military subjects. He was a veteran of the British Army's Peninsular War and 1812 campaigns. However, despite his privileged background, he had developed sympathy for ordinary people, including the democratic ideas of Chartism. This showed a progressive side to his character. Nevertheless, he was sent to the North of England to keep the Chartist insurgency in check. What he wrote in his diary was quite astonishing for someone of such rank:

"As matters stand, I am for strong police, but the people should have universal suffrage, the ballot, annual parliaments, farms for the people, and systematic education. I am opposed to landlordism and capitalism... Manchester is the smoky chimney of the world... If the path to hell is paved with good intentions, it is certainly laid out with Lancashire cotton goods... The people must have rights to be able to protect themselves."[24]

His direct experiences in Ireland during the uprising of the United Irishmen had developed in him a horror of civil war. His letters reveal that he often tried to curb the local magistrates, who were constantly seeking to suppress the movement.

In the face of the Chartist insurgency, Napier was worried about the unreliability of his men. "The Chartists are numerous," he wrote, "and should

---

23 Quoted in M. Beer, p. 51.
24 *The Life of Sir Charles J. Napier*, quoted in M. Beer, pp. 71-72.

one detachment be destroyed the soldiers would lose confidence; they would be shaken, while the rebels would be exalted beyond measure…" He had earlier written to his brother: "…the example of one rising might have been followed throughout England; for the agitation is so general no one can tell the effect of a single shot: all depended on avoiding collision."[25]

In March 1839, the Whigs had submitted a plan to strengthen the forces of law and order through the Country Police Bill, sometimes referred to as the Rural Police Bill, in order to create a national police force. Just ten years earlier, the metropolitan police force, composed of several thousand men, had been created in London. Elsewhere, little existed, forcing local authorities to rely on troops and yeomanry. However, attempts to strengthen the police nationally were viewed with alarm by the Chartists. At the Convention, William Sankey, the delegate from Edinburgh, drew parallels with the experiences in Ireland:

> "[T]his system was first tried in Ireland… Ireland has been for a long period the nursery in which the future legislators of England are sent unfledged to develop the powers of mischief… and now the Lord Lieutenant of Ireland is in fact the independent general of an army appointed by himself, commanded by officers chosen by himself…"

There were also dire warnings from others, including Dr. John Taylor, who declared:

> "You may submit to it in the South of England – the men of the North, I tell you will not… before such a system can be put in force there, you will hear of many a bloody struggle, and when all else has failed and England is subdued, every valley in Scotland will be a battlefield…"[26]

Others also responded in a similar vein. "Every man," declared the veteran William Benbow, "and every boy of twelve years of age, should have a stiletto, a cubit long, to run into the guts of any who should attempt to oppose them."[27] In the face of this, the Convention adopted a resolution proposed by the Democratic Association members stressing that every citizen in England had the right "to possess arms, [which] is established by the highest legal authority beyond all doubt".[28]

---

25 *Life and Opinions of General Sir Charles James Napier*, quoted in D. Thompson, *The Chartists*, p. 72.

26 Quoted in D. Black and C. Ford, *The Chartist Insurrection*, p. 74.

27 A. Briggs, *Chartist Studies*, p. 46.

28 G.D.H. Cole and A.W. Filson, p. 362.

Finally, on 8 May, the Convention decided to leave London and move to Birmingham, despite the opposition of Lovett and the 'moral force' party. O'Connor and O'Brien argued that the body should meet in a central geographical location in case of trouble. But Lovett, for one, was anxious to avoid trouble at all costs. However, the latest news of Henry Vincent's arrest swayed the delegates and the 'physical force' arguments prevailed. The move to Birmingham was sealed. "The people were anxious," stated O'Brien, "that the Convention should meet in Birmingham under the shelter of the guns made by the people there, especially when the time came for the ulterior measures."[29]

Misguidedly, O'Connor chose Birmingham over Manchester or Leeds so as to imbue "its sleepy inhabitants with new revolutionary ardour." In case of danger, any industrial town north of Birmingham, regarded as a bedrock of Chartism, would have been far more secure. Despite this, the replacement delegate from Birmingham guaranteed that "the people of Birmingham were ready for anything, and would stand forth as a wall of brass in protection of the Convention".[30]

CONVENTION SHIFTS TO BIRMINGHAM

On 13 May 1839, the delegates started to arrive in Birmingham and were met with the enthusiastic welcome of an impressive demonstration of 50,000 workers. It looked as if the Birmingham delegate had told the truth. Large crowds gathered in Birmingham's Bull Ring area, traditional for meetings, so as to follow the news from the newly-convened Convention. Birmingham, which had been the centre for 'moral force' Chartism and Attwood's Birmingham Political Union, was clearly beginning to shift its political allegiance as the mood in the town became much more radical.

As soon as the Convention opened, the "ulterior measures" commission issued its report. The debate on the report, together with its recommendations, took centre stage and led to heated disagreements. The original unity of the Convention had now fractured. Support for the Charter was one thing, but how it was going to be achieved was quite another.

The commission's report recommended a list of 'peaceful' revolutionary measures, which included the withholding of rent, rates and excise duties on liquor, the boycott of opponents of the Charter, the withdrawal of deposits from savings banks, with gold to be withdrawn in place of paper notes. In addition, people should not buy newspapers that opposed the Charter. These

---

29 M. Chase, p. 76-77.
30 M. Beer, p. 68.

actions, it recommended, should take place simultaneously – on the same day – throughout the country for maximum effect. It also proposed that workers should refrain from drinking alcohol and beer, which were taxed, thereby reducing revenue to the government. And, finally, the most serious proposal: the people should be armed and plans drawn up for a one-month general strike or 'National Holiday' in the event that the Charter was turned down.

As expected, this opened up a violent debate, exposing the unbridgeable gulf between the 'moral force' minority and the 'physical force' majority. But a decision could not be avoided. The followers of Chartism were demanding concrete answers and a clear strategy as a matter of urgency. It was evident to the majority that, if the Charter was rejected by the Commons, no amount of moral persuasion was going to change the minds of Members of Parliament. If that was the case, what should be done? What was being posed point blank was no secondary matter, but the question of state power. This was the first time that such a question was seriously being raised before the working class in Britain. The records of the Convention reveal a sharp debate and the rapid crystallisation of different tendencies.

While the proponents of 'moral force' attempted to hold their ground, the debate became increasingly bitter, resulting in resignations. The first casualty was James P. Cobbett, a strict legalist, who was horrified at what was being discussed. He was the first to resign, but was shortly joined by the other Birmingham delegates. They were condemned as 'traitors' by the vast majority and the Birmingham Union swiftly elected three others in their place. The 'moral force' party was by this time completely shattered and largely withdrew from the Convention.

In effect, the Convention had now become a forum, debating the pros and cons of revolution and the next steps to be taken. With the departure of most of the 'moral force' supporters, it was now time to clarify the situation in the 'physical force' camp. But precisely at this very moment, when action was demanded, the Convention's weaknesses became exposed. Even amongst the 'physical force' party, confusion reigned. Harney dismissed out of hand the secondary 'measures' being suggested, arguing that the working class did not possess bank accounts, and to prevent them from drinking alcohol would take away their only pleasure in the face of misery. He concluded that the general strike was the only way forward, but this could only be effective if it led to the overthrow of the government, as the workers would otherwise eventually be starved back to work. This was the only logical conclusion of the general strike.

"Let there be no blinking the question", stated Harney. "These are not the times to be nice about mere words: the fact is that there is but one mode of obtaining the Charter, and that is by *insurrection*."[31] In other words, there was no other road open to them. The working class had to be prepared to seize power and it was the responsibility of Chartism to organise it. These views were reflected in the weekly paper, the *London Democrat*, which was full of shrill language. "Organisation won't do it. It won't be the organised masses that will carry the victory," stated the paper, "... the battle will be fought by brigands as they are called."[32] Such ideas were, however, more akin to the anarchist ideas of Proudhon and Bakunin, who based themselves on the lumpenproletariat, rather than the organised working class.

Nevertheless, Harney strenuously argued for a concrete plan of action. According to him, they should participate in the elections, win endorsement from the disenfranchised masses, then organise a mass march on London, together with the 'elected' Chartist MPs, to evict the government and Parliament and take power.

"In the event of Parliament being dissolved before the presentation of the National Petition, or before the *Honourable* (Scoundrel) House have given their decision upon the People's Charter, what should the people do? ... My recommendation is, the Queen's Writ for a new election of members being proclaimed, let the people of each county, city and borough, where democracy hath reared its head, assemble at the place of nomination day appointed and then and there nominate the men of choice...

"When parliamentary elections take place let all the unrepresented elect Chartists. There is no doubt that nine-tenths of the elected will be Universal Suffrage men. To elect representatives without enabling them to take their seats in the legislature would be the veriest farce imaginable. To complete the good work, it will be necessary that each representative should be furnished with a bodyguard of sturdy *sans culottes*, some thousands strong, the number, of course, varying according to the strength of democracy of the district. By the time the whole of the representatives arrived in the environs of the metropolis they would have with them not less than a million men. They would encamp for one night on Hampstead Heath and then march to Parliament Street... 'If the House of Commons should not be dissolved and reject the Charter, what then should the people do?' Your duty, working men, will then be to meet in countless thousands.

---

31 M. Beer, p. 64.
32 Ibid., p. 64.

Every district should send its deputation on a given day to a certain place and march from thence right on to London... At what more fitting opportunity could the Men of the North commence this journey; the weather is fine and good; their hearts are anxiously beating in expectation of the word of command; they want to be free and they know that London must be the battle-field...

"Should the plutocratic-elected scoundrels be fool enough to have taken their places in the tax trap, the voice of the people, crying, 'Make place for better men!' Would scatter them like chaff before the wind, or should they hesitate to fly, the job will soon be settled by their being tied neck and heels and flung into the Thames."[33]

Harney's revolutionary plan was vigorously supported by Major Beniowski, a refugee from the Polish insurrection of 1831, who was chosen by the extreme left of the Convention to lead the insurrection in South Wales. Harney was also supported in the debate by Ryder and Marsden. But the majority were not ready for such a bold move and drew back.

PRESSURE ON THE CONVENTION

During the adjournments of the Convention sessions, Harney and his *Montagnard* supporters used the time to organise local meetings in London, where he appealed for people to arm themselves. Harney spoke at an open-air meeting in Spitalfields wearing his usual Red Cap of Liberty, in solidarity with the French Revolution. Adopting the tactics of the French revolutionaries, he tried to exert pressure on the Convention from the outside. A resolution was passed at Spitalfields and forwarded to the Convention stating that if they had the courage, the Charter could be the law of the land within four weeks. This attempt to twist the arm of the Convention provoked a counter-response to expel Harney and his supporters on the pretext of injuring the Chartist cause by constantly using French revolutionary terms and emblems. However, this proposal was abandoned in favour of a motion of censure, which was passed. But this was a step too far for Harney and provoked the young twenty-two-year-old to resign in disgust.

Julian Harney tried to model himself on Marat and drew unflattering comparisons between the French Jacobin and English Conventions: one led the revolution whilst the other was capitulating. He was a great believer in the propaganda of the deed. "We are betrayed," he exclaimed, and "the traitors

---

33 *London Democrat*, 27 April and 4 May 1839, quoted in M. Beer, p. 65 and T. Rothstein, pp. 46-47.

are ruining the revolution." Other delegates, such as Ryder and Marsden, rushed to support him, stating, without naming names, that "there were only eight honest men in the Convention". With insults flying and tempers flaring, the debate was derailed onto the fruitless issue of the constitutional right to bear arms. As the answer was obvious, a number of delegates said the question was irrelevant. "What would we think of a nation of slaves asking legal opinion as to the right of arming themselves?"[34] they asked, and most signalled agreement with this. Despite some opposition, the Convention passed a resolution stating that the right of people to bear arms was beyond all question.

In the midst of all this, news arrived from Members of Parliament that the Petition, although not voted on yet, would certainly fail. As with a public hanging, this served to concentrate the minds of the Convention. In response, the Convention issued a 'manifesto' that seemed to dismiss the parliamentary route, but then sought to put the question of what to do back into the hands of the workers nationally. While no one could argue against consultation, there also needed to be some leadership from the top. After all, what was the role of leadership, if not to lead? But they dodged their responsibility and there was no direction given. Instead, the statement read:

> "The Convention have no hopes other than in the firmness and energy of the people. Public meetings should be holden in as many places as possible during Whitsun week, to direct what ulterior measures shall be adopted. Delegates from the Convention will attend as many of these meetings as their numbers will allow."[35]

PREPARING A SHOWDOWN

This *Manifesto of the General Convention of the Industrious Classes* was issued by the delegates on 14 May in 10,000 copies. Reflecting the divisions of the Convention, it raised the question of power, but in an ambiguous and vacillating manner:

> "Shall it be said, fellow countrymen, that *four millions of men capable of bearing arms*, and defending their country against every foreign assailant, *allowed a few domestic oppressors to enslave and degrade them?* ... We have sworn, with your aid, to achieve our liberties or die... [B]e assured, the joyful hope of freedom, which now inspires the millions, if not speedily realised, will turn into wild revenge...

---

34 M. Beer, p. 66.
35 M. Beer, pp. 66-67.

the once boasted manufacturers of England will perish by an agent soldiers cannot cope with nor policemen avert... [A]t least, we trust, you will not *commence* the conflict. We have resolved to obtain our rights, '*peaceably, if we may – forcibly if we must*'; but woe to those who begin the warfare with the millions, or who forcibly restrain their peaceful agitation for justice – at one signal they will be enlightened to their error, and in one brief contest their power will be destroyed."[36]

The government, faithfully serving the interests of the ruling classes, was preparing the ground for a showdown. It was busy weighing up the situation, calculating its odds and balancing the chances in military terms. General Napier, who had some sympathy for the Chartists, wrote in his diary of 23 April 1839: "These poor people are inclined to rise, and if they do what horrid bloodshed! This is dreadful work, would to God I had gone to Australia..."[37] He was reluctant to use force against the people given the risk of bloodshed. In June, again betraying his sympathies, he wrote:

> "Good God what work! To send grape-shot from our guns into a helpless mass of fellow-citizens; sweeping the streets with fire and charging with cavalry, destroying poor people whose only crime is that they have been ill-governed and reduced to such straits that they seek redress by arms..."[38]

Typically, as an army man, Napier was looking at things strictly from a military point of view. The government forces clearly had the advantage in terms of weaponry. But the troops would face a popular uprising, which, if the masses acted with determination and courage, arms in hand, no number of troops would be able to stop. Such a stand would, however, require firm and decisive leadership.

The Chartists in Lancashire and Wales seriously took up the call to arm themselves with pikes, cutlasses and muskets. Harney had urged his audiences to carry "a musket in one hand and a petition in the other".[39] Such weapons were now openly traded in the street markets in many industrial areas. In Norfolk, blacksmiths were discovered making pike heads, while Staffordshire Chartists were buying a ready supply of guns from Sheffield. The Loughborough Chartists started a penny-a-week arms club. Peter

---

36 Quoted in M. Chase, p. 72, emphasis in original.

37 *Life and Opinions of General Sir Charles Napier*, quoted in R. Brown and C. Daniels, p. 59.

38 D. Thompson, *The Chartists*, p. 72.

39 R. Challinor and B. Ripley, *The Miners' Association: A Trade Union in the Age of the Chartists*, p. 13.

McDouall ordered twenty muskets from a Birmingham dealer, saying "there would be from five hundred and a thousand more wanted", if the first order was satisfactory. There were reports of significant withdrawals from friendly societies and saving banks to pay for weapons. In other districts, military drilling began to be stepped up, often at night, under the instruction of older, more experienced former soldiers. On 29 April 1839, tensions snapped and workers rose up in revolt in Llanidloes, in mid-Wales, but found themselves isolated. The rising ended in failure, with seventeen Chartists arrested.

Reports poured in from spies and magistrates about the dangerous situation that was developing nationally. There was considerable agitation in governing circles and immediate steps were taken to strengthen the garrisons in the Midlands and the North of England. On 3 May, Lord John Russell, the Home Secretary, issued a Royal Proclamation against military training and drilling and authorised magistrates to confiscate weapons from suspicious persons, and instructed them to declare illegal all those meetings where weapons were present. In addition, the Home Secretary encouraged citizens to form "societies of volunteers for the protection of life, liberty, and property", auxiliary civilian forces to the government.

The plan was to mobilise the middle classes and the shopocracy against the workers. Some well-to-do citizens offered their services, hoping this would lead to them becoming officers in a new yeomanry. They were disappointed to find they were instead simply to be an arm of the constabulary. According to Mather: "Several of the early attempts to set up associations came to grief in consequence of this disagreement as to their character."[40]

Everything was being prepared by the central government for a bloody confrontation with Chartism. But the working class was also ready for action if called upon. During the second half of May, the mood of the workers in the Midlands and the North was reaching boiling point. Reports of arming and drilling swamped the Home Office. James Partington described the worsening situation in Lancashire in a letter dated 3 April 1839:

"Honoured Sirs,

I consider it a duty incumbent upon me to inform you of the Chartist proceedings on Monday last. About four o'clock p.m. five very splendid flags, Caps of Liberty, Death with Cross Bones, mounted upon poles, a band of music, accompanied with a great number of men, women, boys and girls armed with pikes, some with swords, pistols, firelocks with fixed bayonets arrived and halted opposite the Chapel

---

40 F.C. Mather, *Public Order in the Age of the Chartists*, p. 92.

from Hindley and Wigan road, which Motley Group was joined by a number of the 'Westhoughton Fleet'. After brandishing swords, and discharging fire-arms several times in front of the Red Lion Inn, they returned by the same road…"[41]

Such outbursts were occurring all over the country. It should be remembered that there was nothing illegal at this time in simply possessing arms. The Convention was correct in this. There existed a Bill of Rights, which declared "all the subjects which are Protestants may have arms for their defence, according to their condition and as allowed by law". Nevertheless, an armed people posed a clear threat to the government under the circumstances.

Julian Harney and John Taylor were the main speakers at a mass meeting held at Newcastle Town Moor on 20 April 1839. Not long before it started, the authorities attempted to close it down and proceeded to read out the Riot Act four times. From outside the meeting, Thomas Hepburn, the miners' leader, stood up and defiantly attacked the ban, saying: "John Fife, Mayor of Newcastle, I tell you your proclamation is no law. You have no right to prevent us from holding our meetings." Later that year, when John Taylor and other Chartists were arrested, protest strikes were held throughout the North-East, an important reflection of the support for Chartism in the area.

A letter from Newcastle to the Convention reported that:

"[N]early all the colliers in the North are laid in with a stern determination on the part of the men not to commence work again until they have gained their rights. We have done all in our power to try to get them to wait for the commands of the Convention. The answer is that long enough for aught they have to expect from their tyrants. They add, 'We are prepared to commence.' In fact, they have done so…"[42]

It reported that there were 25,000 pitmen from Northumberland and Durham on strike, as well as other workers. This was a clear indication of the mood on the ground. However, it was not possible to keep up the same degree of militancy indefinitely. Prevarication from the Chartist leaders would only serve to eventually dissipate the mood. In such circumstances, it was necessary to strike while the iron was hot, or the opportunity would be missed.

'NATIONAL HOLIDAY'

In the meantime, the National Petition had already been signed by an astonishing 1,280,959 people. The paper with the signatures weighed six

---

41 Quoted in D. Jones, p. 156.
42 Quoted in R. Challinor and B. Ripley, p. 13.

hundredweight (305 kg), and, when laid out, was two miles long. This was an amazing achievement. In fact, it was unprecedented. But the question still remained of what was to be done if the Petition was rejected, which seemed inevitable given the reports from the Radical parliamentarians. There were still lingering illusions that the Commons might, under pressure, come to its senses. But this was never going to happen.

Mass meetings, already planned for 19 May, would be used to gauge the mood. On that basis, it was felt the delegates could decide what to do next. The Convention therefore adjourned amid rumours of general strikes and revolution. An indication of the feeling in the country was reflected in the sales of William Benbow's pamphlet, the 'Grand National Holiday and Congress of the Productive Classes', as well as the sales of Francis Maceroni's book on street fighting, which reached incredible levels. The idea of the general strike or 'National Holiday' had been in circulation for quite some time and had grown in popularity.

Disraeli's characters in *Sybil* accurately reflect some of the feelings and conversations among Chartists at the time. The text is very illuminating:

"Depend upon it," said Gerard, "we must stick to the National Holiday: we can do nothing effectively, unless the movement is simultaneous. They have not got troops to cope with a simultaneous movement, and the Holiday is only machinery to secure unity of action. No work for six weeks, and the rights of Labour will be acknowledged!"

"We shall never be able to make the people unanimous in a cessation of labour," said a pale young man, very thin, but with a countenance of remarkable energy. "The selfish instincts will come into play and will balk our political object, while a great increase of physical suffering must be inevitable."

"It might be done," said a middle-aged thickset man, in a thoughtful tone. "If the Unions were really to put their shoulder to the wheel, it might be done."

"And if it is not done," said Gerard, "what do you propose? The people ask you to guide them. Shrink at such a conjuncture, and our influence over them is forfeited and justly forfeited."

"I am for partial but extensive insurrections," said the young man. "Sufficient in extent and number to demand all troops and yet to distract the military movements. We can count on Birmingham again, if we can act as one before their new Police Act is in force; Manchester is ripe; and several of the cotton towns; but above all I have letters that assure me that at this moment we can do anything in Wales."

"Glamorganshire is right to a man," said Wilkins, a Baptist teacher. "And trade is so bad that the Holiday at all events must take place there, for the masters themselves are extinguishing their furnaces."

"All the North is seething," said Gerard.

"We must contrive to agitate the metropolis," said Maclast, a shrewd carroty-haired paper-stainer. "We must have weekly meetings at Kennington and demonstrations at White Conduit House; we cannot do more here, I fear, than talk, but a few thousand men on Kennington Common every Saturday and some spicy resolutions will keep the Guards in London."

"Aye, aye," said Gerard; "I wish the wooden and cotton trades were as bad to do as the iron, and we should need no holiday as you say, Wilkins. However, it will come. In the meantime, the Poor Law pinches and terrifies, and will make even the most spiritless turn."

"The accounts today from the North are very encouraging though," said the young man. "Stevens is producing a great effect, and this plan of our people going in procession and taking possession of the churches very much affects the imagination of the multitude."

"Ah!" Said Gerard, "if we could only have the Church on our side, as in the good old days, we would soon put an end to the demon tyranny of Capital."

"And now," said the pale young man, taking up a manuscript paper, "to our immediate business. Here is the draft of the projected proclamation of the Convention on the Birmingham outbreak. It enjoins peace and order, and counsels the people to arm themselves in order to secure both. You understand: that they may resist if the troops and police endeavour to produce disturbance."

"Aye, aye," said Gerard. "Let it be stout. We will settle this at once, and so get it out tomorrow. Then for action."

"But we must circulate this pamphlet of the Polish Count on the manner of encountering cavalry with pikes," said Maclast.

"'Tis printed," said the stout thickset man; "we have set it up on a broadside. We have sent ten thousand to the North and five thousand to John Frost. We shall have another delivery tomorrow. It takes very generally."

The pale young man then read the draft of the proclamation; it was canvassed and criticised sentence by sentence; altered, approved; finally put to the vote, and unanimously carried. On the morrow it was to be posted in every thoroughfare of the metropolis, and circulated in every great city of the provinces and every populous district of labour.

"And now," said Gerard. "I shall tomorrow to the North, where I am wanted. But before I go, I propose, as suggested yesterday, that we five, together with Langley, whom I counted on seeing here tonight, now form ourselves into a committee for arming the people. Three of us are permanent in London; Wilkins and myself will aid you in the provinces. Nothing can be decided on this head till we see Langley, who will make a communication from Birmingham that cannot be trusted to writing. The seven o'clock train must have long since arrived. He is now a good hour behind his time."[43]

There was a growing realisation of the importance of the general strike as a weapon in the class struggle. Strikes were of course commonplace. However, a general cessation of labour was on another level altogether and posed the question of power. In such a strike, everything is brought to a standstill and the capitalist state is paralysed. Not a wheel turns, not a whistle blows and not a machine operates without the kind say-so of the working class.

This potential strength was graphically expressed in a Chartist placard, an appeal to the miners to strike:

"To the Colliers of
England and Wales.
Strike! Colliers! Strike for the Charter!

"In your hands is reposed such a power as the tyrants few, who oppress and grind the faces of the poor, cannot stand. Without coal the lordly aristocrat cannot cook his luxurious meal. Without coal the Steam Engine whose iron arm has beggared so many of your poor fellow-countrymen, willing to work – murdered thousands of innocent children in our Cotton Mills yearly – reduced thousands of tender mothers to a worse state than brute beasts, and hung their pale limbs with filthy rags – without coal this giant monster, the Steam Engine, cannot work. Your labour, my honest friends, supplies it with strength, for without Coal it is powerless. Stop getting Coal, for Coal supports the money-mongering Capitalists."[44]

But to regard the general strike simply as 'downing tools and folding arms' was not enough. The working class could not remain on strike indefinitely, and would eventually be starved back to work. The action would have to be

---

43 B. Disraeli, *Sybil*, pp. 276-278.
44 D. Thompson, *The Chartists*, p. 298.

resolved quite quickly one way or the other. During such a strike, in which everything is paralysed, a situation of 'dual power' would exist in society, with the strike committees that would be thrown up challenging the capitalist state. In reality, it would be the embryo of workers' power. In such a situation, either the working class would consolidate power into its own hands, or the ruling class would reassert its control and 'normality' would be restored.

The 'National Holiday', as originally envisaged, was supposed to last one month, long enough, it was hoped, to win the strike. Such a strike, on such a level, could only be regarded as a prelude to a revolutionary overturn. As Engels later explained in discussing this question, the general strike "leads directly to the barricades". Engels reached this conclusion based primarily on the experience of the Chartists between 1839 and 1842. Such an action would not be a *putsch*, the actions of a small minority, but a mass movement of the working class.

An interesting observation about the 'Sacred Month' was made by Robert Lowery, who said:

"Whatever might have been meant by it at first, it meant in the people's minds the chances of a physical contest; not an insurrection or assault on the authorities, but that by retiring from labour, like the Roman plebeians of old to the Aventine-hills, they would so derange the whole country that the authorities would endeavour to coerce them back, and that they would resist the authorities unless their rights were conceded, and thus bring the struggle to an issue. Hence *The Northern Star* and the speakers had advised the people to arm."[45]

GROPING FOR A SOLUTION

Around the Chartist discussions of the general strike emerged the question of a working-class insurrection. Both were interlinked, as Engels observed. The question had been posed but not fully answered. Lowery's suggestion was that the 'National Holiday' would serve to provoke the government, which would in turn provoke a counter blow from the working class. There is no doubt that there were many in the ranks of the Chartist movement who were keen to overthrow the old regime and bring the working class to power. The main problem was how exactly that could be done. They were certainly groping towards a solution, but failed to get clarity. The fact remained that the only real reference points for them to follow were the French Revolutions of 1789 and 1830, and the American Revolution of 1776. The Paris Commune and the Russian revolutions still lay in the future. The bulk of the Chartist leaders

45 P. Hollis, p. 234.

were certainly prepared to go to the end as, after all, they were prepared to risk long imprisonment, transportation, and even death. Unfortunately, they did not fully understand all the implications or draw all the necessary conclusions. They were pioneers and such questions were new to them. Julian Harney and the *Montagnards* were certainly in advance of many, but even they were only groping for a solution. Whatever their shortcomings, they truly displayed élan, courage and initiative, for which they deserve credit and praise.

Lenin, who closely studied the British labour movement, correctly described Chartism as more of an "anticipation". It represented the first real attempts to forge a revolutionary party, but the leadership was still lacking a strategy to succeed. They had little to go on but intuition and the example of the French revolutionaries and the American colonists.

From the beginning of May 1839, the Northern Chartists believed the movement could not be held back any longer. Unstoppable pressure for action was building up. It was like a pressure cooker that was ready to explode. The working class could not be kept in such a state of heightened ferment indefinitely. If action was not organised soon, it would erupt spontaneously.

This was in May, when the Convention hoped Parliament would debate the Petition, and the matter would be clarified one way or the other. And yet, a complication arose. Attwood and Fielden, Members of Parliament, were informed that the Petition would not be presented before the middle of June, and not debated until 14 July. This delay meant that the initiative was slipping from the hands of the Chartists, and much time had been wasted in talking instead of preparing for action.

If there was an appropriate time for a general strike and an insurrection against the government, it would be when Parliament had rejected the National Petition.

Although General Napier held certain Radical views, these did not stand between him and his duty as a soldier and officer. He declared:

> "Conscience should not wear a red coat. When I undertook the command of the Northern District under Lord John Russell, I put all my Radical opinions in my blue coat-pocket, and locked the coat in a portmanteau which I left behind me. I told Lord John this when I went to see him on taking the command."[46]

Within a few years, he would relinquish the Northern command to take up an appointment as Major General of the Indian army. In his place came Major General Sir William Gomm, then followed by Colonel Wemyss.

---

46 D. Thompson, *The Early Chartists*, p. 24.

Throughout May, Chartist meetings were being held everywhere, normally addressed by Convention delegates. *The Northern Star* reported that a crowd of 500,000 assembled at Kersal Moor, then 200,000 on Peep Green in the West Riding, followed by meetings in Liverpool, Newcastle, Blackwood in Monmouthshire, Hull, Northampton, Glasgow Green and on Primrose Hill in London. O'Connor reported he had attended three meetings at which a total of one million were present, which is entirely possible. Most speeches given at these meetings reflected the revolutionary mood at the time. General Napier actually attended the mass meeting at Kersal Moor and found everything in order, but naturally thought the ideas of 'physical force' Chartism delusional. He showed contempt for their boasts: "Physical force! Fools! *We* have the physical force, not they... How little they know of physical force!"[47] While the military under Napier showed restraint, they certainly put on a show of strength.

Hundreds of thousands had attended the Whitsun Sunday meetings on 19 May, where resolutions were unanimously passed regarding the "ulterior measures". Whitsuntide was a traditional holiday, although there were no paid public holidays prior to 1871. Interestingly, even a number of soldiers attended these meetings to support the Charter, but they were not disciplined by the authorities for fear of the public reaction. This fact was symptomatic of the volatility within the armed forces, many of whom came from the working class. The army, after all, is a reflection of society and its class divisions.

Dozens of smaller meetings took place in Brighton, Dalton, Dudley, Haywood, Kendal, Leicester, Southampton, Wilton and Kennington Common along with many other places.

RETURN TO BIRMINGHAM

With the debate of the Charter by Parliament now imminent, the delegates returned to Birmingham on 1 July. It was clear the Convention had received an overwhelming mandate to proceed with action, and John Taylor moved a resolution to enact the "ulterior measures" as agreed, withdrawing money from banks, etc. But he added: "The people have got muskets, but they require bayonets in order to be able to resist cavalry charges."[48] The resolution also included a separate point: "That the members of the Convention meet on 15 July for the express purpose of appointing a day when the Sacred Month or National Holiday should commence."[49]

---

47 Quoted in M. Beer, p. 74.

48 M. Beer, p. 73.

49 Ibid., p. 74.

Fresh from the mass meetings, the Convention got down to business. O'Connor seconded the motion, and stated: "I strongly approve of the Sacred Month when the people might act the part of honourable plunderers instead of being arrant slaves." McDouall wanted the Sacred Month launched as soon as possible and recommended July as the chosen date, being the celebrated month for revolutions. Warden supported the resolution of Bussey, also believing that a National Holiday was tantamount to a national insurrection. Taylor reported a similar view in the areas after attending twenty-six Chartist gatherings in Scotland: "With respect to the Sacred Month, they felt it would be nothing short of physical revolution that would be caused by it."[50] Other delegates also rushed to pledge support to the main resolution. Bussey said it was time to take serious action, as did Fletcher. McDouall therefore called for a much tighter organisation, on the lines of the United Irishmen. Burns intervened, saying: "Such an organisation is necessary. If the government Peterlood the people, we should Moscow the country."[51]

However, within twenty-four hours of this debate, events took a sharp turn in Birmingham. The area of the Bull Ring was flooded with Metropolitan police and all hell broke loose. "The sapient and contemptuous magistrates sent for one hundred policemen from London", explained G.J. Holyoake. "Magistrates oftener break the peace than workmen, as they do in Ireland, as they did at Peterloo in 1819…"[52]

The peace was certainly broken in Birmingham. William Lovett, who was soon to be arrested, also related what had happened:

"When… the agitation for the People's Charter commenced, following the example of their former leaders, the working classes began to hold their meetings also in the Bull Ring. But this of course was not to be endured by the ex-reform authorities; what was one right and legal in themselves was denounced as seditious and treasonable in the multitude. The poor infatuated workers, however, could not perceive the distinction of Birmingham authorities between the two political measures, but continued to meet as usual… At last the governing powers of Birmingham… sent to London to their former friends and allies requesting them to send down a strong posse of the new police to assist them. They came down by rail, and were no sooner out of their vans than they were led on by the authorities, truncheon in hand, and commenced a furious attack upon the men, women and

50 M. Chase, pp. 80-81.
51 M. Beer, pp. 73-74.
52 J. Lindsay and E. Rickword, *Spokesmen for Liberty*, p. 303.

children who were assembled in the Bull Ring, listening peacefully to a person reading a newspaper. This proceeding, as may be supposed, greatly exasperated the people..."[53]

Exasperation led to a showdown with the authorities. It was clear that the government, in league with the Birmingham authorities, had made up its mind to incite the people and then act to crush the movement. A state of emergency was declared, and Birmingham was flooded with police, troops and yeomanry. All meetings were banned. The next morning around eighty Chartists were arrested, including delegates. The Convention protested the police violence and the arrest of its leaders. Posters protesting the actions were produced, signed by Lovett and spread all around Birmingham. This, in turn, provoked his arrest, together with Taylor and Collins. Harney was also taken into custody at Northampton and a military curfew was imposed on Birmingham.

Although most of those arrested were released on bail, tensions were running extremely high. Spontaneous protest strikes broke out, with 25,000 colliers going on strike against the arrests. Clashes soon broke out in Birmingham as workers confronted the military and police. Faced with intense pitched battles, at one point the police were forced to flee after a twenty-minute barrage. This encouraged the workers to take the offensive and news of the Birmingham riot spread rapidly, provoking bloody clashes elsewhere: in Glasgow, Newcastle, Sunderland and a host of Lancashire towns. The Bull Ring outrage "exasperated the democracy all over the county", recalled a Newcastle Chartist. "Then commenced the work of 'preparation'." The head of the Manchester military garrison on 15 July noted that "there have been more Pikes made and sold within the last ten days, than in any former period." Henry Vincent, from Cheltenham, declared: "A crisis is now at hand... Fellow slaves! Rattle your chains!" He confided privately that "a desperate feeling is now abroad – you can have no conception of the intensity – even in this aristocratic town of Cheltenham the people are *ripe* and *ready*".[54]

The Convention was in a state of fury at the assaults and arrests and issued another manifesto calling for the immediate introduction of the "ulterior measures", all with the exception of the general strike. This was clearly a mistake. The Convention could have used this moment to launch a strike,

---

53 R. Brown and C. Daniels, p. 40.
54 M. Chase, p. 84.

but the majority balked at the idea. If ever there was a time to have called such a strike, it was then. The mood was electric and the growth of spontaneous strikes was indicative of the situation. However, the Convention took the strange decision instead to return to London and to convene at Johnson's Tavern, Fleet Street, as the second reading of the Petition was in process in the Commons. This shifted the attention away from the immediate crisis towards the parliamentary field, which tended to defuse the situation.

They could have moved the Convention to an industrial centre where resistance could have been properly organised, but instead chose to return to London, where the state was strongest, simply to hear the inevitable fate of the Petition. This was another miscalculation.

The Petition had been delivered to Parliament a month earlier in several vans. Attwood, when introducing it, pleaded to a hostile House of Commons to support it. Following the so-called debate, Lord John Russell replied with a long speech, attacking those who dared preach violence and anarchy. Daniel O'Connell scandalously joined in the attack on the Chartists, accusing them of high treason with their talk of physical force, at the same time that Ireland was bleeding under British rule.

Finally, the Commons divided and Attwood's motion was resoundingly defeated by the Ayes – 46 and the Noes – 235. The Charter had been decisively rejected. The whole affair was a complete farce. The vote was a clear reflection of the callous opposition of the ruling classes to any parliamentary reform, however small. Attwood, exhausted and disappointed, left Parliament and then dropped out of the movement altogether.

THE GENERAL STRIKE PLAN

Now that the Charter had been overwhelmingly rejected in Parliament, the time once again arrived for decisive extra-parliamentary action. The former road to reform had been decisively blocked and no amount of peaceful persuasion was going to change parliamentary minds. In places like Bolton, Bradford, Pontypool and Newcastle, it was reported that "there existed a sullen gulf between two armed camps". The recalled Convention was, however, sparsely attended, with only half of those eligible in attendance. Several were still in prison, notably Collins, Harney, Lovett, Taylor and Vincent, while some were involved elsewhere in agitation and another group was involved in plotting a conspiracy.

Arrests still continued in the areas. It was felt that the only hope now was a call for national action, a general strike, which would certainly have been answered in the industrial areas, and rapidly spread from there. But there needed to be a clear call. *The Northern Star* called on the Convention to appoint a committee of thirteen to go into permanent session, while the remaining thirty members should tour the country to organise the movement. It was evident that power was not in Parliament, but in the streets. The ruling class would either be forced to immediately capitulate to the movement or it would be overthrown. Very quickly, the mood of the delegates swung behind the idea of a general strike as the only power that could bring the government to its knees. Most, reluctantly, also came to the conclusion that a general strike, if successful, would be a prelude to an insurrection. Therefore, it was not simply a question of a work stoppage, but involved the seizure of state power. That, in turn, posed the perspective of an all-out victory and the sweeping away of the old regime.

Both Neesom and Marsden were strongly of the opinion that a date should be fixed for the general strike. Marsden, a handloom weaver, stated:

> "The working men of the North signed the petition for the Charter, under the impression that the men who spoke for them of the Holy Week were sincere. None of the industrious classes, who signed the petition in this belief, ever thought for one moment that the legislature would grant the Charter. The people expected nothing at the hands of the government – they looked to the determination of this Convention… all they had to do, was to let the country know when the sacred week was to commence."[55]

Marsden posed the question very sharply. Either the leadership would take advantage of the situation or there would be widespread disappointment. The Convention, however, was split, with those Lovettites who still remained simply wanting to protest and proclaim the right of every citizen to resist aggression by armed force. But this was a diversion. Matters had gone far beyond this. As the pressure mounted, there were other waverers, including O'Connor and even O'Brien, who shifted their ground. Lovett personally took no part in the proceedings as he was busy preparing for his trial following his arrest. Hetherington and the London delegates dithered and wanted more information and further discussion.

However, a resolution moved by Robert Lowery proposed that a general strike be launched on a definite date of 12 August without any further delay. Neesom then moved an amendment that the strike date be brought forward to 5 August. But few supported this proposal. Nevertheless, the issues had

---

55 M. Chase, *Chartism: A New History*, p. 63.

become clear. There could be no further prevarication. Unfortunately, under intense pressure, some began to get cold feet. James Moir (Glasgow) strongly advocated the need to test the ground further, as the consequences of such a strike were extremely serious. He felt that everyone needed to be aware of what was at stake. He explained:

> "My personal opinion is that the question before the Convention is one of the most important character. The Sacred Month is, in fact, nothing more nor less than the commencement of a revolution, the end of which no man can foresee."

In this, he was correct. However, he continued:

> "My opinion, therefore, is that before any such thing is recommended the organisation of the people should be carried out much more completely than it is now. It was not enough that some portion, some small portion, of the working classes should be willing to carry out the proposition for a National Holiday; it must be adopted generally, if not universally, or evil and not good would be the result of it. I am of the opinion that steps should be taken to get at least every large town to agree to act upon such a recommendation as that now asked for before such a recommendation can be given."[56]

While these were legitimate concerns, the ground had already been tested, and delay upon delay would only serve to dissipate the movement. They simply exposed the different tendencies present in the Convention between revolutionaries and the more reformist trends.

The doubts of James Moir were countered by other delegates, notably Neesom, Skevington, and Dr. Fletcher, who gave assurances that Bury, Loughborough, Gloucester, Worcester and Somerset were areas in which the workers were clearly in favour of a general strike. But the delegate from Rochdale raised doubts:

> "The question we are discussing is most important. I must first ask, what is the meaning of the National Holiday? Are we to abstain from all manner of work? If so, is the bread baked for a month? Is the corn ground for a month? I deny that is so. The people of Rochdale are of opinion that there is not food enough in South Lancashire to subsist the people for a fortnight. Failure in such a step would properly enough be looked upon as being a proof at once of folly and wickedness. It is of the utmost importance to consider not only the practicality, but also the consequences of such a measure as this."

56 M. Beer, p. 84.

He continued:

> "It had been called a bloodless effort. Those who said so knew better. They know that it must lead to both blood and plunder. I do not say I am against it, but I want to see beforehand what we are to gain by it if unsuccessful. My mind is open to conviction, and although I am of opinion that a general strike is at once impracticable and foolish, the arguments to be brought forward may change my opinion."[57]

But Burns, who belonged to Taylor's grouping, announced:

> "It is no use now to cry 'halt'. Whatever we may do now, we shall run great risks. The purpose of the National Holiday is to show that if we ceased labour the government must cease to govern and the profit mongers to get their profit."

However, the divisions persisted. William Carpenter urged caution, stating he wanted to speak the plain truth, irrespective of the likelihood of being tarred a coward, or even worse. He pointed to the fact that out of fifty-three mandated delegates, only about thirty were present to discuss such a life or death issue. "Where is O'Connor? Where is O'Brien? Craig, D. Taylor, and Frost?" he asked. "The fact is we have come to this subject without due preparation." While the workers of Newcastle and its neighbours, he said, were ready to follow the lead of the Convention, many others were not.

> "Friends, we are deceiving ourselves. Glasgow is not ready, Ashton is not ready, Manchester has given no definite answer, nor has Sheffield. Are we going to let loose hundreds of thousands of desperate and hungry men upon society without having any specific object in view or any plan of action laid down, but trusting to a chapter of accidents as to what the consequences should be? Is this the course worthy of a deliberate assembly? I have made up my mind. I shall oppose fixing a day for the holiday until we have better evidence, first, as to the practicality of the thing, or the probability of its being carried into effect; and next, as to the way in which it is to be employed."[58]

This served to pour cold water over the strike proposal. But in spite of the voices raised against the general strike, Lowery's resolution was surprisingly passed by the Convention and the general strike set for 12 August, some three weeks away. But there seemed little conviction behind the vote. A layer of delegates had great apprehensions about the decision. In fact, the decision

---

57 M. Beer, pp. 84-85.
58 Ibid., p. 86.

brought O'Connor, Taylor, and O'Brien rushing back to London, and they managed to get the Convention to reconsider the matter. Amid allegations of timidity, it was proposed that a committee of seven be formed to discuss the organisation of the general strike. It was also decided to draw up a manifesto. McDouall, furthermore, was most insistent that they link up with the trade unions to ensure the strike's success.

Bronterre O'Brien, having heard the decision to organise a general strike, also came back with a proposal to postpone it. He explained:

> "My absence from the Convention was excused by the circumstance that I was agitating in the North of England and Lancashire. The people are well up to the mark, but I fear they are not ready yet for a general strike. I strongly urge the Convention not to precipitate matters. I should like to see great masses of the population keeping the holiday, but this could not be the case if it were fixed for 12 August. At all events we ought to enquire into the facts and place them fearlessly before the people."[59]

He then put forward a motion to postpone the strike due to a number of problems, such as the large number of arrests, the division of opinion in the areas, insufficient support, and the danger of anarchy. He therefore concluded that it was once again down to the workers themselves to decide.

Following these interventions, opinion in the Convention appeared to be moving towards O'Brien's position, and so it was finally agreed to appoint a committee of ten to reconsider the previous decision. Furthermore, it was decided to once more call on the workers to decide whether or not to strike on 12 August. The Convention then pledged "to co-operate with the people in whatever measures they may then deem necessary to their safety and emancipation". O'Brien's motion was put to the vote and carried by a majority of only six votes; twelve voting in favour, six against, and seven abstaining, reflecting the confusion that still prevailed. Moreover, to make matters worse, the issue of *The Northern Star* for 3 August openly opposed the strike and argued that

> "[T]he country is not for it; there is no state of adequate preparation; there is no proper organisation among the people; they are not able to act in concert with each other; they are not a tenth part of them in possession of the means of self-defence; they are not agreed on their opinions, either as to the practicality or the necessity of the measure."[60]

---

59 M. Beer, pp. 86-87.
60 M. Chase, p. 86.

In the same issue, O'Connor also disparaged the action:

"I do now most emphatically warn you, that the attempt to stop work for a month would either have the effect of subjugating the working men more than ever to the will of their masters, or of terminating in a short and sanguinary sectional struggle, the result of which would be a licence for every rich man to shoot as many poor men as he thought proper."[61]

In practice, this sealed the fate of the strike. It was like the Grand Old Duke of York, who marched his troops up to the top of the hill and then marched them back down again. It clearly demonstrated the failure of a divided Chartist leadership at this crucial time.

If the Convention had been united on this question, this would have galvanised the forces of Chartism, cut across the hesitations and rallied the troops. In this context, united action would have spoken louder than words. There were always going to be doubts and hesitations, that was inevitable. But precisely a firm hand from the leadership would have calmed the nerves and unified the workers. Once the action had started, it would have snowballed. But this vital ingredient, of a firm leadership, was lacking. Even with these confusions, there were many areas that awaited the call for action. Many feared retreat, such as in Bath, where it was reported that "the biggest fear is that the strike will not take place". Bradford was also keen for action, despite the "mischief" of *The Northern Star*. Such was the disgust, some even went so far as to suggest burning the newspaper. Some areas, trying to make the best of it, called marches and demonstrations, but the time for marching had passed, so these were poorly attended. The people were expecting a clarion call for the 'Sacred Month', but nothing came. Under such circumstances, the mood began to dissipate as the confusions and trepidations at the top transmitted themselves down to the workers.

RETREAT AND RE-GROUPING

The retreat from the general strike had serious consequences. With the decision to consult the workers, the majority of delegates left London for the provinces. A central council of seven was chosen to oversee the business of the Convention as it still formally continued to meet. The committee to oversee the strike also remained in the capital to gather reports from the areas, and on that basis, it would make its recommendation for how to proceed. A mere week before the proposed general strike date, on 5 August, the committee

---

61 P. Hollis, p. 235.

issued its report which drew the conclusion: "We are unanimously of opinion that the people are not prepared to carry out the 'Sacred Month' on the 12 August."[62]

The whole thing was deflated. The prevarications in the leadership rubbed off onto the workers, who could sense the mood emanating from the Convention. Instead of reassurance, they sensed doubts and hesitation. The committee's recommendation simply confirmed the retreat. On this basis, the Chartist leadership had no alternative but to call off the general strike. However, the committee believed there remained a strong feeling for at least limited industrial action and therefore recommended a one- or two-day strike, starting on 12 August. During this period, protest meetings and demonstrations could be held. They believed these demonstrations should deliberate:

> "[O]n the present awful state of the country, and devising the best means of averting the hideous despotism with which the industrious orders are menaced by the murderous majority of the upper and middle classes, who prey on their labour."

Their appeal to the trade unions to take part in this limited action ended with the words: "Men of the trades! The salvation of the country is in your hands!"[63]

Strike action did take place on 12 August, with meetings and rallies addressed by Convention delegates, which caused some disturbance in several localities. In Lancashire, Chartists paraded in most cotton towns and forced several factories to close. In the cotton districts around Manchester mass picketing enforced a three-day strike. But in other areas mills continued to work. Bolton was a particular hotbed of the strike. Arising from the disturbances and the reading of the Riot Act, arrests were made. The evidence Baker, a police officer, gave against those arrested was reported in *The Northern Star*, 11 April 1840:

> "A great number of people assembled during the day; and the effect was that the shopkeepers closed their shops, and business was almost entirely suspended...
> On the morning of the 12th, he saw Lloyd about six o'clock addressing a mob...
> He heard him say they were not to cause disturbance, but if interfered with, to act like men determined to have their rights. Let their tyrants see they were not to be frightened into surrender of their birthright, but that they were determined to have it, and willing to die for the cause. They dispersed after that, and assembled

---

62 G.D.H. Cole and A.W. Filson, p. 367.
63 Ibid., p. 367.

again in Market place... Lloyd then addressed them, and said he was not an advocate for rioting, but he would have them remember that the Reform Bill was gained by the riots in Bristol – The mob continued to meet during the day. In the evening many thousands assembled again, and it was such a multitude that the civil force could not contend with... They then paraded the streets, some of them carrying bludgeons. There was great shouting, hooting the police, and creating great terror in the people. Even the shutters were closed. Witness, after the proceedings of the 12th received directions to apprehend the prisoners...

"A police officer named Bradshaw was next called, and stated that the crowd on the 12th of August went about to a number of factories and induced workmen to leave work... The defendants were leaders of the crowd. Would give instances. They fell in rank when Lloyd told them, and they insisted on rescuing him when he told them to be quiet. (A laugh)."[64]

In Newcastle, the Chartists produced a statement with a stark message to the middle classes called 'Address to the Middle Classes of the North of England':

"We address you in the Language of Brotherhood probably for the very last Time... It is your intense and *blind* Selfishness that is rendering almost inevitable a Civil Convulsion. This Fact will be remembered in the Day of Trial. You have not been with us and therefore you are against us. Should the People (and it were folly to doubt it) succeed, they will owe you no gratitude – should they fall you will be involved in their ruin... they will '*disperse in a million of incendiaries*', your Warehouses – your Homes – will be given to the Flames, and one black Ruin will overwhelm England!"[65]

While two people were later charged with sedition for its publication, this did nothing to calm the anger. An equally strident address also appeared two days later, 'To the Middle Classes of Darlington, and its Neighbourhood', warning: "You *are* now on the brink of a *civil war at home*... oh foolish and infatuated men!"[66] This was followed by an 'appeal' for the defence fund amongst local shopkeepers in Bradford warning them that "in all cases of refusal to this respectable request we shall know how to discriminate between our Friends and our Enemies".[67]

After a few days, the strikes inevitably dissipated, and in Lancashire and Manchester the strike was mainly confined to Monday. However, in Bury,

---

64 Quoted in P. Hollis, pp. 236-237.
65 M. Chase, p. 98.
66 Ibid., p. 98.
67 Ibid., pp. 98-99.

Bolton, and Haywood, nine out of ten mills were still out on Wednesday. Eventually even these petered out and returned to work. A great opportunity had been missed, tragically mishandled by the Chartist leadership.

Following the strike, the delegates to the Convention reassembled in London on 26 August, but things seemed to have reached a total impasse, a dead-end. The Petition had been rejected and the general strike abandoned. This led to even further confusion and disarray, as morale visibly ebbed away. Feargus O'Connor's personal authority was deeply affected and the general authority of the Chartist leadership had been badly damaged. It would have been better to have fought, with determination and dignity, and gone down to defeat, rather than to have given in feebly, without a real fight. But defeat was not the inevitable outcome. "Suppose I was wrong," said O'Connor, "in your opinion, do you think that so old a friend should not be allowed a fault."[68] But this was less a "fault" and more a calamity.

As was to be expected, this retreat and confusion served to embolden the government. A number of arrests took place. Lord Broughton urged the judges to act quickly as "the object of the Chartists was to knock us on the head and rob us of our property".[69] In August alone, some 130 Chartist leaders were taken into custody, which included a number of Convention delegates, while others were committed for trial or released on bail. *The Northern Star* spoke of a "reign of terror", which summed up the situation. Chartists were dragged before the magistrates in large numbers, charged with conspiracy to incite people to arms, seditious conspiracy, unlawful assembly, or other such heinous crimes. Many who pleaded 'guilty' were bound over to keep the peace. Several hundred, however, were tried and imprisoned. This list included Vincent, Lovett, Collins, Brown, O'Connor, McDouall, Taylor, Richardson, O'Brien, Carrier, Neesom, and Deegan. Nevertheless, others were allowed out on bail and continued to address meetings and organise activities.

The arrests and resignations had weakened the Convention's numbers still further. This caused greater internal dissent within the leadership and, as a consequence, it was agreed narrowly to dissolve the Convention by twelve votes to eleven. All avenues had been tried and were now blocked.

Nevertheless, in many areas, notably in Wales, the mood was becoming increasingly desperate. There was also a growing level of violence. The arrest of the Reverend Stephens, who was touring the North, added to the bitterness

---

68 Ibid., p. 105.
69 D. Thompson, *The Chartists*, p. 78.

and anger against the authorities. A section of the Chartist leadership sought to put themselves at the head of this movement and looked to organise an uprising in different parts of the country. While O'Brien and Carpenter returned to journalism, O'Connor toured the country agitating, but Taylor, Frost, Burns, Cardo, and Bussey made plans for an armed insurrection. This attempt was to lead to the most famous Chartist event of all, the Newport Uprising of November 1839.

5. THE NEWPORT UPRISING

"Up in Nantyglo and Blackwood in Merthyr and Tredegar, the Scottish
Cattle would scotch a man by breaking his leg when he worked on
when the Union said strike. But the *Funeral of the Scab* was worse than
mutilation, for it spelt death of the soul: A Church of England service
for a non-conformist man. And after the service that man was dead
to the community."
– Alexander Cordell, *Song of the Earth*

"A more lawless set of men than the colliers do not exist… It requires
some courage to live amongst such a set of savages."
– Reginald Blewitt, Whig MP for Monmouth boroughs, 1839

"Do you intend to be freemen or slaves? … Be ready then to nourish
the tree of liberty, WITH THE BLOOD OF TYRANTS. You can get
nothing by cowardice, or petitioning."
– Handbill from May 1839

UNREST IN WALES

Following the strike, the Convention seemed to lose its relevance. With each
successive day, its authority drained away further. It managed to stagger on until
the middle of September 1839, when it finally dissolved. In confronting the
question of power, it seemed to have completely exhausted itself. With the failure
of the general strike, an increasing number of Chartists turned towards the idea
of insurrection, in which South Wales was destined to play a prominent part.

Throughout this period, the Principality of Wales had always been a hotbed
of social and political unrest. "The Welsh are a people almost as impulsive
as the Irish", noted R.C. Gammage.[1] The workers, who had emerged with

---

1 Quoted in R.C. Gammage, p. 68.

the new industries of coal and iron, had certainly acquired a very hard and militant outlook. The dangerous work in the pit and foundry bound the workers together ever more closely. This was combined with a dose of religious Nonconformist fervour, which gave the movement a combative and uncompromising character. Even Henry Vincent thought that Wales, for similar reasons, would make an excellent republic.

Most of the coal mines and iron works in South Wales were owned by the Crawshay brothers, Guest, Bailey and a few other rich families. During the 1830s, iron production in South Wales doubled to almost half-a-million tons a year, and coal output increased correspondingly to meet the rising demand. In the thirty years between 1801 and 1831, the population of Monmouthshire and Glamorgan doubled in number, a pattern replicated in many industrial towns. Working conditions were especially brutal, with punishing work discipline, petty fines deducted from wages, charges for tools, and the notorious truck or company shops that fleeced the workers. Towns like Merthyr were like 'frontier' settlements, filling up with migrant labour, with the workers forced to live in cramped, insanitary conditions. Since the government acted as the naked instrument of the powerful capitalist-masters, many strikes took on an extremely violent character. In June 1831, the epic Merthyr riots, caused by a series of injustices, shook the town.

As Ness Edwards, in his history of the South Wales miners, wrote:

> From 1800 to 1832 the miners of South Wales made many riotous protests against the oppression of their employers. In the summer of 1832, they even started a union, which, however, was ruthlessly suppressed by the employers. But this repression brought forth the secret organisation known as the 'Scotch Cattle,' which struck terror into the hearts of the employers and blackleg workmen.[2]

An eight-week lockout had forced the union underground. The word 'Scotch' refers to the verb, meaning to scotch or to stop. They were forced to fight fire with fire, with no holds barred. They adopted the figure of a red bull's head and horns as a terrifying symbol as they hunted down and dealt with "traitors, turn-coats and others" throughout the industrial valleys of South Wales. They blew up furnaces, beat up blacklegs and employed other acts of terror, similar to the Molly Maguires, who operated in Ireland and the coal fields of Pennsylvania.

The 'Scotch Cattle' were organised into 'herds' and, disguised in animal skins and wearing horns, confronted all scabs who dared oppose them. In

2   N. Edwards, *History of the South Wales Miners' Federation*, vol. 1, p. 1.

their struggle with blacklegs, they would name the culprits and issue them with a public warning:

"To all colliers, Traitors, Turncoats and others. We hereby warn you the second and last time. We are determined to draw the hearts out of all the men above-named, and fix two hearts upon the horns of the Bull; so that everyone may see what is the fate of every traitor – and we know them all. So, we testify with our blood."[3]

These were no idle threats and were taken very seriously by those who dared to betray their own class.

This struggle was brought to life in the novels of Alexander Cordell, especially *The Rape of the Fair Country*, *The Fire People* and *Song of the Earth*. Their activities included fighting against victimisations, strike-breaking, evictions, rack-renting and truck shop violations. This was accomplished using methods which struck terror into the hearts of employers, landlords, magistrates, clerics and those with no character. Their actions proved highly successful, and the authorities found this movement impossible to crush given the support it received from within the local communities. It was this battle-hardened proletariat that became the future revolutionary bedrock of Welsh Chartism.

The police forces in South Wales were few and far between, if not entirely non-existent in many areas, whereas the military was confined to barracks. This lack of government authority added to the region's wild appearance and lawlessness, born out of the hardship of rapid industrialisation. It was therefore fertile ground for Chartism, which was destined to make rapid progress in the valleys of South Wales. It was to provide the workers with hope, a symbol of resistance and something to fight for. It was estimated that in the industrial areas of Glamorganshire and Monmouthshire, as many as one in five people considered themselves staunch Chartists. As expected, Wales became dominated by the 'physical force' variety, just like the North of England. "These are the physical force, or spurious Chartists; who think a Revolution would be a good thing, because it would get rid of all the aforesaid grievances, by a grand explosion…" stated an anonymous correspondent in *The Welshman*.[4]

Armed drilling became a common occurrence, together with mass demonstrations and torchlit processions in the valley areas. In January 1839,

---

3   G.D.H. Cole & A.W. Filson, p. 260.

4   D. Black and C. Ford, *1839: The Chartist Insurrection*, p. 50.

a workhouse was burned down in Narberth, reflecting a growing hatred towards the New Poor Law. It was symptomatic of a rising militancy and class consciousness among the colliers and iron workers. Blackwood colliers had drawn the conclusion that "all other orders are living upon the labour of the so-called lower orders". And workers at the Garndiffaith Union lodge argued for the common ownership of industrial property, "as the Works do not belong to the present proprietors, but to the Workmen, and they would very shortly have them".[5] South Wales was rapidly becoming a cauldron of growing discontent and working-class radicalism.

In April 1839, following a visit by Henry Hetherington, police arrested a group of Chartists in Llanidloes, a flannel-weaving town. An angry crowd formed, which attacked the police and released the prisoners. As Edward Hamer relates:

> "Some of the women who joined the crowd kept instigating the men to attack the hotel – one old virago vowing that she would fight till she was knee-deep in blood, sooner than the Cockneys[6] should take their prisoners out of town. She, with others of her sex, gathered large heaps of stones, which they subsequently used in defacing and injuring the building which contained the prisoners."[7]

Using this incident as a pretext, the authorities flooded the area with troops, and further arrests were made. The leading Chartist Thomas Powell was sentenced to twelve months in prison on trumped-up evidence. A further three men were given sentences of between seven- and fifteen-years transportation for their part in the disturbances. Thirty other convictions were also secured. Local women were also active in this riot, after which three of them, Margaret Meredith, "single woman", Ann Williams, "servant", and Elizabeth Lucas, "widow", were given terms of six months' imprisonment. This was the beginning of a general crackdown. But this was simply like pouring petrol on the fire.

REBECCA RIOTS

In May of the same year, the first 'Rebecca Riots' broke out. Groups of workers, members of a secret society called the 'Hosts of Rebecca', with their faces blackened and dressed in women's clothes, attacked and destroyed the hated toll gates. These gates, established by landlords along roadways,

---

5   J. Charlton, *The Chartists*, pp. 22-23.

6   'Cockney' is used here as a slang term for people from London. In this case it refers to the London Metropolitan Police.

7   D. Thompson, *The Early Chartists*, p. 223.

extracted heavy duties on all goods permitted to pass and were a source of grave disaffection. 'Rebecca' and her daughters no doubt originated from a Biblical reference to Genesis 24:60, a verse which states that the seeds of Rebecca will inherit the gates of those that hate her. This shows how Nonconformism in Wales was intertwined with radicalism, and even terrorism.

The destruction of toll gates, which lasted until the end of 1844, symbolised a more general revolt against the heavy burden of rents, rates and tithes that bore down on the working population. The 'moral force' Chartists were alarmed by the effects of these terrorist actions on the Welsh Chartist movement. "It would be madness, nay it would be worse; it would be traitorism to the hallowed cause of Chartism to mix it up with the present [Rebecca] movement", said one.[8] But they were powerless to prevent this contagion. "The South Wales coalfield," said Home Secretary Viscount Melbourne, "is the most terrifying part of the kingdom."[9] Meanwhile, in 1834 the *Merthyr Guardian* declared that "from Dowlais to Abergavenny … THERE IS NO LAW".[10]

Local authorities sent regular reports to the Home Secretary about the disturbances and growing class hatred. In March, a Newport magistrate sent a report about the distribution of weapons in the area:

"The inquiries I have made only enable me to trace with certainty three distinct packages of guns and muskets, all of which appear to have arrived here from the neighbourhood of Birmingham… I understand that clubs have been recently established in this neighbourhood to which men contribute small periodical payments in order to obtain arms in their town, and I was informed sometime back that guns and muskets were purchased with eagerness at the neighbouring iron works. It is also within my knowledge that active efforts are making to incite the workmen employed at the Collieries to violence and to persuade them that in any course they may pursue they will not be opposed by the soldiers who would not act against them."

He continued:

"There has existed in this town for some months a Chartist Society – some of the members whereof make circuits periodically into the neighbouring villages and mining districts to obtain signatures to the Chartist petition and contribute to the national rent. The missionaries attend at public houses and beer shops where

8   D. Jones, p. 152.
9   J. Davies, *A History of Wales*, p. 376.
10 *Merthyr Guardian*, 14 June 1834.

a party, small or large as the case may be, has been assembled. The missionary expounds to them the grievances under which they labour, tells them that half their earnings are taken from them in taxes, that these taxes are spent in supporting the rulers in idleness and profligacy – that the great men around them possess property to which they are not entitled that these evils are to be cured by the Chartists, but that the people must sign the Chartist petition and contribute to the Chartist rent, that if their demands are not peaceably conceded they will be justified in resorting to force and that they need not fear bloodshed because the soldiers will not act and a letter is normally read to confirm the statement made with respect to the feelings of the soldiery."

He went on to conclude: "I am loath to believe that they will be hurried into actual insurrection… but I would urge strongly on the government the necessity for being fully prepared for an outbreak."[11]

Henry Vincent was chosen by the London Working Men's Association as their missionary to tour Monmouthshire in South Wales. A talented speaker and propagandist, he was destined to become the hero and mentor of the ironworkers and colliers of the area, a man who embodied their aspirations. Everywhere he went, he was received with enthusiasm, and dozens of solid proletarian Chartist cells were established as a result. As Gammage explained:

This impulsive people received Vincent with open arms. He was just the man to rouse all the keener emotions of the masses, whose condition was none of the best, and it was not long before a spark of ire ran from breast to breast, which threatened to ignite into an inextinguishable flame.[12]

This feeling can be seen from Vincent's report following a visit to Herefordshire:

"I then spoke to the people – simplified and explained to them the subject of government – told them of the Convention – and asked them if they approved of what we said, and if they would join with us – they shouted their assent, and swore they would fight for us if government attacked us. We had a most determined display of popular enthusiasm. When the meeting concluded the people cheered us to our inn… One thing I am now convinced of, that if we do not have an almost immediate political and social change, a bloody revolution must take place. The people will not starve much longer. Let their tyrant rulers beware!"[13]

11 D. Thompson, *The Early Chartists*, pp. 226-227.
12 R.C. Gammage, p. 69.
13 M. Chase, p. 66.

Vincent managed to unite the solid Nonconformist element with the adherents of the Scotch Cattle to form the Chartists of Monmouthshire. By the autumn of 1839, there were over 25,000 paid-up Chartists in the area, organised into 100 branches, which met regularly in public houses and hotels. In its embryonic stages, Chartism in Wales, as in many places, was dominated by moderate middle-class radicals, linked to the 'moral force' party. By the middle of 1839, this had changed dramatically with the entry of militant-minded workers from the coal and iron-working valleys of South Wales. Welsh Chartism became a very proletarian movement, which chimed with its 'physical force' tendency.

Apart from Henry Vincent, another key Chartist leader was John Frost, a Newport draper, who had been arrested for his radical views and had developed a considerable local following among the workers. Given his popularity, he had been elected to the town council, then appointed mayor of Newport, magistrate and justice of the peace. This gave him an air of respectability. But when Frost met Vincent during his visits to South Wales in 1838, he was won over completely to the Chartist cause. Soon, Frost was elected as a delegate to the National Convention, and later became its chairman, an honoured position. He was originally from the moderate persuasion, but, despite some misgivings, he ultimately placed himself at the head of the 'physical force' movement.

Both Frost and Vincent were accused by the authorities of using "violent and inflammatory language". As a result, Frost was forced to give up his position as a justice of the peace at the insistence of Lord John Russell, the Home Secretary. This radicalised Frost even further and he eventually joined John Taylor in his support for 'physical force' tactics.

In the meantime, Hetherington, another 'moral force' Chartist, was sent to Monmouth to give a report of the Convention. He urged that the local Chartists avoid "anything illegal". He received an enthusiastic response, but reported that many people were arming and drilling. He heard that an order for 300 muskets had been sent from Newtown to Birmingham, and also believed the 'physical force' men in the area could turn out 600 armed men when required.

Then a sudden twist occurred. Arising from the disturbances at Llanidloes, Henry Vincent was seized by the authorities and imprisoned at Monmouth in early May. He was offered bail with sureties set at £1,000, amounting to a staggering nineteen years' wages for a skilled worker. Being unable to raise such an astonishing amount, he was held by the authorities. Vincent's incarceration had an electrifying effect. It provided a catalyst, which inflamed everyone and intensified hatred against the authorities. It also served to reinforce the idea that nothing would be gained from the 'Reformed Parliament' of landlords and capitalists. It added to the boiling anger. Some 30,000 workers demonstrated in Blackwood, demanding Vincent's release. Things became more intense following the harsh sentences handed out to the accused at Llanidloes. Again, news of further arrests of Chartist leaders, including the radical Reverend Stephens, added to the flames. "But these prosecutions nowhere excited such bitterness of feeling as in Wales", commented Max Beer.[14]

In the build-up to the proposed 'Sacred Month' on 12 August, vast meetings were being held in South Wales, with some 30,000 alone turning out at Dukestown, a reflection of the growing militancy. A concatenation of events: the rejection of the Charter in July, the rioting in Birmingham, Vincent's arrest, the sentences at Llanidloes, the abandonment of the August general strike, and the collapse of the Convention, all combined to exasperate the already fierce class war in the South Wales valleys. Chartist military preparations reached fever pitch. Drilling and the rehearsal of tactics took place under the cover of darkness. The clandestine traditions of the Scotch Cattle were ever-present.

It has been stated many times that the masses enter onto the road of revolution, not armed with a fully worked-out programme for social reconstruction, but with a profound feeling that they can no longer tolerate the situation or its impositions. Patience was at breaking point, which was certainly a common feature, especially in South Wales.

PLANS FOR INSURRECTION

While the masses may not have a conscious plan to change society, a revolutionary leadership certainly needed one. Following the rejection of the Charter, John Frost, together with Julian Harney, Peter Bussey and John Taylor decided to take matters into their own hands. The overwhelming response to his speeches in Cardiff and Merthyr had convinced Frost of the tremendous support for Chartism and, so he reckoned, if the workers did rise up, the army would refuse to open fire. Therefore, he joined the other Chartist leaders – Taylor, Bussey, Cardo, Burns, and Lowery – in a clandestine plan to promote a general insurrection in Yorkshire, Lancashire, Birmingham, Sheffield and South Wales, the details of which still remained hazy. Peter Bussey, on his return to Bradford, called a meeting for 30 September, in

---

14 M. Beer, p. 93.

which, according to Lovett, the delegates were told of plans for an uprising in Wales. They too decided to join the rebellion in the North of England, with a date set for 3 November. There had been some talk of a 'Secret Committee of War' in the summer of 1839.

To help organise an uprising, the Polish exile, Beniowski, a member of the London Democratic Association, was sent to Wales as a military instructor. Other non-commissioned officers were chosen in certain Northern and Midlands towns to assist in drilling and other preparations. On account of government spies, the organisation was, of course, kept secret, along the lines of the United Irishmen. According to the plan, the country was divided into districts, then into groups of ten, 100, and 1,000 men with their own captains. When William Cardo was arrested in November, some of these plans were discovered, but much remained shrouded in mystery, given their covert nature. There were reports from spies to the Home Office that an armed uprising was being planned, but such reports cannot be taken as gospel. While other Chartist leaders testified secret plans existed, this was also denied. What remains a fact is that the South Wales valleys were in a state of near-insurrection. Pike-making and drilling became extensive, while the authorities did not have the forces on the ground to prevent such activities. Certainly, pikes and possibly other weapons were secretly made and stockpiled in local caves at Llyn y Garn Fawr in the Brecon Beacons during the summer of 1839.

Dr. William Price, who assumed the leadership of the Pontypridd Chartists and had travelled to Staffordshire in September to procure arms, told his followers in a valiant speech:

"We have tolerated the tyranny of those who oppose us – landlords, coal owners and the clergy – too long. We must strike with all our might and power, and strike immediately. The time for hesitating is past and the day of reckoning is at hand. Let all cowards go their way, for they have no part to play in the great struggles. Men of the valleys, remember that the principle behind Chartism is the principle which acknowledges the right of every man who toils to the fruits of his labour. The points embodied in the Charter are our immediate demands, but ultimately, we shall demand more. Oppression, injustice and the grinding poverty which burdens our lives must be abolished for all time... We are the descendants of valiant Welshmen and we must be worthy of the traditions which they have passed on to us. It is far better that we should die fighting for freedom, than live as slaves of greed and opulent wealth..."[15]

---

15 D. Black and C. Ford, p. 120.

Central to the preparations for the South Wales rising was the plan to free Henry Vincent by use of force. Frost felt he had no alternative but to put himself at the head of this movement. Apparently, he tried to convince workers that the rising was premature, but his fears were brushed aside. He instead argued for a mass demonstration, but the majority rejected the idea in favour of an armed assault. He then attended a meeting in Nantyglo, where Zephaniah Williams was present, a man who was to play a leading role. The Chartist lodges in Monmouth were now meeting on an almost daily basis, in public and private, and a sizable network of local leaders was being put together. According to a report in *The Charter*, 17 November 1839, carried two weeks after the rising, a local Chartist had a meeting with another Chartist, Jenkin Morgan, at Newport:

> "He told me that I should be in danger if I did not join them, but that if I joined them, I should be in no danger, because Frost's men would attack the soldiers. Upon that I went with him and several other men to the outskirts of the town. He told me that there was powder at Crossfield's warehouse, and I said it used to be kept at Pill, but we found no powder. He also told me that there was to be a rising through the whole kingdom on the same night, and the same hour, and that the Charter would be the law of the land..."[16]

The South Wales men were determined to go through with it to the end. According to David Davies, a veteran of Waterloo who commanded three Chartist brigades, one of which was the Abersychan:

> "The Abersychan Lodge is 1,600 strong; 1,200 of them are old soldiers; the remaining 400 have never handled arms, but we can turn them into fighting men in no time. I have been sent here to tell you that we shall not rise until you give us a list of those we are to remove – to kill. I know what the English army is, and I know how to fight them, and the only way to succeed is to attack and remove those who command them – the officers and those who administer the law. We must be led as the children of Israel were led from Egypt through the Red Sea."[17]

Time was rapidly running out. On Sunday 27 October, Frost informed Dr. Price that the rising was to take place the following Sunday. Frost was very agitated, given the colossal pressure he was under, but there was now no turning back. Peter Bussey, who was having cold feet, sent a message to Frost asking for the uprising to be postponed, but to no avail. "I might as well

---

16 Quoted in P. Hollis, p. 244.
17 Quoted in D. Black and C. Ford, p. 122.

blow my brains out as to try and oppose them or shrink back", stated Frost.[18] The only person with enough prestige who could have possibly curbed the Welsh insurrectionists, or led them, was Feargus O'Connor, but he had left for Ireland in October. On his return to England, the attempted insurrection had already taken place and its leaders were in prison.

According to William Lovett, O'Connor, who he hated, gave encouragement to the insurrection:

> "[Frost was informed that] if the Welsh effect a rising in favour of Vincent, the people of Yorkshire and Lancashire... were ready to join in a rising for the Charter... In anticipation of this rising in the North a person delegated from one of the towns to go to Feargus O'Connor, to request that he lead them on, as he had so often declared he would...
>
> *Delegate* – Mr O'Connor, we are going to have a rising for the Charter, in Yorkshire, and I am sent from ... to ask if you will lead us on, as you have often said you would when we were prepared.
>
> *Feargus* – Well, when is this rising to take place?
>
> *Delegate* – Why, we have resolved that it shall begin on Saturday next.
>
> *Feargus* – Are you all well provided with arms, then?
>
> *Delegate* – Yes, all of us.
>
> *Feargus* – Well, that is all right, my man.
>
> *Delegate* – Now, Mr O'Connor, shall I tell our lads that you will come and lead them on?
>
> *Feargus* now indignantly replied, 'Why, man! when did you ever hear of me, or any one of my family, ever deserting the cause of the people? Have they not always been found at their post in the hour of danger?' In this bouncing manner did Feargus induce the poor fellow to believe that he was ready to head the people; and he went back and made his report accordingly."[19]

Lovett, who had a profound dislike of O'Connor, claimed that O'Connor had gone back on his promise and put out messages that no risings were to take place, then abruptly left for Ireland. We will never know exactly what happened. All we do know is that O'Connor returned to Liverpool on 3 November, the day of the Newport Uprising, but only found out what had happened a few days later.

Towards the end of October, after a huge growth in Chartist numbers, John Frost, William Jones, and Zephaniah Williams had finally decided on an

---

18 Quoted in Ibid., p. 133.

19 R. Brown and C. Daniels, pp. 62-63.

armed attack on 3 November, hoping to capture Newport. The attacking force was composed of three contingents, which would then march on Monmouth to release Vincent. Newport was a convergence town that served the collieries and ironworks, and was therefore of strategic importance. This was most certainly part of a much wider plan, with uprisings planned in different areas of the country, particularly in Lancashire and West Yorkshire. The forces that they were assembling were viewed as part of a massive workers' army that would spearhead a national Chartist uprising. Tens of thousands had already gathered at Dukestown, an indication of the movement's growing support. In the face of this show of strength, Frost had convinced himself that government troops would surrender without a fight. Frost's role in all this was regarded as pivotal, as he was not simply a local leader, but chairman of the National Chartist Convention and therefore respected by all sections of the movement.

As *The Charter* newspaper stated afterwards:

"The ultimate design of the leaders does not appear, but it probably was to rear the standard of rebellion throughout Wales, in hopes of being able to hold the royal forces at bay, in that mountainous district, until the people of England, assured by successes, should rise, *en masse*, for the same objects."[20]

This view was confirmed by Bronterre O'Brien two years later, when he asserted that the 'men of the North' definitely encouraged the Newport rising:

"Frost never intended that there should be an outbreak, but he had been led to expect that in case he was forced to anything of that kind, he should have the sympathy and support of other parts of the country, and the parties who made him believe this were those who sacrificed him."[21]

The Chartist forces were formed into three armed columns, made up of around 20,000 to 30,000 colliers and ironworkers. It was at this time that the young George Shell left his lodgings in Pontypridd to join his contingent and sent a final message to his parents. The columns were further split up into brigades, companies and units, and the men were armed with guns, muskets, pistols, coal mandrills and clubs. They sang songs as they marched over the mountain to Newport:

Then rise, my boys, and fight the foe,
Your arms are true and reason.

---

20 17 November 1839, in P. Hollis, pp. 243-4.

21 *Manchester and Salford Advertiser*, 11 December 1841, quoted in A. Briggs, *Chartist Studies*, pp. 49-50.

We'll let the Whigs and Tories know
That union is not treason.

Ye lords, oppose us if you can,
Your own doom you seek after,
With or without you will stand
Until we gain the Charter.[22]

NEWPORT DEFEAT

The original plan was for a surprise night-time attack. However, faced with worsening weather conditions, the going got tough and the time line changed. Despite these delays, the columns marched in military formation overnight, thousands strong, from Nantyglo, Pontypool, Blackwood, Newbridge and Risca. However, they did not reach Newport until the following morning, 4 November. The authorities had been informed of what was happening and acted accordingly, reinforcing the town with police, special constables and troops from the 45th Infantry Regiment. The unreliable 29th Foot Regiment had been withdrawn and replaced with more reliable, tried-and-tested infantry, which had put down a revolt in cold blood the previous year. The authorities had rounded up local Chartists and held them at the Westgate Hotel in the centre of the town.

The insurgents were informed about the prisoners held at Westgate. Unfortunately, rather than wait for reinforcements, they headed straight for the hotel, anxious to free their comrades. Other contingents were advancing on Newport, and thousands more were still stationed in the surrounding areas. In the end, the early Chartist insurgents crowded around the hotel at around 9 o'clock in the morning, facing about forty government troops who were waiting within. Apparently, the Riot Act was read. Then the troops opened fire, with several volleys, after claiming they had been fired upon. A special constable, who remained inside the Westgate Hotel, wrote:

> "There was a dreadful scene, dreadful beyond expression – the groans of the dying, the shrieks of the wounded, the pallid, ghostly countenances and the bloodshot eyes of the dead, in addition to the shattered windows and passageways ankle-deep in gore."[23]

Without cover, the Chartist insurgents had been dangerously exposed. In the end, faced with several rounds of firing, the crowd scattered and fled.

---

22 M. Beer, p. 97.
23 M. Chase, p. 116.

There were officially twenty dead, some fifty seriously wounded, and many more injured. There were other deaths that were never officially recorded, possibly a further ten, harboured by families and friends. The young George Shell, forcing his way into the Westgate Hotel, was shot several times. Badly wounded, he suffered in great pain for three hours before he finally died. His body was later taken by the authorities, together with the other corpses, and buried under the cover of night in an unmarked grave in the cemetery of St Woolos Cathedral in Newport. The loss of life was higher than at Peterloo twenty years earlier. The leaders of the rising, disorientated by the initial losses, staged a disorderly retreat, pursued by troops. When the musket smoke cleared, and the dead lay all about the ground, it was clear the attack had been defeated.

Thousands of insurrectionists were still stationed in surrounding hillsides and villages. However, the orders to advance never came. Skirmishes lasted for several days afterwards, as more troops were sent to secure the town. Order was restored at the point of a bayonet, under the stewardship of the town mayor. The Newport massacre put an end to the Chartist insurrection in South Wales, although the authorities still believed further attacks were imminent. It also put paid to the idea of a national insurrection. There were rumours circulating that Yorkshire and Lancashire were to rise by the end of the month, which forced Napier to head for Bradford. Certainly, military preparations had taken place. Taylor himself proclaimed to have 900 well-armed men ready for action. There were growing fears among the magistrates of an 'English Newport'. In January 1840, it was reported that the Chartists in the county of Leicestershire were preparing a rising, together with others in the North. This prompted the Leicester magistrates to request that the Home Office arm the special constables. The *Manchester Guardian*, hardly an unbiased source, declared at that time that "a rather extensive conspiracy" had existed, but that "the numbers and means of the conspirators" had been "in most cases as contemptible as their plans were wild and extravagant".[24]

The leaders of the Newport uprising certainly held wider ambitions. Zephaniah Williams had the idea of setting up a British Republic, while others believed in establishing a Chartist Executive Government of England, with Frost as its president. The defeated insurrectionists now found themselves isolated. The Chartists in the north of the country – due to a lack of serious preparation – failed to respond. It is true that revolts later broke out in Sheffield, Dewsbury and Bradford, but these were short lived and

24 Quoted in A. Briggs, *Chartist Studies*, p. 49.

easily suppressed. Rather than giving support to an uprising, *The Northern Star* published an editorial denouncing all insurrectionary plots and called on everyone to "beware of damaging the cause of Frost and his associates... by any outbreak of physical violence".[25] While conspiracies abounded, this put a stop to all insurrectionary plans, at least for the time being.

Many of the South Wales Chartist leaders involved in the uprising were hidden by communities or managed to escape abroad. Posters appeared everywhere with a reward of £100, a considerable sum, being offered for the arrest of John Frost, Zephaniah Williams and William Jones. Eventually, Frost was found near his home, attempting to say farewell to his family. Jones was also arrested, brandishing a pistol, in woodlands near Ebbw Vale. In his pocket was discovered a pamphlet celebrating the Llanidloes rioters. Williams himself was discovered on a ship bound for Portugal. In total, 125 men and women were seized and presented for trial. Sixteen prisoners were indicted for high treason, while twenty-four faced lesser charges of sedition, conspiracy and riotous assembly. The Newport trial was one of the last mass treason trials in British history.

During the nine-day trial, a vile campaign of slander was undertaken by the capitalist press, led by *The Times*, especially against the families of the accused. A Special Commission of judges ruled over the two-week-long proceedings, after which, surrounded by soldiers, Frost, Williams, Jones and five others were found guilty. In sentencing the men, the learned judges placed the black caps of death on their heads. The Chief Justice addressed the eight prisoners, stating they "were to be taken to the place from whence they came, and from thence to the place of execution, there to be hanged by the neck until they were dead – afterwards, their heads should be severed from their bodies, their bodies quartered, and disposed of as Her Majesty should think fit". He then concluded by asking the Lord to have mercy on their souls.[26]

These courageous Chartists of Wales stood their ground and refused to flinch. As they left the courtroom in Monmouth following the sentencing, Williams defiantly shouted to the crowd, "Three cheers for the Charter!" Apart from the death sentences, others were given various prison sentences or bound over for good behaviour. Amy Meredith, the wife of a collier, was arrested and charged alongside her husband with stealing a gun to be used in Newport. Henry Vincent's newspaper, *The Western Vindicator*, was closed down, the last issue of the paper urging all Chartists to do everything to save

25 M. Chase, p. 135.
26 R.C. Gammage, p. 169.

Frost and his comrades from the gallows. As a result, defence committees were established everywhere. In Aberdeen, the news of the death sentences arrived on the Sunday. By the next morning, a petition had been organised that had gained 15,000 signatures before its dispatch to London at 3 o'clock on the Wednesday afternoon. By the end of 1840, many were still serving prison terms in Monmouth gaol, the same place where Vincent was held.

The Newport massacre and the threat of executions, rather than leading to demoralisation and despair, served to intensify the angry mood. Astonishingly, there was increased talk of revenge and insurrection. O'Connor, reflecting the bitterness of the moment, boasted that should Frost and his companions be convicted, and their lives placed at risk, he would "place himself at the head of the English people and carry through a bloody revolution to save Frost".[27] The days in the run-up to the announcement of the sentences imposed on the Welsh Chartists were the most dangerous. "The days between the verdict of 'guilty' on Frost, pronounced on 9 January, and the calling of the three men for sentence were some of the tensest in the whole period", wrote Dorothy Thompson.[28] It was at a time when there were numerous secret negotiations taking place in the North, especially at Dewsbury in West Yorkshire. Men in the area were expecting to stage their own uprising either during or after the trial of Frost, Williams and Jones. The Sheffield Rising took place on the night of 11-12 January, three days after the end of the trial, and similarly at Dewsbury, but these soon fizzled out. Samuel Holberry and Robert Peddie were sentenced to two years imprisonment, along with others, for their parts in the attempted uprisings.

The government became aware of the grave situation, and although vengeful local magistrates demanded the severest of measures against the Welsh leaders, there were those who urged caution for fear of turning the men into martyrs. It became increasingly clear that executions, together with the mutilation of the condemned men, could easily inflame the situation, resulting in further social unrest. As Lt. Colonel Pringle Taylor wrote to the Marquis of Anglesey on 27 January 1840:

> "I cannot however but confess my alarm at the position in which the Government and the country may possibly be placed, if, through the event of Mr Frost's execution, the sympathy of the Chartists was to be re-excited…"[29]

---

27 D. Black and C. Ford, p. 178.
28 *The Early Chartists*, p. 249.
29 Quoted in R. Brown and C. Daniels, p. 54.

SENTENCES COMMUTED

An enormous public outcry served to change certain minds at the top of government. On 1 February, the Cabinet discussed the question and cooler heads prevailed. The men were saved from the gallows, and their death sentences commuted to transportation for life. This proved a wise decision for the ruling class under the circumstances. The mood in the country was an angry one, with talk of sedition and plans to rescue the men. Had the executions taken place, who knows what would have happened? Napier noted that the decision was politically astute, and prevented increased bitterness and strife. "The moment any Chartist is convicted, whether it be Frost or any other," wrote Napier, "this warfare is to begin and all labour instantly to cease…" He added: "It would not stop Chartism if they were all hanged… Chartism cannot be stopped…"[30]

Lord Broughton recalled in his diary that when the cabinet heard the news about a recommendation for mercy, they were initially unanimous in their opposition to leniency. They believed the men should all be hanged. However, in a further meeting, Lord Normandy reported that Chief Justice Tindal had told him that:

> "[I]t would be advisable for the government to consider whether under all the circumstances the lives of the criminals might not be spared. This opinion produced a great effect, and even Lord Melbourne confessed that it would be difficult to execute the men after such a hint…"[31]

For them, the choice between transportation and hanging was a tactical question, nothing more. It had nothing to do with morality or sentiment.

This decision to grant leniency stands in marked contrast to the decision seventy-five years later when the 1916 Easter Rising in Dublin was put down in cold blood and its leaders executed, including the wounded James Connolly. Too injured to stand, he was strapped to a chair and shot. This eventually led to a bloody guerrilla war and the partition of Ireland. Nevertheless, whatever their thoughts, the decisions of the ruling class are always based on a cool, ruthless calculation, and certainly had nothing to do with pity. William Gladstone, a Tory, who originally opposed the 1832 Reform Act and defended the slave trade, now favoured flexibility, and was to comment later: "Please to recollect that we have to govern millions of hard hands: that it must be done by force, fraud or goodwill…"[32]

---

30 P. Hollis, Class and *Class Conflict in Nineteenth Century England: 1815-1850*, p. 233.
31 Quoted in D. Thompson, *The Chartists*, p. 82.
32 Quoted in J. Saville, *The British state and the Chartist Movement*, p. 223.

However, there is always a sting in the tail. On reaching Port Arthur in Van Diemen's Land (modern-day Tasmania), John Frost was immediately sentenced to two years' hard labour for making a disparaging remark about Lord John Russell, the Home Secretary. After serving sixteen years in the penal colonies and following a campaign, Frost and his comrades were eventually granted pardons in 1854. Williams and Jones would remain in Tasmania, while Frost returned to Britain.

The Newport rising was over in a relatively short period of time, but this is in the nature of insurrections, which are normally not drawn-out affairs, but decided one way or the other very quickly. The deliberate attempt to downplay the rising must not be allowed to minimise this truly historic event. To begin with, the Newport rising was the greatest armed clash between government forces and the British people in the whole of the nineteenth century. Newport was clearly a proletarian uprising of, in the main, colliers and iron workers, with some 30,000 workers on the move, behind whom stood a mass movement of hundreds of thousands. Given the secrecy surrounding the rising, nothing was committed to writing. However, there is enough evidence to show that the intention was to take other towns, including Cardiff, Abergavenny, Brecon and Monmouth. Given the total numbers on the march, this would have been entirely feasible. If successful, this would have been a beacon to Chartists in other parts of the country and would have posed an extremely serious threat to the government.

The fact remains that the uprising went down to defeat. The reasons might be many, but as the enigmatic William Blake explained: "Hindsight is a wonderful thing, but foresight is better". Engels, who related a point raised by Harney a few years later, thought that "Frost's plan being betrayed, he was obliged to open hostilities prematurely. Those in the North heard of the failure of his attempt in time to withdraw."[33] This is of course difficult to prove. However, whatever the weaknesses in terms of poor communication, indecision, and delays, the Newport rising must be seen as the first generalised insurrection of the new industrial proletariat. It certainly reflected the insurrectionary mood of the times, and not only in South Wales.

Although defeated, defiance remained, even in Newport, where in May 1841, it was reported that flowers were left at the unmarked graveside of the victims.

---

33 F. Engels, *The Condition of the Working Class in England*, MECW, vol. 4, p. 518.

"Sunday week, being Palm Sunday, the graves in our churchyard were decorated with flowers and evergreens. The most conspicuous were those in which the men who were shot in the late Chartist riots were buried; and at the head of each grave were placarded the following lines written on a large sheet of paper.

"Here lie the valiant and the brave,
That fought a nation's right to save;
They tried to set the captives free
But fell a prey to tyranny!

"Yet they shall never be forgot,
Though in the grave their bodies rot;
The Charter shall our watchword be
Come death or glorious liberty!"[34]

The death in particular of seventeen-year-old George Shell captured the popular imagination. His sacrifice was immortalised in verse:

"All foes are conquered when we conquer fear,
As did bold Shell, who braved the bloody bier.
To gain his rights he took the manliest course –
The plain straightforward argument of force!
Vengeance is now our cry. Remember Shell!
We'll live like him – at least we'll die as well."[35]

ARRESTS CONTINUE

The leniency displayed towards John Frost should not disguise the fact that the government was still proceeding to take firm measures against the Chartist movement. It was a case of stick and carrot, but clearly more stick. The Chartist Convention issued a *Manifesto*, which stated in no uncertain terms: "The mask of *constitutional liberty* is thrown aside, and the form of despotism stands hideously before us..."[36] Between April 1839 and June 1840, 380 Chartist leaders in England and sixty-two in Wales were arrested and sentenced to terms of imprisonment from three months to transportation for life. The vast majority of these were industrial workers involved in textiles, iron and coal mining. On 3 August 1839, four Chartists who had been involved in the Birmingham riots a month earlier were taken for trial at the Warwick assizes. Again, they were condemned to death, but their sentences

---

34 D. Thompson, *The Chartists*, pp. 86-87.
35 M. Chase, p. 120.
36 D. Thompson, *The Chartists*, p. 83.

were reduced to transportation for life. Lovett and Collins also stood trial, the former carrying out his own defence. They argued that the people had the *right* to assembly and free discussion. However, they were each sentenced to twelve months imprisonment. Stephens and McDouall were tried at the Chester assizes.

McDouall, who was accused of street fighting and incitement to procure arms, conducted an admirable defence of Chartism lasting five hours. He was found guilty and sentenced to twelve months' imprisonment. Messrs. Thompson, gun manufacturers of Birmingham, together with Mitchell and Davies of Stockport, and Higgins of Ashton, were indicted for sedition, attending illegal meetings, disturbing the peace, and unlawful possession of arms. They were found guilty and sentenced to eighteen months. John Holmes was found guilty of walking at the head of a procession with a Red Cap of Liberty on a pole. Edward Riley was convicted of military training and riot near Manchester. T. Radcliffe was indicted for seditious conspiracy and riot near Wigan and found guilty. J. Fairplay was tried for illegal training, and was convicted. Some twenty or thirty others were put on trial, found guilty of similar offences and sentenced to varying terms of imprisonment.

Throughout these Chartist trials was heard the simple language of ordinary workers, devoid of legal terminology, who provided a vivid description of the distressing conditions experienced by the working class. One of those accused, George Lloyd, a carpenter, described the sufferings of working people in front of a jury in Liverpool, who, on hearing their plight, were moved to tears. Other trials took place in March and April 1840, in which O'Connor was sentenced to eighteen months imprisonment in York Castle for conspiracy. Bronterre O'Brien received the same sentence. The veteran William Benbow, after conducting a ten-and-a-half-hour defence, was found guilty and sentenced to sixteen months in prison, having already served eight months awaiting trial. The twenty-five-year-old Samuel Holberry, who tried to seize Nottingham, received four years imprisonment. Two years later, after suffering horrible hardship, he died alone in his prison cell. His wife, Mary, was also arrested, but later released. She gave birth to a baby boy, who died while Samuel was still in prison. These examples provide a glimpse of the brutal hardships that the Chartists endured, real heroes who made colossal sacrifices for their cause.

Samuel Holberry's funeral in Sheffield attracted 20,000 workers according to the local paper, but *The Northern Star* estimated 50,000, which formed a massive procession to the cemetery at Attercliffe where he was laid to rest.

There were many bands and banners on the solemn procession. On the name-plate attached to his coffin was inscribed the words, "Samuel Holberry, died a martyr to the cause of Democracy, 21 June 1842, aged 27".

Standing at the graveside, Julian Harney delivered the oration:

"Our task is not to weep… our task is to act; to labour with heart and soul for the destruction of the horrible system under which Holberry has perished… Swear as I now swear, that neither persecution, nor scorn, nor calumny; neither bolts nor bars, nor chains, nor racks, nor gibbets; neither the tortures of a prison death-bed, nor the terrors of the scaffold, shall sever us from our principles, affright us from our duty, or cause us to leave the onward path of freedom; but that come weal, come woe, we swear, with hearts uplifted to the Throne of Eternal Justice, to have retribution for the death of Holberry; swear to have our Charter law, and to annihilate forever the blood-stained despotism which has slain its thousands of martyrs, and tens of thousands of patriots, and immolated at its shrine the lovers of liberty and truth."[37]

Those who were imprisoned experienced horrendous conditions and a miserable diet. At Beverley prison, Robert Peddie's punishment involved spending six weeks in complete silence, working a treadmill, in the full view of spectators outside the prison, which then became three months of stone-breaking. Prisoners sentenced to hard labour walked the treadmill for at least six hours a day. Certain prisons used the treadmills to power water pumps and grind corn. At Chester Castle, the Chartist prisoners were kept below ground level, where water ran down the walls. Those not sentenced to hard labour were forced to work for their meals, usually four-hour stints on the treadmill. Special relief funds were established by the Chartists to alleviate the plight of those incarcerated and their families. O'Connor himself gave a proportion of the profits from *The Northern Star* to those imprisoned. Of course, those transported to Australia faced even more atrocious conditions, beatings and barbaric work. Quite a number were not able to endure the long arduous sea journey and perished before their arrival.

In the aftermath of the Newport rising, John Taylor withdrew from the movement altogether and died shortly afterwards. Peter Bussey left for America. Many others abandoned hope and emigrated. At the same time, Thomas Phillips, the Mayor of Newport, was presented with a purse of 2,000 gold sovereigns, made a freeman of the City of London, and then knighted for bravery by Queen Victoria. The ruling class always reward their own

---

37 Quoted in R.C. Gammage, p. 216.

and those who bend the knee. Meanwhile, the authorities took measures to close down the Chartist press, starting with Henry Vincent's paper. As a result, between 1839 and 1840, the following papers ceased publication: *True Scotsman, Operative, Charter, Champion, Southern Star, London Despatch, Western Vindicator,* and the *Northern Liberator.* In their place emerged two weeklies, *The Scottish Chartist Circular* and *English Chartist Circular.* In 1842, the weekly *British Statesman* appeared.

"The Chartists swear they will not let the ball drop", wrote General Charles Napier in his diary. "I believe them, but they must show more pluck to make anything of it; they seem to have shown none at Newport, and nine or ten have been killed."[38]

The defeat of the Newport rising certainly represented a setback for the movement nationally. It emerged out of the need to break out of the impasse, especially with the failure of the general strike. After all, was the Chartist slogan not 'peaceably if we may, forcibly if we must'? With the peaceful road blocked, the question of force came very much to the fore.

As far as official histories were concerned, the sooner the rising was forgotten, the better. H.W. Dulcken's history, *A Picture History of England…Written for the Use of the Young* (1866), gave the Newport rising one brief sentence: "It was quickly suppressed, and the Chartist leaders, who, in other times, would undoubtedly have been hanged, were transported beyond the seas."[39] Elsewhere, it did not even merit a mention. Others simply wrote it off as a petty misadventure, nothing more. Margaret Cole termed it "the pitiful little insurrection".[40] The present Newport City Council website records the views of Chris Williams, Professor of History at Cardiff University: "The Battle of the Westgate was a bloody and not especially brief struggle, but it clearly resulted in the defeat and confusion of the Chartists and discredited the physical force strategy." But this judgement of Newport discrediting 'physical force' is wide of the mark, as we shall see. In fact, it was the 'moral force' that came out discredited.

What is true is that, with the defeat in Newport, the leadership arrested, and the movement in disarray, what could be described as the first phase of Chartism had come to an end.

---

38 D. Jones, p. 157.
39 J. Saville, p. 203.
40 M. Cole, *Makers of the Labour Movement,* p. 95.

6. THE FIRST EVER WORKING-CLASS PARTY

"Plunder is the object. Plunder is likewise the means."
— Duke of Wellington on Chartism

"My time has been occupied with odious business arising from the mad insurrection of the working classes…"
— Robert Peel

"I protest against the insolence of those who dare to lecture the working classes on their 'immorality' while they themselves live by the most immoral system that this earth was ever afflicted with--a system which bases the wealth, luxuries and pleasures of the few, upon the poverty, crime and misery of the many."
— Julian Harney

LAUNCHING THE WORKERS' PARTY

It is often said that defeated armies learn well. The events of 1838-39 were certainly a watershed for the Chartist movement. Despite all the threats of a general strike, an armed insurrection and mass protests, Parliament still refused to budge over the Charter. It was clear from the intense repression and the arrest of leading Chartists that the intention of the government was to behead the Chartist movement. The more middle-class layers had already deserted the cause. This situation, therefore, led to a rethink about the future strategy and tactics of Chartism, especially among the tops of the movement, many of whom were languishing in prison. It was therefore a critical time, a time to digest the experiences and draw some vital lessons. Would Chartism survive such wholesale persecutions? What was to be done next? It was necessary to face up to some hard facts and make some difficult decisions.

The leadership was also forced to reconsider the very structure of the Chartist movement. The organisation had certainly been plagued by weaknesses. A loose-knit organisation, both locally and nationally, was totally unsuitable for unified national action. The task of a reorganisation and the creation of a centralised party therefore became a burning question. "Centralisation and organisation are the weapons of the government," said McDouall, "and until you can successfully imitate their tactics, you never can reduce their power."[1]

The onset of an economic slump and growing distress once again gave an impetus to Chartism. It became urgent to put the movement on a much sounder footing. Therefore, a conference to consider the question of reorganisation was called in Manchester on 20 July 1840, composed of twenty-three delegates from the Midlands and the North of England. Different plans were drawn up and put forward by a number of Chartists, including O'Connor, O'Brien, Burns, McDouall and William Benbow. O'Connor was in favour of strengthening the Chartist press, and in particular turning *The Northern Star* into a daily morning paper, but few shared his conviction. Bronterre O'Brien favoured the formation of an electoral machine, which would attempt to make a breakthrough on the parliamentary front. McDouall argued for the Chartist movement to organise amongst the different trade unions, so as to strengthen its roots in the organised working class. Lovett and Collins, on the other hand, drew up plans to convert Chartism into an educational association that would publish tracts, set up libraries, and train teachers. Lastly, Benbow's plans were considered unsuitable and not made public.

In a sideswipe at the movement's 'physical force' members, Lovett and Collins issued a circular to the Chartist rank and file complaining amongst other things that:

> "[O]ur public meetings have on many occasions been the arenas of passionate invective, party spirit, and personal idolatry, rather than public assemblies for deliberation and discussion, dissemination of knowledge, and inculcation of principles. We need political power to enable us to improve to any extent our material condition, but we need also sobriety and moral culture."[2]

This immediately provoked O'Connor, who launched a frontal attack on their proposals, accusing them of being part of a middle-class scheme for

---

1 D. Jones, p. 60.
2 M. Beer, p. 110.

destroying Chartism. He also denounced a plan by Henry Vincent, who wanted all Chartists to become teetotallers. As one Chartist humorously quipped, the Charter does not lie "at the bottom of a glass of water".[3] Furthermore, O'Connor went on to disparage the idea of Christian Chartist Churches, most of which had been established in Scotland.

Finally, after five days of heated deliberations, on 24 July, an agreement was reached to transform the Chartist movement root and branch. It proposed to amalgamate the Chartist groups into a single national political party, modelled on some of the trade unions. This change would mark a qualitative leap forward and served to establish the first ever working-class party in history, which became known as the *National Charter Association of Great Britain* (NCA).

This decision represented a decisive move in the direction of the independent political representation of the British working class. It was a forerunner of the great working-class parties of the future. The landlords, bankers and capitalists had their own political parties, the Whigs and Tories, which represented their class interests. It was therefore time for the working class to establish its own political party that would represent its specific class interests. It was a revolutionary idea for its time and showed a leap forward in the political understanding of the working class. The founding of such a party – in effect, what can only be described as a revolutionary party – to fight for working people had never been envisaged before. There had been societies and clubs, even revolutionary underground organisations, but never before an open political workers' party operating on a national scale.

The proletarian character of the Chartist movement was further confirmed by the formation of such a party. "Our movement is a labour movement, originated in first instance by the fustian jackets, the blistered hands and the unshorn chins", stated Feargus O'Connor. He was absolutely correct in this. This reorganisation, as expected, greatly shocked the ruling class, who saw it as a direct threat to their system of property, power and prestige. Rather than sever the head from the Chartist movement, as intended, they were witnessing its rebirth on a higher level.

The formation of the National Charter Association meant the end of parochial formations with all their limitations. The National Association meant a national party, with its own national rules, national structures and twenty-two-point national constitution. It had an organised national subs-paying membership, who were recruited after signing a declaration

---

3 *An Anthology of Chartist Literature*, p. 361.

and agreeing to pay two pence a quarter, and who worked in hundreds of branches that were established all over the country.

The branches, or 'classes', as they were known, would each be formed of ten members and met on a weekly basis, some more frequently, in homes, schoolrooms, church halls, coffee houses, as well as public houses and inns. Each branch elected an executive, branch secretary, and treasurer, who would collect one penny a week from each member. Each town was divided into wards and divisions, with aggregate meetings held on a monthly basis. Each town would have a council of nine members, including officers, to co-ordinate matters, which would receive half the money collected for local purposes. By its very nature, it was a highly democratic movement, in which positions were normally rotated between members. As a report from Dumfries and Maxwelltown explained:

> "The business of the Association is managed by weekly meetings of its members and in accordance with a provision of its constitution, which declares that there shall be no presidents, vice-presidents, or leaders of any description, a chairman is elected at each meeting from the members present; but special committees are occasionally appointed, and a secretary, treasurer, etc, with special and strictly defined powers, every three months."[4]

At a national level, there was an executive committee of seven members, including a secretary and treasurer. This was to provide permanent professional leadership, which was to be elected by the whole party membership and would receive a full-time salary. The general treasurer would publish a statement of accounts once a week in the Chartist newspapers to ensure accountability and transparency. This represented a fundamental departure from the past and revealed a greater professionalisation of the organisation. The fact that a leader, such as Feargus O'Connor, was to be elected by the rank and file of the movement, every year, as part of an elected executive, was previously unheard of. In the past, popular leaders such as William Cobbett or Henry Hunt had simply appointed themselves and were never accountable to anyone.

However, some of the organisational proposals for the new party had to be dropped for legal reasons, in order to prevent government reprisals. The Corresponding Society Act of 1799, for example, had made it illegal for any society to have branches. If local bodies elected their delegates to a National Executive, they were deemed branches and would fall foul of the law. Simply calling branches 'classes' provided little protection. Therefore, strictly

---

4   D. Jones, p. 77.

speaking, the NCA was constantly pushing against these legal boundaries. Moreover, they figured, if the Anti-Corn Law League was allowed to exist as a national organisation, why should they not be permitted? The difference was obvious. The League did not constitute a threat to the established order, whereas Chartism did. In any case, any attempt by the Whig government to outlaw the organisation could provoke an almighty explosion, which they were keen to avoid until they were sufficiently prepared. Despite the legal hurdles, the plans adopted by the Manchester conference gave the organisation a definite centralised character. This national character was essentially a reflection of a national identity as well as a new working-class self-awareness.

RECRUITMENT

At the end of the conference, the National Charter Association was formally launched. An appeal was then made for the supporters of Chartism to join its ranks and work for its aims. It took some time for the party structures to be firmly established. By October 1841, there were 16,000 members enrolled, which rose to 30,000 by December, and to 40,000 in February 1842. By August, more than 50,000 members had enrolled into the party, organised in some 400 classes. What is more, as the Executive Committee wrote at the time:

> "We have attached to our Association many thousands who, as yet, have not taken out their cards, but who on every occasion, where a demonstration of strength is necessary, muster in such overwhelming numbers as to out vote the expediency-mongers in their own strongholds."[5]

The Chartist movement drew support from a host of party meetings, up to 600 a week, according to James Leach, the new chairman of the NCA Executive Committee. This foundation of a mass party of the working class certainly marked one of the main high points of Chartism.

"But events were now about to occur, which were calculated to rekindle the old fire of the Chartist movement", wrote Gammage.[6] The impetus for this was the release from prison in July 1840 of a number of Chartist leaders, including Lovett, Collins and McDouall. In the same month, in honour of Lovett and Collins, a mass demonstration was held in Birmingham, which was two miles long, with crowded streets, and well-wishers hanging from lamp posts, windows and rooftops. It ended with a great banquet of 800

5 B.N. Ponomorev, *The International Working Class Movement*, pp. 316-7.

6 R.C. Gammage, p. 184.

people, with toasts, speeches and songs. Other celebratory meetings also took place in different parts of the country.

The release of McDouall from Chester Castle was also a cause for great celebration and merriment, with a giant procession in Manchester once again followed by a dinner. "He [McDouall] was not going to allude to the dungeon into which he had been thrown by the Whigs", reported *The Northern Star*, 22 August 1840.

> "He despised them and their dungeons too. (Great cheering). They had laboured hard and long to destroy him; but, though a small person, his body had the strength of iron, and his spirit had been unbroken by all their machinations. (Cheers.) He had gone through their dungeons, and had felt their force; but he had forgot their prosecutions and he remembered only them. (Long and tremendous cheering.) From the moment he left his dungeon gates he swore in his heart he would have revenge. (Tremendous cheering.) He should not have that species of revenge which was implied by the general acceptance of the term – his revenge would be to see the Charter the law of the land – to contend, peaceably, if he must – yes, peaceably if he must – (laughter) – for the great principles to carry out which they were united, and for which he hoped all present were prepared to suffer, and, if necessary, to die. (Cheers.)"[7]

In Glasgow, tens of thousands formed a vast procession to honour the released prisoners, which was addressed by McDouall, Collins and George White, who had also recently been released. Once again, many meetings and rallies were held across the country, which reunited and fired-up the Chartist movement. This provided an important impetus for the new National Chartist Association. A popular song from 1840, published in *The Northern Star*, went as follows:

> Hurrah for the masses,
> The lawyers are asses,
> Their gammon and spinach is stale!
> The law is illegal,
> The Commons are regal,
> And the Judges are going to jail,
> Hurrah for the masses!
> The lawyers are asses,
> The Judges are going to jail.

---

7   D. Thompson, *The Early Chartists*, pp. 160-161.

Hurrah for the masses!
The lawyers are asses,
We'll cut off the gasses,
And shiver the glasses,
And eat sparrow-grasses,
And fill our carcasses,
And kiss all the lasses,
And rob all that passes –
There are no upper classes,
The Judges are going to jail![8]

ELECTION TACTICS

In the Manchester conference, a proposal had been put forward by Bronterre O'Brien that, in the event of a general election, Chartist candidates should stand, attend all public meetings to argue their case, and then move amendments and raise objections against the other parties. Support for this tactic was overwhelming, and it became a hallmark of the NCA's electoral strategy. Then, suddenly, in the summer of 1841, the Whig government was indeed forced to call a general election following a vote of censure moved by Robert Peel. The election proved a golden opportunity to try out the new approach. The Chartists had long displayed an open hatred towards the government of Lord Melbourne, and Whiggery in general. "The vile, bloody Whigs", as *The Northern Star* called them. "A Whig is a political shuffler, without honour, integrity, or patriotism", stated the *Chartist Circular*.[9]

However, the question was posed about how to behave towards the opposition Tories. Could the Chartists play one bourgeois party off against the other to further their cause? They certainly had enough support to possibly decide the outcome in certain seats. This tactic of supporting one party over another had been tested in the spring of 1841 at a by-election in Nottingham. The Whig government candidate was challenged by the Tory Mr. Walter, who was also the editor of the *Times*. The Chartists threw their support behind Walter's campaign and he won the seat by 278 votes. Whether their intervention had been enough to determine the outcome of the election is open to question. However, the Whigs soon raised a hue and cry: "The Chartists are allies of the Tories!" The Chartists were accused of selling their soul to the devil by siding with the deadliest enemies of freedom. This issue provoked a deep controversy, in

---

8   *The Northern Star*, 8 February 1840, in *The Anthology of Chartist Literature*, pp. 33-34.
9   *An Anthology of Chartist Literature*, p. 329.

particular between O'Connor and O'Brien, both of whom were still in prison at that time. O'Connor leaned on the masses' hatred of the Whigs and advocated a policy of supporting Tory candidates against them. O'Brien opposed him, saying to support or vote for the Tories was to become a tool of theirs. He said that the same was true for the Whigs, and that the only true Chartist policy was to vote for neither party, except in cases of mutual advantage.

Gammage went a step further, arguing that:

> "[W]e would never coalesce with either party *on any terms whatsoever*. To do so is almost the height of inconsistency. What, to say the least, can be more ridiculous than supporting a friend with one vote, while you support, it may be, a most deadly enemy with the other? Such a policy as this never yet accomplished the slightest permanent good. It may be that a victory is for the moment gained, but it is a victory worse than defeat. Can any good ever come by linking together truth and error, virtue and vice? If there are but three men of right principles, let them stand or fall by those principles; it at least secures them the respect even of their foes."[10]

What Gammage was attacking was a policy of so-called 'lesser evilism'. In practice, a case could always be made of one party being more 'progressive' than another. But this approach only served to sow illusions in one or other of the propertied parties. Given that the Whigs and Tories both represented property interests, to support one or the other would unnecessarily tie the hands of the working class. Either way, it meant supporting an enemy. Such a policy could easily backfire and thus damage the Chartist cause. Gammage stood for maintaining an independent class position and a 'plague on both your houses' as the way forward. It is no accident that this policy of 'lesser evilism' was later used to justify workers' support for the Liberal Party and held back the development of an independent party of labour for many years.

However, at this time, given the deep-seated hatred towards the Whigs, there was quite a bit of support for O'Connor's position. In an opportunistic manner, the Tories, who at that time represented landed interests at that time, often supported factory and social legislation that hurt the interests of the industrialists. Also, the Whigs' anti-working-class record was fresh in people's minds: after all, they had thrown Chartist leaders in prison, promoted the New Poor Law and enacted the treacherous Reform Bill. It must be said that O'Connor's policy of support for Tory candidates brought with it endless confusion, and a sizable minority openly opposed this line, thus leading to increased division in the ranks of the Chartists.

---

10 R.C. Gammage, p. 193.

A London Chartist conference, which violently attacked the Whigs, recommended the 'lesser evil' policy:

"It is better at times to submit to a real despotism than to a government of perfidious, treacherous, and pretended friends. We are natural enemies to Whiggism and Toryism, but being unable to destroy both factions, we advise you to destroy the one faction by making a tool of the other. ...elect Chartists or upset a ministerial hack."[11]

In other words, fight for the Charter, but if all else fails, oppose the government candidate. But a 'lesser evil' was still evil. 'Better an open enemy than a false friend!' went the saying. In reality, the conference of Londoners wanted to support, not the Tories, but the 'progressive' Whigs and Radicals. However, O'Brien dismissed them as simple "knowledge-mongers"!

In the general election, *The Northern Star* published a list of recommended candidates to support, including parliamentary Radicals. Roebuck stood for Bath and was successful; Colonel Thompson for Hull and was defeated; Oakly and Duncombe were returned for Finsbury; Fielden and Johnson for Oldham. Henry Vincent contested Banbury and got fifty-one votes, with the winner obtaining 124. McDouall contested Northampton and polled 170 votes, out of a constituency of about 2,000. At Newcastle, Bronterre O'Brien was proposed as the Chartist candidate while still in prison and got the largest show of hands by far, much more than those who were eventually elected by the restricted suffrage. Julian Harney and Pitkeithly contested the hustings against Lords Morpeth and Milton in the West Riding. They certainly carried public opinion in favour of the Charter, if not the seats.

In many other places, Chartists put up their own candidates, who appeared at the hustings alongside the other parties. After delivering their election addresses, they would ask the audience to vote for them by a show of hands, irrespective of whether they had the vote or not. This practice may seem very odd to us today, but it had a long tradition, supposedly as an attempt to involve the non-electors in some kind of consultative capacity. In 'normal' times, such practices went unnoticed, but in these stormy times such hustings became mass meetings, drawing in thousands of people. It was here, amongst the mass of people, that the Chartists made their mark.

As expected, the Chartist candidates politically defeated their well-to-do opponents in argument, and in almost every case they carried the majority in their favour at the hustings, which exposed the gulf between those able to

---

11 M. Beer, p. 116.

vote and those excluded from the franchise. This was excellent propaganda, where the Chartists, who invariably won the show of hands, called on the authorities to recognise them as the victors – to no avail, of course. The defeated Whigs and Tories would simply call for a 'constitutional' ballot of electors to finally decide the result, which they invariably won in every case. Following this farce, the Chartist candidates would storm off the platform, their job done in exposing the rigged system. It was clear that if the masses had the vote, the Chartists would have gained 100 seats in Parliament.

In the end, the Tories won the general election with almost a 100-seat majority. Despite a number of Radical sympathisers in Parliament, not a single Chartist candidate was returned. As expected, the Tories, when faced with a choice, withheld their votes from Chartist candidates. They had no need of Chartist support. "The distance between Whigs and Tories is but slight; but between Tories and Chartists, there is in principle an almost immeasurable distance", wrote Gammage.[12] Above all, there was a fundamental class difference between Chartism and the parties of landlords and capitalists. It was therefore dangerous for O'Connor and others to blur the principled differences between the parties, as this only served to sow disunion. As Gammage explained:

> Had it not been for the pro-Tory policy recommended by O'Connor, the election of 1841 might have conferred immense benefit on the cause. Had the Chartists never taken a single candidate to the poll, but left the Whigs and Tories to fight their own battles, standing aloof from both, and contenting themselves for the time being with carrying their men by show of hands, they would have necessarily increased their influence, and have laid the foundation for future triumph."[13]

In this, Gammage was certainly correct. Far better to remain aloof from the electoral squabble between, in effect, two species of reptile.

Towards the end of the summer, on 30 August 1841, Feargus O'Connor and Bronterre O'Brien, having completed their sentences, were released from prison. This gave a further impetus to the movement. On his release, O'Connor received, at his own request, a suit of fustian cloth, to symbolise his attachment to ordinary factory workers. "These are, indeed, times to try men's souls", he said. "If the principle is worth living for, it is worth dying for, and therefore worth persecution-bearing."[14] Given his personal standing, he

---

12 R.C. Gammage, p. 195.

13 Ibid., p. 194.

14 *An Anthology of Chartist Literature*, p. 338.

immediately assumed the leadership of the National Charter Association. An unknown Welsh woman Chartist composed a poem 'The Lion of Freedom' to commemorate the occasion. The first stanza read:

"The lion of freedom comes from his den,
We'll rally around him again and again,
We'll crown him with laurels our champion to be,
O'Connor, the patriot of sweet liberty."[15]

At the same time as O'Connor's release from prison, William Lovett separated himself from the Chartist movement. He believed the new NCA "illegal", and ended up dropping out of politics altogether to become a teacher and educator. "London is rotten", retorted O'Connor. Lovett's separation from the movement marked the complete extinguishing of the remnants of the right-wing 'moral force' grouping.

Others were equally disgusted by Lovett and his like, and expressed their strong opinions on the matter. As John Watkins explained:

"Imprisonment seems to operate a change in the minds of some Chartists; they go into prison like lead into the Alchemist's furnace and come out transmuted into a more refined metal. The truth is, after draining all the support possible from the working classes, they take their principles to a higher market and find purchasers in the middle classes. They are then used as decoys, not unwittingly, like the poor birds used by fowlers, but with a full knowledge of their foul purposes, for, like the fox having lost their own tails, they would fain persuade others to reduce themselves to the like pitiful and ludicrous condition. How disgusting and degrading is this; but they are paid for it."[16]

'New Movers' was the term Watkins used for these turncoats.

"The New Move became a sewer, a common sewer, to drain and carry off dregs, and so far, it was useful to our body. It became, and now is, a refuge for the destitute – a kind of Botany Bay to which we transport all convict Chartists.

"No contraband goods for us – no smugglers – no gang of coiners to coin false principles for us… He that is not with us is against us."

He did not want to associate with any "pussy-cat Chartists".[17]

---

15 *The Northern Star*, 11 September 1841.
16 *An Anthology of Chartist Literature*, p. 341.
17 Ibid., pp. 342-343.

FIRE AND WATER

As mentioned, the question of class independence was a powerful theme running through Chartism from its very inception. But it became more pronounced as the movement developed. Prior to the Reform Act of 1832, the struggle was regarded as 'the people versus the corrupt aristocracy', where the interests of the working class were subordinate to those of the middle classes. However, the experience of 1832 exposed the role of the 'grasping middle classes' and destroyed this alliance. Nevertheless, at one time or another, the Chartist leaders certainly flirted with the idea of forming an alliance with a section of the 'progressive' middle classes. This was particularly the case with the right wing of the movement around Lovett.

This was openly displayed at the 'Complete Suffrage' meeting of Sturge in Birmingham. As Henry Solly wrote:

> "[T]he Chartist delegates were as much surprised as gratified to find that not only Mr Sturge … but even this sturdy Rochdale capitalist, were willing to meet them and their demands in a friendly and conciliatory spirit. Yet how much depends in such cases on the character of the leaders. With Sturge at the head of the one side and Lovett on the other, it was not wonderful that mutual confidence was speedily established, difficulties were smoothed away, concessions, where necessary made…"[18]

But given the open hostility shown by both sides, suggestions of unity were ruled out in this period. The working class hated the middle-class Radicals, and they, in turn, had contempt for the working class. As Blackwood's *Edinburgh Magazine* of September 1839 stated:

> "The working classes have now proved themselves unworthy of that extension of the suffrage for which they contend, and that, whatever doubts might formerly have existed on the subject in the minds of well-meaning and enthusiastic, but simple and ill-informed men, it is now established beyond all doubt, that Universal Suffrage in reality means nothing else but universal pillage… What the working classes understand by political power, is just the means of putting their hands in their neighbour's pockets…"[19]

It was nevertheless still felt that there were some questions, such as the repeal of the Corn Laws, over which different classes could unite together in a common cause. The initiative for this was taken by a Birmingham Chartist, Joseph Sturge,

18 H. Solly, *These Eighty Years'*, quoted in R. Brown and C. Daniels, p. 106.
19 Quoted in R. Brown and C. Daniels, p. 98.

who persuaded a group of supporters to launch an invitation under the title of *Reconciliation between the Middle and Labouring Classes.* This was an attempt to combine the repeal of the Corn Laws with an extension of the suffrage. Of course, Lovett was very much attracted to the idea of using this group as a bridge to the Anti-Corn Law League. When Sturge organised a meeting in London, Lovett was invited. Arising from this, a further conference was organised in Birmingham, this time addressed by Sturge, Bright, Spencer, Lovett, Collins, Vincent and O'Brien. O'Brien's attendance was especially surprising, given his previous opposition to the mixing of banners with the political representatives of the middle class. This was an incredible about-face, which opened him up to attack. "Great numbers of the working classes were however kept aloof from it, by the abuse and misrepresentation of *The Northern Star...*" wrote Lovett in his autobiography.[20] In the meeting, there was a suggestion of establishing another organisation to promote the Charter, but the Bradford delegates – all Chartists – who attended regarded any such idea as heresy. Despite this, the conference agreed to set up the 'National Complete Suffrage Union'. This proposal was inevitably met with ferocious opposition by Feargus O'Connor and many others. There was not going to be any meeting of minds between the Chartists and the Anti-Corn Law League, the "black-hearted murderers", who were involved in the Peterloo Massacre. As a result, for his attendance at the Birmingham meeting, O'Brien was branded a traitor, a theme taken up in *The Northern Star.* As a result of its internal contradictions, Sturge's organisation split and had disappeared from the scene by the end of the year.

The question of class independence became a burning issue, a reflection of a growing class consciousness. Meetings of the Reform Associations were aghast by the degree of class hostility towards them during the 1830s. 'We don't want any gentlemen to represent us, we can represent ourselves', was the usual refrain. Under O'Connor's guidance, despite his indecisiveness on certain issues, *The Northern Star* became the standard-bearer for class independence. This was a powerful weapon, as the paper's circulation reached more than 40,000 a week, outselling all others. O'Connor asserted that all agitation before 1835, including from the London Radicals, had been linked to the careers of middle-class leaders. Chartism, he said, was something completely different, an organisation based on the working class. "From this moment," stated Engels, "Chartism was purely a workingmen's cause freed from all bourgeois elements."[21] Engels hoped and worked for the next step,

---

20 Ibid., p. 105.
21 MECW, vol. 4, p. 523.

which he believed was a union of Socialism and Chartism, "the reproduction of French Communism in an English manner".[22]

Feargus O'Connor, given his forceful personality and control of *The Northern Star*, dominated the Chartist movement throughout this period. Without doubt, just like many others, he put his body and soul into it. He promoted and popularised the National Charter Association and used his colossal authority to pull the movement together. In doing so, he brooked no opposition, and took up the battle-cry 'one party, one programme'. In speeches and in print, this was O'Connor's common theme. He was therefore against distractions, as he saw it, and for "out-and-out Chartism". He had nothing but contempt for separate Teetotal, Church or Knowledge Chartism, which he described as complete "humbug".

He stated:

> "If Chartists you are, Chartists you remain; you have work enough without entering into the new maze prepared for you … get your Charter, and I will answer for religion, sobriety, knowledge, and house, and a bit of land into the bargain…"[23]

Under his leadership, at least in the first period, O'Connor tended to keep Chartism on the straight and narrow, although on occasions he too succumbed to the temptations of opportunism, as we saw with his electoral support for the Tories.

THE SECOND PETITION

> "Sons of poverty assemble,
> Ye whose hearts with woe are riven,
> Let the guilty tyrants tremble,
> Who your hearts such pains have given.
> We will never
> From the shrine of truth be driven."
>
> (A Chartist song by William Jones)[24]

1842 came to be a further milestone, the opening of a momentous chapter in the history of Chartism. "We are arrived at an awful crisis," stated a report of a government spy, "the day and hour is at hand when there must be a mortally

---

22 Ibid., p. 527.
23 D. Jones, p. 55.
24 J. Lindsay and E. Rickword, p. 310.

Bloody Revolution."[25] Such reports were mostly spiced up, but the situation was nevertheless unquestionably bad. "The spring of 1842 was fearful", wrote Thomas Cooper. "The lack of employ continued; and the people grew either despairing or threatening."[26]

Given this new development, the Executive Committee of the National Charter Association made plans to draw up a new National Petition. On 12 April 1842, Chartist delegates attended a Convention in London to agree on its wording. The first National Petition had contained no social or economic demands. This time it was felt the petition needed to be broadened to include these questions. This was opposed by the Scottish delegates, but was agreed by the vast majority. The wording and tone of the new petition was far wider in scope and more revolutionary in content than the previous one:

"That in England, Ireland, Scotland, and Wales thousands of people are dying from actual want; and your petitioners, whilst sensible that poverty is the great exciting cause of crime, view with mingled astonishment and alarm the ill provision made for the poor, the aged, and the infirm; and likewise perceive with feelings of indignation, the determination of your honourable House to continue the Poor Law in operation, notwithstanding the many proofs which have been afforded by sad experience of the unconstitutional principle of the Bill, of its unchristian character and of the cruel and murderous effects produced upon the wages of working men and the lives of the subjects of this realm.

"Your petitioners would direct the attention of your honourable House to the great disparity existing between the wages of the producing millions and the salaries of those whose comparative usefulness ought to be questioned, where riches and luxury prevail amongst the rulers and poverty and starvation amongst the ruled. With all due respect and loyalty, your petitioners would compare the daily income of the Sovereign Majesty with that of thousands of working men of this nation; and whilst your petitioners have learned that Her Majesty receives daily for private use the sum of £164 17s.10d., they have also ascertained that many thousands of families of the labourers are only in receipt of 3 3/4d. per head per day. Your petitioners have also learnt that His Royal Highness Prince Albert receives each day the sum of £164, while thousands have to exist on 3d. a day. Your petitioners have also learned with astonishment that the King of Hanover daily receives £57 10s while thousands of taxpayers of this country live on 2 3/4d. per head per day. Your petitioners have with pain and regret also learned that the Archbishop of

---

25 M. Chase, p. 192.
26 Ibid., p. 201.

Canterbury is daily in receipt of £52 10s. per day, whilst thousands of the poor have to maintain their families upon an income not exceeding 2d. per day...

"That notwithstanding the wretched and unparalleled condition of the people, your Honourable House has manifested no disposition to curtail the expenses of the State, to diminish taxation, or promote general prosperity...

"Your petitioners complain that the hours of labour, particularly of the factory workers, are protracted beyond the limits of human endurance, and that the wages earned, after unnatural application to toil in heated and unhealthy workshops, are inadequate to sustain the bodily strength and to supply those comforts which are so imperative after an excessive waste of physical energy.

"That your petitioners also direct the attention of your honourable House to the starving wages of the agricultural labourer, and view with horror and indignation the paltry income of those whose toil gives being to the staple food of the people.

"Your petitioners deeply deplore the existence of any kind of monopoly in this nation, and whilst they unequivocally condemn the levying of any tax upon the necessities of life and upon those articles principally required by the labouring classes, they are also sensible that the abolition of any monopoly will never unshackle labour from its misery until the people possess that power under which all monopoly and oppression must cease...

"From the numerous petitions presented to your honourable House we conclude that you are fully acquainted with the grievances of the working men; and your petitioners pray that the rights and wrongs of labour may be considered with a view to the protection of the one and the removal of the other; because your petitioners are of opinion that it is the worst species of legislation which leaves the grievances of society to be removed only by violence or revolution, both of which may be apprehended if complaints are unattended to and petitions despised."[27]

The reference to "violence and revolution" was a distinct reminder of the real threat that was posed by the rejection of the Chartists' demands. But the ruling class was also determined to resist the Second Petition as it had the first. This did not deter the forces of Chartism. On the contrary, efforts were stepped up as never before. A host of lecturers and organisers toured the length and breadth of the country: Christopher Doyle, James West and William Jones in Yorkshire, Cockburn in Newcastle, Williams in Durham and Sunderland, John Leach in Lancashire, Julian Harney, Jonathan Bairstow,

---

27 P. Hollis, *Class and Class Conflict in Nineteenth Century England: 1815-1850*, pp. 219-221.

Thomas Cooper and A. Taylor in the central counties, John Mason and George White in Birmingham, Joseph Linney in Bilston, T. Wheeler, Ruffy Ridley and Smallwood in London and Mogg in Shropshire. These were only a small portion of a long line of lecturers who were very popular among the working class. They provided the organisational backbone of Chartism.

Following a colossal drive covering cities, towns and villages, the Second Petition was signed by an astonishing 3,315,752 people. A partial breakdown can be seen in Table 5.1. There was not a single industrial area in which there was not a large number of workers supporting the Charter.

Table 5.1

Place	Signatures
London and suburbs	200,000
Manchester	99,680
Newcastle	92,000
Bradford	45,100
Glasgow and Lanarkshire	78,062
Birmingham	43,000
Leeds	41,000
Norwich	21,560
Rochdale	19,600
Preston	24,000
Oldham	15,000
Bolton	18,500
Ashton	14,200
Leicester	18,000
Huddersfield	23,180
Sheffield	27,200
Liverpool	23,000
Stalybridge	10,000
Stockport	14,000
Burnley	14,000
Brighton	12,700
Merthyr Tydfil	13,900

The paper on which the petition was written, when laid end to end, was six miles long. This was an amazing feat, given that the total adult population in

England and Wales at this time was only around 8.5 million. The signatories represent nearly forty per cent of the adult population. Compare this to the total votes cast in the 1841 general election – a mere 593,445. The Petition from any point of view was clearly a powerful expression of the will of the people. According to the *Times*, 50,000 persons marched on Parliament to present the Petition and demand its adoption. *The Northern Star* reported ten times that number, reflecting a truly massive procession that shocked the authorities, who were taken off guard. On delivery, the Petition was broken up into parts and laid out on the floor of the House of Commons, as it was too large to enter the chamber. This made the room look "as if it had been snowing paper", according to one observer.

The Petition was allowed to be carried into Parliament while it was still in session, to the alarm of many parliamentarians, unaccustomed as they were to its size and presentation. The clerk then had to read the petition aloud. It was then formally introduced into the House of Commons by Thomas Duncombe, who spoke at length about its virtues, including a history of the Radical movement, especially the dissatisfaction after the 1832 Reform. He was supported in his intervention by other sympathetic Radicals and free traders. In opposition, there were only two speeches of note from the government, one from Thomas Macaulay, the Secretary of State for War, and the other from Lord John Russell. Both dismissed the so-called 'will of the people'. Macaulay's speech was a classic defence of private property as the basis of civilisation and all known progress:

> "I am opposed to universal suffrage. I believe universal suffrage would be fatal to all purposes for which government exists and for which aristocracies and all other things exist, and that it is utterly incompatible with the very existence of civilisation…
>
> "The Government would rest upon spoliation… What must be the effect of such sweeping confiscation of property? No experience enables us to guess at it. All I can say is, that it seems to me to be something more horrid than can be imagined. A great community of human beings – vast people would be called into existence in a new position; there would be a depression, if not an utter stoppage of trade, and of all those vast engagements of the country by which our people were supported, and how it is possible to doubt that famine and pestilence would come before long to wind up the effects of such a state of things. The best thing which I can expect, and which I think everyone must see as a result, is that in some of the desperate struggles which must take place in such a state of things, some strong military despot must arise, and give some sort of protection – some security to the property which may remain…

"The petitioners ask for supreme power; in every constituent body throughout the empire capital and accumulated property is to be placed absolutely at the foot of labour. How is it possible to doubt what the result will be? Such a confiscation of property and spoliation of the rich will produce misery, and misery will intensify the desire for spoliation."[28]

Lord John Russell took a different approach in challenging the 'democratic' threat. For him only the great and powerful – the patricians – had the ability and intelligence to govern:

"I am aware that it is a doctrine frequently urged, and I perceive dwelt upon in the petition, that every male of a certain age has a right, absolute and inalienable, to elect a representative to take his place among the members in the Commons House of Parliament. I never could understand that indefeasible and inalienable right. It appears to me that that question, like every other in the practical application of politics, is to be settled by the institutions and the laws of the country of which the person is native. I see no more right that a person twenty-one years of age has to elect a Member of Parliament than he has to be a juryman or to exercise judicial functions, as the people used in some of the republics of antiquity.

"These things, as it appears to me, are not matters of right; but if it be for the good of the people at large, if it be conducive to the right government of the State, if it tend to the maintenance of the freedom and welfare of the people that a certain number, defined and limited by a reference to a fixed standard of property, should have the right of electing members of parliament, and if it be disadvantageous to the community at large that suffrage should be universal, then I say that on such a subject the consideration of public good should prevail and that no inalienable right can be quoted against that which the good of the whole demands. And *as our society is very complicated and property very unequally divided, it might come that a parliament issued from Universal Suffrage might destroy or shake those institutions which are of the utmost value in holding society together…*"[29]

PARLIAMENT'S REJECTION

Despite the millions who signed the petition supporting the Charter, when it was finally put to the vote in the Commons, it was rejected by 287 against and forty-nine in favour. The vote represented a vote against the 'rabble', those without a property stake in the country, and a vote against those who would subvert private property. The political representatives in Parliament of

---

28 M. Beer, p. 136, Chase, p. 206.
29 Ibid., pp. 136-137, my emphasis added.

Capital and the landed aristocracy could not permit the 'anarchy' of universal suffrage at any cost.

The size of the vote against the petition was not totally unexpected. Some Chartists had illusions that the force of 'public opinion' would be sufficient to guarantee success, but that was a naive hope. On hearing the result, O'Connor, as usual, sounded a defiant tone:

> "Be not intimidated! Be not downhearted!! Be not influenced by the House of Commons' defeat. We are 4,000,000, aye and more. Never lose sight of the fact that we are 4,000,000 and more. How proud was I to call you 2,000,000 just twelve months ago, when the prison walls separated us, and how doubly proud must I now be to call you 4,800,000!"[30]

O'Connor was certainly capable of rallying the crowd and raising their spirits. The question was posed, as before, what should be done now?

There were many, including in government circles, who believed that the country was once again on the brink of revolution. Discontent had reached record levels, and was rising. Wages were falling despite the efforts of trade unions. For workers, it was like the labour of Sisyphus, a never-ending battle on all fronts. The staggering revelations of the conditions of women and children in the coal mines, highlighted by Lord Ashley, added to the bitterness. *The Spectator* encapsulated the dilemma felt by many in an article titled 'More factories – more pauperism'. Even Gladstone, as vice-president of the Board of Trade, felt the need to declare:

> "It is one of the most melancholy features in the social state of this country that we see beyond the possibility of denial that while there is at this moment a decrease in the consuming powers of the people, an increase of privation and distress of the labouring and operative classes, there is at the same time an enormous accumulation of wealth in the upper classes, a constant increase of capital."[31]

It was precisely the 'Two Nations', as described by Disraeli.

Under these conditions, Chartist propaganda, explaining that the salvation of the working class was to be found through direct political means, was gaining ground. In the issue of *The Northern Star* following the Charter's rejection by Parliament, we read:

> "Three-and-a-half millions have quietly, orderly, soberly, peaceably, but firmly asked of their rulers to do justice; and their rulers have turned a deaf ear to that

---

30 M. Beer, p. 138.
31 M. Beer, p. 140.

protest. Three-and-a-half millions of people have asked permission to detail their wrongs, and enforce their claims for RIGHT, and the 'House' has resolved they should not be heard! Three-and-a-half millions of the slave-class have holden out the olive branch of peace to the enfranchised and privileged classes and sought for a firm and compact union, on the principle of EQUALITY BEFORE THE LAW; and enfranchised and privileged have refused to enter into a treaty! The same class is to be a slave class still. The mark and brand of inferiority is not to be removed. The assumption of inferiority is still to be maintained. The people are not to be free."[32]

Amidst this feeling of angry dejection, the idea of a general strike was once again popularised. Again, blocked on the parliamentary front, the scene was set for an industrial showdown. Towards the end of July 1842, factory workers near Manchester, at Ashton, Stalybridge, and Hyde held a meeting to discuss what should be done in the face of growing attacks. Most speakers were in favour of a strike against the masters' proposal for a twenty-five per cent wage cut. For those workers, and many others, this was intolerable. They felt enough was enough. They were at the end of their tether. This provided the spark that was to set off a forest fire, and lead to a spontaneous general strike, famously named locally as the 'Plug Plot' strike.

---

32 J. Charlton, *The Chartists: The First National Workers Movement*, p. 34.

1. Feargus O'Connor

2. Thomas Paine   3. Robert Owen

4. The General Convention of 1839

5. James Bronterre O'Brien

' The body of the people, I do think,
  are loyal still,'
But pray, My L—ds and G—tl—n,
  don't shrink
From exercising all your care
  and skill,
Here, and at home,
  TO CHECK THE CIRCULATION

OF LITTLE BOOKS,

Whose very looks—
Vile ' *two-p'nny trash,*'
  bespeak abomination.
Oh! they are full of blasphemies
  and libels,
And people read them
  oftener than their bibles.

6. William Hone's 1820 satirisation of the censorship speeches in parliament

7. Richard Carlile   8. Henry Hetherington

9. Sketch from a Chartist church sit-in demonstration

10. Henry Vincent

11. A commemorative poster of
Thomas Attwood

12. 1836 trial

13. George Julian Harney

14. William Lovett

15. John Frost in court   16. Dr. Peter Murray McDouall

17. The Special Commission of the Assize, 1842

18. William Jones   19. Zephaniah Williams

20. 1839 Newport Rising

WANTED

1000 Courageous Volunteers

To the cause of Liberty,

Who, like the printer of this bill, are willing to brave *the despotic power of* TYRANNY, and defeat the odious attempt now making to suppress the *cheap* Papers, written for the People, by the " POOR MAN'S GUARDIAN " and the " REPUBLICAN," and all other cheap publications devoted to the *interests* of the WORKING CLASSES; thereby, in fact, striking a death blow at the Liberty of the People, and the Press, by means of that MOST ODIOUS of Castlereagh's *odious* " SIX ACTS," which the present WHIG *Attorney-General* himself, who now endeavours to enforce it, declared that *" Severe as it was, it could not effect what its proposers-contemplated unless they put a* DAGGER TO THE THROAT, AND WRESTED THE PEN FROM THE HAND OF THOSE WHO COULD WRITE."

Englishmen! The POOR MAN'S GUARDIAN and the REPUBLICAN appeal to you to support them in their *determination* to DEFY the despotic laws of a SELF-ELECTED TYRANNY, which are *more atrocious and arbitrary* than the Ordonnances of CHARLES X. which DESERVEDLY lost that tyrant his Throne.

None of the TRADE have *declined* selling the future papers of the *Poor Man's Guardian* and the *Republican;* the trade and the public, therefore, can be supplied as usual at *No.* 13, *Kingsgate Street, Holborn;* and at such other *patriotic* places as may have sufficient *honest courage* to present them for sale. More than ONE THOUSAND Englishmen have already, at public meetings, pledged themselves, if necessary, to become sellers.

Hetherington, Printer, 13, Kingsgate Street, Holborn.

21. Poster requesting volunteers for the *Poor Man's Guardian*

22. Reverend R.J. Stephens

23. The Preston massacre, 1842

24. William Cuffay

25. Thomas Cooper

26. Karl Marx   27. Friedrich Engels

28. Another scene of the Preston massacre, 1842

The Northern Star,
AND LEEDS GENERAL ADVERTISER.

VOL. I. No. 3.   SATURDAY, DECEMBER 2, 1837.   PRICE FOURPENCE HALFPENNY, Or FIVE SHILLINGS PER QUARTER.

THE FACTORY QUESTION.

TO THE PEOPLE OF HALIFAX
AND ITS PARISH.

LARGEST TEA AND COFFEE TRADES
IN YORKSHIRE.

COFFEES,
LUMP SUGARS AND SPICES.

TWO HUNDRED AND THIRTY THREE
CHESTS AND BOXES OF TEA

THE COFFEE TRADE.

OTTLEY AND COMPANY,
2, SOUTHGATE, HALIFAX.

LONDON AND PARISIAN FASHIONS.

SOUTH LANCASHIRE DELEGATE MEETING.

MORISON'S PILLS.

PUBLIC CAUTION.
BEWARE OF IMITATIONS.

THE BREWERS.

STEPHEN DICKINSON.

29. Front page of *The Northern Star*, organ of the Chartists

30. Ernest Jones

31. The Chartist Convention of 1848

32. Phillip McGrath

33. Henry Vincent

34. Chartist procession, 1848

35. A Chartist demonstration attended by the police, 1848

36. Daguerreotype of the meeting on Kennington Common, 1848

37. Another view of the Kennington Common meeting

38. The procession and petition of 1842

7. THE 1842 GENERAL STRIKE

"I lectured in a barn where there were two pigs outside and two
policemen inside. The pigs grunted, the policemen grumbled and the
people were gratified. The policemen were sent for by an old lady who
either imagined we were going to storm the house or steal the pigs.
The pigs remained unmolested to digest the first Chartist lecturer ever
to address the swinish multitude..."
– McDouall in *The Northern Star*, January 1842

"Real Chartism is Labour against Capital."
– George White, Birmingham Chartist

"They flatter themselves that Chartism was crushed, as if their batons
had the power to kill a principle!"
– Thomas Frost, Forty Years' Recollections

FIRST GENERAL STRIKE IN HISTORY

The great 'Plug Plot' strike erupted in 1842, a decisive year, and one
characterised by colossal turmoil. This strange name was used to describe
the actions of strikers, who removed the 'plugs' from the boilers and brought
factories to a standstill in August of that year. Beginning as a dispute over
wage cuts, it quickly took on a political form and spread throughout the
industrial areas. To describe it as a 'plot' is a bit far-fetched, however, as it
certainly had more of a 'spontaneous' character.

This strike wave nevertheless grew into an all-out general strike. No one
planned it as such, least of all the Chartist leaders. It just happened, as most
strikes do. The pressures had built up over the previous period and reached
explosive levels. The proposed wage cuts simply acted as the catalyst for the
movement. Whether the employers thought they could get away with it is

an open question. What is true is that the ground had certainly been laid by Chartist activists for an extensive period before the strike broke out. All that was required was the initial spark. In the sudden and sharp turn of events, characteristic of such a strike, working-class consciousness changes very rapidly from day to day, almost from hour to hour. It was at this point that the struggles of Chartism dovetailed with the aims and struggles of the trade unions to culminate in a political general strike.

The 'Plug Plot' strike was not only the first general strike in Britain, a political one at that, but the first on such a scale in any country. It was a time when British workers, as a class, put a decisive stamp on the situation by bringing the main industrial areas of the country to a standstill.

There is some highly revealing dialogue in *Sybil*, which deserves a mention:

"I am thinking what a mistake it was to have moved in '39." Sybil sighed.

"Ah! You were right, Sybil," continued Gerard; "affairs were not ripe. We should have waited three years."

"Three years!" exclaimed Sybil, starting; "are affairs riper now?"

"The whole of Lancashire is in revolt," said Gerard. "There is not a sufficient force to keep them in check. If the miners and colliers rise – and I have cause to believe that it is more than probable they will move before many days are past – the game is up."

"You terrify me," said Sybil.

"On the contrary," said Gerard, smiling, "the news is good enough; I'll not say too good to be true, for I had it from one of the old delegates who is over here to see what can be done in our north countree."

"Yes?" said Sybil, inquiringly, and leading on her father.

"He came to the works; we had some talk. There are to be no leaders this time, at least no visible ones. The people will do it themselves. All the children of Labour are to rise on the same day, and to toil no more, till they have their rights. No violence, no bloodshed; but toil halts, and then our oppressors will learn the great economical truth as well as moral lesson, that when Toil plays, Wealth ceases."[1]

This certainly reflected the mood and expectations at the time. At its height, the strike movement embraced up to half-a-million workers and covered an area from the Scottish coalfields to the tin mines of Cornwall. "It lasted twice the length of the 1926 General Strike, and was the most massive industrial action to take place in Britain – and probably anywhere – in the nineteenth century", wrote Mike Jenkins, without any exaggeration.[2]

---

1   B. Disraeli, *Sybil*, pp. 312-313.
2   M. Jenkins, *The General Strike of 1842*.

In terms of everyday life, 1842 was probably one of the most difficult years on record. It was the beginning of what was to become the 'Hungry 'Forties', a deep-seated and decade-long depression punctuated with ups and downs. The new slump had a devastating effect on wages and employment. In the main factory areas, Lancashire in particular, wage levels were being driven down to levels much lower than ten years before. Weavers' wages had been reduced by as much as eighty per cent over the previous twenty years. Unemployment in some towns reached up to half of the working population, together with workers subsisting on short-time, which had become an epidemic. In Stockport, unemployment reached seventy-five per cent. The New Poor Law had made life even harsher, as workers and their families were driven to the verge of starvation. Soup kitchens, becoming widespread, dispensed thousands of gallons of thin broth to the poor each day. It was reported that some families were so desperate they had to survive on tea leaves and bread. If they were lucky, they might get a pennyworth of liver or three-halfpenny worth of what was known as 'black fat'. According to the *Manchester Guardian*:

> "It is absolutely impossible to convey an idea of the amount of suffering among the poor for thirty miles around. It is admitted on all sides to be very great and, if not speedily remedied, will involve all classes in one common ruin."[3]

This 'common ruin' was very real. As the leader of the August strike, Richard Pilling, recalled:

> "I have seen in the factory in which I worked wives and mothers working from morning to night with only one meal; and a child brought to suck at them thrice a day. I have often seen fathers of families coming in the morning till night and having only one meal, or two at the farthest extent. This was the state we were in at the time of the strike."[4]

It was this that pushed the workers of Stalybridge over the edge. On 4 August they walked out, raising loud cheers for the Charter, *The Northern Star* and Feargus O'Connor. This bears witness to the fact that the strike was not simply a question of wages and conditions. The issue of the Charter was raised repeatedly and reflected the deep roots of Chartism in the working class. It became a political strike with a political aim, of which the fight against wage cuts formed a part. Of the forty-three recorded speeches made in the run up

---

3 *Manchester Guardian*, 20 April 1842, quoted in R. Challinor and B. Ripley, pp. 24-25.

4 G.D.H. Cole and R. Postage, *The Common People*, p. 299.

to the strike, from 26 July to 7 August, only two were given by speakers who were not Chartists. This shows the leading role that the Chartists played, at least at a local level. They gave the strike its political content and helped fertilise it with Chartism. This clearly reflects, as in every mass movement, how the working class learns in action, and how consciousness is transformed on the basis of events.

The strikers marched on factories in Ashton and succeeded in calling out the workers, in what could be described as a rolling action. This tactic was used to spread the strike, as strikers paraded from factory to factory, closing them down in the process. Eventually, such was their success that they formed a huge procession as they converged on Manchester. It became an unstoppable wave that swept all before it.

On the outskirts of the town, the strikers were met with soldiers under the command of Colonel Wemyss, who had succeeded Sir Charles Napier. The troops were accompanied by the magistrates, who were ready to read the Riot Act as required. But the strikers, given their vast numbers, were allowed through after pledging to keep the peace, which served to strengthen their morale and self-confidence. They soon divided into small groups and went from factory to factory, calling on workers to join the strike. This proved highly successful, and Manchester established itself as the strike centre. Very quickly, the strike spread outwards to Lancashire, Warwickshire, Staffordshire, The Potteries and into Wales. It was even reported that in Wales, workingmen's benefit clubs were once again ominously buying muskets and other weapons.

Disraeli vividly described what was unfolding in *Sybil*, which was published three years after the strike:

> The whole of the North of England and a greater part of the midland counties were in a state of disaffection; the entire country was suffering; hope had deserted the labouring classes; they had no confidence in any future of the existing system. Their organisation, independent of the political system of the Chartists, was complete. Every trade had its union, and every union its lodge in every town and its central committee in every district...

> Never such a gaunt, grim crew. As they advanced, their numbers continually increased, for they arrested all labour in their progress. Every engine was stopped, the plug was driven out of every boiler, every fire was extinguished, every man was turned out. The decree went forth that labour was to cease until the Charter was the law of the land: the mine and the mill, the founders and the loom-shop, were, until consummation, to be idle: nor was the mighty pause to be confined to these great enterprises. Every trade of every kind and description was to be

stopped: tailor and cobbler, brush maker and sweep, tinker and carter, mason and builder, all, all...[5]

According to *The Northern Star*, the organiser and prime mover of the strike was Richard Pilling, a handloom worker with a radical background. His first initiation into radical politics was his participation in the Peterloo demonstration, which ended in a massacre. The destruction of the jobs of the handloom workers by the power looms pushed Pilling into the factory system. He joined the Ten-Hour movement, read Cobbett, Sadler and Oastler, and became a trade union agitator and Chartist, which earned him the sack from his job. In 1841, he obtained work at Ashton, where wage cuts had reduced the wages of workers to a pitiful seven shillings a week. The following year, faced with a further round of cuts, he organised strikes at Ashton and Stalybridge, which spread throughout the district and became the basis for the August general strike.

At the same time, the Scottish miners were drawn into the strike as the movement continued to spill out in all directions. There were even rumblings in London, where nocturnal meetings of Chartists in Lincoln's Inn Fields were taking place in solidarity.

In March 1842, some sixty-four trade union delegates had attended a Chartist meeting in Manchester, showing how the unions were drawing close to the Chartists. Similarly, William Beesley, who edited the miners' paper and considered himself a staunch Chartist, tried to get the colliers in the North East to come out on strike for the Charter. He was subsequently arrested and tried at Lancaster, along with Feargus O'Connor and fifty-seven others. He was accused of advocating an armed insurrection at a mass meeting. At his trial, Beesley ended his appeal to the court with a defiant speech: "You may lock me up in prison, but the moment I get out I will begin again advocating my principles ... Let ten thousand convictions be obtained against me and I will still be a Chartist."[6]

"CLOSE EVERY MILL!"

As the strike began to bite, a mass meeting was held on Mottram Moor in Greater Manchester, and addressed by Chartist leaders. It was agreed to send out flying pickets to strengthen the strike, an indication of the level of organisation and consciousness of the workers. The chairman of the meeting ended the proceedings with the call:

---

5 *Sybil*, pp. 319-320.
6 R. Challinor and B. Ripley, p. 19.

"You people have been told the evils we labour under and I am requested also to tell you that tomorrow morning a meeting will take place at Stalybridge at five o'clock in the morning, when we will proceed from factory to factory, and all hands that will not willingly come out we will turn them out. And friends, when we are out, we will remain out, until the Charter, which is the only guarantee you have for your wages, becomes the law of the land. I hope to meet you all tomorrow morning at Stalybridge; when we will join hand in hand at this great National turn-out."[7]

The influence of Chartism in the trade unions was an indication of a growing thirst for radical ideas in the working class. In most workshops, "politics were the general theme for discussion and conversation", wrote Daniel Merrick, a framework knitter from Leicester. "A Chartist newspaper was taken weekly… The universal feeling of these operatives was that so long as they were kept in a state of political bondage, they would simply be the tools of the classes of society above them in social status." They would break for tea at five o'clock, which left some time for discussion:

"Some would seat themselves on the winders' stools, some on bricks, and others, whose frames were in the centre, would sit on their 'seat boards'. Then they would commence a general discussion upon various matters: political, moral, and religious. After tea, a short article would be read from *The Northern Star*, and this would form the subject matter for consideration and chat during the remainder of the day."[8]

Such agitation was especially promoted by Peter McDouall, who, of all the Chartist leaders, saw most clearly the importance of links with the trade unions. He was, in effect, the trade union 'organiser' of Chartism, and promoted caucuses in the unions. As Max Beer explains:

"He tried to group together working men who were already Chartists in Chartist associations on the basis of their trades, to permeate the trade unions with the Chartist spirit, so that they should eventually form the basis of the agitation. Organisation on these lines was carried out to a considerable extent both in London and Manchester. Combined Chartist and trade organisations existed in these districts down to the end of 1842."[9]

Again, this brief comment completely cuts across the myth argued by some historians that the trade unions were kept completely separate from Chartism.

7   J. Charlton, p. 31.
8   A. Briggs, *Chartist Studies*, p. 127.
9   M. Beer, p. 109.

This myth was propagated by Henry Pelling in his famous *History of British Trade Unionism.*[10]

By the second week of August, everything had come to a halt. Even workers at Sharp, Roberts & Co, which at this time was the largest factory in the world, were involved. For over fifty miles around Manchester, Britain's second-largest city, the din of the factories was silenced. Furnaces went cold, power looms stopped, mines were closed, wheels came to a standstill, and the hated factory bell fell silent as groups of workers went from mill to mill, shutting down production. The strike was rock solid, especially in the large textile mills and engineering works, although small firms were also affected. Even the shops were closed.

Where resistance was found to the strike, the force of the strikers was brought to bear. Systematically, such resistance was broken down, potential strike-breakers dealt with and, as a precaution, plugs removed from boilers. Even in these cases, violence was very much the exception, as the strength of the movement was enough to produce the necessary results. It was a case of class war being pursued with vigour. The chief magistrate, Daniel Maude, wrote:

"Number of mills were turned out with such expedition and by such insignificant bodies, as shown that the hands in (I believe) the majority of instances were ready to go out at the first invitation, and rendered it generally impossible for any force to be brought to the required point in time to prevent such a result."[11]

This readiness 'to go out' reflected the real mood on the shop floor. They had lost all fear of the overseers and masters. Every step they took brought with it a change within themselves and in those about them. Solidarity was on the order of the day. To many it seemed that nothing would ever be the same again. This confirms what Lenin would say many years later: "An ounce of experience is worth a ton of theory."

An unknown Ashton millworker, who was turned out on the Monday, joined the strikers the following morning. He described the events in a remarkable letter, which conveys a real flavour of the situation:

"Tuesday 9th: Met at 5 o'clock, went to Oldham, Hyde, Manchester, Stockport, and Newton lees – Hurst and all other places round about and stopt every Mill in them – Soldiers and police trying to stop us, took a sword from one of the Soldiers, broke it in pieces, made bloody noses for the policemen. Wednesday 10th: Went

10 H. Pelling, *A History of British Trade Unionism*, p. 43.
11 J. Charlton, p. 31.

to Gossop Dale, stopt every Mill there. Masters thought to stop *us* got knocked down… We get plenty of something to eat, the Shops are open, they give us what we want. Today: Aug 11th to Stockport, they are stopt, but we go a parading the Streets like Soldiers 6 a breast. News from Manchester: Bloody fights, Soldiers ready to fight for the people, police the same. Now's the time for Liberty. We want the Wages paid 1840. If they won't give it us, Revolution is the consequence. We have stopt every trade – Tailors, cobblers – Brushmakers – Sweeps, Tinkers, Carters – Masons – Builders – Colliers &c and every other trade. Not a Cart is allowed to go through the Streets."[12]

The workers were feeling their class power, a collective power, as everything around them ground to a halt. Nothing happened without their consent. Their mood of confidence was contagious, affecting every worker alike, including those never before involved. The threat of 'revolution' by the millworker was not a throwaway remark, but made in deadly earnest. Of course, there were some casualties, which was inevitable, as strikers clashed with troops in Preston and Blackburn, resulting in the death of six workers and several more wounded. But the movement still continued, carrying all before it, like an unstoppable lava flow from an erupting volcano. It certainly had all the characteristics of a developing revolutionary situation.

STRIKE RAPIDLY SPREADS

From Manchester, the rolling strikes quickly spread north and south through extensive picketing. As it spread, the democracy of the strike movement was reflected in the extraordinary mass assemblies held every morning to hear speeches and gather reports: 3,000 in Stalybridge, 14,000 in Ashton, 10,000 in Oldham, 20,000 in Manchester, and 30,000 in Rochdale. This guaranteed the unity of the strike. Early on there was a realisation that this was no ordinary strike, and the idea soon caught on of using the struggle to secure the Charter. This reflected the 'molecular' thinking taking place in the masses as they increasingly felt their power. Every day brought a new experience. It was regarded as a once-in-a-lifetime opportunity, which must not be passed up. A victorious strike over wages would bring temporary relief, but a victory for the Charter would mean a permanent betterment. This was the idea not only at the top of the movement, but widely held among the rank-and-file. On 10 August, the strike in Manchester suddenly evolved into a mass general strike. The movement had gone far beyond the immediate issues and, through the Charter, had posed the question of power. This was

---

12 M. Chase, p. 215.

not the view of a minority, but a general feeling amongst the majority of strikers, whose consciousness was being rapidly transformed.

Of course, there existed a small minority in the Chartist leadership who still feared that the general strike would alienate middle-class opinion, but they kept their heads down. In reality, the initiative of the struggle for the Charter had passed from the Chartist leaders to the trade unions and the workers on the ground. On Thursday 11 August, in the Carpenters' Hall, Manchester, some 350 worker delegates attended a regional conference of the metal trades and passed the following resolution:

"1) That this meeting pledges itself not to sanction any illegal or immoral proceedings. 2) That this meeting deprecates the late and present conduct of those employers who have been reducing wages, thereby depriving the labourers of the means of subsistence, and also destroying the home trade; but at the same time we cannot, nor do we sanction the conduct of those individuals who have been going about destroying property, and offering violence to the people. 3) That it is the opinion of this meeting that, until class legislation is entirely destroyed, and the principle of united labour established, the labourer will not be in a position to enjoy the full fruits of his own industry. 4) That it is the opinion of this meeting the People's Charter ought to become the law of the land, as it contains the elements of justice and prosperity; and we pledge ourselves never to relinquish our demands until that document becomes a legislative enactment."[13]

This resolution of the leaders at Manchester, the heartland of the dispute, was very clear in fighting for the People's Charter and the end to repressive class laws. This strike was not only political, but had clear revolutionary overtones. On the same day as the Manchester conference, the town of Bacup was bordering on a state of outright insurrection.

A procession of people, amounting in number to two thousand, entered the town by the Rochdale road, armed with sticks, and immediately visited the several mills, demanding that the hands should turn out. Half an hour after they had entered the town, every mill to the number of twenty was at rest; and the invading parties then went round in detachments to the various shops. Many of the doors were locked; but by persuasion and threats they got them opened, and demanded provisions, which the shopkeepers seemed afraid to refuse, and which they accordingly distributed. At Stalybridge, a crowd of from three to four thousand people paraded the streets, and went from mill to mill, crying, "Turn them out, turn them out"; an order which was speedily obeyed. From Stalybridge

---

13 R. Brown and C. Daniels, p. 80.

they proceeded to Dukinfield, stopping every mill which lay in their way, both leading to and in the town. They then went to Ashton, and proceeded in a similar line of conduct, running about from mill to mill and brandishing their sticks…

On the 11th the Stalybridge men proceeded to Saddleworth, to the number of eight hundred, stopping all the works on their line of march, and causing the middle class the utmost consternation.[14]

In Preston, following a strike meeting, workers continued to picket even the smallest workplaces. This forced the local magistrates to act and call on thirty of the 72nd Highlanders, who were quartered in the town, to intervene. As the soldiers proceeded down Fishergate, their path was blocked by an immense crowd of strikers. Workers' self-discipline had overwhelmingly replaced the need for sporadic violence, although physical confrontation, when unavoidable, certainly took place.

Proceeding down Fishergate and Lune street the soldiers were pelted by the people with showers of stones, upon which they faced about with the view of effecting a dispersion, which they made great efforts to achieve. The chief of the county constabulary told them that the Riot Act would be read; but a stone was immediately thrown, which knocked the Riot Act out of the Mayor's hand. Showers of stones flew from all sides at the military. The Mayor, however, succeeded at last in reading the Riot Act, the stones meanwhile flying about him. The chief constable then informed the people that the Riot Act had been read. Women filled their aprons with stones, and brought them to the men, who from other streets threw them over the houses, causing very great annoyance, and harassing the military. It was in vain that the soldiers attempted to disperse them. All attempts to do so by a mere display of force were ineffectual, and the Mayor at last gave the order to fire.

At the first discharge many of the people fell to the ground; the rest did not run away, but stood for two or three minutes in a state of consternation, as though they had not power to stir from the spot. Four were shot dead, and many others were wounded. The remainder speedily dispersed, and the military returned to their quarters.[15]

The Home Secretary, Sir James Graham, fell over himself to congratulate the mayor on his courage and for restoring order in face of this riotous behaviour. The evidence of the Chief Constable of Preston was given at the trial of

---

14 R.C. Gammage, pp. 220-221.
15 Ibid., pp. 221-222.

Feargus O'Connor and fifty-eight others, which confirmed the manner of the shootings:

> "'At length the mayor ordered the soldiers to fire. I did not hear what was the word of command; but they did fire.'
> 'What was the consequences of the firing?'
> 'I saw several of the foremost of the mob drop in the street.'
> 'How many rounds did they fire?'
> 'I don't know the exact number; they did not fire in a body but by platoons. The mob stood mute; they did not attempt to run; they stood for some minutes as if thunder-struck.'
> 'How long did they stand?'
> 'About two or three minutes.'
> 'I believe some were killed?'
> 'Yes.'
> 'How many?'
> 'Four died immediately and a fifth man who was wounded had his leg taken off.'"[16]

Such were the daily scenes of the strike, peppered with clashes, as it spread from factory to factory and from town to town. Either workers willingly joined the strike, which was the case most of the time, or they were picketed out, which achieved the same result. Some places were besieged by armed strikers. Where they could, workers entered the factories to remove the plugs from the boilers, and extinguished fires, effectively stopping the engines and shutting down the works. Where employers attempted to obstruct the strike, they were threatened with the burning down of their mills. Such threats, real or imaginary, were enough to guarantee compliance. In some cases, the military were called to protect and guard the factories. This was normally sufficient to settle matters, and work ground to a halt. For fifty miles around Manchester, the scene was the same. A vast area of England's industrial heartland was, in effect, in a state of open warfare between the workers and the authorities. Despite the actions of the police, the forces of the state were continually being thrown back. Troops were having to rush from place to place, overstretched by the scale of the strike movement.

While the success of the strike had made it a *cause célèbre* of the working class, it produced terror in the ruling circles, including among the royal family, who were quaking in their shoes. A flustered Queen Victoria issued a Royal Proclamation on 13 August:

---

16 R. Brown and C. Daniels, p. 82.

"In divers parts of Great Britain great Multitudes of lawless and disorderly Persons have lately assembled themselves together in a riotous and tumultuous manner, and have, with Force and Violence, entered into certain Mines, Mills, Manufactories, and other Places, and have, by Threats and Intimidation, prevented our good Subjects therein employed from following their usual occupations and earning their Livelihood; We, therefore, being duly sensible of the *mischievous consequences* which must inevitably ensue, as well to the Peace of the Kingdom as to the Lives and Properties of our Subjects, from such wicked and illegal practices if they go unpunished, and being firmly resolved to cause the laws to be put in execution for the punishment of such offenders, have thought fit by the advice of our Privy Council, to issue this proclamation, hereby strictly commanding all Justices of the Peace, Sheriffs, Under Sheriffs and all other Civil Officers whatsoever within the said Kingdom, that they do use their utmost endeavours to discover, apprehend, and bring to Justice, the Persons concerned in the riotous proceedings above mentioned."[17]

It offered rewards of £50 for each person convicted.

The authorities employed every means to undermine the strike. One such policy, advocated by the Duke of Wellington, was to sow mistrust and division among strikers. Government spies were widely engaged in this pursuit. In addition, information was wormed out of prisoners, who were held in custody, and used to spread discord. "If once these rioters were aware that their plans were discovered, their secrets known, and their evil advisers watched," stated Home Secretary Graham, "distrust would be sown amongst them, and the efficacy of your repressive force would be greatly augmented."[18] It was the old policy of 'divide and rule', perfected by the British ruling class in Ireland and elsewhere.

COMMITTEES OF ACTION

In many places, workers established strike committees which asserted their control over the area. Workers could really sense their power. At previous meetings, strike leaders had emerged. These leaders now called on workers to elect delegates to a Great Delegate Conference for 15 August. This, in practice, was an extended strike committee meeting, and, if it had been developed by linking together all local committees, it could have provided the embryo of workers' power and the beginnings of a workers' state. In Lancashire, following the French example, 'Committees of Public Safety'

17 Ibid., pp. 83-84.
18 F.C. Mather, quoted in A. Briggs, p. 389.

were formed. These committees dealt with employers' requests for exemption from the strike for various reasons. Such was their power that factory owners had to come cap in hand to them for help and permission. This resulted in licences being issued in certain cases, allowing the partial resumption of essential production, as deemed necessary by the committee.

These strike committees exercised day-to-day authority and became an effective power in the region. This was certainly a definite form of workers' control, if not containing elements of dual power. The word 'soviet' was as yet unknown in the working class. It would not become known for another sixty-five years, when such committees emerged in the Russian revolution of 1905. In the 1920s and in the 1926 British general strike in particular, these committees took the name of 'Councils of Action'. Such committees or councils were being thrown up in the developing general strike of 1842, the earliest examples of these organs of power.

In the Delegate Conference, delegates representing eighty-five trades from the strike centres of Lancashire and Yorkshire met to discuss the pressing situation. The meeting, representing workers in action, was like a democratic workers' parliament, and was on a higher level than anything that had come before. It was like a modern version of the Putney Debates. Each of the delegates' mandates were scrutinised very closely and only *bona fide* delegates were given official sanction. Outside the conference hall, thousands of workers crowded around, eagerly waiting for any news from the assembly. These workers were deliberately harassed by troops, who had been given orders to disperse them by the magistrates. But this led to a stand-off and the conference continued its business until the following day.

The central question of whether the general strike should be restricted to wages or continued as a fight for the Charter was again raised. Although most delegates held limited mandates from their workplaces, the overwhelming majority came out in favour of achieving the Charter. To be precise, out of the eighty-five delegates present, fifty-eight declared for the Charter, nineteen decided to abide by the decision of the meeting, seven voted to make it a strike over wages, and one, while in favour of the Charter, had no instruction and therefore abstained. The threatening presence of troops outside the conference only served, if anything, to strengthen their resolve. As soon as the meeting had taken this historic decision, the magistrates ordered that the gathering immediately be dispersed by the troops.

Sir James Graham, the Home Secretary, was behind this move. He regarded the conference as the centre of the general strike, a centre that needed to be dealt with. "It is quite clear that these Delegates are the Directing Body," he said, "they form the link between the Trade Unions and the Chartists, and a blow struck at this Confederacy goes to the heart of the evil and cuts off its ramifications."[19] But the closure of the conference was somewhat late. Despite five delegates being arrested and warrants being issued against four others, the stable door had been closed after the horse had already bolted. The conference had reached a definite conclusion, which it started to broadcast to all and sundry.

Following the meeting, its chairman, Alexander Hutchinson, immediately issued a general call to the Trades of Manchester and the surrounding districts:

"We hasten to lay before you the paramount importance of the day's proceedings. The delegates from the surrounding districts have been more numerous at this day's meeting than they were at yesterday's; and the spirit of determination manifested for the people's rights has increased every hour. In consequence of the unjust and unconstitutional interference of the magistrates our proceedings were abruptly brought to a close by their dispersing the meeting, but not until in their very teeth we passed the following resolution:

"'The delegates in [the] public meeting assembled do recommend to the various constituencies which we represent to adopt all legal means to carry into effect the People's Charter. And further, we recommend that delegates be sent to the whole of the country to endeavour to obtain the co-operation of the middle and working classes in carrying out the resolution of ceasing labour until the Charter be the law of the land.'

"Englishmen! Legally determine to maintain the peace and the well-being of the country, and show, by the strict adherence to our resolutions, that we are your representatives.
[signed]
"Alexander Hutchinson,
"Charles Stuart.
"Manchester, 16 August 1842."[20]

Hutchinson was also the general secretary of the smiths' trade union and editor of the *Trades Journal*. He was an Owenite socialist and committed Chartist. During the strike, he played a prominent role, together with Richard Pilling and many others who had a long history in political and trade union

---

19 J. Charlton, p. 46.
20 M. Beer, pp. 145-146.

activity. These men in turn provided the direct link between Chartism and the mass strike, as well as a leadership with deep roots in the working class.

A national general strike to secure the Charter, inherent in the situation, was occurring throughout the industrial North and other areas. From the Manchester trades meeting, it looked as if William Benbow's dream was coming true. While there were few Chartists who had ever read his pamphlet, its phrases were on everyone's lips, and every speaker made use of it. The bond between the strike and Chartism was strong. According to Richard Otley at his trial, "in the manufacturing districts there are, at least, four out of every five of the working classes, that either are actually Chartists, or hold Chartist principles."[21] Above all, the call to extend the general strike came from the trades of Manchester, the 'town of high chimneys', which could be regarded as the British Petrograd. It was regarded as the most radical place in the country, and therefore the centre of the British revolution. The area was the heart of industrial Britain and the storm centre of the British working class.

REVOLUTIONARY SPEECHES

There were many great speeches made during these momentous times, often by ordinary workers inspired by the revolutionary mood on the ground. Probably the most memorable speech was by Thomas Cooper, a self-educated worker and Chartist leader. He spoke to an immense crowd in The Potteries, while standing on the Crown Bank in Hanley. In his autobiography, he described what happened. As usual, he began his speech by quoting from the Bible:

"I took for a text the sixth commandment: 'Thou shalt do no murder' – after we had sung Bramwich's hymn, 'Britannia's sons, though slaves ye be', and I had offered a short prayer.

"I showed how kings, in all ages, had enslaved the people, and spilt their blood in wars of conquest, thus violating the precept, 'Thou shalt do no murder'.

"I described how the conquerors of America had nearly exterminated the native races, and thus violated the precept, 'Thou shalt do no murder'.

"I recounted how English and French and Spanish and German wars, in modern history, had swollen the list of slaughtered and had violated the precept, 'Thou shalt do no murder.'

"I decided our own guilty Colonial rule, and still guiltier rule in Ireland; and asserted that British rulers had most awfully violated the precept, 'Thou shalt do no murder'.

---

21 J. Charlton, p. 37.

"I showed how the immense taxation we were forced to endure, to enable our rulers to maintain the long and ruinous war with France and Napoleon, had entailed indescribable suffering on millions, and that thus had violated the precept, 'Thou shalt do no murder'.

"I asserted that the imposition of the Bread Tax was a violation of the same precept; and that such was the enactment of the Game Laws; that such was the custom of primogeniture and keeping of land in the possession of the privileged classes; and that such was the enactment of the infamous new Poor Law.

"The general murmur of applause now began to swell into loud cries; and these were mingled with execrations of the authors of the Poor Law. I went on.

"I showed that low wages for wretched labourers, and the brutal ignorance in which generation after generation were left by the landlords, was a violation of the precept, 'Thou shalt do no murder'.

"I asserted that the attempts to lessen the wages of the toilers underground, who were in hourly and momentary danger of their lives, and to disable them from getting the necessary food for themselves and families, were violations of the precept, 'Thou shalt do no murder'.

"I declared that all who were instrumental in maintaining the system of labour, which reduced poor stockingers to the starvation I had witnessed in Leicester, and which was witnessed among the poor handloom weavers of Lancashire, and poor nail-makers of the Black Country, were violating the precept, 'Thou shall do no murder'.

"And now the multitude shouted; and their looks told of vengeance – but I went on, for I felt as if I could die on the spot in fulfilling a great duty – the exposure of human wrong and consequent human suffering. My strength was great at that time, and my voice could be heard, like the peal of a trumpet, even on the verge of a crowd composed of thousands."

He addressed another meeting the next morning in the presence of 8,000 striking miners. At that meeting, John Richards, a seventy-year-old Chartist and member of the first Convention, proposed the resolution "that all labour cease until the People's Charter becomes the law of the land". The resolution was adopted by a mass show of hands with not a single vote against. They then marched on to Longton, picketing out those few potters who were still operating.[22]

There were clashes in Halifax between strikers and the forces of law and order. Here, the women played a key role in resisting the troops. Faced with

---

22 Quoted in R. Challinor and B. Ripley, pp. 30-31.

the military, "thousands of female turnouts... poorly clad and not a few marching barefoot" refused to move when the Riot Act was read, defying the soldiers ordered to kill them. Eventually, cavalry cleared the streets, "cutting down or riding over all who stood in their way". Frank Field watched the strikers passing along the Bradford to Halifax road:

> "The sight was just one of those it is impossible to forget. They came pouring down the wide road in thousands, taking up its whole breadth – a gaunt, famished-looking, desperate multitude, armed with huge bludgeons, flails, pitch-forks and pikes, many without coats and hats, and hundreds upon hundreds with their clothes in rags and tatters... As the wild mob swept onwards, terrified women brought out all their bread and eatables, and in the hope of purchasing their forbearance, handed them to the rough-looking men, who crowded to the doors and windows. A famished wretch, after struggling feebly for a share of the provisions, fell down in a fainting condition in the doorway where I was standing. A doctor, who lived close at hand, was got to the spot as soon as possible, but the man died in his presence. One of his comrades told us that the poor fellow had eaten raw potatoes at Ovenden after being without food for two days."[23]

INSURRECTIONARY MOOD

Without question, the industrial North and the Midlands were in a state of insurrection. The strike was spreading uncontrollably. Its breadth and scope were remarkable. The other main centres of the country – Scotland, Wales, and London – were not far behind the storm centres of the North as workers joined the strike. In fact, many sections were streaming out. In Scotland, for example, Clackmannanshire colliers pledged to "never again produce a pennyworth of wealth till the People's Charter be law". One hundred pits in Lanarkshire were also on strike against wage cuts. Airdrie and Fife collieries followed suit.

In every sense, the general strike was a Chartist strike. The mood on the ground was described in a letter written by William Corah, who brandished a Chartist flag at the Watford Road demonstration in Leicester:

> "Leicester, 18 August 1842
>
> Dear Father,
>
> Spread the Charter through the land. Let Britons bold and brave join hand in hand. I write you these few lines to inform you of my circumstances: my wife is on the point of Death. She has got the Fever, and I am altogether in an unsettled

---

23 M. Chase, p. 218.

State. I must now inform you of the State of our town, we have had meetings every Night this week consisting of from 2 to 3,000 men. Yesterday morning a body of persons came round to our shop and fetched us out. They then commenced to fetch the cut up hands and the wrought hose hands out, they assembled at Night to the tune of 20,000 men or upwards and swore that by the Ghost of many a murdered Englishman and English woman, they would work no more till the People's Charter becomes the charter of the land. They are assembled this moment in the Market Place, and before the day is over, they mean to fetch the Bread and Beef where it is to be had. They are going round now. I am just informed while I am writing that they are stopping all the mills and factories and God speed the plot, you will see that I am working Gloves at William Adama, Burnleys Lane, Church Gate, Leicester. I remain your Son and Brother Chartist,

[signed]

William Corah

N.B. They are all Chartists here.

Please to send this directly to Sam Lintwilers, Ashby Road, Loughborough."[24]

The mass meeting gathering at Market Place was ordered to disperse and the Riot Act was read. As the police moved in, the crowd withdrew, only to reform later at the Recreation Ground. This, in turn, was broken up by the yeomanry, but once again the mass meeting reformed on the other side of town. It was like a game of cat and mouse. The following day, hundreds of strikers attempted to march on Loughborough, but were stopped by troops, and the 'Battle of Mowmacre Hill', as it became known, broke out.

In this unprecedented struggle, what more could you ask of the working class? They were prepared to strike and fight for the Charter to the bitter end. All that was needed was a concerted national lead by the National Charter Association, to draw all the threads together in conjunction with the trades, get access to weapons, and mobilise the forces to overturn the old order. The workers felt their power and in many industrial areas, at least for the moment, they were the masters of the house. But the Chartist leadership nationally were completely thrown off guard. They were taken by surprise by this sudden turn of events which they never anticipated or prepared for.

At this point, by pure coincidence, a representative Chartist meeting was being held in Manchester to unveil a monument commemorating Henry Hunt. The Chartist leadership had suddenly become aware of what was happening as the shutdown became obvious. "Not a single mill at

---

24 Quoted in A. Briggs, *Chartist Portraits*, p. 113.

work!" exclaimed John Campbell, the secretary of the NCA, as he entered Manchester, where every chimney was smokeless. "Something must come out of this, and something serious too!" he said.[25] The way he posed the issue showed that he had no idea what was required, he only knew that "something" was.

On 17 August, the Chartist delegates met secretly in a chapel. The original business about Henry Hunt's commemoration was dropped in favour of a discussion on the general strike movement. At first, on hearing the news of the trades' conference, which had pledged allegiance to the Charter, the delegates were overwhelmingly in favour of helping to mobilise the workers. According to Thomas Cooper, everyone believed that "the time had come for trying, successfully, to paralyse the government". According to him: "In the streets, there was unmistakable signs of alarm on the part of the authorities. Troops of cavalry were going up and down the principal thoroughfares, accompanied by pieces of artillery, drawn by horses."[26]

Peter McDouall seized the initiative and proposed that the Chartist conference fully support the resolution of the trades, including the promotion of a general strike until the Charter became the law of the land. This was eagerly seconded by Cooper, who also believed that the strike was evolving into an all-out national struggle. In the debate, it was stressed that, in face of inevitable government repression, the workers would be forced to defend themselves arms in hand. The Chartists therefore had a duty to do all they could to help the strike to succeed.

But while several delegates, such as Thomas Cooper and James Leach, strongly supported the motion, it was opposed by none other than Feargus O'Connor, who poured cold water on the idea. "We are not met here to talk about fighting", he said. "We are met to consider and approve the resolution of the trades", as if one precluded the other.[27] He became obsessed with the notion that the strike had been instigated by Anti-Corn Law League factory masters for their own ends. Even if this had been the case, the strike, the aims of which embraced the Charter, was now a fact. "I would never have counselled the present strike," he said, "but as we have been assailed in our peaceful position you have no alternative but to bow or resist the tyrant's will." O'Connor seemed to be facing in two directions, but eventually sided with resistance. This was a time for clear and bold thought,

25 *Class and Conflict*, p. 288.
26 R. Brown and C. Daniels, p. 85.
27 M. Beer, p. 147.

but O'Connor proved incapable of providing such leadership, and instead spread ambivalence and confusion. They were making heavy weather over what needed to be done.

This prevarication gave the green light to the Rev. William Hill, the then editor of *The Northern Star*, who firmly intervened against both Cooper and O'Connor, latching onto the idea that the strike had been promoted by the Anti-Corn Law employers. He called for complete opposition to the strike:

> "I wonder that so a clear an intellect as Cooper's should dream of fighting. Fighting! – the people have nothing to fight with, and would be mown down by artillery if they attempted to fight. The strike has originated with the Anti-Corn Law League, and we should simply be their tools if we helped to extend or prolong the strike. It could only spread disaster and suffering. I move an amendment that we entirely disapprove of it."[28]

This intervention was not surprising, as Reverend Hill ascribed everything to the Anti-Corn Law agitation and saw its influence everywhere! He was then followed by Richard Otley of Sheffield, who also downplayed the strike's potential for success:

> "How could poor, starving weavers be expected to fight? If we endeavoured to form battalions for fighting, the people would need food and clothing – they would need arms and powder and shot; they would very likely have to bivouac in the fields – anyhow could poor weavers be expected to do that? It would kill them in a few days."[29]

He seemed to forget that hundreds of thousands of workers were fighting and looking for support.

But even Julian Harney, the admirer of Marat and the French Revolution, and friend of Major Beniowski, was disorientated. His head was in a complete spin, surprised by the sudden turn of events. Instead of urging maximum support, he warned of dangers, real or imaginary. He even came out against the use of physical force, believing it to be premature and therefore doomed to fail. Rather than providing clarity and determination at this critical juncture, he vacillated and drew back. In the end, he returned to Sheffield where he pursued his opposition to a possible insurrection. "Are you ready to fight the soldiers?" Harney asked a mass meeting. "You may say that this is not the question but I tell you that it would be the question. I do not think

---

28 Ibid., p. 148.
29 Ibid., p. 148.

you are. I am ready to share your perils but I will not lead you against the soldiers."[30]

In his book, *Chartist Portraits*, the historian G.D.H. Cole argues that "Harney was essentially right", and minimises the depth of the strike movement.[31] But this is more a reflection of Mr Cole's own scepticism and outlook than the reality on the ground. What the situation lacked was clear leadership, particularly at such a crucial time. To draw a parallel, similar advice was given by Georgi Plekhanov to the Russian workers in 1905 who, when faced with the tsarist state, in his opinion, "should not have taken up arms". But the working class is not a tap that can be simply turned on and off when it is thought convenient. And there is no such thing as a thermometer that can be placed under the tongue of history to see if the time is ripe for revolution. This has to be estimated by weighing up the concrete situation. What is clear is that they were facing an unfolding political general strike, the likes of which they had never seen before. If a revolutionary situation can be defined as the forcible entry of the masses onto the scene, then this was certainly an example of one.

REVOLUTIONARY CONDITIONS

Thomas Cooper, who had travelled around the country speaking at meetings, and was very much in touch with the real mood on the ground, came out vigorously in favour of McDouall's proposal:

> "I would vote for the resolution because it meant fighting and I saw it must come to that. The spread of the strike would and must be followed by a general outbreak. The authorities of the land would try to quell it; but we must resist them. There was nothing now but a physical force struggle to be looked for. We must get the people out to fight; and they must be irresistible if they were united."[32]

However, it appears that only Peter McDouall, Cooper and James Leach had any grasp of what was taking place and what needed to be done. McDouall was in touch with the mood of the masses after addressing assemblies of 100,000 people, as well as small rural ones. It was these three leading Chartists who understood the real gravity of the situation.

When it came to the vote, Hill's amendment only received six votes. The conference instead decided to give support to the decision of the trades to

---

30 J. Charlton, p. 39.

31 G.D.H. Cole, *Chartist Portraits*, p. 281.

32 J. Charlton, p. 40.

strike. Even O'Connor who was equivocal now voted in favour. However, this resolution of support needed to be put into practice. It was a time for action. After the vote, the meeting believed there needed to be unity and therefore agreed that the minority would be bound by the majority decision. This was democratic centralism, or unity in action. It reflected the democracy of the movement, but also the need for centralism. It was like a trade union strike vote: once agreed, the decision was binding on everyone. There was no room for doubters or blacklegs, who had to accept the view of the majority. The resolution, which reflected more 'sympathy' than resolve, reads as follows:

> "Whilst the Chartist body did not originate the present cessation from labour, the conference of delegates from various parts of England express their deep sympathy with their constituents, the working men now on strike, and that we strongly approve the extension and continuation of the present struggle till the People's Charter becomes a legislative enactment, and decide forthwith to issue an address to that effect, and pledge ourselves on our return to our respective localities to give a proper direction to the people's efforts."[33]

On the same day, the Executive of the National Charter Association also issued an address, which was an appeal for action. It deserves to be quoted in full, so as to present its flavour:

> "Brother Chartists – The great political truths which have been agitated during the last half-century have at length aroused the degraded and insulted white slaves of England to a sense of their duty to themselves, their children, and their country. Tens of thousands have flung down their implements of labour. Your taskmasters tremble at your energy, and expecting masses eagerly watch this the great crisis of our cause. Labour must no longer be the common prey of masters and rulers. Intelligence has beamed upon the mind of the bondsman, and he has been convinced that all wealth, comfort, and produce, everything valuable, useful and elegant, have sprung from the palms of his hands; he feels that his cottage is empty, his back thinly clad, his children breadless, himself hopeless, his mind harassed, and his body punished, that *undue riches*, luxury, and gorgeous plenty might be heaped on the palaces of the taskmasters, and flooded in the granaries of the oppressor. Nature, God, and reason, have condemned this inequality, and in the thunder of a people's voice it must perish forever. He knows that labour, the real property of society, the sole origin of accumulated property, the first cause of natural wealth, and the only supporter, defender, and contributor to the greatness of our country, is *not possessed of the same legal protection which is*

---

33 M. Beer, p. 148.

given to those lifeless effects, the houses, ships, and machinery, which labour alone have reacted. He knows that if labour has no protection, wages cannot be upheld nor in the slightest degree regulated, until every workman of twenty-one years of age, and of sane mind, is on the *same political level as the employer*. He knows the Charter would remove by universal will, expressed in universal suffrage, the heavy load of taxes which now crush the existence of the labourer, and cripple the effects of commerce; that it would give cheap government as well as cheap food, high wages as well as low taxes, bring happiness to the hearthstone, plenty to the table, protection to the old, education to the young, permanent prosperity to the country, long-continued protected political power to labour, and peace, blessed peace, to exhausted humanity and approving nations; therefore it is that we have solemnly sworn, and one and all declared, that the golden opportunity now within our grasp shall not pass away fruitless, that the chance of centuries afforded to us by a wise and all-seeing God, shall not be lost; but that we now do universally resolve never to resume labour until labour's grievances are destroyed, and protection secured for ourselves, our suffering wives, and helpless children, by the enactment of the People's Charter.

"Englishmen! The blood of your brothers reddens the streets of Preston and Blackburn, and the murderers thirst for more. Be firm, be courageous, be men. Peace, law, and order have prevailed on our side – let them be revered until your brethren in Scotland, Wales, and Ireland are informed of your resolution; and when the universal holiday prevails, which will be the case in eight days, then of what use will bayonets be against public opinion? What tyrant can then live above the terrible tide of thought and energy, which is now flowing fast, under the guidance of man's intellect, which is now destined by a Creator to elevate his people above the reach of want, the rancour of despotism, and the penalties of bondage. The trades, a noble, patriotic band, have taken the lead in declaring for the Charter, and drawing their gold from the keeping of tyrants. Follow their example. Lend no whip to rulers wherewith to scourge you.

"Intelligence has reached us of the wide spreading of the strike, and now, within fifty miles of Manchester, every engine is at rest, and all is still, save the miller's useful wheels and the friendly sickle in the fields.

"Countrymen and brothers, centuries may roll on as they have fleeted past, before such universal action may again be displayed; we have made the cast for liberty, and we must stand, like men, the hazard of the die. Let none despond. Let all be cool and watchful; and, let continued resolution be like a beacon to guide those who are not hastening far and wide to follow your memorable example...

"Let no man, woman or child, break down the solemn pledge; and if they do, may the curse of the poor and starving pursue them...

"Our machinery is all arranged, and your cause will, in three days, be impelled onward by all the intellect we can summon to its aid; therefore, whilst you are peaceful, be firm; whilst you are orderly, make all be so likewise; and whilst you look to the law, remember that you had no voice in making it, and are therefore the slaves to the will, the law, and the price of your masters.

"All officers of the Association are called upon to aid and assist in the peaceful extension of the movement, and to forward all monies for the use of the delegates who may be expressed all over the country. Strengthen our hands at this crisis. Support your leaders. Rally round our sacred cause, and leave the decision to the God of justice and of battle."[34]

While powerfully expressed, there was little more in the appeal than support for extending the strike. It mentioned little in the way of concrete proposals as what to do next, certainly not the question of political power.

THE QUESTION OF POWER POSED

Throughout August, the strike was being rolled out from town to town in endless waves, involving hundreds of thousands of workers in the Midlands, Lancashire, Cheshire, Derbyshire, Yorkshire, and the Scottish coalfields. Striking pickets travelled the counties reinforcing the strike, which had assumed unprecedented proportions. The country had never seen anything like it before. It was an astonishing display of working-class power. A young worker, Ben Wilson, made his way towards Halifax amid the factory stoppages:

"I was much surprised when I saw thousands marching in procession, many of whom were armed with cudgels... I then made my way to Skircoat Moor, where I had heard there was to be a large meeting held, and when I arrived, I saw such a sight as I had never seen there before, the moor being literally covered with men and women."[35]

Although the epicentre of the strike was Manchester, Ashton and Stalybridge, it had spread far beyond that. In areas not directly affected, including London, there was still solidarity with the strikers. Charles Darwin, the author of *On the Origin of Species*, was one of those caught up in the trouble and was

---

34 R. Brown and C. Daniels, pp. 86-88, and R.C. Gammage, p. 219.
35 J. Charlton, p. 29.

hemmed in at Gower Street. As Adrian Desmond and James Moore explain in their biography of Darwin:

> For three days, from 14-16 August, battalions of Guards and Royal Horse Artillery marched up through central London to the new Euston Station to put down the riots in Manchester. The troops were trailed by jeering crowds. The commotion was terrible as they passed Darwin's road, with screams of "Remember, you are brothers," and "Don't go and slaughter your starving fellow countrymen." By the time the battalions reached Gower Street, the demonstrators were hemming them in, with gangs everywhere. The streets were frightening, even with a huge police presence. Each day the situation worsened. On the 16th the station (only a few hundred yards from the house) was actually blocked and the troops repeatedly charged the crowds to clear a way in... For days on end, up to ten thousand demonstrators massed on the commons all over the capital. Working men and women milled about the streets, shouting and cheering.[36]

To witness such scenes in the capital city was truly alarming for the ruling class, with sordid stories even reaching the ears of the young Queen Victoria, who noted in her diary on Saturday, 13 August 1842:

> Both Children appeared at our luncheon. Papa thinks the Baby so like Albert.
>
> The accounts from Manchester are dreadful – such disturbances, as also in some other parts, near Sheffield, &c.
>
> Drove out with Papa & Alexandrine, Albert & Ernest, &c, riding. We drove to the Stud & showed Papa all the horses. We also looked at the Hunters. I never felt anything like the heat.
>
> On returning, found Sir Robert Peel & some of the other Ministers had come down for a Council, & I found a box from Sir Robert, in my room, in which he wrote that 3 Magistrates had come to Town this morning, giving an account of the bad state of things in Manchester, and expressing their anxiety that something should be done before the 16th inst, the anniversary of a great mob fight, which took place there in 1819 [The Peterloo massacre], and some great explosion is dreaded for that day.[37]

She wrote to Sir Robert Peel, the Prime Minister, demanding he act, and:

> "[S]urprised at the little (or no) opposition to the dreadful riots in the Potteries... at the passiveness of the troops... they ought to act, and these meetings ought

---

36 A. Desmond and J. Moore, *Darwin*, p. 297, Quoted in J. Charlton, p. 30.

37 https://www.open.edu/openlearn/history-the-arts/history/social-economic-history/queen-victoria-on-the-chartists

to be prevented… everything ought to be done to apprehend Cooper and all the delegates at Manchester."[38]

She remained in close contact with Peel during the strike, urging repression of the 'multitude' at every opportunity.

The Queen's strictures had the effect of extracting the maximum penalties. For the crime of burning down the house of the Reverend Dr. Vale – a clergyman and coal owner – six men were sentenced to be transported for twenty-one years each. Added to the sentences passed on others for their complicity, a total of 189 years' imprisonment was imposed. "Measured in terms of human suffering," states Dr. Wearmouth, "the Rev. Dr. Vale had lived in a most costly house."[39]

"I have not had a spare moment since the close of the session", wrote the pestered Peel to Brougham on 21 August. "My time has been occupied with odious business arising from the mad insurrection of the working classes…" He was convinced that "force alone can subdue this rebellious spirit", a view reinforced by the Duke of Wellington and Her Royal Highness.[40]

Within days, the strike had finally reached its zenith. But the leadership did not know what to do next. It could not simply tread water. In such a titanic struggle, time was of the essence. Either the strike would advance towards taking power, or it would inevitably retreat. If carried to its conclusion, it could have been an historic victory for the working class, but unfortunately the Chartist leadership lacked any perspective for power. There was no clearly defined road to take, and confusion reigned. Two years later, Engels explained that the general strike had failed, not due to a lack of courage or determination, but the "want of a clearly-defined object" on the part of the working class. He explained:

> The thing had begun without the working men having any distinct end in view, for which reason they were all united in the determination not to be shot at for the benefit of the Corn-Law repealing bourgeoisie. For the rest, some wanted to carry the Charter, others, who thought this premature, wished merely to secure the wages rate of 1840. On this point, the whole insurrection was wrecked. If it had been from the beginning an intentional, determined working men's insurrection, it would surely have carried its point.[41]

---

38 Quoted in R. Challinor and B. Ripley, p. 35.
39 Ibid., p. 35.
40 Quoted in A. Briggs, *Chartist Studies*, p. 388.
41 MECW, vol. 4, p. 521.

Towards the second week of the strike, the momentum began to wane. Still, even then, workers were coming out, as in Bradford and other places. The picketing was still very effective. However, on 16 August, a sizable flying picket in Burslem was forcibly broken up by dragoons and special constables, resulting in over 200 workers being arrested. It was an indication that the state was determined to break the strike.

The general strike inevitably faced problems, especially as the momentum waned. While at a local level organisers were able to give direction to the movement, national direction was floundering. There were also logistical problems of communication between areas and the central leadership. The forces of the state were well armed, while workers had access to only basic forms of defence, although the armouries could have been targeted. A class appeal to the soldiers could also have had an effect. Food was in short supply, which added to the increasing pressure on the strikers and their families. Direct assistance from the NCA was very uneven, with little in the way of support from *The Northern Star*. Some leaders were even hostile to the strike, as in the case of the Reverend William Hill, the editor of *The Northern Star*. All of this added to a lack of direction at a crucial time.

HIGH POINT

"The working men who had no special aim, separated gradually, and the insurrection came to an end without evil results", explained Engels.[42] O'Connor's role was pivotal, given his colossal authority. However, his vacillations and hesitations served to expose his limits. It is not for nothing that Marx said that insurrection is an art, which means it has to have a clear aim and plan. But these elements of consciousness, premeditation, and planning were clearly lacking.

From the point of view of the working-class struggle, the general strike of 1842 marked a high-point of the movement. It was a popular working-class rebellion against the capitalist system. "In the heat of the struggle," noted Max Beer, "the political and revolutionary idea gained the upper hand over the purely industrial view."[43] The world had never before experienced such an action of the new working class in terms of its scale and degree of class consciousness. Workers had learned more in a day than in the previous decade. Moreover, it served to reinforce the growing chasm between the class instincts of the proletarian masses and the bourgeoisie.

---

42 MECW, vol. 4, pp. 521-2.

43 M. Beer, p. 143.

The government was terrified that the country, at least in the North, was on the brink of all-out civil war. State repression, as far as they were concerned, had to be stepped up if the situation was to be salvaged. Large military reinforcements were therefore poured into Manchester, the West Riding and The Potteries. At this crucial moment, it was the government that took the initiative to act to break the strike movement. The Home Secretary, Graham, had taken the decision to arrest several trades delegates. The National Chartist Association conference was also broken up, and sixty delegates arrested, including James Leach and Thomas Cooper. McDouall managed to evade arrest by escaping to France. Hutchinson, meanwhile, was taken into custody.

In the meantime, more troops were dispatched to the North, the epicentre of the movement, including some drawn from Ireland. The Lord-Lieutenant of Worcestershire stated that "all meetings in large numbers in present circumstances have a manifest tendency to create terror and to endanger the public peace, that as such they are illegal, and upon notice given that they will not be allowed to be held, they ought to be dispersed."[44]

By 20 August, the tide had turned. The back of the strike movement had been broken. Only isolated pockets of strikers now held out, as the strike began to retreat and eventually crumble. In Manchester, the movement began to disintegrate, despite the weavers holding out until 26 September. Other areas also held out, especially in south-east Lancashire, but with depleted resources and government repression, many desperate strikers drifted back to work. "So deep was the distress, so universal the hunger, that they had to eat the dead carcasses of cows dug up after they were buried", stated William Beesley.[45] The largest strike in Britain's history effectively came to an end in the last week of August.

As for the ruling class, their feelings were summed up later by Sir James Graham:

"We had the painful and lamentable experience of 1842 – a year of the greatest distress, and now that it is passed, I may say, of the utmost danger... We had in this metropolis, at midnight, Chartist meetings assembled in Lincoln's Inn Fields. Immense masses of people, greatly discontented and acting in a spirit dangerous to the public peace... What was the condition of Lancashire? ... All the machinery was stopped... For some time, troops were continually called on, in different parts of the manufacturing districts, to maintain public tranquillity... For three months

---

44 F.C. Mather, quoted in A. Briggs, pp. 388-389.
45 Quoted in R. Challinor and B. Ripley, p. 27.

the anxiety which I and my colleagues experienced was greater than we ever felt before with reference to public affairs."[46]

But a defeat is a defeat. For the working class, the failure of the general strike had an inevitable impact on morale. Despite all the exertions and potential for victory, which was within their grasp, they had been driven back to work to face the wrath of the employers. The masters had reasserted their control once again and were determined to turn the screws. Although the workers were not completely cowed, they were feeling exhausted. Their efforts had come to nothing. Apathy began to set in as 'normality' was restored. This is always the mood after the defeat of a major movement. It takes time for the wounds to heal, but heal they do.

WOMEN WORKERS

As mentioned earlier, one of the weaknesses of the Charter was that it only mentioned the struggle for the vote for adult men. Nevertheless, this was no barrier to the involvement of working women in the Chartist movement. They regarded Chartism as their struggle too. Starting with the East London Democratic Association, many women were drawn into membership, especially the marginalised silk weavers of Spitalfields, an industry which involved whole families. Women workers, who constituted a significant percentage of the labour force, turned out in great numbers to join their menfolk in this united struggle. After a hard day's work in the factories and the mills, tens of thousands of women turned out to rally to the Chartist cause.

Women, after all, were a key part of the workforce. The bulk of those employed in the cotton mills of Lancashire were women. They worked in the mines, the bowels of the earth, causing a woman to say to Thomas Bald: "O, sir, this is sore, sore work. I wish to God the first woman who had tried to bear the coals had broken her back, and none would have tried again."[47]

Throughout history, women have played a key role in revolutionary movements. They participated in the Radical movement, often in women's classes, and could also be found in the illegal trade unions. In 1791 Mary Wollstonecraft wrote a blistering attack on Edmund Burke titled *Vindication of the Rights of Men, in a letter to the Right Honourable Edmund Burke*, which upheld the ideals of the French Revolution. In the same year, she wrote her *Vindication of the Rights of Women* (published 1792). Female Reformers were out in strength at St Peter's Field in Manchester in August 1819.

---

46 Quoted in A. Hutt, *This Final Crisis*, p. 53.
47 M. Ramelson, *Petticoat Rebellion*, pp. 27-28.

Women played a considerable part in all three Charter campaigns, where, once more, they formed Women's Charter Associations. They were to be found in large numbers in the torchlit processions to demonstrations on the moors and out-of-way places, at which some of them spoke. These were proletarian women. "But all these stormy events touched upper- and middle-class women not one iota", continues Ramelson.[48]

Women took the initiative to organise themselves into separate Chartist groups. The first female Charter Association was established in Birmingham in 1838 with a membership reaching 1,300, and more than 100 women's associations were established in the early years of the movement. Women played their full role, alongside the men, in marching and organising, as well as in physically confronting the authorities. "Woman can no longer remain in her domestic sphere. For her, home has been made cheerless, her hearth comfortless, and her position degrading", stated a resolution adopted by the women Chartists of Bethnal Green.[49]

Many women were drawn into activity when women's committees monitored the shops under the Convention's 'exclusive dealing' policy, where Chartists would prevent shopping at businesses unsupportive of the cause. In Barnsley, every Chartist meeting began with "an index to exclusive dealing", in which the names of shopkeepers who had contributed to the Reverend Stephens' defence fund were read out. "Let every shop and shopkeeper be noted in a book kept for the purpose, stating names, residence, trade and whether Whig or Tory; also, another book containing the names of those friendly to the cause of the people..." stated the manifesto of the Female Political Union in 1838. This was directly linked to the battle cry: "'Tis better to die by the sword than by famine, and we shall glory in seeing every working man of England selling his coat to buy a sword or a rifle to be prepared for the event..."[50]

There were certainly many Chartists who strongly believed that not only men, but women too, should have the vote. A number even campaigned for it, including R.J. Richardson who, while in prison, wrote a pamphlet called *Rights of Women*. It is a fine document, which graphically describes the slave-like working conditions faced by women in the mines, factories and mills. He argued forcefully:

"Ought women to interfere in the political affairs of the country? ...

---

48 Ibid, p. 70.
49 M. O'Brien, *Perish the Privileged Orders*, p. 47.
50 Quoted in D. Thompson, *The Chartists*, p. 137.

I do most distinctly and unequivocally say – YES! And for the following reasons:
First, because she has a natural right.
Second, because she has a civil right.
Third, because she has a political right.
Fourth, because it is a duty imperative upon her.
Fifthly, because it is derogatory to the divine will to neglect so imperative a duty."[51]

He went on to look at the plight of women in different settings and trades. "How disgusting it was", he wrote, that women were used as pack animals, not least in the coal mines, where they were forced to work in the most confined spaces, "where they squat down on their knees, and sometimes in a half reclining position, for the purpose of hewing with a small pick" the coal from the seam, and had to drag heavy loads underground.

The coal owners, of course, saw things differently. Lord Londonderry, "the miners' friend", for example, argued that, as some seams were too low for ponies, they were naturally suited to female labour. As animals could not be used, women had to drag the loads. When Parliament passed a law against women working in mines, it was simply ignored. One Wigan owner dressed his women workers "in male attire, having jackets and trousers in place of the linsey petticoats".[52]

Richardson stated:

"Many years before the age of puberty, are they taken to these hell-holes to earn their little pittance, in order to enable the parents to purchase the miserable sustenance which the rapacity of the capitalist deigns to allow them to support the cravings of Nature…"

He described the lot of women as "outrages upon humanity".
He appealed:

"Rouse you, and let future historians record your zeal in the cause of human redemption, and you will confer a perpetual obligation on posterity. Debased is a man who would say women have no right to interfere in politics, when it is evident, that they have as much right as 'sordid man.'"[53]

The whole pamphlet is worthy of being reprinted today as an inspiration to women workers in their fight for a better life.

---

51 Quoted in D. Thompson, *The Early Chartists*, p. 115.
52 R. Challinor and B. Ripley, p. 213.
53 Quoted in D. Thompson, *The Early Chartists*, p. 121.

Another Chartist who addressed the question of women was John Watkins, who wrote in his *Address to the Women of England*:

"So far from being excluded from taking part in politics, women ought to be allowed to vote; not wives – for they and their husbands are one, or ought to be as one – but maids and widows..."[54]

This revealed the common conception that husbands and wives were as one politically, as dependants. But those who were single, and therefore independent, should have the vote. This misconception was not universal. Many made the obvious point that Britain was ruled by a woman, who was also married, but no woman had any political rights. "If a woman can rule," explained James Hyslop, a Scottish weaver, "surely women could and should have the vote."[55]

Working women did not see their interests as separate from the men. Their fight was regarded as a joint endeavour in opposition to employers and capitalist politicians. After all, they worked together in the factories and mills, being exploited together. They were of a similar mind. To get involved was the natural thing to do, and it included whole families. The idea that a 'woman's place is in the home' was breaking down and being challenged. Women had a mind of their own. As a woman Chartist from Newcastle declared:

"We have been told that the province of woman is her home and that the field of politics is to be left to men; this we deny; the nature of things renders it impossible and the conduct of those who give the advice is at variance with the principles they assert."[56]

When Julian Harney addressed the Democratic Festival in June 1839, he told the women of Newcastle that "good as the men of Cumberland were, the women were better men of the two".[57] At around the same time, it was reported that in the Lancashire area "women were now in a state of progress, and were purchasing pikes in large numbers". The delegate from Hyde announced that his society had 300 men and 200 women, but that the women were much better than the men.

Women turned out in droves for the mass meetings and demonstrations. They joined in the mass picketing and fearlessly confronted the police and

---

54 Ibid., p. 125.
55 Ibid., p. 126.
56 *The Northern Star*, 9 February 1839, quoted in D. Black and C. Ford, p. 62.
57 D. Thompson, *The Chartists*, p. 139.

soldiers' bayonets when necessary. *The Manchester Guardian* reported a scene from Halifax:

> "Perhaps the women were at this encounter the more valiant of the two; approaching to the very necks of the horses they declared they would rather die than starve, and if the soldiers were determined to charge, they might kill them."[58]

Clearly, this participation was a tremendous advance in a society in which women had no rights of citizenship. The more women broke out of the home, whether in work or in the Chartist movement, the more they stood on their own two feet and became independent. Their involvement in the struggles of Chartism was part of this process, bringing many working-class women into activity for the first time, allowing them to play a broader role than ever before. It was a liberating experience. This was extremely progressive, since women are doubly oppressed: as workers and as women. Women being involved in such a militant movement was an enormous challenge to the existing morality and norms of behaviour promoted by government, press and pulpit.

When Chartism first emerged, women did not need any encouragement to stand up for themselves. In May 1839, Elizabeth Neeson of the London Female Democratic Association stated:

> "[We] consider it our duty to co-operate with our patriotic sisters in the country to obtain the Universal Suffrage in the shortest possible time [and] to annihilate the cruel, unjust and atrocious New Poor Law (miscalled!) Amendment Bill, to support with any means in our power any patriot engaged in the great struggle for freedom who may need our assistance and to destroy forever this cruel murdering system of transporting our children to the burning sands of Africa or immuring them in the horrid cotton hells and treating them worse, for no other crime than that of being poor. Sisters and friends, we entreat you to shake off that apathy and timidity which too generally prevails among our sex (arising from the prejudices of a false education) ... To those who may be, or appear to be, surprised that females should be daring enough to interfere with politics, to them we simply say that, as it is a female who assumes to rule this nation in defiance of the universal rights of man and woman, we assert in accordance with the rights of all, and acknowledging the sovereignty of the people our right, as free women (or women determined to be free) to rule ourselves."[59]

---

58 *The Manchester Guardian*, 20 August 1842, quoted in J. Charlton, p. 29.
59 *The Northern Star*, 11 May, 1839, quoted in D. Black and C. Ford, p. 64.

Four months later, after a demonstration in favour of the general strike, the *Nottingham Mercury* spoke disparagingly of "these harpies, whose expressions on every occasion, whose oaths and blasphemy, groans and yells, really made us blush for the feminine sex of England..."[60] This expressed the loathing of the bourgeois establishment for the activities of the 'no nonsense' proletarian women.

At this time, a period of heightened activity, *The Northern Star* reported on the situation in Bradford:

> "The female radicals of the Bradford district, amounting to upwards of 600, walked in procession through the principal streets headed by a band of music and banners... at the head of the procession there was carried by a woman a large printed board with the words 'exclusive dealing'..."

When the time came, they also rolled up their sleeves and joined in the confrontations with the police and military. In the Preston disturbances "women filled their aprons with stones, and brought them to the men... It was in vain that the soldiers attempted to disperse them", noted Gammage.[61] Once involved, they were in many ways more determined than their menfolk. Thompson Cooper, a Wolverhampton surgeon, explained how the women in the coalfields were the backbone of the strike. "The women, particularly, were exceedingly inveterate in urging their husbands to hold out, saying they would rather live on potatoes and salt than give in."[62]

In 1842, John La Mont said it was time to:

> "[S]uggest... such changes as the probable extension of the Suffrage to sane minded males of eighteen years of age instead of twenty-one, already provided by our Charter; and enfranchisement of females – notwithstanding the amount of blackguardism, folly and coercion which will be arrayed against this by the aristocratic *debauches*."[63]

When the NCA was established, it was open to men and women alike, and many women took up membership. In 1843 the *English Chartist Circular* wrote that "hundreds of women had enrolled in the NCA". This was the high point of women's involvement. When the movement was on the wane, women's involvement also fell. As soon as it came to life, so did the

---

60 Quoted in D. Thompson, *The Chartists*, p. 138.
61 R.C. Gammage, p. 221.
62 Quoted in R. Challinor and B. Ripley, p. 26.
63 Quoted in D. Thompson, *The Chartists*, p. 124.

participation of women members. They certainly regarded the fight for the Charter as a class and social question which would bring about the liberation of both men and women.

In many ways, there was a close bond between men and women in the Chartist struggle. As George White noted to a friend:

> "I have spent nearly four years out of the last ten in gaol for Chartism. My wife is a glorious trump and seconds my views. She would perish of starvation rather than degrade me in my absence... Is this not happiness to a man like me?"[64]

Of course, women Chartists were attacked and ridiculed by figures of the establishment. *The Times* for instance called them "Hen Chartists". In the mind of the Reverend Francis Close, the woman was worse than the man. He condemned "a bad mother" as more mischievous "than a bad father". He went on: "What a curse are such women to the country! Their children must grow up revolutionists, for they have been taught revolution at home!"[65]

This involvement of women, often at the sharp end, was also carried over into the trade union struggles. Miss Ruthwell, a radical woman from Bradford, was one of these outstanding figures. In a speech to the newly-formed National Association of United Trades for the Protection of Labour, it was reported:

> "The time was approaching when the mind of the Power-Loom Weavers would arise above their thraldom; and she now warned the employers that the day was fast approaching when the tyranny practised on them would end forever and the sun of freedom and virtue rise to shine refulgent to the end of time... While she had a tongue to proclaim the wrongs of sisters in slavery; while a drop of British blood flowed in their veins she would strive for the emancipation of her class and ere long they would find that the female workers in Bradford would be a powerful auxiliary in the onward march to 'a fair day's wage for a fair day's work'. Miss Ruthwell sat down loudly cheered."[66]

This was the voice of working-class women aroused to militant class action. Chartism certainly helped to bring such women to their feet. The deeper the mass movement, the more the oppressed are drawn into its embrace. In the process, they are transformed by the experience of the struggle.

---

64 Quoted in D. Thompson, *The Chartists*, p. 144.

65 Ibid., p. 147.

66 Ibid., p. 136.

This brings to mind the words of Charles Fourier, the French utopian socialist, often quoted by Marx, that the measure of social progress in society can be gauged by the progress of women toward liberty. The actions of Chartist women contributed an important step in this direction.

STRIKE AFTERMATH

With the government clampdown, mass arrests followed the general strike defeat. Given the disruption and alarm over anarchy and rebellion, the ruling class was blinded by hatred. They believed that the 'insolent' working class needed to be taught a lesson it would never forget. "Arrest or arraignment was the lot of every leader or speaker among the Chartists or trade unionists, and of every working man suspected of complicity in the strike movement", explained Max Beer.[67] All in all, 1500 arrests took place in the North West alone, and many more nationally, of whom 200 men and women were transported to Australia for terms between seven years and life. Others received varying prison sentences to give them a taste of the dungeon. The strike leader, Richard Pilling, who was charged with sedition, conspiracy, tumult and riot, faced the death penalty.

In Liverpool, the assizes had sentenced eleven men to transportation and had imprisoned 115. It was presided over by Lord Abinger, who was beside himself with rage against the Chartists and expressed himself in vitriolic terms:

"The doctrines promulgated by the Chartists were doctrines of perfect insanity, and no man but a fool or a knave could promulgate them... the establishment of the Charter would become an odious tyranny... They [the executive of the NCA] ... wanted to carry the principle of the Charter... that is to say the labouring classes who have no property are to make the laws for those who have property."[68]

In October, 651 prisoners appeared before the courts. Only 125 of them were acquitted, while the bulk received sentences of between a few months to two years. Some seventy-nine prisoners were sentenced to transportation to the penal colonies in Australia. A further 800 were released after a short period in captivity or rushed through the police courts, while 710 were tried at the assizes in York, Lancaster, Stafford, Chester and Liverpool. The repression had led to the death of Samuel Holberry in York prison. Workers were also victimised at their jobs, and about 100 Merthyr Chartists were given the sack from their work at the iron foundry.

---

67 M. Beer, p. 151.
68 Quoted in J. Charlton, p. 47.

Sir James Graham was delighted that he had "brought the Chartists into a strait". But there was also disquiet in ruling circles. "The state of affairs is somewhat improved," he noted, "at least the insurrection is overawed; but the rebellious spirit is unbroken."[69]

This "rebellious spirit" was noticed by Cooke Taylor when he visited the areas in September, in the strike's aftermath. He was surprised to see that there was little sign of demoralisation. "The operatives are disappointed at the result of their late proceedings, but they are certainly not daunted; on the contrary, they boast of the great strength they displayed and the sympathy they met in almost every direction."[70]

This shows how the working class learns from its experiences, defeats as well as victories. It takes time for the workers to digest these events, but digest them they do. As is said, nothing is wasted in history.

The ruling class was still haunted by this unbroken "spirit" and continued to regard the situation in the gravest terms possible. From all their reports, it was clear that the Chartists still had widespread support in the industrial working class. This support was now tempered and hardened. The ruling class sought to deal with it by again attempting to sever the Chartist head from the body. As a consequence, some fifty-eight Chartist leaders had been arrested, including O'Connor, Harney, Hill and Cooper. They had their trials postponed until the following March, with the authorities hoping to secure life sentences. However, when they were eventually brought before the Lancaster Assizes, the defendants were freed on a legal technicality in the flawed indictment. Cooper was not so fortunate and, after being acquitted in Lancaster, he was sentenced to two years' imprisonment for seditious speeches at Staffordshire. He defended himself with vigour, addressing the jury for ten hours. When he was brought before the Court of Queen's Bench, he spoke for a further eight hours, but was eventually halted by the irate judge. McDouall, who had a price on his head, had evaded capture and escaped to Brighton, then to France, where he remained in exile for two years. It was a bitter pill to swallow.

"I am sorry that Feargus escaped", wrote the Queen's husband, Prince Albert of Saxe-Coburg and Gotha, to Sir Robert Peel. "Still, the effect of the trial is satisfactory."[71] Under pressure from the meddling Royals, Prime Minister Peel was looking for ways in which to suppress the Chartists,

---

69 M. Chase, p. 224.

70 J. Charlton, p. 49.

71 M. Chase, p. 241.

especially their 'subversive' newspapers. "Are we not now able to pounce with effect upon some of the vile trash of which the enclosed is a specimen", wrote Peel to Graham on 15 October 1842. Two months later he was urging the Home Secretary to "go to the extreme verge of the Law" in suppressing "revolting infidel publications and placards".[72]

But no amount of repression would diminish the underlying hatred felt by the lower orders towards their so-called betters. The class hatred remained intense and there was a profound questioning of the system. Richard Pilling was not alone in his criticisms of capitalism, made at his own trial at the Lancaster Assizes in March 1843. There, he launched a stinging attack:

> "Overproduction; intolerably long hours of labour; competition and the beating down of wages; unemployment and poverty in the midst of plenty; the employment of children and juvenile labour and the break-up of the family; lack of independence and control; the reification of human beings under commodity production; the many tyrannical and hypocritical actions of the cotton manufacturers – their insensitivity to the sufferings of operatives, blind adherence to the tenets of orthodox political economy, opposition to combination among workers and their frequent victimisation of labour activists... and their abhorrence of Chartism."[73]

A speech made by Pilling, and taken down by a constable, was read out at the trial to prove that he was the ringleader of the strike:

> "Fellow Townsmen, for I may so call you, having lived amongst you so long and having been at so many meetings attended by thousands, and having been in prison, I do not know whether it would be safe for me to own it or not; but I may avow that I have the honour to be the father of this movement and the sole cause of your being ladies and gentlemen at the present time; for the masters of Ashton had thought proper to offer a reduction of twenty-five per cent upon their wages. I then caused the bellman to go round and call the meeting swearing by the God of Heaven that, if the reduction took place, we would annihilate the system and cause the day of reckoning. I then addressed a meeting of 12,000. I later went to Stalybridge and addressed a meeting of 10,000. I then addressed a meeting at Hyde of 10,000 and at Dukinfield of 5,000. At every meeting they came to a resolution to work no more till they got the same wages as they had in February 1840... In the course of the last three weeks I have addressed upwards of 300,000 in different parts of Lancashire and Cheshire. When we went to Droylsden and

72 A. Briggs, *Chartist Studies*, p. 393.
73 J. Charlton, p. 49.

Manchester, and the people of Droylsden swore by the God of Heaven they would not work anymore until they had got their price of 1840. They then came to Stockport and caused all mills to be stopped.

"You must be sure and sick out, and not go to your work; for if you do, the masters will crush you down... I know the law of conspiracy and there never was a good thing got, but someone had to suffer for it. But they may put me in prison for I don't care a damn for being within the prison walls..."[74]

Richard Pilling also displayed his defiance by conducting his own defence: "And, now, Gentlemen of the jury, you have the case before you; the masters conspired to kill me, and I combined to keep myself alive."[75]

This whole episode underlined the indisputable fact that Chartism was first and foremost a class-conscious revolutionary movement, which drew towards itself the most self-sacrificing elements within the working class. Chartism became closely related to the mass hotbeds of revolt over the New Poor Law, the Ten-Hour Bill movement, as well as to the fight for trade union rights. According to the historian Max Beer, "the expressions Chartist, Socialist, trade unionist and working man were synonymous terms".[76]

CALM BEFORE STORM

In the years following the 1842 general strike, Chartism was largely treading water. The movement was catching its breath, so to speak, and so this period should be regarded as an interregnum, a relative calm before the storm of 1848.

Of course, there were some losses. There were those activists, disappointed by the failure to win the Charter, who shifted their attention from politics to trade unionism. In November 1842, the Miners' Association of Great Britain and Ireland was founded, in which the Chartist leaders – O'Connor and Duncombe – played a supporting role. This was followed by other trade unions – the Potters' Union (1843), the Cotton Spinners Association (1843) and the National Typographical Association (1845). Also, in the same year, a new general organisation was founded for the first time in a decade – the National Association of United Trades (NAUT), which became a focal point for the smaller and less well organised trades. The NAUT deserves to be remembered as the first trade union body to suggest the creation of a working-class party based upon the trade unions.

---

74 R. Brown and C. Daniels, pp. 91-92.

75 P. Hollis, p. 298.

76 M. Beer, p. 104.

As Challinor and Ripley explain:

So, the general strike of 1842 played a dual role: it helped to create the conditions for the growth of trade unions like the Miners' Association and, at the same time, it made Chartism more favourable, more responsive, more helpful to the trade unions than it would otherwise have been..."[77]

The Whig governments, in power for most of the decade between 1830 and 1841, had allowed the Corn Laws to remain in place. However, the agitation for repeal became intense and, with the support of the Whigs and sections of the Tories, repeal was eventually pushed through in January 1846, to the manufacturers' delight. At a single stroke, it had removed the thirty-year-long split in the ruling class, which had become a festering sore. But Peel's actions also split asunder the old Tory party, which was against repeal, and kept it out of power for more than twenty years. The revolt against Peel was led by the youthful Benjamin Disraeli, who was later to re-establish the Tory Party, not as a party of the landowners but as the party of industrial capital and imperialism. Peel, now isolated, was forced to resign on 27 June 1846, leading the way for the Whigs to assume power under Lord John Russell. The support of the Peelites gave Russell a comfortable working majority, with Lord Palmerston as foreign secretary and the Marquis of Lansdowne as Lord President of the Council, both of whom were Irish landlords.

Corn Law repeal was wholeheartedly welcomed by the manufacturing bourgeoisie, who saw free trade as the road to new markets and greater profits. They were not wrong: thanks to this legislation, the export of Lancashire cottons rose from £141,000 in 1843 to £1,000,000 in 1854. Nothing now stood between the British manufacturer and world markets. Some workers were fooled into believing that they would benefit from lower prices. However, there was no fall in wheat prices, as predicted, with the average for the five years from 1851 to 1855 at 56s. compared to 54s. 9d. in the five years from 1841 to 1845. It was not until 1870, with the opening of the wheat belt of the US Midwest by the railways, that large quantities of corn were imported.

Prior to the abolition of the Corn Laws, with the working class suffering from long working hours, the question of shorter hours had become a burning issue. However, the Short Time campaign that had been established attracted all sorts of middle-class moralists and do-gooders, who were led in Parliament by Michael Sadler, a Tory MP. When he lost his seat, the lead was

---

77 R. Challinor and B. Ripley, p. 43.

taken by Lord Ashley, later to become the Earl of Shaftesbury, the aristocratic philanthropist. The Conservative press in the industrial areas favoured the Ten-Hours Bill, while the Liberal press believed it disastrous to industry, reflecting once again a division between landowning and industrial interests. On this issue, the landlords attacked the manufacturers mercilessly, as they saw it as a means of getting back at them for the repeal of the Corn Laws. The Short Time Committees attracted the likes of the barnstorming Richard Oastler, a Tory, but also trade unionists, like John Doherty. Mass meetings were held and Parliament was petitioned.

But the wheels of Parliament move ever so slowly. Therefore, the agitation for shorter hours was carried on outside of Parliament, involving mass demonstrations, such as one of 100,000 workers at Wibsey Low Moor, near Bradford. At that time, 30,000 children paraded the streets of Leeds with placards proclaiming 'The Ten Hours Bill', and singing:

> We will have the Ten Hours Bill,
> That we will, that we will,
> Else the land shall ne'er be still,
> Never still, never still,
> Parliament say what they will,
> We will have the Ten Hours Bill,
> We want no Commissioning,
> We will have the Ten Hours Bill.

Given the inhumane overwork in the factories, especially of children, this campaign produced a wave of working-class activism. The Chartists, of course, supported it. O'Connor declared:

> "The ten-hour proposals will later on be regarded as a measure of the power of the working men. It is an attempt to initiate a series of laws which will curb the new order of things that has been produced by machinery, and which will place it at the service of the whole of society, instead of letting it act solely to the advantage of a single class."[78]

As expected, the factory owners put up a fierce resistance, in alliance with such Radicals as the Quaker John Bright. As we saw earlier, eminent economists, like Nassau Senior, claimed that profits were made "in the last hour" of work, so passing the Ten-Hour Bill would immediately bankrupt the whole of British industry. This opposition was represented by the 'free-traders'.

---

78 Quoted in M. Beer, p. 12.

Cynically, Lord Ashley put himself at the head of this Ten-Hour movement to prevent it falling into the wrong hands. He worked with the most moderate and respectable church-and-king types, and argued with the workers involved "that all should be carried on in a most conciliatory manner... that there should be no strikes, no intimidation and no strong language against their employers either within or without the walls of Parliament". Ashley later confessed: "From the first hour of my movement to the last, I had ever before me, and never lost sight of it, the issue of a restoration of a good understanding between employer and employed."[79]

In the end and through these safe channels, the Ten Hours Act of 1847, limiting the hours of textile workers, was finally passed by a block of anti-free traders, landowners and a section of the capitalists. Ashley wrote in his diary: "I may rejoice and heartily thank God that the operatives of Lancashire and Yorkshire, suffering as they are, remain perfectly tranquil."[80]

Engels recognised that this reform over hours had been carried due to a split in the ruling classes. He explained:

> "Did they carry it from any sympathy with the people? Not they. They lived, and live, upon the spoils of the people. They are quite as bad, though less barefaced and more sentimental, than the manufacturers. But they would not be superseded by them, and thus, from hatred towards them, they passed this law which should secure to themselves popular sympathy, and, at the same time, arrest the rapid growth of the manufacturer's social and political power."[81]

Of course, Engels was not opposed to the Ten-Hour Bill, but demanded greater protections for the working class, arguing instead for an Eight Hours' Bill. He added significantly: "The working classes will have learned by experience that *no lasting benefit whatever can be obtained for them by others, but that they must obtain it themselves by conquering, first of all, political power.*"[82]

However, the industrialists never stopped their relentless efforts to nullify the Ten-Hour Act. Finally, they succeeded, through a combination of resistance and a legal loophole. While the Act had stipulated a maximum of working ten hours for women and children, it did not refer to ten *continuous* hours, or the same ten hours. This allowed employers to find a loophole in the law by using children in relays, which allowed for much longer hours overall,

---

79 T. Rothstein, p. 77.

80 Ibid., p. 78.

81 F. Engels, 'The Ten Hours' Question', MECW, vol. 10, pp. 273-274.

82 MECW, vol. 10, p. 275.

and kept adults at work from 5.30 in the morning until 8.30 at night. This served to annul the 1847 Act altogether, and provoked massive anger in the working class.

In 1850, Lord Ashley's reputation was badly tarnished when he was forced to accept the Ten-and-a-Half Hours compromise Act, regarded as a betrayal by most in the industrial areas. The indignation was so deep in Halifax that a meeting passed the following resolution:

> "That in the opinion of this meeting Lord Ashley has basely and treacherously betrayed the interests of the factory children. After breaking faith with the factory operatives, we have no more confidence in my Lord Ashley… That we, the delegates, take this opportunity of expressing our utmost contempt and indignation to his Lordship, for the scandalous, abominable and disgraceful manner he has manifested in having betrayed the factory cause. And we also take this opportunity of ringing this as the last death knell betwixt Ashley, his colleagues, and the factory operatives, and bid the man everlasting adieu."[83]

The 'relay' system was not done away with in the factories until the amending Act of 1853. A further piece of legislation introducing a genuine ten-hour maximum working day was not secured until 1874, some twenty-five years later. Nothing was ever given easily or freely by the ruling class, except under intense class pressure.

THE LAND PLAN

Following the state repression after 1842, Chartism underwent years of soul searching. The boot was now on the other foot, and the movement was feeling the isolation. In 1843, O'Connor made a telling remark about the prevailing mood:

> "[M]uch indeed of what was called enthusiasm has apparently subsided – the glare of the torch has gone out. Processions and demonstrations, instead of being necessary 'to keep up the steam', are abandoned with the feeling that they are but little worth – and flags and banners perhaps may yield to what seems to be general necessity. Be it so – they have done their work – and well!"[84]

He emphasised the point that "Chartism is not dead, but sleeping".

Another factor in this ebb in the fortunes of the Chartist movement was the economic recovery starting in 1843. While support for the Charter was

---

83 J.L. Hammond and B. Hammond, *Lord Shaftesbury*, p. 140.
84 D. Thompson, *The Chartists*, p. 129.

still solid, the movement stagnated. As with all setbacks, it took time for the movement, starting with the activists, to get their bearings and digest the experience.

After his time in prison in 1841, O'Brien was in poor health. Although he resumed writing and lecturing, he had lost his old flair. His participation in Sturge's meeting reflected his political decline, and resulted in a clash with O'Connor. He moved to the Isle of Man, where there was no stamp duty, to set up a print shop. He eventually returned to England and was elected as a delegate to the Chartist Convention of 1848, but soon resigned. He had completely lost his bearings. His best years as editor of *The Poor Man's Guardian*, a powerhouse of ideas, were far behind him. Sadly, he abandoned his original perspective of social revolution for the blind alley of reformism. The old flame had been extinguished. As we will observe elsewhere, the hardships of revolution, then retreat, are a great devourer of people. It uses up people, some physically, some morally. This was unfortunately the case with Bronterre O'Brien, the father of Chartism.

McDouall had left for France, and others drifted from the movement. This served to dislocate the Chartist leadership. As with all defeats, the more conservative features began to come to the fore, including the more utopian schemes. The historian Mark O'Brien makes an interesting point: "It is at this stage of the Chartists' history that it is most true to say that Chartism anticipated every future development of the working-class movement over the next century-and-a-half."[85] In this "anticipation" he sees the revolutionary aspects mixed up with the more backward and even reactionary elements, which arose from these difficult years.

The decline of the movement was also reflected in the fall in paper sales, most notably of *The Northern Star*. O'Connor had moved the paper from Leeds to McGowan of Great Windmill Street in London, and had changed the paper's name to *The Northern Star and National Trades Journal*, to give it greater appeal to the members of trade unions. He removed the Reverend Hill and appointed Julian Harney as its editor, who, as we have seen, was not only left-wing, but also held the most internationalist outlook among the Chartists.

In these years, while certain leaders drew revolutionary conclusions from their experiences, others, represented by O'Connor, became increasingly backward-looking. This outlook was particularly reflected in his scheme

---

85 M. O'Brien, *Perish the Privileged Orders*, p. 57.

called the 'Land Plan', which was to dominate things for the next few years. It was a plan for agrarian reform and was discussed at a meeting in Birmingham in September 1843, which, despite some objections, expressed its support for the plan.

Land ownership had always been a burning question. From the early Middle Ages to the Diggers of Gerrard Winstanley, the land was always regarded as common property stolen from the people of England. Since then, through robbery and violence, land ownership had been concentrated in the hands of the aristocracy and gentry. Industrialisation had produced a massive urban population with few, if any, links with the countryside. O'Connor's land proposal could be seen as an alternative to the horrors of the factory system and capitalist exploitation. The Land Plan had therefore a certain attraction for workers. This attempt to return to Merry England, of 'back to the land', promised to "make a paradise of England in less than *five years*". The plan to give workers and their families their own four-acre plots seemed for many like a dream come true.

As John Noakes wrote to *The Northern Star*:

"English soil is the property of the people, from whom our aristocrats seized it either by force or by trickery. The people must see that their inalienable right to property prevails; the proceeds of the land should be public property and used in the interests of the public. Perhaps I shall be told that these are revolutionary remarks. Revolutionary or not, it is of no concern; if the people cannot obtain that which they need in a law, they must get it without law."[86]

The idea clearly drew on the experiences of Robert Owen and his communist colonies. Owenism had been a strong current within the workers' movement, although Owen, following his failures, had turned towards the trade unions as the way forward. However, O'Connor's Land Plan differed markedly from Robert Owen's colonies in the sense that it was based on individual ownership, while Owen's was more collective and communistic. In any case, O'Connor made it abundantly clear that his idea had nothing to do with Owenism or Socialism. He proudly declared:

"My plan has no more to do with Socialism than it has with the Comet. I am advocating the co-operative system, not the principle of Communism. My plan is entirely opposed to the principle of communism for I repudiate communism and socialism."[87]

---

86 Quoted in MECW, vol. 6, pp. 307-308.
87 P. Hollis, p. 309.

In effect, O'Connor had become the voice of the smallholder. But such was the attraction that some 75,000 men and women within a two-year period spent their entire savings on weekly subscriptions to the project.

"Would it be for your advantage," asked Henry Vincent at a meeting in Watford, "that your fields of waving corn, in which the happiest years of your life have been spent, should be superseded by the smoke of chimneys, the clash of machinery, all the squalid filth and poverty of manufacturing hells?" The reply, of course, was a resounding "no".[88]

The Chartist conference in April 1845 discussed and endorsed the Land Plan, founding the Chartist Co-operative Land Society. Its object, as stated, was:

> "To purchase land on which to locate its members in order to demonstrate to the working classes of the kingdom, firstly, the value of the land as a means of making them independent of the grinding capitalist; and, secondly, to show them the necessity of securing the speedy enactment of the People's Charter, which would do for them nationally what the society proposes to do sectionally; the accomplishment of the political and social emancipation of the enslaved and degraded working classes being the prominent object of the society."[89]

'The Land, the Land, the Land', was the cry of thousands who existed on nine or ten shillings a week. A once-in-a-lifetime investment seemed to be a realisable dream for many. They answered the call of lecturers who toured the country promoting the scheme. With the Land Plan, O'Connor's popularity was now at its height.

> The Lion of Freedom is come from his den;
> We'll rally around him, again and again;
> We'll crown him with laurel, our champion to be:
> O'Connor the patriot, for sweet Liberty!
>
> – From 'Lion of Freedom', a popular song about Feargus O'Connor

They did not only compose songs in his honour, many even named their children after him. *The Northern Star* printed a dialogue between a Mrs King of Manchester and Richard Webb, a registrar of births and deaths:

> Mr Webb – What is the child to be called?
> Mrs King – James Feargus O'Connor King.

---

88 Quoted in A. Briggs, *Chartist Studies*, p. 291.
89 Quoted in M. Beer, p. 156.

Mr Webb – Is your husband a Chartist?

Mrs King – I don't know, but his wife is.

Mr Webb – Are you the child's mother?

Mrs King – Yes.

Mr Webb – You had better go home and consider it again; for if the person that you are naming your child after was to commit high treason and get hanged, what a thing it would be.

Mrs King – If that should be the case, I should then consider it an honour to have my child called after him, so that I shall never have him out of my memory so long as the child lives; for I think Feargus O'Connor a great deal honester man than those who are punishing him.

Mr Webb – Well, if you are determined to have it named after him, I must name it; but I never met such an obstinate lady as you before.

Mr Webb then registered the child by the above name.[90]

With the cash capital raised plus bank loans, half a dozen large estates were purchased and divided up into small holdings. The allocation of the plots was determined by ballot. Those chosen would receive funds to purchase equipment and stock to work the land. These plots would then become part of a collective or co-operative settlement where the landholders could share their endeavours for the good of the community. From the profits more land for settlement would be bought, from which new profits would be recycled, and so on.

"The land belongs to the people", declared O'Connor. "It is the people's heritage. Kings, princes, lords, and citizens have stolen it from the people. The law of nature is on the side of the people. Usurpation is the work of the rich and powerful."[91]

O'CONNORVILLE

A Chartist colony was established in Heronsgate, Hertfordshire, which took the prestigious name of O'Connorville. Another, called Charterville, was set up near Witney, Oxfordshire. O'Connor, ever flamboyant, appropriately headed his letters from his estate as "From Paradise". *The Northern Star* urged:

"Courage, poor slaves! deliverance is near.

Oh! she has breathed a summons sweeter still:

Come! take your guerdon at O'Connorville!"

---

90 Quoted in D. Thompson, *The Chartists*, p. 146.

91 M. Beer, p. 155.

The agrarian plan had three successive titles, (1) Chartist Co-operative Land Society, (2) National Co-operative Land Company and (3) National Land Company, which showed its evolution from an agrarian collective to an investment company. On this basis, O'Connor founded his Land Reform Joint Stock Company. In 1847, he explicitly stated: "Peasant proprietorship is the best basis of society."[92]

But there was no sea change. The venture was not short of critics, especially its business management. Attacks on the scheme came especially from the bourgeois newspapers. *The Dispatch, Lloyd's Newspaper, Manchester Examiner, Nottingham Mercury* and *The Nottingham Journal* all attacked the scheme, as well as O'Connor.

However, there were also critics inside the Chartist movement. Some, like Thomas Cooper, who had been a close ally of O'Connor, now believed the plan was delusional and would bury Chartism. As there was no real control over it, balance-sheets were published irregularly and in an incomplete form. The business operation was all at sea. There were those like Julian Harney, who criticised the plan's backward-looking idea, which was unlikely to succeed in a country that was rapidly industrialising. "It is equality, not feudalism," wrote Harney in *The Northern Star,* "which is the hope of the many... the 'golden age' is before, not behind us."[93] Others, like Bronterre O'Brien, condemned the scheme as extending "the hellish principle of Landlordism", which would only serve to benefit a small minority, and "destroy the principle of United Action".[94] Many others saw it as a diversion from the Charter, as a back-to-the-land movement that could not be a solution to the problems of the working class as a whole. The vast majority would inevitably be excluded from the scheme. O'Brien correctly called instead for the land to be nationalised for the benefit of everyone, not simply smallholders.

There was no love lost between O'Brien and O'Connor, who lambasted each other. O'Brien wrote:

"But the strangest thing of all is that the philanthropic Feargus should have dragged millions of people after him to torch-lit meetings, demonstrations, etc, all attended with great sacrifice of time and money, and caused the actual ruin of thousands through imprisonment, loss of employment, and expatriation, when all the while he had only to establish a 'National Chartist Co-operative Land

---

92 M. Beer, pp. 155-6.
93 *The Northern Star,* 14 February 1845.
94 A. Briggs, *Chartist Studies,* p. 339.

Society' to ensure social happiness for us all, and when, to use his own words in last week's *Star*, he had discerned that 'political equality can only spring from social happiness'. Formerly, he taught us that social happiness was to proceed from political equality; but doubtless when his land-bubble has burst, he will have the old or some other new creed for us."[95]

O'Connor was not slow to retaliate against his critics, especially in the pages of *The Northern Star*. He organised mass meetings, including one in the Hall of Science in Manchester, which held between three and four thousand people. At such gatherings, when O'Connor attacked his critics, there were cries of "Oh, the villains!" Again, he went on the offensive:

> "[V]illains who quaff your sweat, gnaw your flesh, and drink the blood of infants, suppose that I too would crush their little bones, lap up their young blood, luxuriate on woman's misery, and grow fat upon the labourer's toil. No, I could go to bed supperless, but such a meal would give me the nightmare; nay, an apoplexy."

O'Connor tested the audience's confidence in him. He said: "I have now brought money with me to repay every shareholder in Manchester." (Shouts of "Nay, but we won't have it!") "Well, then, I'll spend it all." (Cries of "Do, and welcome!")

"For more than three hours did O'Connor address the crowded and excited meeting," explained Gammage, "which was so densely packed before he commenced, that the reporters had to be pushed through the windows into the hall."[96]

As always, the Chartist poets captured the moment:

Come let us leave the murky gloom,
The narrow, crowded street:
The bustle, noise, the smoke and din,
To breathe the air that's sweet.
We'll leave the glorious palaces
To those miscalled great;
To spend a day of pleasure on
The People's First Estate!

The banners waving in the breeze,
The bands shall cheerfully play,

95 G.D.H. Cole, *Chartist Portraits*, pp. 259-260.
96 R.C. Gammage, p. 288.

Let all be mirth and holiday
On this our holy day.
Unto the farm – "O'Connorville,"
That late was "Herringsgate,"
We go to take possession of
The People's First Estate![97]

But this euphoria did not last long and the bubble soon burst. The government was taking a close interest in O'Connor's affairs and, in June 1844, Parliament appointed a select committee, which included O'Connor, to examine the Land Company's workings. As expected, this revealed serious shortcomings. The committee therefore recommended, given gross anomalies, that the Company's affairs should be wound up. The publication of its findings was devastating and completely undermined O'Connor's standing, including his cherished Land Plan. The scheme suffered a complete collapse.

Despite O'Connor's initial optimism, the demise of the Land Plan left those with shares penniless and effectively destitute. The parliamentary inquiry nevertheless cleared O'Connor of any corruption. Only later did it emerge that the government had actively worked to sabotage the Land Plan so as to discredit O'Connor. This is how the ruling class reacts to potential threats. For them, all is fair in love and war. Leaving these intrigues aside, every attempt to create 'islands of socialism' in the sea of capitalism was always doomed to fail. Robert Owen's 'Harmony Hall' at Queenwood, in Hampshire, went into deficit and collapsed in 1845. This was also true of many co-operatives, which had to adapt to the methods of capitalism or go bankrupt. They were a variety of 'utopian socialism', dreamed-up schemes, not rooted in the real development of society. While the 'back to the land' campaign was no solution to problems arising from industrial capitalism, it nevertheless did draw attention to the failure of the social system and its inability to provide even the basic necessities of life. It was for this reason that it incurred the animosity of the ruling class, which viewed it as a threat to the rights of the private ownership of land. Against such attacks, Engels, of course, publicly defended O'Connor and the Chartists.

BETTER TIMES AHEAD

As with all defeats and setbacks, and 1842 was no exception, personal animosity, frictions and squabbles tend to come to the surface. Leaders began to look for someone to blame and turned on each other. O'Connor

---

97 J. Arnott, 'The People's First Estate', *The Northern Star*, 1 August 1846.

repeatedly clashed with O'Brien and Cooper for different reasons. O'Brien responded in like fashion. Cooper, in turn, threatened to exacerbate the conflict with O'Connor by moving a resolution to the Chartist Convention demanding greater accountability of the Executive, and specifically that officers of the Land Society were to be banned from holding positions in it. This greatly increased tensions. To make matters worse, he then stated that, if the resolution were rejected, he would propose another, calling on the NCA to abandon the doctrine of physical force, which, according to him, "[had] filled the public mind with an aversion to Chartism".

This was a step too far and a real indication of demoralisation and Cooper's accommodation with liberalism. But it was the last part of the resolution that contained the real sting in the tail: "That this Convention regards Feargus O'Connor as unworthy of the confidence of Chartists, and thereby earnestly warns British working men of the folly and danger of union with him."[98]

As a consequence of this open frontal attack, all hell broke loose and every effort was made to silence Cooper. The pages of *The Northern Star* denounced him as a traitor and called on Chartists to speak out, urging that he be expelled from the Convention. As a result, hundreds of resolutions poured in from the localities to the offices of *The Northern Star*, most of which showed total confidence in O'Connor and nothing but contempt for his accuser, expressed in the most lurid terms imaginable.

The Conference where the showdown was to take place was held in Leeds on 3 August 1846. When Cooper rose, he tried to get a hearing but was denounced from all sides as a "rascal, scoundrel, liar, hypocrite", and many other epithets. A motion was moved by a young man, new to the Chartist movement, to expel Cooper. The name of the mover was Ernest Jones. He was to become the most left-wing leader of Chartism, but on this occasion he was one of O'Connor's right-hand men. When the move to expel Cooper was put to the vote on a show of hands, the conference chair declared it passed unanimously. But Cooper refused to budge from the hall. The meeting was instead adjourned and Cooper found his readmission to the conference barred. "It was utterly in vain that any man attempted to shake the confidence of the Chartists in O'Connor; that confidence became wider spread and firmer every day", wrote Gammage, who was present at the event.[99]

When a movement is in the doldrums and things are not going forward, the stale atmosphere often leads to acrimony, and this was a clear example

---

98 R.C. Gammage, p. 275.
99 R.C. Gammage, p. 283.

of that. Difficulties become magnified and differences widened in such a situation. It would require a sharp turn in the objective situation for things to revive and fortunes to change. Despite these internal troubles, Chartism and *The Northern Star* were still held in high regard, not least by revolutionaries on the Continent. *The Northern Star* published a letter from the German Democratic Communists of Brussels on 25 July 1846, which congratulated O'Connor on his electoral showing in Nottingham, where, as usual, he won in the hustings, but was defeated at the poll.

> "We hesitate not a moment in declaring that the *Star* is the only English newspaper… which is free from National and religious prejudice; which sympathises with the democrats and working men… all over the world; which in all these points speaks the mind of the English working class… We hereby declare that we shall do everything in our power to extend the circulation of *The Northern Star* on the Continent, and to have extracts from it translated in as many continental papers as possible."

The letter was signed by Friedrich Engels, Phillippe Gigot, and Karl Marx.[100]

As the year 1847 opened, there were plans to draw up a new National Chartist Petition and the collecting of signatures was being planned systematically all over the country. This coincided with a new economic crisis, wage cuts and rising unemployment. As Engels noted:

> "Consequently, meetings of discontented workers are rapidly increasing. *The Northern Star*, the organ of the Chartist workers, uses more than seven of its large columns to report on meetings held in the past week; the list of meetings announced for the present week fills another three columns."[101]

But as the Petition campaign was getting going, it was suddenly cut across by the announcement of a general election, in which about thirty candidates stood on Chartist principles. As usual, they made a good showing by winning on a show of hands in the hustings. Harney made a great display in Marylebone, where he challenged Lord Palmerston, the Foreign Secretary. Harney carried a majority on a show of hands, but declined to go to the poll. Ernest Jones stood in Halifax against a Tory and a Whig, again overwhelmingly winning the vote by a show of hands. When forced to stand in the polls, he picked up a very respectable 280 votes to the winners' 511 and 507 votes, remarkable considering few workers, if any, had the vote.

---

100 MECW, vol. 6, p. 59.
101 MECW, vol. 6, p. 305.

However, the greatest triumph of all, and cause for great celebration, was the amazing election victory of Feargus O'Connor as Member of Parliament for Nottingham. Remarkably, he managed to defeat the Whig minister, Sir John Cam Hobhouse. O'Connor polled 1,257 votes to Hobhouse's 893 on an extremely limited franchise. This single event boosted the cause of Chartism nationally, and placed the movement back on the map. In the person of O'Connor, real Chartism entered Parliament for the first time. During his time in the Commons he was to carry on a ferocious one-man opposition, especially on Irish issues. His relentless attacks on the government inside and outside Parliament were a constant reminder that 'the Lion' was still very dangerous and far from caged.

Chartism was rising as a force once again in the country. The collection of signatures for the National Petition was again stepped up in a frantic bid to outdo the Petition of 1842. O'Connor, ever the optimist, was now confidently predicting that there would be 5 million signatures before it was presented to Parliament.

"There is no possible room for doubt as to the social-revolutionary aim of Chartism up to the year 1845", wrote Max Beer.[102] In fact, this was the fundamental aim of Chartism up to its very end.

Towards the end of November 1847, Marx and Engels addressed an international meeting in London to mark the anniversary of the Polish Uprising of 1830. Julian Harney also addressed the meeting. During his contribution, Engels made the point: "I have lived in England for a number of years now and openly aligned myself with the Chartist movement during this period." He concluded: "The English Chartists will be the first to rise because it is precisely in England that the struggle between the bourgeoisie and the proletariat is the most intense."[103] The meeting ended with a singing of the *Marseillaise*. Everybody joined in, standing with hats off. It was a small sign that things were beginning to move. Within two months, revolution was sweeping the whole European Continent. Everything was about to dramatically change.

---

102 M. Beer, p. 45.
103 MECW, vol. 6, p. 389.

8. 1848: A CRITICAL YEAR

> To aid this cause we here behold
> British and French agree,
> Spaniard and German, Swiss and Pole
> With joy the day would see
> When mitres, thrones, misrule and wrong
> Will from this earth be hurled
> And peace, goodwill and brotherhood
> Extend throughout the world.
> – John Arnott, *The Northern Star*, September 1846

> Rise Britons rise with indignation.
> Hark! Hark!! I hear the clanking chains
> That bind a generous nation,
> Where martial law and terror reign.
> – 'Ireland in Chains', *The Northern Star* April 1846

> "The Jacobin of 1793 has become the Communist of today."
> – Karl Marx, 'Speech to the Democratic Association', February 1848

TURMOIL IN IRELAND

1848 began quietly enough. But this was deceptive. "We are sleeping on a volcano … A wind of revolution blows, the storm is on the horizon", stated the French thinker Alexis de Tocqueville in January 1848, clearly a very perceptive comment at that time. It was simply the calm before the storm, a *raging* storm that was going to sweep across the whole of Europe.

Social discontent was already brewing in Ireland, a land which had long suffered under the iron heel of the British state, as a colonial vassal of the English landlords. Her fate was bound ever more securely by the Act of Union with England in 1801, imposed shortly after the bloody repression of the United Irishmen's rebellion. However, by the 1840s, retribution and famine fanned the flames of revolt. Daniel O'Connell, the recognised leader of Irish nationalism in that period, was skilfully able to channel this discontent and use it as a bargaining chip with the British ruling class. However, following his death in May 1847, new and more militant forces began to emerge. In particular, Chartism began to make headway in Ireland, with links to local revolutionary organisations – Young Ireland and the Irish Confederation. Young Ireland emerged in opposition to O'Connell's moderation and had founded a new militant organisation, the Irish Confederation.

Although ruled by a Viceroy, the abolition of the Irish Parliament permitted Irish political representation in the British Parliament. This served merely to bloat the number of bigoted Orange peers in the House of Lords, described by Bishop Berkeley grimly as "vultures with iron bowels". Their tenacious opposition towards the persecuted Catholic majority in Ireland was unyielding. Their cruelty was unsurpassed.

In Ireland, the introduction of anti-Catholic laws went to extraordinary lengths to crush the spirit of the Irish. Take the case of the Irish Privy Council in 1719, which attempted, although unsuccessfully, to substitute castrations for brandings as the penalty for unregistered Catholic priests. The *Penal Codes* were repressive laws aimed at Catholics, excluding them from the vote and banning them from official life. Oppression of the Irish peasantry by absentee landlords was a matter of course, leading to the hellish conditions and the starvation they experienced. "How do you govern it?" demanded Macaulay in the House of Commons on 19 February 1844. "Not by love but by fear ... not by the confidence of the people in the laws and their attachment to the Constitution but by means of armed men and entrenched camps."[1]

Free trade between Ireland and England, imposed by the Act of Union, destroyed most of Ireland's local industry, reducing it to a colony that simply supplied cheap food, mainly to Britain, as well as cheap labour. Marx referred to Ireland in Volume One of *Capital* as "an agricultural district of England" supplying the latter with "corn, wool, cattle, industrial and military recruits". Violence was rife in the island of Ireland with Whiteboy outrages and state repression following one another in quick succession. The famine gave a new desperate twist to Irish misery.

The English ruling class viewed the relationship between the countries somewhat differently. As *The Times* stated on 1 April 1848:

---

1   C. Woodham-Smith, *The Great Hunger*, p. 12.

"Instead of degradation [Ireland] has found equality and union. That which depressed other nations has elevated her. If she talks of privileges, she has none but what England gave her and England shares with her. Law she had none but that which she owes to England."[2]

Until this moment, there had been no Chartist movement in Ireland. This was mainly due to the influence of Daniel O'Connell MP, lawyer and bourgeois nationalist, who led the Irish struggle. He was hostile to Chartism, as he was towards revolution in general. He used every means possible to keep Chartism out of Ireland, and was so successful that he even boasted in the House of Commons that:

"England was discontented and disaffected – Ireland was tranquil. England was distracted by lawless bands of physical force Chartists. Ireland did not seek to attain her ends by violence, by resistance to the law, by destruction of property."[3]

Friedrich Engels was deeply interested in Irish affairs and followed them closely. He was extremely impressed by the mass following of Daniel O'Connell, which he believed was being deliberately squandered. He wrote:

How much could be achieved if a sensible man possessed O'Connell's popularity, or if O'Connell had a little more sense and a little less egoism and vanity! Two hundred thousand men [who had attended his rallies], and what men! Men who have nothing to lose, two-thirds of them not having a shirt to their backs, they are real proletarians and *sans culottes*, and moreover Irishmen – wild, headstrong, fanatical Gaels. If one has not seen the Irish, one does not know them. Give me two hundred thousand Irishmen, and I could overthrow the entire British monarchy.[4]

Engels was pointing to the revolutionary fervour in Ireland, to the determination and courage of the ordinary people. If this was harnessed, it could lead to revolutionary change, and not only in Ireland, but throughout the British Isles.

Clearly the growing troubles in Ireland posed a serious threat to Britain. The ruling class felt that they were sitting on a powder keg of social discontent and growing anger, aggravated by national oppression. Not least, the British army had a high proportion of Irishmen in its ranks, who were susceptible to radical moods and were therefore regarded as unstable and potentially

2 J. Saville, p. 39.
3 T.A. Jackson, *Ireland Her Own*, pp. 228-229.
4 K. Marx and F. Engels, *On Ireland*, p. 33.

dangerous. Irish repression, like a running sore, had always stirred the Radical cause in England. This time was no exception.

The plight and agony of Ireland led to large public meetings held in London in favour of Irish freedom. At every stage the Chartists, headed by Feargus O'Connor in Parliament, had vigorously opposed the Irish Coercion Act, which was one of the most repressive laws ever imposed on the country. Eventually, the law was only passed by a mere fourteen votes, partly as a result of O'Connor's relentless actions. The Chartists had correctly regarded the Coercion Act not only as a threat to the Irish, but also to the working class of England, Scotland and Wales. Their struggle was therefore a common one. It was no accident that the demand for the repeal of the Act of Union between Britain and Ireland was contained in the Chartist Petition of 1842, which, as we have seen, attracted three-and-a-half million signatures.

With O'Connell's death, and the ineptitude of his son, the struggle for Repeal increasingly fell to the Chartist leader, Feargus O'Connor. His key role in organising opposition in Parliament to the Irish Coercion Bills added to the prestige of Chartism in the eyes of the Irish, which was something the British authorities desperately wanted to avoid. It is no accident that in the very first issue of *The Northern Star* in January 1848, O'Connor published an address from himself directly to the Irish people, calling for the unity of the Irish with the English working class to win the Charter and achieve independence for Ireland.

At this time, Ireland was still suffering from the worst famine in living memory, which began in earnest in 1845. Rack-renting landlords had driven up rents and driven millions into destitution. Land had been turned over to cash crops, and subsistence farming was only good for growing potatoes. The potato blight destroyed Ireland's potato crop and led to utter devastation. Tens of thousands of starving paupers were driven off the land. Countless numbers of starving peasants perished in ditches and on roadsides. The Irish faced a holocaust. To escape starvation, tens of thousands emigrated to New York, Liverpool, London, Glasgow, Manchester, Birmingham and the four corners of the globe. Large crowds of desperate, starving Irish wretches wandering the streets of London and the industrial North was a common sight. "It looks as though the Irish will not die of hunger as calmly next winter as they did last winter", wrote Engels. "Irish immigration to England is getting more alarming each day. It is estimated that an average of 50,000 Irish arrive each year."[5] Prepared to accept lower wages due to their absolute

---

5   MECW, vol. 6, p. 309.

destitution, the animosity between the Irish and other workers increased, stirred up by the employers.

The Irish famine could have been resolved, as there was plenty of wheat available in Ireland. The problem was that this grain was reserved only for export to England, and the British ruling class held the position that on no account was it to be used to relieve the starving Irish. There were public works, but the Irish would have to pay for them, and they were then closed down within a year. The British government believed that, if nothing was done, the market would resolve the problem. Although they were not prepared to supply food to the Irish, they were still very eager to call out the troops to keep the population in check. As a consequence of all this inaction, Ireland was devastated. Through starvation and emigration her population fell dramatically, from over 8 million, to 6.5 million by the time of the census in 1851. Measured in terms of deaths, the famine was Europe's most deadly in the nineteenth century. Sir Charles Trevelyan, the callous head of the British Treasury and a true Malthusian, told the starving Irish that nothing could be done due to "the operation of natural causes", while he announced a further reduction in famine relief.

Daniel O'Connell's death served to heal the rift between the Irish and English radical movements. It proved to be a watershed. Chartist speakers in Ireland, who had previously been shunned, were now welcomed with open arms. Many Irishmen had, after all, provided important leadership to Chartism, both locally and nationally. It is no accident that the greatest support for Chartism was in towns and regions with high Irish concentrations. This new-found unity between the Irish national struggle and Chartism, welcomed by the working class, was regarded as a serious threat by the English government. The growing danger of insurgency in Ireland led by a new militant leadership caused alarm in London.

UNITED IRISHMAN

John Mitchel, a leading member of both Young Ireland and the Irish Confederation, which had been established in January 1847, decided to break away to form his own party, launching a paper called *The United Irishman*. This preached vengeance against the English government and sought to "prepare the country for rebellion". Lord Clarendon was referred to in the paper as "Her Majesty's Executioner General and General Butcher in Ireland". Mitchel took as the motto for the paper the words of Wolfe Tone:

"Our independence must be had at all hazards. If the men of property will not support us, they must fall; we can support ourselves by the aid of that numerous and respectable class of the community, the men of no property."[6]

In other words, the Irish national liberation struggle would mean an armed struggle, even street warfare, against the British state. The newspaper created a sensation in England as well as in Ireland. Mitchel openly appealed for Chartist support, and the Chartist movement was ready to provide it. As T.A. Jackson comments:

"In England the Chartists sold Mitchel's journal as one of their own. Chartism in England became a 'danger' again, while the Confederate Chiefs in Ireland discovered that the mass of their supporters were becoming Mitchelites, almost to a man."[7]

Mitchel and his comrades in the Confederation Clubs began to establish Charter Associations in Irish towns. The Confederation had seceded from O'Connell's Repeal Association shortly before his death, and increasingly took the lead. Likewise, an Irish Democratic Confederation appeared among Irish workers in England, which attracted those considered the more extreme elements. *The United Irishman* became at the time the most widely circulated paper in Ireland, even reaching into the military and police barracks.

The British government, the Catholic hierarchy, and the remnants of the Repeal Association were outraged at Mitchel's actions, which they regarded as beyond the pale. This was compounded by news of the overthrow of the French monarchy and the establishment of a Republic, and the enthusiastic reception it received from Irish Confederates, Chartists and Radicals in both countries. There were clear concerns about the spread of revolution from all quarters.

The example of the French Revolution was uppermost in Irish minds. Now the Confederation Clubs seized the initiative and began to march, drill and collect arms. They quickly established fraternal links with the French revolutionaries. The Irish tricolour was in fact modelled on the French flag, designed in green, white, and orange. It was first displayed in Waterford, and then at a public meeting in Dublin, where it was greeted with wild enthusiasm. Lord Russell expressed fears that "some attempt may be made in Dublin to emulate the barricades of Paris... The Irish are not the French but they have a great knack of imitation."[8]

---

6   M. Fegan, *Literature and the Irish Famine 1845-1919*, p. 53.

7   T.A. Jackson, *Ireland Her Own*, p. 252.

8   J. Saville, p. 81.

The Chartists had sent James Leach to Dublin in January 1848. In contrast with the past, he was received with great enthusiasm, which served to strengthen the bonds between them and the Irish Confederates. Alarmed by this collaboration, as well as by the revolution on the Continent, the English government introduced new repressive legislation which simplified the laws against 'sedition' and 'treason'. It changed the offence of 'misdemeanours' into 'treason' and 'felony', which carried long terms of transportation instead of the customary death penalty. There were no longer to be distinctions between 'political' prisoners and ordinary criminals.

The Irish had not only sent over their starving masses to England but also their rebels, many of whom entered the trade unions and joined the Chartists. This Irish bloody-mindedness was recorded by one English employer, who gave evidence before a parliamentary commission:

> "Where there is discontent, or disposition to combine, or turnouts among the work people, the Irish are the leaders; they are the most difficult to reason with and convince on the subject of wages and regulations in the factories."[9]

As stated, the first issue of *The Northern Star* for 1848 carried an address from O'Connor to the Irish people. He spoke not only as an Irishman but as a democrat and Chartist. He explained that the struggle for Irish freedom was linked with achieving the Charter. "There can be no doubt that henceforth the mass of the Irish people will unite ever more closely with the English Chartists and will act with them according to a common plan", wrote Engels.[10]

For the English establishment, the mixing of revolutionary Irish republicanism with inflammatory Chartism was a deadly concoction. Added to this mix were the revolutions in Europe, which were overthrowing monarchs and governments. The revolutionary reverberations in Britain in 1848 can only be understood as part of this international situation.

EUROPEAN REVOLUTION

"Do you not feel – how should I say it – a revolutionary wind in the air?" asked De Tocqueville.[11] He was certainly in touch with the mood sweeping France. Within a matter of weeks, the monarchy had been overthrown by an insurrection. One by one, the monarchies of Europe were swept aside by popular revolts, led mostly by the proletarian 'mob'. A revolutionary wave

---

9   M. O'Brien, *Perish the Privileged*, p. 6.

10 MECW, vol. 6, p. 449.

11 *Le Moniteur*, 30 January 1848.

was sweeping all before it, affecting Poland, the German states and Austria, the Czech lands, Hungary, the Italian states, as well as France. This sent an ice-cold chill down the spine of the British bourgeoisie.

"Glory to God, our Europe was not to die but to live!" wrote Carlyle in *Chartism*.[12] It can be said that 1848 was the most revolutionary year of the nineteenth century, in which the working class appeared on the scene to play an increasingly independent role. "For us, too, the tocsin sounds", stated the editorial in *The Northern Star* on 26 February 1848.

The revolutions on the Continent were aimed at clearing away absolutism and all the old feudal rubbish. Marx's articles in the daily *Neue Rheinische Zeitung* of 1848 were a steadfast defence of the extreme left wing of the democratic movement. As Marx and Engels explained in regard to tactics in the *Communist Manifesto*:

> The Communists fight for the attainment of the immediate aims, for the enforcement of the momentary interests of the working class; but in the movement of the present, they also represent and take care of the future of that movement.[13]

These revolutions failed because the bourgeoisie, fearing the workers, betrayed the people and preferred instead capitulation and compromise with the nobility. Marx explained its role:

> The big bourgeoisie, which was all along anti-revolutionary, concluded a defensive and offensive alliance with the reactionary forces, because it was afraid of the people, i.e. of the workers and the democratic bourgeoisie.[14]

At the time, Marx and Engels looked forward to the intensification of the revolutionary wave carried forward by the workers. They saw in the successful bourgeois-democratic revolution the prologue to a new proletarian revolution. But with its defeat, which ushered in a period of reaction, this perspective was cut across. Despite this, they looked to an eventual turn in the situation. In Germany, Marx explained, everything "will depend on the possibility of backing the proletarian revolution by some second edition of the Peasant War."[15]

During the 1848 Revolution, the Chartists expressed their admiration for the revolutionary line of Marx's newspaper. As *The Northern Star* of 24 June 1848 wrote:

---

12 J. Lindsay and E. Rickword, *Spokesmen for Liberty*, p. 316.

13 MESW, vol. 1, p. 136.

14 MECW, vol. 7, p. 74.

15 K. Marx 'Letter to Engels', 16 April 1856, MECW, vol. 40, p. 41.

"The *Neue Rheinische Zeitung*... which announces itself 'the organ of democracy', is conducted with singular ability and extraordinary boldness; and we hail it as a worthy, able, and valiant comrade in the grand crusade against tyranny and injustice in every shape and form."

The white heat of the European Revolution made the British ruling class tremble at its close proximity, a mere twenty or so miles across the English Channel. In fact, they were even more frightened than they had been in 1839 and 1842 when events were confined to Britain. In contrast, the news of the new French Republic was enthusiastically celebrated by Radicals and Chartists alike. A joint meeting was organised by the Executive of the National Charter Association and the far-left Fraternal Democrats. It was held in the White Hart tavern in Drury Lane, the headquarters of the German Workers' Educational Association.

An eyewitness report of the meeting from Thomas Frost gives a flavour of the proceedings:

Suddenly, the news of the events in Paris was brought in. The effect was electrical. Frenchmen, Germans, Poles, Magyars, sprang to their feet, embraced, shouted, and gesticulated in the wildest enthusiasm. Snatches of oratory were delivered in excited tones, and flags were caught from the walls, to be waved exultantly, amidst cries of '*Hoch! Eljen! Vive la République!*' Then the doors were opened, and the whole assemblage... with linked arms and colours flying, marched to the meeting place of the Westminster Chartists in Dean Street, Soho. There another enthusiastic fraternisation took place, and great was the clinking of glasses that night in and around Soho and Leicester Square...[16]

BLEAK AGE

After 1842, trade had revived somewhat and the unrest had died down. But, in addition to the events on the Continent, the winter of 1847-48 was particularly bitter, and proved to be the opening of a depressed year. It was, in the words of the Hammonds, an altogether "Bleak Age". Diseases of all kinds were widespread, including influenza, bronchitis, pneumonia and smallpox. Henry Reeve noted in his diary at the end of 1847: "Remarkable depression in the last months of this year in society; general illness; great mortality; innumerable failures... want of money... a curious presage of the impending storm..."[17] Such difficult times also resulted in increased

---

16 T. Frost, *Forty Years' Recollections*, pp. 128-129.

17 R. Brown and C. Daniels, p. 124.

Chartist activity, and great gatherings took place in London and the provinces.

Such was the increased interest that no hall existed in London that was large enough to hold the crowds who flocked to hear the Chartist speakers. As a result, Chartist open air assemblies once again sprang up. In early March there were reports of rioting, including in Manchester, Oldham and Glasgow. In Manchester, crowds stormed the workhouses and demanded the release of the inmates. In Glasgow, the demonstrators marched through the streets crying 'Bread or Revolution!' Faced with such crowds, the Riot Act was read and the military were called out. At Bridgetown in Glasgow several people were shot dead.

On 2 March, a mass meeting took place in Lambeth, in South London, which drew thousands and was addressed by O'Connor, Harney, Jones, Szonakowski and others. A resolution was passed protesting against any English government interference in the French Republic, and an address to the French people was approved unanimously. The meeting then took the decision to present the address in person by sending a fraternal delegation to Paris composed of Harney, Jones and McGrath.

This created a diplomatic storm with the British government. Lamartine, the President of the Republican government, received a protest from Lord Palmerston following offensive remarks made by a minister, who, having met with the Chartists, suggested that the Peel government did not have the confidence of the British people. Lamartine was forced to apologise for this indiscretion. But when Lamartine was presented with an Irish flag by a delegation from Ireland, this once again provoked a furious response from the British. Lamartine retreated, but Palmerston sent a further message telling the French in no uncertain terms to "abstain from interfering or meddling in any manner whatever with the internal affairs of the United Kingdom".[18] As a result, when Smith O'Brien arrived with a further Irish delegation in March, they were told bluntly by Lamartine to expect no help or encouragement from the French, a comment which was made public.

In Britain, meetings were nevertheless held up and down the country as republican slogans circulated widely among the Chartists. Thousands attended open air meetings in London at Stepney Green, Clerkenwell Green, and Bethnal Green. Despite being banned by the police, a rally was held in Trafalgar Square on 6 March, which, according to Gammage, ended with three cheers for the people of Paris and for the People's Charter. However,

18 J. Saville, p. 87.

rioting again broke out in Glasgow and London, where there were clashes with the police. In Glasgow, gunsmiths and bakers' shops were looted, and even barricades were thrown up, resulting in the Riot Act being read. In the fighting that followed, three demonstrators lost their lives. In Manchester, there was also rioting, which broke "the profound tranquillity", according to *The Examiner*.

Other Chartist rallies were held in Newcastle, Dumfries, Sunderland, Bath, Nottingham, Birmingham and a host more. They all enthusiastically cheered the people of Paris. Interestingly, the Birmingham meeting, which took place indoors, was also addressed by Joseph Sturge, who had recently returned from Paris. Obviously intoxicated by the experience, he approved of "the soldiers who refused to fight against their quiet and peaceful fellow citizens. He hoped the time was coming when soldiers would not fire upon people who demanded their rights."[19] A great gathering was also held on Kennington Common, attended by 20,000 people with a heavy police presence. The general public were urged to stay away, while 4,000 police were dispersed in or around the Common. In a foretaste of what was to come, bridges across the Thames were guarded by several hundred police, as were the Bank of England and Buckingham Palace. At the rally, Ernest Jones announced the plans of London Chartists to accompany the third National Petition to Parliament with a procession of at least 200,000. Other mass meetings, which pledged allegiance to the French Republic and the Charter, followed in Blackheath, Preston, Birmingham, Manchester, Bradford, South Shields, Stockport, Sheffield and other places. In Southampton, open-air meetings were held every night amid great excitement. Even in Newport, South Wales, where Chartism had been dormant following the failed uprising, meetings were held to advance the Charter.

Julian Harney announced an appeal – a challenge – in the pages of *The Northern Star*:

"How long, Men of Great Britain and Ireland, how long will you carry the damning stigma of being the only people in Europe who dare not will their freedom. Patience! The hour is nigh! From the hill-tops of Lancashire, from the voices of hundreds of thousands has ascended to Heaven the oath of union, and the rallying cry of conflict. Englishmen and Irishmen have sworn to have THE CHARTER AND REPEAL, OR VIVE LA RÉPUBLIQUE!"[20]

---

19 Ibid., p. 92.

20 M. O'Brien, p. 82.

Encouraged by the events taking place, Benjamin Wilson painted a picture of what was happening in the country:

> "I have been a woollen weaver, a comber, a navvy on the railway, and a barer in the delph [quarryman] that I claim to know some little of the state of the working classes… It was said by its enemies that Chartism was dead and buried and would never rise again, but they were doomed to disappointment. A great many people in these districts were arming themselves with guns and pikes, and drilling on the moors. Bill Cockcroft, one of the leaders of the physical force party in Halifax, wished me to join the movement, I consented and purchased a gun, although I knew it to be a serious thing for a Chartist to have a gun or pike in his possession. I had several years practice in shooting, as the farmer for whom I worked supplied me with gun, powder and shot for the purpose of shooting birds in summer. I saw Cockcroft who gave me instructions how to proceed until wanted, which did not occur as the scheme was abandoned…"[21]

This account gives you a real sense of the situation. There was clearly a revolutionary mood developing again in the working class, despite the previous lull. And sections of workers were taking practical steps to acquire weapons.

Ominously, the Earl of Clarendon, representative of the government hardliners, wrote to Sir George Grey on 16 March, saying he would welcome a confrontation "that we might have done with it one way or another".[22] This idea of a short sharp blow against Chartism certainly had currency in a section of the ruling class. The idea of a showdown was becoming more common.

RALLYING THE CAUSE

Monster meetings in different parts of the country once again passed resolutions supporting the Charter and the National Petition. Following speeches, they proceeded to elect delegates to a new Chartist Convention being planned in London. As a result of these renewed activities, signatures to the Petition began to pour in. On 1 April 1848, O'Connor published a defiant appeal in *The Northern Star* to the Chartist ranks, urging them to harness their energies and prepare for the battle ahead. He began with the bold statement:

> "Onward, and we conquer,
> "Backward, and we fail!
> "The People's Charter and No surrender!

---

21 R. Brown and C. Daniels, p. 135.
22 J. Saville, p. 92.

"Old Guards! As I believe in my soul that the time has now arrived when we are entitled to the fruits of our thirteen years' labour, I call upon you to perform that duty which your own order, 'the fustian jackets, the blistered hands and unshorn chins', expect from your hands. It is impossible, as it would be immoral, that the labouring classes of England, the most oppressed of any country in the world, should allow the present manifestation of their order throughout the world to pass unnoticed or unimproved by them... I would rather die than give up one particle of the Charter.

"Still, remember that our movement is a labour movement, originated in the first instance by the fustian jackets, the blistered hands and the unshorn chins. Further, I would not give a fig for the Charter if we were not prepared with a solid, social system to take the place of the artificial one which we mean to destroy; and it was good that we did not succeed earlier with the Charter, before we were ready with the new social system. Look at France; the great trouble of the Provincial Government is the organisation of labour. As so will it be in Prussia, where the people are rejoicing over their victory over Frederick William IV, while the latter is really laying the foundation for a stronger military power. But in addition to the Charter we have land reform, which will give bread to the working men when the Charter is carried. The Charter and the Land! Those are our objects. Protect us in our work, People of England! Sign the Petition!"[23]

These were stirring words. But there was a growing number, blooded by the strike of 1842, who were determined to move in the direction of revolution. Military-style drilling and the gathering of arms were taking place all over the country on a much wider scale than before. The Continental revolutionaries had shown how to rid themselves of the ruling powers through revolution. The Chartists reasoned: if revolutionaries had toppled monarchies in Europe, why couldn't they topple their own rotten establishment? Once more, the question of what should be done when the Petition was rejected was posed. Harney, who was representing Nottingham at the Convention, reported that his area was arguing that this must be the last ever Petition. The time for petitioning was over. It was a time for action.

On 3 April, the third Chartist Convention opened in the John Street Institution, Fitzroy Square, London. The Convention was being held in abnormal circumstances, at a time when almost every European capital was consumed by revolution. These were stirring times indeed! McGrath was elected president of the Convention, and the number of delegates was again

---

23 *The Northern Star*, 1st April, 1848.

restricted to forty-nine so as "to escape the penalties of the Convention Act". Delegates duly presented their reports, and a committee was appointed to get the monster National Petition ready for delivery to the Commons a week later, on Monday 10 April. The Petition was on the same lines as in 1842. It stated:

> "Labour is the source of all wealth. The people are the source of all political power. The worker has the right to the produce of his labour. Taxation without parliamentary representation is tyranny. The resources and economic means of a country are best developed and administered most advantageously by the means of laws which are made by the representatives of the working and the industrious classes. In recognition of these principles, the Chartists demand that the People's Charter should become the law of the land."[24]

This time, the National Petition had attracted an unprecedented number of signatories. In fact, as O'Connor had predicted, over 5,000,000 had signed it. This was a startling achievement, without parallel, and reflected a renewed enthusiasm for the Charter. The Petition was divided into four large bundles so as to make it more manageable to transport. Such was its size that O'Connor stated it took himself and four other persons to lift the largest bundle. The Petition had been weighed and was found to weigh 5 hundred weights and 84 pounds (264.88 kilos). Of course, when it came to Parliament, no matter the size, weight or indeed number of signatures, the vested interests of the propertied classes would far outweigh any appeal from ordinary people.

The Convention then heard and debated the reports from delegates. Edmund Jones, the delegate from Liverpool, said the workers there saw the choice facing them as either bankruptcy or revolution. H. Smith reported that if no other town would start a revolution, Liverpool would. Both expressed the belief that they would only attain the Charter at the point of a bayonet. Similar reports were given from Dundee, Oldham, Wolverhampton, Bilston and Dudley, all of which said the workers were ready to obey the lead of the Convention. Lund said the Chartists of Lancaster were also prepared to adopt extreme measures. Those from Mirfield reported the feelings from a mass meeting, that if the military were let loose in Ireland, the Chartists should be let loose here in England. West reported that the people were in a desperate position, facing starvation on less than half wages. The people of Stockport were also of the opinion that this should be the last Petition. They also reported

---

24 *The Northern Star*, 1 April 1848.

that they had never witnessed such a state of unease and restlessness, and that excitement for the Charter was running very high. Reynolds stated that if the Petition was rejected, this would mean a "declaration of war against labour". If the National Petition was rejected, the consensus was that the Convention should not disperse but should be prepared to take up the reins of government. Once again, the question of a revolutionary overturn was being posed.

On 5 April, the Convention issued a printed poster to be put up around London, appealing to the Irish to join the Chartist procession the following Monday:

> "Irishmen resident in London, on the part of the democrats in England we extend to you the warm hand of fraternisation; your principles are ours, and our principles shall be yours... Look to your fatherland, the most degraded in the scale of nations. Behold it bleeding at every pore under the horrible lashings of class misrule! What an awful spectacle is Ireland, after forty-seven years of the vaunted Union! Her trade ruined, her agriculture paralysed, her people scattered over the four quarters of the globe, and her green fields, in the twelve months just past, made the dreary grave yards of 1,000,000 famished human beings. Irishmen, if you love your country, if you detest these monstrous atrocities, unite in heart and soul with those who will struggle with you to exterminate the hell-engendered cause of your country's degradation – beggary and slavery."

It ended with the plea that "the eyes of *Europe are fixed upon you*" and, in an internationalist appeal, stated that a massive demonstration would strike a "moral blow" in achieving "liberty and happiness to every sect and class in the British Empire".[25]

As before, the intention was to march with the National Petition and present it to the House of Commons. The Chartist leadership presumed that it was business as usual, but they were mistaken. The government was not going to make the same mistake as on the previous two occasions, and took steps to counter the Chartist plans by mobilising the full force of the state.

Things were being posed sharply. What we have is two irreconcilable classes facing one another. It was a contest for supremacy. However, one class, the bourgeoisie and its representatives, had drawn all the necessary conclusions from past experience. They were about to act accordingly. Meanwhile, the other class, the working class and its representatives, had failed to do so, proceeding on the same lines as before. This was a grave mistake on the part of the Chartist leadership.

---

25 J. Saville, p. 104.

O'Connor informed the Convention that he had been told by an Alderman in the Commons that there was a danger he would be assassinated on Monday, the day of the Kennington rally, if they proceeded. He had replied to the Alderman that, were he to be murdered, shootings and reprisals would take place all over the country. He made it plain that, despite the threats, he would remain in the front row of the procession whatever the consequences.

What were they proposing if the Petition was rejected by Parliament, as was expected? Rather than organise a general strike and move to displace the government, the Chartist leadership avoided this and looked for 'peaceful' means. They even had illusions that the monarchy might save them, which was very naive. Therefore, O'Connor proposed that simultaneous meetings take place to call on the Queen to dismiss her bankrupt Ministry and form another that would introduce the Charter if it was rejected. If that failed, O'Connor stated that he would sooner die than not win the Charter!

This, however, still did not answer the question: if all else failed, what should be done? This gave rise to a heated debate, despite the shortage of time, with many proposals and amendments being put forward. One from Reynolds proposed "that in the event of the rejection of the Petition, the Convention should declare its sittings permanent, and should declare the Charter the law of the land."[26] After a long discussion, the Executive settled on the amendment of Ernest Jones, who was regarded as O'Connor's close ally, and the rest were withdrawn. The Convention then proceeded to agree on five proposals: 1) If the Petition was rejected, the Convention would prepare a National Memorial to the Queen requesting the dissolution of the present Parliament, and the formation of a Cabinet of those willing to enact the Charter; 2) that another body, a National Assembly, be convened, consisting of delegates elected at public meetings to present the Memorial and continued in session until the Charter became law; 3) simultaneous meetings to be held on 21 April to adopt the Memorial and elect delegates to the National Assembly; 4) the National Assembly to meet in London on 24 April; 5) the present Convention to continue until the opening of the National Assembly.

To say the least, this was quite a convoluted plan which attempted to exhaust all the legal options. In this, the Chartist leaders were in danger of diffusing the movement. This National Assembly, as envisaged, was in effect another name for a provisional government, which, if carried to its conclusion, would pose a direct challenge to the state. But it would take

26 R.C. Gammage, p. 308.

more than a mere announcement to overthrow the British state. Lastly, the Convention formally agreed that a mass meeting would still go ahead on Kennington Common as planned, and from there a procession would take the National Petition to the House of Commons, with Feargus O'Connor at its head. This was to be a peaceful demonstration and a show of popular support, nothing more. A host of meetings were held in London, where the Convention was taking place, to build for this event.

However, the plan still left things very much up in the air. The idea of a show of strength must have a conclusion. If the Charter was rejected, the matter could only be resolved by the working class taking power. But apart from the proposal for a National Assembly, the Convention delegates, despite their militant language, dodged this question. This prevarication allowed the government to seize the initiative.

PROCESSION BAN

The aim of the government was to sow panic and demoralisation among the Chartists by banning the demonstration, under the pretext of avoiding possible trouble. All persons were warned to comply with the law of the land. This manoeuvre was roundly condemned by O'Connor in the Commons as sabotage, but the government remained firm. Their actions were designed to nip the movement in the bud and allow them to show their teeth. In doing so, they used the press to whip up opposition to the Chartists, especially amongst the middle classes. The government then made preparations for this 'show of strength' by swearing in thousands of special constables and reinforcing the powers of the state. Their strong-arm plans were bolstered by alarming reports of drilling and other subversive activities from different parts of the country. "I hope your artillery is in good order", wrote Sir George Grey to Clarendon. "It is very important to do without the soldiers but if it is necessary to use them, the artillery is the most formidable and efficient arm."[27]

In Ireland, John Mitchel deliberately changed the name of the *United Irishman* to the *Irish Felon*, as an affront to the law, and its language remained as outspoken as ever. On Sunday 9 April, at a meeting in Victoria Park, Ernest Jones, the main speaker, also showed defiance, stating:

> "If the government touch one hair of the head of the delegates – If they place them under arrest, or attempt the least interference with their liberty – every town represented by the delegates, would be in arms in less than twenty-four hours [tremendous cheers]. If I were to be killed, or wounded, or arrested, the

27 J. Saville, p. 82.

moment the intelligence arrived at Halifax the people would rise and disarm the troops – and 100,000 Yorkshiremen would march upon London [enthusiastic cheers]. So help me God, I will march in the first rank tomorrow, and if they attempt any violence, they shall not be twenty-four hours longer in the House of Commons."[28]

At this point, there were no plans to arrest or disrupt the Convention, but the situation remained very fluid. The government's main aim was to ban the procession, the easiest target, to force the Chartists to retreat, and to sow the maximum confusion. In the Commons, Sir George Grey, in his capacity as Home Secretary, was asked whether the meeting on Kennington Common would, as well as the Chartist procession, also be illegal. Sir George replied that this would depend upon the character of the meeting. The idea was nevertheless freely broadcast that physical force was being planned by the Chartists, which was not the case, but the government intended to regard such a threat seriously and would deal with it effectively.

Trevelyan, in an internal letter, outlined the government's plan to prevent the Chartist demonstration. The main component was a show of brute force:

"The stream of Chartists on Monday should be turned off *at a distance* from the Houses of Parliament and the Public Offices, and the whole of Whitehall and Parliament should be filled with Special Constables. The head of the Chartist column should be met *by a body of Special Constables*, and the Chartists should be made to see that there is a power in the Society itself sufficient to put them down. It should be shown that as the disaffected are bandied and organised, so are the well-affected. The National Guards – the middle classes – can *keep* the upper hand, if proper arrangements are made, but it would be difficult for them to recover their position if once the Chartists got the upper hand, and the end would be attained only through a fearful civil war."[29]

At the same time, the press was being used to whip up anti-French and patriotic fervour, while warning of the dangers of Jacobinism. "There is no doubt," wrote *The Illustrated London News*, "a deep under-current of Communism – theories respecting property that may produce a war of classes."[30] *The Times* published a letter from an English resident in Paris, dated 27 February, which also expressed fears about Socialism and Communism:

---

28 Ibid., p. 105.
29 Ibid., p. 96.
30 Ibid., p. 97.

"It is important to recollect that the present revolutionary tendencies are social rather than political – aiming at equality of possessions, or an equal distribution of the national revenue, rather than the mere establishment of democratic institutions. This is the alarming feature in the present condition of France. In England, Socialist opinions and feelings have not as yet a definitive shape; they are rather dispositions or tendencies than distinct theories or formulae...

"I can assure you that my fears of Socialism, or Communism, are anything but fanciful. The late violent explosion was caused mainly by the severe and extensive distress of the Parisian *ouvriers*; and by the opinion, widely spread amongst them, that the government and the wealthier classes might and ought to have prevented it."[31]

It seemed to confirm the assertions of the *Communist Manifesto* that the spectre of communism was haunting Europe, but this time it was used to engender panic in the middle classes.

The Chartist Convention, lacking clarity, was now beset with doubts. It reconvened to consider this provocative move by the government. There was further confusion as they planned to go ahead with the mass meeting in Kennington, but they made no mention of the procession to Parliament. When reports reached the Convention that the mass meeting and procession were, according to the government, to openly carry arms, a delegation was hurriedly sent to see the Home Secretary and reassure him that this was definitely not the case. When Harney informed the Convention that a man in London had got an order for 30,000 staves, the news was received with groans of disapproval. The Convention was determined to avoid a physical confrontation, at all costs. They were clearly on the back foot and eager to placate the authorities.

Of course, weakness invites aggression. The government was clearly looking for any pretext for a confrontation or, at least, if not a confrontation, then a complete capitulation. The Chartists were either to be crushed or humiliated, the choice was theirs. The government was not going to allow them to march, victory style, to deliver their National Petition to Parliament as on previous occasions. They had been wrong-footed in 1839 and 1842 and they were not going to be wrong-footed this time round. The government felt that any weakness they showed would simply encourage the Chartists and their revolutionary co-thinkers across the Channel. Therefore, a firm stand was decided upon.

---

31 Ibid., p. 98.

The dilemma facing the Chartist leadership was a reflection of a lack of perspective for how to take power. There were attempts to skirt around the problem, but this simply exposed their weakness. They had failed to raise the question of a general strike if Parliament rejected the five-million-strong Petition, which would have been essential if they were serious in their intentions. This failure arose not so much from a lack of will as a lack of experience. There was no historical precedent from which they could draw upon. The revolutions of 1789 and 1830 in France were bourgeois revolutions, one social and the other political. While they could learn lessons from them, a proletarian revolution was on a different level. Above all, there needed to be an understanding of how and when to mobilise the working class, which needed serious preparation and a clear strategy for taking power. The Chartist leaders were pioneers, which was both a strength and a weakness.

KENNINGTON COMMON

Finally, the glorious 10 April arrived, the day of the mass meeting at Kennington Common and the planned procession. From early on, the government had turned the whole city into an armed camp. As R.C. Gammage, an eyewitness to these events, explained:

"The ever-memorable 10th of April arrived, and vast preparations were made by the government. Besides the regular troops quartered in the metropolis, others poured in from Windsor, Hounslow, Chichester, Winchester, and Dover. The marines and sailors of the Royal Navy at Sheerness, Chatham, Birkenhead, Spithead, and other government towns, as well as the dockyard men, were kept under arms. The Thames police kept watch upon the mercantile marine, lest they should show any leaning towards the Chartists.

"Heavy gun-batteries were brought from Woolwich, and placed at various points. The marines were stationed at the Admiralty. Many of the troops were disposed of secretly, to be ready in case of necessity. The mounted police were armed with broad swords and pistols. All the public buildings were put in a state of defence. Two thousand stand-of-arms were supplied to the general post-office, for the use of the clerks and officers of that department, who were sworn in as special constables; and the officials at other public places were equally well provided. All the steam vessels were ordered to be ready for any emergency, in order to convey troops. At the Tower the guns were examined, the battlements strengthened by barricades, and the troops held in readiness to march at a minute's notice. The labourers at the docks were sworn in as specials. The city prisons were guarded by the military, and the churches were converted into barracks. The public vehicles were generally withdrawn from the streets. In the city, seventy thousand persons were sworn in as special constables, and military officers commanded them. The royal carriages and horses, and other valuables, were removed from the palace. The military force amounted to nine thousand men."[32]

The Royal Family had been shunted off to the Isle of Wight, at the government's request, although Palmerston still fretted for their safety as "the Solent Sea is not impassable". The government had also put the aging Duke of Wellington, the 'Iron' Duke, formally in charge of the Capital's security, and he prepared an open display of military force. Incidentally, Wellington's title of 'Iron' Duke was gained not for his role at Waterloo, but because of the iron shutters he put over his windows. On this occasion, he was, in reality, the 'front-man', while the real leadership decisions were taken by Sir George Grey and the Lieutenant-General Lord Fitzroy Somerset, the Military Secretary.

The bridges across the river Thames provided the main point of concentration of state forces, guarded by foot and horse police, and a sea of special constables. Some 120,000 of these specials had been newly sworn in. They in turn were backed up by troops at close quarters but kept in reserve. Government ministers were clearly in no doubt about the gravity of the situation. There was a great deal at stake. Events across the Channel had badly shaken them and they needed to regain their composure. Clarendon wrote to Grey, "the future is so menacing, that I feel sure you will not appeal in vain to the 'Haves' in England against the 'Have nots'".[33]

Public opinion was being whipped up against the Chartists, emphasising their links to the unruly Irish and the French Jacobins. The middle classes were frightened out of their wits and rallied to the cause of 'law and order' against the common rabble, who they regarded as a threat to life and limb, as well as property. The shopocracy were particularly anxious, many of whom volunteered as special constables.

Feelings among the propertied classes were running high, despite the government preparations. Colonel C.B. Phipps, on his way to report to Prince Albert, Queen Victoria's husband, observed the situation on his journey:

"This morning, which was very beautiful, brought all kinds of sinister reports; even at Windsor before arriving at London by the train I was informed that immense bodies of people were collecting, and that all the bridges would be occupied by troops and Gun pointed, and that an immediate battle was expected. Coming

---

32 R.C. Gammage, pp. 312-313.
33 J. Saville, p. 108.

from Paddington Station to Buckingham Palace the town certainly wore a most warlike appearance – all the Park Gates were closed and each guarded by a Picquet of the Foot Guards, with haversacks and Canteens upon their backs, prepared for actual service. At Buckingham Palace I heard that very large bodies have assembled at Kennington Common, and that numerous additions were marching towards the meeting in different directions."[34]

Clearly, the government was well prepared for their display of strength, although they were nevertheless concerned to find out about any possible disloyalty among the soldiers. But it was also clear that the Chartists were not prepared for a serious clash, which they were determined to avoid like the plague. The demonstration, after all, was never intended to be the starting-point for an insurrection. They had only turned out the numbers as a show of support for the Charter, and nothing more. The balance of forces was against them. They felt hemmed in on all sides. But this was also a reflection of their failure to prepare seriously for such an eventuality. It was abundantly clear what Parliament would do. The only course of action was to meet the challenge, which needed to be prepared in advance, involving a general strike. There comes a time, as Danton explained, when audacity is needed.

Despite the government's plans, crowds of Chartists met at certain locations, mainly Stepney Green, Finsbury Square, Russell Square and Clerkenwell Green, with their bands and banners, as part of a number of feeder marches on their way to Kennington Common. On their arrival, they were met by 6,000 police and 8,000 specials. Among them, oddly enough, was the future Napoleon III, the first president of France. The approaches to Westminster Bridge were strongly guarded, and the Bridge was covered with government posters announcing that no procession would be allowed to accompany the Petition to Parliament. The crowds, unperturbed, assembled on the Common with music and banners proclaiming 'Liberty, Equality, Fraternity', 'Ireland for the Irish', and other demands of the Charter.

Meanwhile, in another part of London, a procession was being formed behind a massive cart, fully decorated, to convey the 5,000,000-strong National Petition to its destination. This was followed by a second cart, drawn by six horses, which contained a host of Convention delegates. Then, a mass of workers and their families fell in behind them, eight abreast. The march headed along Tottenham Court Road to the National Land Company's offices at 144 Holborn to pick up the Petition, and then carried on through Holborn and

---

34 Ibid., p. 106.

Farringdon to Blackfriars Bridge. After some time, they reached Kennington Common, where a massive crowd of between 150,000 and 200,000 had assembled, who immediately burst into cheering as the procession arrived.

On arrival, O'Connor was called upon to see the Commissioner of Police, who informed him the meeting could proceed, but the procession to Parliament was officially banned. He was told that the police and troops would stop it by force if necessary, but the responsibility was his. At the sight of this, the crowd became agitated as it was rumoured that O'Connor had been arrested.

Thomas Frost, who was present, records the moment:

> I was standing near the van in which were the members of the Executive Council and many delegates of the National Convention, with the piled-up rolls of the petition, when I heard a cry of "they have got him!" And a wild rush was made towards the western side of the common. Looking in that direction, I saw the giant form of Feargus O'Connor – he and Wakley were the two tallest men in the House – towering above the throng, as he moved towards the road, accompanied by a courageous inspector of police. There was a cry repeated through the vast throng that O'Connor was arrested; a moment of breathless excitement, and then a partial rolling back of the mass of human forms that had suddenly impelled itself towards the road. The tumult subsided; but no one knew as yet what was the situation at that moment.
>
> Presently O'Connor was seen returning, and his reappearance was hailed with a tremendous shout. He mounted the van, and in a few words explained the state of affairs to an anxious throng. He had had an interview with Sir Richard Mayne at the Horns Tavern, and concessions had been made on both sides. The government had consented to allow the meeting to be held without molestation, and the honourable member for Nottingham had promised to use his influence with the masses for the purpose of inducing them to abandon the intended procession to the House of Commons with the petition. I breathed more freely when I heard this arrangement announced, and I have no doubt that it was a welcomed relief to the majority of those assembled from the painful suspense that had been felt while the ultimate intentions of the government remained unknown.[35]

TACTICAL RETREAT

The mass audience was obviously under the impression that, following the speeches, they would accompany the Petition to Parliament. As a result, O'Connor was forced, with some difficulty, to explain the tactical retreat.

---

35 T. Frost, *Forty Years' Recollections*, pp. 137-138.

"Now everything depended on his skill as an orator," stated Max Beer, "and it did not fail him."[36] He used his great authority to address the crowd, pointing to the massive number of signatures collected, while taking the opportunity to explain the change of plan: that the Petition would now be taken to the Commons by members of the Executive. He asked for the crowd to remain on the Common. Again, he asked if they were determined to see the Charter introduced and for them to show their hands in support. As expected, a forest of hands were raised in favour. O'Connor then congratulated them for their good sense and concluded, "though I may be stretched on the rack, I will smile terror out of countenance – go on conquering and to conquer, until the People's Charter had gloriously become the law of the land", which was received with rapturous applause.[37]

Then Ernest Jones rose to second what O'Connor had proposed, and, after pacifying the assembled mass, called on them to continue their exertions. Other leaders in turn addressed other sections of the crowd to carry the message. There were some angry protests, such as cries of 'no more petitioning', but little came of them. When the meeting concluded, the Petition was placed in three cabs and the Chartist Executive accompanied the signatures to the House of Commons. The whole day passed off peacefully, but an opportunity had been missed.

William Cuffay, the only black Chartist to play a leading role in the movement, was taken by surprise at the decision and spoke in strong language against it, saying the delegates were a set of "cowardly humbugs". When McGrath, who was chairing the proceedings, declared the event at an end, a section of the audience rushed the platform, including Cuffay. Some in the crowd supposedly cried over to Cuffay: "Come – we will lead if you will follow, come weal, come woe." But it was too late for that and the meeting dispersed.

While the capitalist press, especially *The Times*, was full of anti-Chartist derision, they failed to mention the large body of London-Irish Confederates, who paraded under a green flag on their way to Kennington in defiance of the law. The Chartist and Irish Confederate, Robert Crowe, recalled that "we marched over the bridges eight abreast, on our way to Kennington Common, but no sooner did the procession pass over than the police and soldiery took possession of the bridges..."[38] The London-Irish held a rally at the end of the Kennington meeting, which was addressed by Julian Harney. They then

---

36 M. Beer, p. 170.
37 R.C. Gammage, p. 316.
38 M. Chase, p. 302.

marched in an orderly fashion back the way they had come across the bridge, without any police obstruction.

Nevertheless, the ruling class were more than delighted with the outcome. They believed the Chartists had been humiliated and forced to retreat in the face of a mightier force. They hoped that this was sufficient to turn the tide and put any prospect of revolution to bed. "A physical force revolution is thus, we hope, become an impossibility, never again to be attempted", wrote the *Nonconformist*.[39]

The events and consequences of 10 April 1848 at Kennington have become twisted in the telling. The novel *Alton Locke* by Charles Kingsley, a Christian Socialist and former Chartist, has added to the mythology surrounding the Chartist demonstration. The book contains a background story of the Chartist movement from 1844 to 1848. In the preface, published in 1854, Kingsley penned a personal but distorted and one-sided picture of the deep dejection and dampened spirits felt by some Chartists. The conclusion he reached was that the defeat at Kennington constituted a rejection of the Chartist ideals to change society, arguing instead for salvation through the embrace of Christian beliefs. In the chapter headed 'The Tenth of April', he described the scene that was to become the accepted view for decades to come:

"The practical common sense of England, whatever discontent it might feel with the existing system, refused to let it be hurled rudely down, on the mere chance of building up on its ruins something as yet untried, and even undefined. Above all, the people would not rise. Whatever sympathy they had with us, they did not care to show it. And then futility after futility exposed itself. The meeting which was to have been counted by hundreds of thousands, numbered hardly its tens of thousands; and of them a frightful proportion were of those very rascal classes, against whom we ourselves had offered to be sworn in as special constables. O'Connor's courage failed him after all. He contrived to be called away, at the critical moment, by some problematical superintendent of police. Poor Cuffay, the honestest, if not the wisest, speaker there, leapt off the wagon, exclaiming that we were all 'humbugged and betrayed'; and the meeting broke up pitiably piecemeal, drenched and cowed, body and soul, by pouring rain all the way home – for the very heavens mercifully helped to quench our folly – while the monster petition crawled ludicrously away in a hack cab, to be dragged to the floor of the House of Commons amid roars of laughter..."[40]

---

39 J. Saville, p. 114.
40 Ibid., p. 201.

This account of 'folly' from an apostate of Chartism is an attempt to ridicule the Kennington Common event and disparage the Chartist movement. The masses did not rise up, accused Kingsley, when there was no actual intention or plan for the masses to rise up. The numbers attending, he claims, were wildly over-exaggerated. That may be so. O'Connor stated there were between 400,000 and 500,000 present. While there may be exaggerations, Kingsley's assessment is based on 'official' estimates, which, as we know, tend to grossly underestimate numbers. Things were 'contrived' and 'courage' evaporated, and so on and so forth. This description is more a reflection of Kingsley's personal pessimism and demoralisation and his search for spiritual escape than a description of the real situation. In *Alton Locke*, the character Lady Eleanor asks the protagonist a question: Is he still a Chartist? He replies: "If by a Chartist you mean one who fancied that a change in mere political circumstances will bring about a millennium, I am no longer one. That dream is gone – with others." Instead, he talks of loving his brothers and personal morality as the way forward for society, more in the mould of a sermon. Others who deserted the movement at this time were also drawn to individual solutions: the virtues of self-help, hard work, sobriety and thrift. This represented an abandonment of Chartism and the collective struggle in favour of personal salvation and individual betterment. No doubt this mood deeply affected a certain layer, but mostly of middle-class adherents.

Another lesser-known novel by Thomas Frost, *Forty Years Recollections: Literary and Political* (1880), expresses a completely different view:

> Three weeks had passed since the popular demonstration on Kennington Common, and the political atmosphere had become still, but it was not serenity – it was the oppressive density which harbingers the storm. They flattered themselves that Chartism was crushed, as if their batons had power to kill a principle! They had conquered without striking a blow – the victory was due to the wonderful unanimity, which had banded in close phalanx the swindler, the gambler, the pugilist, the brothel-keeper, the stock-jobber, the bill discounter, the profit-monger, the usurer, and the factory ogre. But in reality, their victory was illusory…

Interestingly, he then describes a meeting of workers in a Drury Lane coffee shop, called to discuss the impasse. The chairman argued for the use of force, ending with the question: "Will you resist it [tyranny], or will you continue to hug the chains that bind you, and will bind your children, and your children's children, unless you determine to break them?" Another spoke of the need to respect the law: "Let us show, by our respect for the laws, that we are worthy of being invested with the power of appointing those by whom they shall be made", but he was interrupted by an old man. He was followed by another, arguing for physical force:

"Does the government depend upon moral force for support? If it did, it might be reasonable to oppose it by moral means: but it relies, not on argument, but on bayonets and grapeshot, and hence the physical force at its disposal must be encountered by the physical force of the people… But it is objected that the course proposed is illegal; was there ever a revolution without infraction of the laws? – and was there ever any great measure of constitutional reform gained without an insurrection, either general or partial?"

He answered himself: "In the history of the world it has not been otherwise."[41]

This revealed support for actually taking power. The mood was there for such an undertaking, but it was squandered. Unless the movement had clear goals, the meetings and rallies, however large, would eventually dissipate, especially if there was no end in sight.

Much has been made of the fact that many workers were signed up by their workplaces as special constables for the Kennington demonstration, leading historians to conclude that the working class was in favour of the status quo and law and order. For instance, 700 workers employed by the Lancashire and Yorkshire Railway Company were sworn in as special constables. However, the next day, these workers held a mass meeting to protest this enrolment and passed the following resolution:

"Resolved, first: That we, the workmen of the Lancashire and Yorkshire Railway Company, do disapprove of the abrupt manner in which we were called up to be sworn in as special constables by the authorities, and that we did fully expect to be treated as men capable of comprehending right from wrong.

"Secondly: That this meeting is of the opinion that it is in the interest and duty of all classes to protect life and property, and that we, the workmen of the Lancashire and Yorkshire Railway Company, do pledge ourselves to do so, as far as it is in our power lies, providing the middle class do pledge themselves to protect our capital, namely, our labour.

"Thirdly: That it is the opinion of this meeting that the present distress of the working classes arises from class legislation, and that it is their unanimous opinion that no permanent good can be effected for the community at large, until the working classes are fully and fairly represented in the Commons House

---

41 *An Anthology of Chartist Literature*, pp. 272-276.

of Parliament, and that intelligence and virtue are the proper qualification of a representative. The workmen here present do pledge themselves to offer no resistance to any body of men who may struggle for such a representation."[42]

The Chartist Convention met the day after the Kennington Common demonstration. A committee was appointed to select delegates to visit the different areas and prepare the election of a National Assembly, but such a measure appeared too little and too late.

In the meantime, O'Connor presented the National Petition to the Commons, explaining it contained 5,700,000 signatures, nearly double the size of the 1842 Petition. But as soon as this was done, things were set in motion to block it. Thirteen stationer's clerks examined the Petition and announced to uproar and derision that there were not 5,700,000 signatures as claimed, but only 1,975,496. O'Connor challenged the findings, saying it was not possible for the clerks to count that number of signatories in such a short space of time.

The clerks had also rejected any signature submitted by a woman, who apparently had no right to sign it. In a particular section containing 10,000 signatures, 8,200 were women's, and were therefore discounted. Many signatories, it is true, were illiterate and could not write their name, but wrote what they thought was sufficient. But the authorities excluded them. That said, even the two million signatures that were declared 'officially' genuine were still double the size of the electorate that had voted for the sitting House of Commons. These 'representatives' of the people did everything in their power to sabotage the Petition from the people. 'All's Fair in Love and War', states the proverb, and this was certainly true in this case. The Commons were not going to be dictated to by the rabble or their signatures.

In the Commons, O'Connor used robust language to challenge the ruling, and in reply he was personally abused and attacked by a member of the scrutiny committee. Following this, O'Connor stormed out of the House. When the scrutiny member rose to apologise for his use of choice language, O'Connor was nowhere to be seen. Bizarrely, the Speaker of the Commons demanded that O'Connor be brought back to the House to hear the apology. The Sergeant in Arms was then sent to detain O'Connor and accompany his return. Once back in the House, following the apology, O'Connor made a blistering acceptance speech and then withdrew to derision. On the other hand, Sir George Grey, the Home Secretary, was cheered to the rafters and

---

42 Quoted in the *Manchester Examiner*, 18 March 1848, J. Saville, p. 117.

lauded in the Commons for his handling of the Chartist threat. Bloodshed had been averted, preventing unwelcome martyrs, and the Petition had been sufficiently ridiculed and discredited.

The government then chose this exact moment to introduce its own emergency legislation into the Commons, the Crown and Government Security Bill. This new Bill served to redefine and extend the offence of treason, making seditious language a felony, punishable by transportation for life or any period not less than seven years. The government was determined to tighten the screws on existing laws. The Bill was introduced on 10 April and the vote was speedily taken with 295 in favour and forty against. It passed the Lords unanimously and received Royal Assent on 22 April, a mere twelve days later. The government then proceeded to introduce an Alien Bill, which was also passed without any fuss. Consideration was then given to the suspension of *Habeas Corpus*, but Palmerston felt it was unnecessary.

The rapid speed with which these class laws were rushed onto the statute books was quite remarkable. William Cuffay was to comment in amazement "how anything to abridge the rights of the working classes can be passed in a few hours."[43] In contrast, the Chartists had to wait almost fifteen months more before the Chartist Petition was finally debated and voted on, reflecting the contempt of the authorities. On 3 July 1849, a mere seventeen members voted in favour of the Petition, the lowest number ever, and 222 voted against. They were more determined in their opposition than ten years earlier.

HARDENING MOOD

Despite the eagerness of certain historians to sign its death certificate, Chartism did not come to a sudden end in April 1848. Many official historians view the Kennington demonstration as no more than a farce. Even G.D.H. Cole, who is very good generally in dealing with this period, describes the event as a "wholly inglorious fiasco".[44] But this is not how contemporaries saw it. Although it was certainly a setback and retreat, it was not a decisive defeat, or a "fiasco", for that matter. In the country at large, the retreat on the day had remarkably little effect on morale. The House of Commons could have its little joke, of course, and the press could wallow in its 'great' victory, but in the North, in particular, the mood was hardening. There was no deep demoralisation, as some would think. We should recall that a few months earlier Chartism had been regarded as a spent force, mired in the

---

43 M. Chase, p. 314.
44 G.D.H. Cole, *A Short History*, p. 118.

Land Plan scandal, but by April, it had rapidly re-emerged at the centre stage of British politics. The display of numbers at Kennington Common was not decisive either way. The Convention continued to meet to prepare a National Assembly as the next step. Mass meetings were again held all over the country. There were 30,000 in Edinburgh, and another 30,000 in Paisley. In Aberdeen, a Chartist National Guard of 1,000 people was set up, ready to defend the proposed Assembly should it declare itself a Parliament. So, on the ground, among the millions of Chartist sympathisers, little had changed.

When the National Assembly finally met on 1 May 1848, it did not remain on the scene very long. In the end, the debates among its sixty members became rather fruitless, and there was little appetite to petition the Queen for her to dismiss her ministers and introduce the Charter. O'Connor, who originally supported the idea, now turned *volte-face* and denounced the plan. This confusion reinforced the lack of clear leadership or direction. Finally, on 13 May, the Assembly voted to dissolve and for its members to return to their constituencies. The newly elected Executive of the NCA oversaw the overhaul of the apparatus of the party's national organisation, reorganising the locals into groups of ten, with a team leader more responsive to underground conditions or immediate actions.

Once again, the Chartists discussed the idea of an insurrection. On two occasions, 12 June and 15 August, plans were laid for such an uprising, but, while serious clashes did occur, they were abandoned. The country, especially in the North, was still in a state of ferment and armed detachments – Chartist National Guards – were forming in Aberdeen, Dundee and Edinburgh, while drilling was taking place elsewhere. So much for the death of Chartism! An Edinburgh Chartist, Donald Mackay, told a Dundee rally: "It was absolutely necessary to overturn the government, or in a short time they would all be starved (loud applause). Moral force was all humbug."[45] The mood in the North of England increasingly resembled the period 1838-39, a picture far removed from one of demoralisation.

News finally arrived at the end of May from Ireland that John Mitchel had been arrested for sedition, along with Smith O'Brien and T.F. Meagher, who were charged with making seditious speeches. While the jury failed to reach an agreement in the case of O'Brien and Meagher, the Irish administration took no such chances with Mitchel. He was charged under the new Treason-Felony Act, recently introduced onto the statute books. The jury was packed, with Catholics excluded, and he was finally sentenced to fourteen years'

45 M. Chase, p. 316.

transportation. Within twenty-four hours, under the cover of darkness, he was immediately deported out of the country in a prison ship *en route* to Australia. This attack on Mitchel provoked a storm of protest, and serious talk of insurrection in Ireland.

On receiving the news, the English town of Bradford, which had a large Irish population, was practically in a state of open rebellion. Under the leadership of two Irishmen, 2,000 local Chartists battled successfully with police and special constables, who were armed with cutlasses. The Chartists met them with bludgeons and a hail of stones. The forces of law and order, many injured and bloodied, lost control of the situation. Four days later, when McDouall went to speak there, some 2,000 workers marched from Halifax to join Bradford's 10,000 Chartists in a semi-military show of strength, accompanied by bands, tricolour flags and pikestaffs. It was a remarkable display of popular anger, but it is not clear if it was part of any planned uprising. At the mass meeting, where people marched in military formation, many with pikes, the working class was called on to arm themselves. Once again, the question of an uprising was in the air.

Things looked threatening throughout Yorkshire, where drilling went on in broad daylight. A delegate meeting of Yorkshire and Lancashire Chartists passed a motion in favour of the formation of a National Guard as an insurance against government attacks. At Wilsden, some three thousand men drilled and, according to Gammage:

> [M]arched in military array, preceded by black banners, surmounted by pike heads, and a resolve was manifested to resist by force any attempt to arrest the leaders. At Bingley, two of such leaders were rescued by a body of two thousand persons. The magistrates of Bradford issued a proclamation against such proceedings, and an attempt was made to arrest Lightowler, and a person called 'Wat Tyler', who had manufactured a large number of pikes. The attempt failed, and a severe fight took place between the people and special constables, and afterwards the police. The military were at last called out; the Chartists still fought with their bludgeons, but at last they retreated before the military force, happily without loss of life.[46]

A number were later arrested and charged with drilling, but not without resistance. In fact, when confronted, they threatened to shoot the constables. They later surrendered and were dispatched to York Castle by train, where they were incarcerated. Meanwhile, in Leeds, mass meetings openly recommended arming and drilling, and as a result were cautioned by the magistrates. The

---

46 R.C. Gammage, p. 333.

meeting in Manchester was banned by the authorities, who needed to call in troop reinforcements. Gathering crowds, after leaving work from the mills, ripped up paving stones to throw at the police. A body of Chartists from Oldham, having left to join the meeting, fully armed with pikes, bludgeons and other weapons, were persuaded to turn back. In Leicester, clubs were being formed, which also began to acquire weapons. In Liverpool, the authorities stationed gunboats in the Mersey, and the mayor called for *Habeas Corpus* to be suspended in the city. "In the provinces," explained Gammage, "things began to look very threatening."

London was definitely another flashpoint for the movement, where the Irish played a key role. Meetings followed in London at Bethnal Green, London Fields, Victoria Park and Bishop Bonner's Fields. But the authorities were prepared and the meetings were dispersed by force, as in Croydon. There were, however, skirmishes, especially at Clerkenwell and Finsbury, with nightly disturbances. As James Cornish, who seemed to have been a special constable, recalled: "…the police were nearly run off their legs to keep order." Another constable, Alfred Andrew, reported on the scenes at Bethnal Green:

> "At eleven o'clock Nova Scotia Gardens contained about 900 or 1,000 persons of the lowest and most abandoned class, who had met to listen to a speech by a well-known inciter of the people. The first attempt to disperse this dangerous mob proved only partially successful; the mounted police arrived; a cowardly attack was instantly made upon them and the constables by a shower of stones; and after a severe conflict some of the aggressors were captured. On attempting to repulse a mob in a street in Gibraltar Walk, the scene became of a most alarming nature. Every tenement furnished a number of persons who threw missiles at the officers, and yelled and hooted at them in terms of the most appalling execration. The Queen, her progeny, the present Government, with that of the late Premier's, the constitution of the country, the representatives of Parliament, and the Lords Spiritual and Temporal were denounced as accursed, and loud complaints were made of the necessity for a complete social revolution by an equal distribution of the wealth of the country. A feeling of insatiable revenge was repeatedly uttered against the special constables, as standing in the way of the growing desire for a revolution in England… I heard large numbers of the misguided mob express a determination to conquer the police force at a forthcoming suitable occasion…"[47]

---

47 R. Brown and C. Daniels, p. 133.

"NEITHER DEAD NOR ASLEEP"

These serious troubles were giving rise to renewed fears in the ruling class. After all the gloating after Kennington Common, they began to draw some worrying conclusions. "Chartism is neither dead nor sleeping", stated *The Times* on 2 June. "The snake was scotched not killed on the 10th of April. The advancing spring had brought with it warmth, vigour, and renovation."[48] The Chartists were again on the move.

The entry of 3 June 1848 in the diary of Charles Cavendish Fulke Greville, who was clerk to the Privy Council, exposed these fears at the highest levels.

"The Government are now getting seriously uneasy about the Chartist manifestations in various parts of the country, especially in London, and at the repeated assembling and marching of great bodies of men. Le Marchant told me that… lately, accounts have been received from well-informed persons, whose occupations lead them to mix with the people, clergymen – particularly Roman Catholic – and medical men, who report that they find a great change for the worse amongst them, an increasing spirit of discontent and disaffection, and that many who on the 10th of April went out as special constables declare that they would not do so again if another manifestation required it."

This was a dangerous state of affairs. In effect, the special constables were refusing to be used against the people, which was bordering on mutiny. This could not have come at a worse time for the authorities. Such splits in the state apparatus were a reflection of the pressures and divisions in society. But this was not the end of the matter, as Greville continued:

"The speeches which are made at the different meetings are remarkable for their coarse language and savage spirit they display. It is quite new to hear Englishmen coolly recommend assassination, and the other day a police superintendent was wounded in the leg with some sharp instrument. These are new and very bad symptoms, and it is impossible not to feel alarm when we consider the vast amount of the population as compared to the repressive power we possess…"[49]

This summed up a serious dilemma for them. Unrest was increasing, but the forces of repression were becoming increasingly unreliable. With dissatisfaction growing more widespread, workers were boldly taking to the streets, risking life and limb, to defy the authorities. The situation was far more

---

48 M. Chase, p. 319.

49 C. Greville, *A Journal of the Reign of Queen Victoria from 1837 to 1852*, vol. 3, pp. 188-90, in R. Brown and C. Daniels, pp. 135-136.

serious than the Kennington Common gathering, which the government had easily contained. That was a single event, whereas now Chartist disturbances were breaking out across the entire country. It was thought that Whitsun Monday, when simultaneous meetings were planned, could be the time appointed for a national uprising. But, fortunately for the ruling class, it passed without serious incident. In June, Ernest Jones issued an appeal:

> "Endeavour to spread the movement. Let every district council take a note of all places in their district that do not contain a Chartist local. Let them send missionaries to inquire into the local circumstances; hire a room, hold a lecture, and use every means to establish a branch. If but one man is converted, the seed is down – he will bring others."[50]

In June, the government chose to act by declaring a ban on all public meetings. In response, Chartist demonstrations were organised to defy the government ban. Again, if there was a time to call a general strike, it was now. However, failure to do so would mean another opportunity being lost. As the government stepped up the pressure, arrests began in earnest. "The world has become nothing better than a great lunatic society", said Robert Owen. The government had managed to restore its nerve and act decisively, a quality lacking in the Chartist leadership.

From May to October 1848, "a reign of terror swept over England", wrote Max Beer.[51] State repression was now used to its fullest extent to break the back of Chartism. There were wholesale arrests of Chartists, including Ernest Jones, John Fussell, Alexander Sharpe, Joseph Williams, and W.J. Vernon, all on charges of sedition for speeches at Clerkenwell Green. They were put on trial and all found guilty. Fussell was given two years and three months for allegedly advocating private assassination. All were bound over for two or three years, except Fussell, who was bound over for five years. Williams got two years and one week. Vernon received a two-year sentence, and Sharpe got two years and three months. The judge sentenced Ernest Jones to two years' imprisonment and sureties of £200. For the rest, it was £150, with all men bound over to keep the peace for five years. The arrests were followed by more trials and long sentences. *The Northern Star* of 15 July summed up the first group of trials as: "A rancorous Whig Attorney-General, a partisan Judge, and a middle-class jury, steeped in hatred towards everything savouring of Chartism..." The arrests of the left-wing Chartist

---

50 *An Anthology of Chartist*, p. 360.
51 M. Beer, p. 173.

leaders at this particular time effectively prevented any regrouping of the revolutionary forces.

Punch produced a 'Song of the Sedition', two verses of which ran:

"Come, all lovers of Sedition for its own delightful sake;
Come, all disaffected rascals, a disturbance let us make;
Come, at midnight let us meet, ye revolutionary crew,
With no purpose in particular but rioting in view.

"Let us shout 'Assassination!' Whilst our Fussell recommends
Our approval of the sentiment – and take the hint, my friends;
Let us shriek aloud for pikes, and with the Patriot sympathise,
Who suggest flinging vitriol into British soldiers' eyes."[52]

At this time, events in Ireland were hurtling towards a confrontation. The arrest of John Martin, Mitchel's life-long friend and the editor of *The Irish Felon*, provided the catalyst for this movement. "Intense excitement reigned in Ireland," states Gammage, "the manufacture of pikes going on briskly." The Commons passed a bill to suspend *Habeas Corpus* in Ireland, which was followed by a whole wave of arbitrary arrests. The radical press was ruthlessly closed down, including *The Irish Tribune* and *The Irish Felon*.

As the repression intensified, the Irish Confederates were faced with a stark choice: either to be arrested one by one, or to issue the call for a general uprising against the British. The leaders looked for support in the country, but in the famine-stricken areas there was little. The Catholic clergy used their influence to curb any thought of revolt. There was some support in the towns, but there were few weapons with which to resist. As a result, some hundreds of insurrectionists gathered at Tipperary, determined to make a heroic stand. But given the balance of forces, it was hopeless and the revolt ended in failure. The leaders were then hunted down, charged with treason and transported. Martin himself got sentenced to fourteen years transportation.

Simultaneously, despite the arrests and clampdown, plans were rapidly put in place for an insurrection in England, beginning in London. However, in August the uprising was foiled by a government *agent provocateur*. Caches of weapons were found in various places, including in the St. James Churchyard, Clerkenwell. This led to the arrest of six conspirators – known as the Orange Tree conspirators – all of whom were sentenced to transportation, while fifteen others received prison sentences of between eighteen to twenty-four months.

---

52 J. Saville, p. 180.

The employment of government spies was extensively used as a means of entrapping Chartist insurgents, including in this case. The informant, known as 'Lying Tom' Powell, was used to bring the Orange Tree men to justice. 'Lying Tom' infiltrated the Chartist movement, urging them to break the law and regularly reported his progress to the Police Commissioners. "I encouraged," he said, "and stimulated these men, in order to inform against them. I gave the men some bullets. I gave balls to Gurney. I gave him half a pound of powder. I also cast some bullets and gave them to him."[53] His embroidered testimony led to further arrests and more trials. McDouall was picked up in Aston. He was tried for sedition, conspiracy, and riot. Found guilty, he was sentenced to two years with hard labour and imprisoned in Kirkdale gaol.

In September the London Chartists were brought to trial. Again, on the evidence of police spies, Downing, Cuffay, Fay and Lacey were found guilty. They vehemently protested against the government frame-up, but to no avail. William Cuffay stated:

"I say you have no right to sentence me... Everything has been done to raise a prejudice against me, and the press of this country – and I believe of other countries too – has done all in its power to smother me with ridicule. I ask no pity. I ask no mercy. I expected to be convicted, and I did not think anything else. But I don't want any pity. No, I pity the Government, and I pity the Attorney General for convicting me by means of such base characters. The Attorney General ought to be called the Spy General, and using such men is a disgrace to the Government; but they only exist by such means. I am quite innocent."[54]

Baron Platt then sentenced the guilty men to be transported for life, whereupon Fay cried: "This is the baptism of felony in England."[55] A string of others received similar sentences.

While William Cuffay was languishing in Tasmania, his poor wife Mary Ann, also an active Chartist, became destitute and was forced to enter the workhouse. She was finally granted leave to join her husband, and her passage was paid for by Chartist subscriptions. Once pardoned in 1856, Cuffay and his wife decided to stay in Australia, where he found work as a tailor. His last public appearance was in 1866, speaking in opposition to the state administration. "I'm old, I'm poor, I'm out of work, and I'm in debt, and

---

53 See M. Beer, p. 338.
54 R.C. Gammage, p. 340.
55 M. Beer, p. 340.

therefore I have a right to complain", he declared to the audience, who he addressed as his "fellow-slaves".[56] He remained active in the Australian labour movement until his death in the Brickfield's Invalids Depot in 1870, aged eighty-two.

Special Assizes were also held in Chester and Liverpool, where Chartists were tried on charges of conspiracy and sedition. All received long sentences. Some were even charged with levying war against the Queen, and transported for life. Again, the principal witness used against them was a spy named Ball, but his evidence was so contradictory that he did more harm than good to the prosecution's case. There were other trials at York and Edinburgh, again with the evidence of informants used to convict those accused. Such was the extent of the arrests that, of the twenty delegates elected to the Chartist National Assembly, at least fourteen had been arrested. With such repression on an unprecedented scale, the government succeeded in overwhelming the Chartist movement.

Samuel Kydd, in a statement from the Executive Committee, wrote:

"The reign of terror progresses, and grows searching and dreadful. So close has our political atmosphere become, that men are almost suffocated. So crowded are rumours, following in quick uncertainty: so fearful the thrilling doubts and stifled fears of every man we meet, that it requires courage even to think steadily, and boldness and nerve to direct order from this motley chaos..."[57]

This systematic clampdown meant a dramatic and fundamental change in the situation. The questions of revolution and counter-revolution are closely related. With the failure of the Chartist leaders to organise a revolution, the pendulum swung back in the opposite direction. "By the end of 1848 all prospects of a British Revolution had disappeared, and over most of Europe the revolutionary cause was going down to defeat", wrote G.D.H. Cole.[58]

O'Connor viewed these setbacks with dismay. He became despondent and increasingly influenced by the proponents of the 'Little' Charter, which he had initially denounced as "a four-legged animal".[59] With the Charter overwhelmingly rejected in Parliament, out of despair, a disorientated O'Connor now made overtures to Joseph Hume, the archetypal middle-

---

56 M. Chase, p. 311.

57 *The Northern Star*, 5 August 1848, quoted in *An Anthology of Chartist Literature*, p. 357.

58 G.D.H. Cole, *Chartist Portraits*, p. 290.

59 M. Beer, p. 332.

class parliamentary Radical. This open class collaboration was condemned by the left wing of Chartism, including Gammage, who was very critical of O'Connor's leadership and his embrace of the Suffrage Association.

Given O'Connor's unacceptable backsliding, there was a concerted attempt to re-establish the Chartist movement on firm ideological principles, led by Harney and Jones. O'Connor became increasingly preoccupied in trying to explain away the collapse of his Land Scheme. He also disparaged the revolutionary movements that had taken place. This shift to the right led to Harney's resignation as editor of *The Northern Star* in May 1850. Defying O'Connor, Harney reconstituted the Chartist Executive later in the year, and included new members, Thomas Clarke and Samuel Kydd, who became a full-time worker for the party.

ERNEST JONES

Ernest Jones (1819-1869) came late to the Chartist movement and therefore did not possess the weak features and baggage of Owenism or Jacobinism. He came from a privileged aristocratic background, which, in fairness to him, he sacrificed for the movement. He refused to accept any remuneration for his many lectures and dedicated himself to Chartism. Like many other outspoken leaders in 1848, Jones was soon arrested for sedition, unlawful assembly and riot. He defended himself in terms that certainly would not have endeared him to the judge: "You think Chartism is quelled", he said to the Bench. "Learn that it is stronger than ever. While oppression reigns, Chartism resists. While misery lasts, Chartism shall flourish and when misery ceases the Charter will be law."[60]

Ernest Jones was imprisoned for two years. He entered prison as a left-wing radical democrat, but he emerged from his cell as a revolutionary socialist. On Jones' release in July 1850, Harney summed up his political transition in an editorial in his new paper, *The Red Republican*:

"In 1848, ERNEST JONES was sent to prison for having spoken figuratively and with a poet's licence, of the coming day when the green flag of Chartism should fly over Downing Street. In 1850, the released patriot was received by thousands of Yorkshiremen under waving folds of the red banner. The change in the popular symbol was vastly significant. In 1848, a Chartist Convention was content to ask for the Charter, and nothing but the Charter, leaving the social question to the chances of the future. In 1851, the delegates of the people (at the Manchester Convention) lift up their voices for THE CHARTER AND SOMETHING

60 Ibid., pp. 346.

MORE… Propositions which the mind of every thinking man can compass, have been enunciated by the Executive, adopted by the Convention and will speedily evoke the action of the people. Behold, the victors of the 'Tenth of April' – behold the fruits of your victory."[61]

Ernest Jones was incarcerated in Tothill Fields prison, Millbank, under the most barbaric of conditions. He was extremely fortunate to have survived the ordeal. In fact, the two others sentenced alongside him both died in prison. It is certainly worth quoting the testimony of Ernest Jones himself:

"I was kept for more than two years in separate confinement on the silent system, most rigidly enforced – so rigidly that for an involuntary I was sent for three days to a dark cell on bread and water. For the first nineteen months, I was kept without books, pen, ink, or paper, and had to sit out that time in a cell, twelve feet by seven, locked up in solitude and silence, without even a table or chair. To this cell (the day cell) were three windows, two without glass but with rough wooden shutters, through which the wind and snow and rain of winter blew all over the place. My night cell was of far smaller dimensions, 9 feet by 4 feet. Its window was unglazed – its shutters did not meet the window frame nor each other by one or two inches. There was an aperture over my bed 18 inches by 12 inches, through which the snow and rain fell on me as I slept, saturating my clothes with moisture, so that often the water dripped from them as I put them on. The bed itself was a sack of straw with a piece of carpeting. From this bed I had to go, when I rose at five in the morning, across two yards in my shirt and trousers only, to wash and dress in the open air, after getting wet through in the rain and snow while dressing, and sitting all day in my wet clothes in my fireless cell; for during the first twelve months I was allowed no fire in my day cell. During the intense frost of '49, I had to break the ice in the stone trough in which I was compelled to wash, in the same water, frequently, that other prisoners had used. The diet was so poor, and often of so revolting a kind, that at last I was unable to walk across my cell without support, through loss of strength. Neither fork nor knife was allowed at meals, and I had to tear my food with my fingers. Bent to the ground with rheumatism, and racked with neuralgia, I applied for permission to have a fire, but this was denied me, as already stated, till the second year of my imprisonment. Then I became so weak that I was compelled to crawl on all fours if I sought to reach the door of my cell to knock for assistance. On one occasion I fell against the grate, and had a narrow escape of being burned to death. It will be remembered that in the year of 1849, the cholera raged so fearfully in London that in one day 417 persons died.

---

61 S. Harrison, pp. 124-125.

During the height of the plague, while suffering from bowel complaint, I was sent to a darkened cell, because I did not pick the oakum that was brought to me as my daily task... During all this time, after the first few weeks, I was allowed to hear from my wife and children only once every three months..."[62]

Incredibly, he survived, while many others perished from a similar ordeal. O'Connor, to his credit, raised the matter of Jones' confinement in the House of Commons, and there was a campaign to obtain a general amnesty for political prisoners. In defiance of the authorities, Jones fashioned an inkwell from soap and pinched some materials from the prison governor's office, where he had been put to work. In prison, he wrote poetry, and his best known, 'The New World', was partly written using his own blood as ink.

Immediately following his release, Jones wrote defiantly in *The Northern Star* with the appeal to "Organise! Organise! Organise!" He continued: "You may tell them, in the speech for which you arrested me I spoke of a *green* flag waving over Downing Street. I have changed my colour since then – it shall be a *red* one now."[63]

NEW LEADERSHIP

Chartism was clearly facing grave difficulties after the defeat of the 1848 Revolution in Europe, as well as the failure of the Irish insurrection. This had cast a blanket of reaction across the entire continent, including Britain. Jones' incarceration had also deprived the Chartist movement of a key leader at a crucial time. Harney, who had remained free, carried the banner of the left wing and attempted on his own to reorganise the party. This was at a time when O'Connor came into conflict with this left wing, who he regarded as a challenge to his authority. O'Connor, in fact, became increasingly cantankerous. There were a lot of arguments between him and Harney. O'Connor's speeches became less and less coherent. He was already suffering from mental illness and did not participate in the central council meetings. His leadership role had now become a barrier to any advancement. His rows with Harney and Jones centred around his rejection of socialism, which he saw as a diversion from the Charter. O'Connor contemptuously attacked Harney and Jones as "Socialists first and Chartists second."

It was at this time, in June 1850, that Harney launched *The Red Republican*, then the *Friend of the People* newspaper. Also, elections were held in the Chartist party for nine executive places, where Reynolds had come top of

---

62 M. O'Brien, pp. 91-92.

63 *An Anthology of Chartist Literature*, p. 361.

the poll with 1,805 votes, with Harney on 1,774, and Jones on 1,757 votes. O'Connor was also elected but received fewer votes, 1,314, an indication of his declining popularity. Discontent had been brewing for a period, resulting in this change at the top.

Sadly, in his final years O'Connor was a shadow of his former self. He was exhausted after more than a decade of continuous exertion, sacrifice and stress. He had become a tragic figure. Throughout his leadership of the Chartist movement, he displayed a brilliant class instinct, which allowed him to play the role he did. He was able to articulate the feelings of the masses, and in that sense was a true mass leader. He nevertheless lacked a theoretical vision, which led him to make mistakes. His resistance to socialism also created problems. For his broader ideas he relied on others, including Bronterre O'Brien, the Chartist theoretician. He finally gave up the ownership of *The Northern Star* in April 1852, which put an end to his control over the paper after a stormy existence of fifteen years. He also spent an increasing amount of time abroad.

When O'Connor became seriously ill, he entered a mental asylum at the request of the Commons authorities and was therefore forced to give up his parliamentary seat. He died penniless three years later in August 1855. Public subscription raised enough to cover the funeral costs. Some 50,000 people followed his hearse to Kensal Green, one of the last great Chartist demonstrations in London. "He lived and died for us", read several banners accompanying the coffin. A Red Liberty Cap was placed on top of the main standard. Thus passed away Feargus O'Connor, Chartism's most outstanding mass leader, who withstood the arrests, imprisonment, and persecution of the English ruling class, and whose energies helped galvanise the "fustian jackets, unshorn chins and blistered hands" into the first proletarian mass movement in Britain.

With O'Connor out of the picture, the younger generation began to assert themselves within the Chartist movement, especially the talented Julian Harney and Ernest Jones. Their task was to re-create the movement as a unified national organisation on a sound political basis. Under the influence of Marx and Engels, they certainly made their mark. They stood for "the Charter and something more", namely the need for social change. It was a play on O'Connor's slogan "the Charter and nothing more." They constituted a new socialist leadership that took Chartism in a new direction.

This led to opposition and then splits. For instance, O'Connor's supporters, who repudiated Jones and Harney, held their own miniature conference in Manchester in January 1851, against the express wishes of the Executive of the

National Charter Association. The majority of this event, which could hardly be described as a 'conference', took a conciliatory reformist stand in regard to collaboration with the middle classes. Numerically it only consisted of O'Connor and *seven* others, supposedly representing four localities, and even these were far from united. Engels, who actually attended the meeting as an observer, described the event as "sheer humbug". In the end, the Manchester people roundly denounced the "Communist Chartism" emanating from London, a clear indication of the direction in which they were travelling.

On the other hand, the official Chartist Convention took place in London from 31 March to 10 April 1851, where the supporters of the revolutionary line of Harney and Jones were in the clear majority. This Convention, attended by fifty-three NCA locals, adopted a new programme for the party, a 'Programme of the Charter and Something More', which openly proclaimed radical policies and socialist aims. It noted that:

> "A political change would be inefficacious, unless accompanied by a social change; that a Chartist movement, unless accompanied with social knowledge, would result in utter failure; that we cannot claim or receive the support of the labourers, mechanic, farmer or trader, unless we show them that we are practical reformers; that power would be safely vested in Chartist hands; that we know their grievances, and how to redress them..."[64]

The programme included the nationalisation of the land; the separation of Church and State; national, secular, and compulsory education; public maintenance of the unemployed; entitlement to relief for the aged and infirm; abolition of the National Debt; abolition of the standing army and the arming of the people; and abolition of capital punishment. It also advocated that the co-operatives be joined in a national union and demanded that all taxes be levied on land and accumulated property. In many ways it was very similar to the programme contained in the *Communist Manifesto*. Only two delegates opposed the Executive, Harney and Finlen, who were in favour of nationalising the land without any compensation to the existing owners. "The programme adopted by the Convention was vastly superior to any adopted by previous Conventions", stated Gammage.[65]

Although O'Connor attended some sessions, suffering from ill health, "he was very little noticed".[66] It was the high point of Harney's leadership, as well

---

64 K. Flett, *Chartism After 1848*, p. 114.
65 R.C. Gammage, p. 372.
66 Ibid., p. 373.

as of socialist ideas within Chartism. Influenced by Marx and Engels, the Chartists learned that real change could only come by taking up economic and social demands and linking them to the transformation of society. "Jones now attempted to make the NCA a more or less Marxist working-class party", state Cole and Filson.[67]

Both Harney and Jones stubbornly held up the red banner of revolutionary socialism, despite O'Connor's opposition. In these years, they constituted the outstanding representatives of the left wing of Chartism, turning their attention towards scientific socialism. With O'Connor absent, the socialist tendency made rapid progress. Harney wrote:

> "Emancipation of labour is the only worthy object of political warfare... that those who till the soil shall be its first masters, that those who raised the food shall be its first partakers, that those who build mansions shall live in them..."[68]

Engels wrote frequently for Harney's *Democratic Review*, which had become, in effect, the theoretical organ of left-wing Chartism. A high point was reached when the *Red Republican* published for the first time an English translation of the *Communist Manifesto*, bringing its ideas to the attention of the advanced sections of the British working class.

However, the strengthening of reaction everywhere and the decline in the Chartist movement at home created difficulties. As Engels explained much later, "the industrial prosperity which had been returning gradually since the middle of 1848 and attained full bloom in 1849 and 1850 was the revitalising force of a re-strengthened European reaction".[69] 1848 proved to be the last peak of Chartist mass activity, but that is a judgment made in hindsight.

Given the many difficulties, these certainly constituted the 'dog days' of Chartism. Marx and Engels recognised the problem and had drawn the conclusion in the autumn of 1850 that "a new revolution is possible only in consequence of a new crisis".[70] But the crisis was delayed. Instead, there was a sharp revival of the economy and renewed prosperity, which was to have its own profound consequences. But how long this interregnum would last was not known.

---

67 G.D.H. Cole and A.W. Filson, p. 373.
68 J. Strachey, pp. 348-9.
69 MECW, vol. 27, p. 507.
70 MECW, vol. 27, p. 508.

9. TWILIGHT AND LEGACY

"I believe that the less enlightened portions of the working classes feel little sympathy with political rights, unless they can be made to see the results in social benefits: I believe they do not yet fully understand the connecting link between POLITICAL POWER AND SOCIAL REFORM; I believe there is little use in holding before them the Cap of Liberty, unless you hold THE BIG LOAF by the side of it."
– Ernest Jones on his release from prison, July 1850

"With the Charter, national ownership of land, currency and credit, people would soon discover what wonders of production, distribution and exchange might be achieved by associated labour, in comparison with individual labour. Thence would gradually arise the true social state, or the realities of socialism, in contradiction to the present dreams of it."
– Bronterre O'Brien, January 1847

"A frightful hobgoblin stalks through Europe. We are haunted by a ghost, the ghost of Communism."
– *The Communist Manifesto*, as published in *Red Republican*, June 1850

THE SOCIALIST YEARS

In 1850, when Ernest Jones emerged from two years' imprisonment, he tried to make sense of what had happened, especially the splits and divisions that had taken place. After much deliberation, he concluded: "Thus, in every transition state, from one set of thoughts to another, a certain loss, a certain retardation is experienced... It is one of these stages of transition through which we have now passed." This assessment was one of the most sober and balanced at the time. Political organisations and parties have to navigate and adapt to the changing conditions, which can often provoke internal crises and splits. Some people are able to adapt while others, stuck in their old ways, tend to resist or drop away, being replaced by new blood. "This is hardly ever done without a certain amount of disruption, disorganisation, and strife", explained Jones.[1]

Political struggles in general, including factional struggles within a party, do not take place in a vacuum. They are carried on under the pressures of social forces and reflect the ebb and flow of the class struggle to one degree or another. This was confirmed in the struggle within Chartism. Nevertheless, above all it is through such a process, however painful, that clarity is finally reached and things can move forward on a far sounder basis.

Interestingly, this was an idea expressed by Lassalle in a letter to Marx around this time: "Party struggles lend a party strength and vitality; the greatest proof of a party's weakness is its diffuseness and the blurring of clear demarcations; a party becomes stronger by purging itself."[2]

In fact, Lassalle had borrowed this idea from Hegel. As Engels wrote some years later:

> Naturally, every party leadership wants to see successes, and this is quite a good thing. But there are circumstances in which one must have the courage to sacrifice momentary success for more important things...

> Moreover, old man Hegel said long ago: A party proves itself victorious by splitting and being able to stand the split. The movement of the proletariat necessarily passes through different stages of development; at every stage part of the people get stuck and do not rejoin in the further advance...[3]

This accurately reflected the process Ernest Jones recognised in the Chartist movement at this stage.

Of course, there are plenty of philistines and unity-mongers who are repelled by such a notion. However, the spurious and deceptive 'broad church' idea of 'all-inclusiveness', so beloved by the reformists, is a recipe for paralysis, especially for its left wing. Its features are of a loosely-knit, heterogeneous organisation utterly incapable in this form of accomplishing the revolutionary overthrow of capitalism. Far better the creation of a homogeneous party, which is based on sound principles and knows what it wants, than a hodgepodge of interests pulling in different directions.

---

1   G.D.H. Cole, *Chartist Portraits*, p. 350.
2   'Letter from Lassalle to Marx', 24 June 1852.
3   Marx and Engels Selected Correspondence, pp. 284-285.

Events, and even shocks, can help to clarify and sharpen ideas and forge a principled unity. Chartism had certainly 'purged' itself of many on the right and the centre, which was a positive development. There had been a number of casualties along the road, as Jones had noted. It was therefore important for him to understand what had happened, and draw the necessary conclusions, so as to prepare for the rebirth of Chartism on a higher level. Above all, the movement needed sound perspectives as a guide. It needed to know where it was heading and be able to establish a unity of purpose. As Engels later pointed out: "In 1848 there were but a few people who had any idea at all of the direction in which this emancipation was to be sought."[4] It was through Harney and Jones, the advanced cadres of Chartism, that Marx and Engels tried to provide such clarity.

"George Julian Harney shares with Ernest Jones the distinction of having been the first English Marxists," states the labour historian G.D.H. Cole, "and the most determined to assert the cause of Chartism in proletarian terms."[5] This is without doubt true.

Following the defeat of the European revolution, Marx and Engels had arrived in England in late 1849. They were to spend the rest of their lives there. They helped to guide the Chartist movement at this difficult time through their contact with its key leaders. Before leaving Geneva, Engels had written to Julian Harney to say they were both coming to London. By this time, Marx and Engels were leading members of the Communist League, had already published *The Communist Manifesto*, and had lived directly through the experience of the 1848 Revolution. While keen to deepen their knowledge, they were also eager to expand their influence, and explain their theories of historical materialism, class struggle and revolutionary change. England was the country where capitalism was the most advanced, which had brought into being a powerful proletariat. It was therefore a prime candidate for a socialist revolution, in which revolutionary Chartism could play a decisive role.

The influence of Marx and Engels, especially on Harney and Ernest Jones, was to help take Chartism in a new socialist direction. Under the guidance of these young men, the politics of these Chartist leaders shifted sharply to the left. Harney had, on Engels' suggestion, become a correspondent of the Brussels Communist Committee. In making this proposal, Engels wrote that he considered him a true internationalist, revolutionary, republican and Communist. Marx and Engels came to regard Harney, given his established

---

4   MECW, vol. 27, p. 511.
5   G.D.H. Cole, *Chartist Portraits*, p. 298.

position within Chartism, as a key to the British working-class movement and thereby the British revolution.

But Harney was beset by doubts. He wrote to Engels questioning his estimation of him:

> "You say I am 'anti-national', 'revolutionary', 'energetical', 'proletarian', 'more a Frenchman than an Englishman', 'Atheistical, Republican, and Communist'. I am too old a soldier to blush at this accumulation of virtues credited to my account, but supposing it to be even as you say, it does not follow that I am qualified for 'leadership'. A popular chief should be possessed of a magnificent bodily appearance, an iron frame, eloquence, or at least a ready fluency of tongue. I have none of these... I am but one of the humble workers in the great movement of progress, as such I desire to be considered."[6]

Harney nevertheless recognised certain qualities in Engels that he trusted, not least his clear ideas, and therefore was prepared to assist:

> "For myself I have confidence in your discretion as well as your zeal, and as far as my humble abilities, and time will permit I am willing to aid you in the manner you suggest..."[7]

This kept the door open to a collaboration that would hopefully bear fruit.

This relationship between all these men – Marx, Engels, Harney and Jones – was to play an important role in shaping the last phase of Chartism. In 1845, Harney had become the editor of *The Northern Star*, which maintained coverage of important events in Europe with articles by Engels, Mazzini, Louis Blanc and many others. In the years after 1848, however, the weekly circulation had fallen to 1,200 copies, a reflection of the decline in the readership of Chartist publications.

When he was removed from *The Northern Star*, Harney decided to launch a new paper, *The Red Republican*. The effort to maintain it was a truly colossal endeavour. Due to the prohibitively high government tax on newspapers, the paper was issued as an unstamped quarto, which was always in danger of falling foul of the law. It contained reports of labour disputes and oriented its content towards the trade unions in an effort to win wider support. In doing so, Harney emphasised more than simply the fight for reforms. He linked this struggle to the question of the overthrow of capitalism, and the working class taking political power. He announced:

---

6   MECW, vol. 38, pp. 535-536.

7   MECW, vol. 38, p. 536.

"It is not any amelioration of the condition of the most miserable that will satisfy us: it is justice to all we demand. It is not the mere improvement of the social life of our class that we seek: but the abolition of classes and the destruction of those wicked distinctions which have divided the human race into the princes and paupers, landlords and labourers, masters and slaves. It is not any patching and cobbling of the present system we aspire to accomplish, but the annihilation of that system, and the substitution instead of an order of things in which all shall labour and all enjoy, and the happiness of each guarantee the welfare of the entire community."[8]

As we have seen, it was Harney who published the first English translation of *The Communist Manifesto* in November 1850 with the note saying that it was "the most revolutionary document ever given to the world". The translation was made by Helen Macfarlane, who was probably the most influential woman in the Chartist movement. *The Times* newspaper hastened to warn its middle-class readers against:

"[C]heap publications containing the wildest and most anarchical doctrines… in which religion and morality are perverted and scoffed at, and every rule of conduct which experience has sanctioned, and on which the very existence of society depends, is openly assailed."[9]

Harney's decision to launch *The Red Republican* was a further open challenge to the O'Connorites. Its aim, he announced, was to "popularise the principles of Red Republicanism, to unfurl a banner, announce a faith, and clear the way for those more powerful who will follow". In the first issue of the paper, he boldly stated its aims:

"Will they charge us with being 'enemies to order'? We shall prove that their order is an 'organised hypocrisy'. Will they charge us with contemplating spoliation? We shall prove that they themselves are spoliators and robbers. Will they accuse us of being 'bloodthirsty democrats'? We shall prove our accusers to be remorseless traffickers in the lives of their fellow creatures…"[10]

In their own way, both Harney and Jones tried to popularise the ideas of scientific socialism, with which they were becoming increasingly familiar. Jones was also a poet who used poetry and song to explain these ideas, which was very well received. Following the approach of Shelley's 'Song to the Men of England', Ernest Jones' 'The Song of the Low' deals with the exploitation

---

8 *Red Republican*, 12 October 1850, quoted in Harrison, p. 125.

9 F. Wheen, *Karl Marx*, p. 255.

10 M. O'Brien, p. 105.

of different layers of the working class, agricultural labourers, miners, builders and weavers. It points to the difference between what they produce in terms of value and what they receive in wages, the very essence of capitalist exploitation.

We're low – we're low – we're very, very low,
As low as low can be;
The rich are high – for we make them so –
And a miserable lot are we!
And a miserable lot are we!
A miserable lot are we!

We plough and sow – we're so very, very low,
That we delve in the dirty clay,
Till we bless the plain with the golden grain,
And the vale with the fragrant hay.
Our place we know – we're so very low,
'Tis down at the landlord's feet:
We're not too low – the bread to grow
But too low the bread to eat.

We're low – we're low – we're very, very low, etc

Down, down we go – we're so very, very low,
To the hell of the deep sunk mines.
But we gather the proudest gems that glow,
When the crown of a despot shines;
And whenever he lacks – upon our backs
Fresh loads he deigns to lay,
We're far too low to vote the tax
But we're not too low to pay.

We're low – we're low – we're very, very low, etc

We're low, we're low – mere rabble, we know,
But at our plastic power,
The mould at the lordling's feet will grow
Into palace and church and tower –
Then prostrate fall – in the rich man's hall,
And cringe at the rich man's door,
We're not too low to build the wall,
But too low to tread the floor.

We're low – we're low – we're very, very low, etc

We're low – we're low – we're very, very low,
Yet from our fingers glide
The silken flow – and the robes that glow,
Round the limbs of the sons of pride.
And what we get – and what we give
We know – and we know our share.
We're not too low the cloth to weave –
But too low the cloth to wear.

We're low – we're low – we're very, very low, etc

We're low, we're low – we're very, very low,
And yet when the trumpets ring,
The thrust of a poor man's arm will go
Through the heart of the proudest king!
We're low, we're low – our place we know,
We're only the rank and file,
We're not too low – to kill the foe,
But too low to touch the spoil.
We're low – we're low – we're very, very low, etc.

EARLIER CONNECTIONS

Marx and Engels had previously set foot in England to attend the London Congress of the Communist League in late November and early December 1847. While Marx was in London, *The Northern Star* reported on a speech he made to the Fraternal Democrats. "Dr. Marx, the delegate from Brussels, then came forward, and was greeted with every demonstration of welcome, and delivered an energetic oration in the German language."

In his speech, Marx declared:

"I have been sent by the Brussels Democrats to speak with the Democrats of London to call on them to be holden a *Congress of Nations* – a Congress of working men to establish Liberty all over the world ... The Democrats of Belgium and the Chartists of England were the real Democrats, and the moment they carried the six points of their Charter the road to liberty would be opened for the world. Effect this grand object, then, you working men of England and you will be hailed as the saviour of the whole human race."[11]

Through the columns of the Chartist newspapers, the eyes of the Chartist rank and file were opened to events on the Continent. The Fraternal Democrats

---

11 *The Northern Star*, 4 December 1847, quoted in M. Beer, p. 165.

was formed in September 1845, its most active members being Julian Harney and Ernest Jones – the former acting as its secretary. This body, together with its successor, the International Association, were the forerunners or pioneers of the First International. As Theodore Rothstein wrote:

> The International was born in England, and it is on English soil that we have to look for its preceding history… It was in England that the proletariat first acquired a deep sense, not only of its solidarity with the workers of other countries, but also of the imperative need for concerted action in the fight against capitalist society, based upon this solidarity.[12]

The most important English fraternal visitors at the London Congress of the Communist League were precisely Julian Harney and Ernest Jones. It was at this historic event, held at the Red Lion public house in Great Windmill Street, that Marx and Engels were asked to draw up the famous *Communist Manifesto* which became the founding document of the communist movement. The first edition of 2,000 copies in German were run off at a print shop in Liverpool Street in early February 1848, a few weeks before the outbreak of the European revolution. Although remarkably concise, the *Manifesto* provides a comprehensive world outlook and the real basis of scientific socialism. As opposed to idealised schemes and utopian communes, the authors explained that socialism was rooted in historical development and the struggle of the working class, the gravediggers of capitalism.

The authors of the *Manifesto* stressed the importance of working-class parties, specifically the Chartists in England, and how Communists should work to influence the workers' movement. This explained their very close relationship with Harney and Jones and their patient approach in trying to convince them of these ideas. Harney had a group of friends in Manchester who Engels was trying to cultivate politically, and this revealed his friendly pedagogical approach. "I shall try to start up a small club with these fellows, or organise regular meetings to discuss the *Manifesto* with them", he wrote.[13]

In these years, Marx and Engels were striving to build an international revolutionary organisation or party of the working class arising from the international character of the class struggle. For them, theory and practice were inseparably linked. "Philosophers have only interpreted the world, in various ways. The point, however, is to change it", Marx famously explained.[14]

---

12 T. Rothstein, *From Chartism to Labourism*, p. 125.
13 MECW, vol. 38, p. 264.
14 MESW, vol. 1, p. 15.

They therefore proposed to organise an international conference in Brussels in September 1848. There even exists a letter from Julian Harney to Marx, dated 18 December 1847, announcing this proposal. The proposal had the unanimous support of the Fraternal Democrats, the German Working Men's Association in London, and the national and metropolitan Chartist Executives. In early March, both Harney and Ernest Jones visited Marx in Paris, after which Marx wrote to Engels informing him that a Central Committee had been formed. However, this conference and these plans were cut across by the unfolding European revolution.

This growing influence of Marxism – of scientific socialism – on the left wing of Chartism was bearing fruit. Between 1849 and 1850, Harney published a magazine, *The Democratic Review,* to which Engels contributed regularly. Both Marx and Engels used it to disseminate their views of socialism to a broader audience and to explain what was taking place on the Continent. It was in this journal that Engels wrote his *Letters from Germany,* as well as his *Letters from France,* concerning his personal experiences as a direct participant in the revolutions of 1848. They made quite an impact on the Chartist left wing. *The Northern Star* commented favourably, saying these letters "will do much towards promoting the good work of international fraternity".[15] The following month, the newspaper stated:

> "Letters from France and Germany are decidedly the most important of the contents of this number of the *Democratic Review.* The disclosures concerning the designs of the European despots, and the proofs given to the progress of the revolutionary spirit in France and Germany, stamp these letters as inexpressibly valuable. The letter from France has but one fault – its brevity."[16]

The following month's review concluded that "the Letters in the present number show that great events are at hand".[17] Other newspapers, including *People*, also carried favourable reviews.

At this time, Harney and Jones fully embraced the ideas of communism. As explained, they had already participated in the Congress of the Communist League in London. With the demise of O'Connor, they worked to mould the movement towards their way of thinking. In April 1850, Harney joined Marx and Engels, together with the French Blanquist refugees, in establishing the

---

15 *The Northern Star*, 5 January 1850.
16 *The Northern Star*, 2 February 1850.
17 *The Northern Star*, 2 March 1850.

'Universal League of Revolutionary Communists' in London. Its first statute boldly declared that:

> "[T]he main aim of the association is the downfall of all privileged classes, the substitution of those classes to the dictatorship of the proletarians by keeping the revolution in continual progress until the achievement of communism, which shall be the final form of the constitution of the human family."[18]

Interestingly, this is one of the earliest references to the dictatorship of the proletariat and the permanent revolution, reflecting a sharpening of their views even in relation to the *Communist Manifesto*, which simply states that its first task is to "raise the proletariat to the position of ruling class, to win the battle of democracy".[19] But with the split in the Communist League and the sectarianism of the Blanquists this initiative did not last long.

REVIEW OF CHARTISM

At the end of 1850, Marx and Engels published a review of Chartism in the German *Neue Rheinische Zeitung*, which revealed much about the state of Chartism, and the division between the opportunist and revolutionary tendencies within the movement:

> The present organisation of the Chartist Party is similarly in a state of dissolution. The members of the petty bourgeoisie who still adhere to the party, together with the labour aristocracy, form a purely democratic faction whose programme is limited to the People's Charter and a number of other petty-bourgeois reforms. The mass of the workers who live in truly proletarian conditions belong to the revolutionary Chartist faction. The leader of the former faction is Feargus *O'Connor*, and the leaders of the latter are Julian *Harney* and Earnest *Jones*. The elderly O'Connor, an Irish squire and self-styled descendant of the old kings of Munster, is a true representative of Old England, despite his origin and his political tendencies. His whole nature is conservative and he most emphatically hates both industrial progress and revolution. All his ideals are patriarchal and petty-bourgeois to the core. He unites in himself countless contradictions which are resolved and harmonised in the form of a certain banal common sense and which enable him year in, year out, to write his endless weekly letters in *The Northern Star*, each of which is in open conflict with its predecessor...

> The main bone of contention between the two Chartist factions is the land question. O'Connor and his party want to use the Charter to accommodate some

---

18 MECW, vol. 10, p. 614.

19 MESW, vol. 1, p. 126.

of the workers on small plots of land and eventually to parcel out all the land in Great Britain. We know how his attempt to organise this parcelling out on a small scale by means of a joint-stock company failed. That propensity which every bourgeois revolution has to break up large landed estates gave the British workers the impression for a while that this parcelling out was something revolutionary, although its corollary is the unfailing tendency of small properties to become concentrated and succumb in face of large-scale farming. The revolutionary faction of the Chartists opposed this demand for parcelling out with the demand for the confiscation of all landed property, and insists that it should not be distributed but remain national property.[20]

In *The Red Republican*, Harney boldly explained:

> "*Chartism* in 1850 is a different thing from Chartism in 1840. The leaders of the English Proletarians have proved that they are true Democrats, and no shams, by going ahead so rapidly in the last few years. They have progressed from the idea of a simple political reform to the idea of a Social Revolution."[21]

This was an important turning-point. Harney's decision to publish the *Communist Manifesto* confirmed the direction in which he was travelling. These ideas were having a stimulating effect in the movement and were becoming increasingly influential. In fact, a key layer of left-wing Chartists saw this as the way forward. Ernest Jones intervened boldly in the discussions, having joined the staff of *The Red Republican*. He explained:

> "Therefore, the capitalists of all kinds will be our foes as long as they exist, and carry on against us a war to the very knife. Therefore, they must Be Put Down. Therefore, we Must have class against class – that is, all the oppressed on the one side, and all the oppressors on the other. An amalgamation of classes is impossible where an amalgamation of interests is impossible also… CLASS AGAINST CLASS – all other mode of proceeding is mere moonshine."[22]

Prior to this, as we saw in previous chapters, socialism in England had been dominated by Owenism, a Utopian trend which, while progressive, was abstract and ahistorical. It made damning criticisms of capitalism but offered little in regard to a viable solution. Engels had summed up the problem as early as 1844:

---

20 MECW, vol. 10, pp. 514-515.

21 M. O'Brien, p. 102.

22 Ibid., p. 102.

Hence it is evident that the working men's movement is divided into two sections, the Chartists and the Socialists. The Chartists are theoretically the more backward, the less developed, but they are genuine proletarians all over, the representatives of their class. The Socialists are more far-seeing, propose practical remedies against distress, but, proceeding originally from the bourgeoisie, are for this reason unable to amalgamate completely with the working class. The union of Socialism with Chartism, the reproduction of French Communism in an English manner, will be the next step, and has already begun. Then only, when this has been achieved, will the working class be the true intellectual leader of England. Meanwhile, political and social development will proceed, and will foster this new party, this new departure of Chartism.[23]

In other words, Chartism was a revolutionary movement, but unfortunately lacking a clear revolutionary theory. While it had a socialist colouration, it had no clearly defined social theory, apart from rudimentary ideas, and therefore lacked coherent direction. O'Connor, for one, harked back to peasant ownership and an idyllic past in his Land Plan. O'Brien had a far clearer vision, but even he lacked a rounded-out understanding. Harney and Jones, under the guidance of Marx and Engels, could provide a solution to this weakness, but on the one condition that they remained politically steadfast in the face of difficulties.

O'Connor, like a bear with a sore head, withdrew. His opportunist wing was eventually defeated. Harney, Jones and those around the Fraternal Democrats took control of the National Chartist Association, transforming it in the process into a socialist party. This was reflected in the 1851 Chartist Convention, where the socialist tendency reached its peak. This was, however, the last important Convention ever held.

The Northern Star, heading for oblivion under O'Connor's stewardship, now called for the abandonment of the Charter and proclaimed that the word Chartist was "offensive to both sight and taste". This was correctly denounced by Jones, who fought back through the columns of his *Notes to the People*, hoping to salvage the movement and turn it further in a socialist direction. Things got very heated, confused and difficult at this point.

The growing difficulties that beset the Chartist movement also served to undermine the confidence of its most revolutionary representatives, starting with Julian Harney. He began to lose his political bearings. Thus the relations between him and Jones deteriorated, as Harney began to shift, one step at

---

23 MECW, vol. 4, pp. 526-527.

a time, in the direction of the petty-bourgeois democrats. At this point, O'Connor decided to sell *The Northern Star*. Harney, keen to take advantage, bought and merged it with his *Friend of the People* to produce a new paper, *The Star of Freedom*.

The idea that Jones and Harney would establish a Chartist paper under their joint auspices had broken down in February 1851. This led to a bitter quarrel between Jones and Harney, who were now producing rival newspapers. Jones accused Harney of attempting to undermine his new *People's Paper*, which had superseded his *Notes to the People*. This friction generated considerable animosity, as the general sales of Chartist literature were in decline, and there was little room for two socialist weekly papers.

This quarrel, described by Marx as a "cockfight", proved to be the last straw in the relationship and finally cemented the break between the two former comrades. Despite all this, Harney's paper only lasted until December 1851 before it closed down.

This eventual split between Jones and Harney, who had been up until then had been intimate friends and political collaborators, can be put down at least in part to the difficult objective situation. But Harney was also looking for a short-cut. It is a law that in the midst of grave difficulties, having to fight against the stream, the less steadfast will hesitate, waver finally and depart the scene. This, unfortunately, was Harney's fate. It is worth explaining this schism in more detail.

Harney's friendship with the worst muddle-heads around Louis Blanc, Mazzini, Blanqui, Barbes, and the German émigrés, who in turn had courted the Chartist leaders, had led to increasing friction with Marx and Engels. Marx, who was a clear thinker, was particularly irritated by this political backsliding and such shenanigans. Harney's links with these confused and demoralised elements meant that he was in practice taking sides against Marx and Engels, who were attempting to hold the line politically and theoretically. "I am tired of Harney's untiring public flattery of 'the little great men'", wrote a frustrated Marx. Engels himself reported on "somewhat strained relations with Harney," while "Jones, however, a fellow quite unlike Harney, is wholly on our side and is at present expounding the *Manifesto* to the English."[24]

The émigré circles in London had been especially affected by the defeat of the 1848 revolutions. They brought with them an atmosphere of demoralisation which even infected the Communist League, becoming

---

24 MECW, vol. 38, p. 380.

embroiled in intrigues, all kinds of conspiracies and petty tittle-tattle. The stagnant political situation in this period was getting increasingly stale and inward-looking. As time went on, Marx and Engels' disdain for the émigrés became more pronounced. "One comes to realise more and more that emigration is an institution which inevitably turns a man into a fool, an ass and a base rascal..." wrote Engels in a letter to Marx. "It is a real SCHOOL OF SCANDAL AND MEANNESS in which the hindmost donkey becomes the foremost saviour of his country."[25]

Marx and Engels fully understood what was happening. Until the objective situation changed, there was little that could be done. An open breach took place on the Central Board of the Communist League in September 1850, where Marx and Engels were completely isolated. They eventually decided to separate themselves from this demoralised milieu, turn their backs on 'popularity' as they had always done, and concentrate on more important matters. "I'm tired of them and wish to employ my time as productively as possible", wrote Marx.[26] Engels replied to Marx: "At long last we again have the opportunity – the first time in ages – to show that we need neither popularity, nor the SUPPORT of any party in any country, and that our position is completely independent of such ludicrous trifles. From now on we are only answerable to ourselves."[27] He added that "the main thing at the moment is to find some way of getting our things published", which showed a keen desire to widen their audience.[28]

In May 1851, a conference to reorganise the Chartist movement took place in Manchester. It was a five-day conference "to raise the Chartist cause once more". A new Executive of full-time members was chosen, composed of Jones, Gammage, and James Finlen. William Grocott, formerly secretary to the Miners' Association, now fulfilled this role as secretary on the Executive. By this time, Harney had dropped off the Executive. What was left of the other fragments soon disappeared.

Given Harney's increasing confusion and capitulation to émigré moods, Marx and Engels tried to base themselves on Ernest Jones who maintained, at this time, a consistently revolutionary position. Engels wrote to Marx in March 1852 about their relations with Ernest Jones and the current state of the Chartist movement, which had entered a further period of decline:

---

25 MECW, vol.38, p. 287.

26 MECW, vol. 38, p. 245.

27 MECW, vol. 38, p. 289.

28 MECW, vol. 38, pp. 290-291.

Judging by everything I see, the Chartists are in a state of complete dissolution and collapse and at the same time experience such a shortage of usable people that they will either fall apart entirely and break up into cliques, hence must practically become a mere tail of the financials [bourgeois radicals of the Financial Reform Association], or some competent chap must reorganise them on an entirely new basis. Jones is moving in quite the right direction and we may well say that, without our doctrine, he would never have discovered how, on the one hand, one can not only maintain the only possible basis for the reconstruction of the Chartist Party – the instinctive class hatred of the workers for the industrial bourgeoisie – but also enlarge and develop it, so laying the foundations for enlightening propaganda and how, on the other, one can still be progressive and resist the workers' reactionary appetites and their prejudices.[29]

This last point about resisting "prejudices" was a warning against opportunism and the chase after popularity at the expense of principles, something which has always plagued the movement.

NOTES TO THE PEOPLE

Engels, along with Marx, was trying to grapple with the problems confronting the British labour movement. Jones issued his own paper, called the *Notes to the People*, which was highly praised and became the only real organ of Chartism. The paper appeared weekly between May 1851 and May 1852 and was the clearest expression in Chartist journalism of a 'social democratic' standpoint, which at that time meant a consistent revolutionary point of view. The period of its publication coincided with the time when Jones was most closely associated with Marx. It contained signed and unsigned contributions from Marx and Engels, and their influence can be seen throughout the paper. Marx either collaborated on or directly dictated many of the articles on economics. He even shared the editorship with Jones for several weeks. As a result of this collaboration, both Marx and Engels came to regard Jones as Chartism's "most talented representative".[30]

The *Notes to the People* is full of reports from all over the country about trade disputes, strikes, grievances and trade union actions. Jones appealed to the working class to furnish him with this important information about the class struggle. He wrote:

"Give me the means, that is, give me the information and these 'Notes' shall be as complete an exposition of labour's wrongs, rights, and remedies, as it is possible to

29 MECW, vol. 39, p. 68.
30 MECW, vol. 38, p. 502.

put in print. I may say this, because what I want is, that the workingman should SPEAK FOR HIMSELF, and none can describe a want so well as he who suffers from it.

"Surely, such an exposition of the labour question, such an all-comprehending, general survey is required. Such the class-press cannot or will not give. Such the means are offered for in this publication."[31]

At the same time, Harney's paper, *The Friend of the People*, was becoming politically confused. It even carried an article attacking Chartism as a class movement, arguing instead for it to be a national movement. It reduced itself to the guiding principle of "Justice – Immutable, Universal, Eternal", with no class content whatsoever. Marx wrote to Engels after receiving a copy of Harney's paper: "I do not know whether our *ex-dear* [Harney] sent me his little paper in order to wring our hearts or whether, out of spite towards us, he has become even more tritely democratic than we would have believed possible."[32]

In the autumn of 1852, Harney went so far as to launch a 'National Party', the purpose of which was to campaign for general suffrage, while specifically repudiating the other five points of the Charter and its social demands. But the venture completely flopped. It had all the hallmarks of the so-called 'Little' Charter, which had been previously pushed by Cobden, Bright and the reformist elements in order to split the Chartist movement. This seems to have been lost on Harney who was becoming increasingly erratic. Marx and Engels' break with Harney was not a personal squabble, as some maintain, but a political one. From 1853, Harney had all but severed his links with Chartism. He had abandoned his paper and had gone to live in Scotland.

Marx and Engels concentrated their efforts and hopes on the firm revolutionary elements, as represented by Ernest Jones. The Chartists, under Jones' leadership, needed to turn their backs on the squabbles and intrigues and face afresh towards the working class. It was with this in mind that Marx urged Jones to shift the centre of their agitation towards the working-class industrial areas. Jones "should begin by *forming* a party, for which purpose he must go to the manufacturing districts", Marx wrote to Engels.[33] On the basis of such activities, there were still prospects for re-establishing Chartism as a working-class party in Britain.

---

31 E. Jones, *Notes to the People: 1851-1852*, back sleeve.
32 MECW, vol. 39, p. 30.
33 MECW, vol. 40, p. 210.

As part of this orientation, Jones correctly emphasised the strategic importance of a paper, which would act as a collective organiser, agitator and propagandist. It would provide the 'scaffolding' around which a new movement could be built. In an article titled 'Why is a *People's Paper* Wanted?' he wrote:

> "The very first, the most essential requisite of a movement is to have an organ to record its proceedings, to communicate through, with its several branches – to appeal through, to exhort through, to speak through, to defend through, and to teach through. It is the fundamental bond of union, the ensign of progress, and the means of organisation. It is that which gives a party a local habitation and a name – it is that which enables it to hold up its head amid the whirl of parties, and to keep its various elements together… A movement that has not the mighty organ of the press at its command is but half a movement – it is a disenfranchised cause, dependent on others, pensioned on others, pauper on others for the expression of its opinions."[34]

Without a paper, Jones explained, the Chartist movement could not be sustained. The winding up of *Notes to the People* due to lack of funds made this an urgent task. He therefore made a financial appeal for £500 to launch "a really Chartist organ". This was backed up with the statement:

> "Let every reader remember the object for which this paper is started. Let him remember that it is established by public subscription of the sons of toil. Let him remember that we are precluded from the usual copiousness of advertisement and publicity… Let him canvass among friends and acquaintances. Let him remember that this is indispensable, and to be of use must be immediate and then a surer success will attend this paper of the people than attends even the gold-supported papers of the wealthy classes."[35]

The People's Paper was finally launched in May 1852 as the successor to the *Notes* and as the weekly organ of revolutionary Chartism. "*The People's Paper* is on the up and up and, for the time being, financially secure", noted Marx the following May.[36]

In June of that year, Jones wrote a letter to Marx, which contained an assessment of the situation and his campaign to re-establish the movement:

> "My Dear Marx, … Tomorrow, I start for Blackstone Edge, where a camp meeting of the Chartists of Yorkshire and Lancashire is to take place, and I am happy to

---

34 S. Harrison, p. 138.
35 Ibid., p. 138.
36 MECW, vol. 39, p. 325.

inform you that the most extensive preparations for the same are making in the North. It is now seven years since a really national gathering took place [in the same location] on that spot sacred to the traditions of the Chartist movement, and the object of the present gathering is as follows:

"Through the treacheries and divisions of 1848, the disruption of the organisation then existing, by the incarceration and banishment of 500 of its leading men – through the thinning of its ranks by emigration – through the deadening of political energy by the influence of brisk trade – the national movement of Chartism had converted itself into isolated action, and the organisation dwindled at the very time that social knowledge spread. Meanwhile, a labour movement rose on the ruins of the political one – a labour movement emanating from the first blind groupings of social knowledge. This labour movement showed itself at first in isolated co-operative attempts; then, when these were found to fail, in an energetic action for a ten-hour's bill, a restriction of the moving power, an abolition of the stoppage system in wages, and a fresh interpretation of the Combination Bill. To these measures, good in themselves, the whole power and attention of the working classes were directed. The failure of the attempts to obtain legislative guarantees for these measures has thrown a more revolutionary tendency in the labour-mind of Britain... Strikes are prevalent everywhere and generally successful. But it is lamentable to behold that the power which might be directed to a fundamental remedy, should be wasted on a temporary palliative. I am, therefore, attempting, in reorganising with numerous friends, to seize this great opportunity for uniting the scattered ranks of Chartism on the sound principles of social revolution."[37]

It was reported that, despite stormy weather, 3,000 attended the Blackstone Edge meeting in Halifax, where they decided to constitute themselves as a Chartist Delegate Council. Jones went on to hold further meetings at Skircoat Moor, Mount Sorrell and Nottingham Forest, attracting the attention of the bourgeois press. In Preston, Jones spoke at a meeting of 15,000 mill workers who had been locked out by their employers, and raised the question of a general strike:

"What gives the capitalist this tremendous power? That he holds all the means of employment... This means of work is, therefore, the hinge on which the future of the people turns... It is a mass movement of all trades, a national movement of the working classes, that can alone achieve a triumphant result... Sectionalised and localised your struggle and you may fail – nationalise it and you are sure to win."[38]

---

37 Quoted in MECW, vol. 12, pp. 135-136.
38 Quoted in MECW, vol. 12, p. 462.

At Blackstone Edge, Jones announced the sad death of Benjamin Ruston, a worker who had chaired Chartist meetings on that very spot. When his funeral took place, upwards of 200,000 workers attended. Marx remarked: "To those who know nothing of English society but its dull, apoplectic surface, it should be recommended to assist at these working men's meetings and to look into those depths where its destructive elements are at work."[39]

In these years, Marx and Engels paid close personal attention to developments in the British working class, especially the attempts to revive Chartism despite its general decline. This explains the time they spent and efforts they made assisting its revolutionary wing and helping to guide its initiatives throughout this period. However, it should be understood that neither Marx nor Engels were blind to the colossal undertakings that would be required to rebuild the Chartist movement on sound foundations. They appreciated how few "able people" there were, but they looked to Jones as the person best placed to accomplish this task.

Nevertheless, the circulation of the *People's Paper* barely reached 3,000 copies, which failed to cover its costs, and Jones was forced to search for subscribers and launch a new fighting fund. Each week recorded a deficit. Therefore, penny-a-week collections were organised to keep the paper going in the Chartist areas. Activities and collections were faithfully recorded. One supporter of the paper, who signed himself "A Working Man, Nottingham", wrote:

> "As a beginning I now send, and mean to send *sixpence* a week myself towards its support. In addition to this I am collecting in my shop and among all the readers of the paper in my locality that I know, their weekly PENNY."[40]

Marx contributed to the paper and assisted Ernest Jones with editing and organisational issues, particularly in its early days. As well as publishing Marx's articles, the paper also reprinted the most important articles by him and Engels from the *New York Daily Tribune*.

THE MASS MOVEMENT

In 1853, a strike movement swept the country. Jones, with a group of fellow Chartists, attempted to create a broad workers' organisation called 'The Mass Movement'. The aim of this was to unite the unions and the unorganised sectors, in order to co-ordinate the strikes. To launch the initiative, they

---

39 MECW, vol. 12, p. 173.
40 *People's Paper*, 30 July 1853.

established a Labour Parliament that met in Manchester in March. It set up an Executive of five members, including Jones. Marx himself was invited to attend the Parliament as an honorary delegate, but was unable to be present. However, a letter from Marx hailing the initiative was read out to the meeting. "The news of this great fact will arouse the hopes of the working classes throughout Europe and America", he wrote.[41]

Unfortunately, the attempt to found 'The Mass Movement' failed, because the majority of the trade union leaders opposed the idea of associating the trade unions with a political struggle. By the summer of 1854, the strike movement had ebbed, which also undermined the project. The Labour Parliament was wound up. Marx wrote in a letter to Engels:

> There is no denying the extent of Jones' energy, persistence and activity, yet he goes and spoils everything by the way he cries his wares, by his tactless striving after pretexts for agitation and his anxiety to be ahead of the time. If he can't agitate in reality, he seeks an appearance of agitation, improvises MOVEMENTS after MOVEMENTS (so that, of course, everything remains at a standstill) and periodically works himself up into a state of fictitious exaltation. I have warned him, but in vain.[42]

Ernest Jones, mainly through his own impatience, was seeking to revive the party single-handedly by his own efforts. But by then, the Chartist movement was steadily haemorrhaging support among the workers. Rather than retrench and prepare for better times, Jones was clearly looking for shortcuts to build the movement where no shortcuts existed. After all, an army does not advance all the time. Sometimes it has to dig in, build up its reserves and prepare for the future advances. But Jones' search for shortcuts tended to lead him astray by seeking desperately to keep alive an agitation that was less and less effective. This prompted Marx to write to Engels saying that Jones was acting very stupidly and making unnecessary mistakes and compromises. The road to opportunism is littered with those looking for short-cuts.

> "Now instead of using the crisis to replace a badly selected pretext for agitation by real agitation, he clings to his nonsense and shocks the workers by preaching collaboration with the bourgeoisie, while he is far from inspiring the latter with the slightest confidence. Some of the radical papers are cajoling him in order to ruin him completely."[43]

41 MECW, vol. 13, p. 57.
42 MECW, vol. 39, p. 523.
43 Selected Correspondence, p. 98, MECW, vol. 40, p. 210.

The summer of 1855 recorded what was probably the last ever Chartist-led demonstration in London, leaving aside the funeral of Feargus O'Connor. It was called against Sunday trading observance and attracted a crowd of over 100,000. It reflected an attempt to engage once again in popular mass agitation. In this instance, Marx praised Jones and the Chartists for refusing to unite with the bourgeois Radicals on this question and defending class independence. However, the exertions of Jones and the Chartists to generate revolutionary feelings in the working class could not stop the decline of the movement. Chartism was being increasingly squeezed from all sides. The economic growth was having an effect in relieving some of the suffering and allowing a certain softening of social relations. Despite these increasing difficulties, Marx continued his efforts to encourage his Chartist allies and bolster their morale so as to keep their faith in the future proletarian revolution.

In early 1856, however, Jones attempted to reorganise the National Charter Association, suggesting that conferences and elections be suspended and that he and James Finley be appointed to their positions for life. Although this was endorsed by the membership, it led to bitter opposition, especially from Manchester. Marx and Engels also criticised such methods, which would not solve the problems the movement faced. For them, there was no organisational solution to a political problem. In this, they were to be proved correct. Jones moving away from Marx and Engels meant relations became strained and they stopped contributing to his paper.

The People's Paper heroically soldiered on for the next five years, with ups and downs and different printers. On 4 September 1858, it finally ran out of capital and closed its doors. In these years the paper, with Jones at its head, struggled to hold together a disintegrating Chartist movement. He had kept "the old flag flying", until, according to the memoirs of W.E. Adams, "he was almost starved into surrender".[44]

Despite the frosty relations, in April 1856 Marx attended a dinner hosted by Jones at the Bell Hotel in the Strand in celebration of the fourth anniversary of the publication of *The People's Paper*. There, he delivered a famous speech of international solidarity, outlining the historic and revolutionary mission of the working class:

There is one great fact, characteristic of this our nineteenth century, a fact which no party dares deny. On the one hand, there have started into life industrial

---

44 K. Flett, p. 154.

and scientific forces, which no epoch of the former human history had ever suspected. On the other hand, there exist symptoms of decay, far surpassing the horrors recorded of the latter times of the Roman Empire. In our days, everything seems pregnant with its contrary. Machinery, gifted with the wonderful power of shortening and fructifying human labour, we behold starving and overworking it. The newfangled sources of wealth, by some strange weird spell, are turned into sources of want. On our part, we do not mistake the shape of the shrewd spirit that continues to mark all these contradictions. We know that to work well the newfangled forces of society, they only want to be mastered by newfangled men – and such are the working men.

He talked of the "old mole" of Revolution that can work so fast and out of sight.

The English working class are the first-born sons of modern industry. They will, then, certainly not be the last in aiding the social revolution provided by that industry, a revolution, which means the emancipation of their own class all over the world, which is as universal as capital-rule and wages-slavery ... All the houses of Europe are now marked with the mysterious red cross. History is the judge – its executioner, the proletarian.[45]

Marx was hoping that the developing economic crisis would help once more to reignite the Chartist movement, believing that the slump would in all likelihood be worse than that of 1842. He explained:

But no sooner will its effects be generally felt among the working classes, than the political movement which has more or less been dormant among these classes over the past six years, leaving behind only the cadres for a new agitation, will spring up again..."[46]

Unfortunately, due to the prolonged economic upturn, this proved a forlorn hope.

During this time, Ernest Jones began to suffer from increased demoralisation. He vacillated and, just like Harney, began to make opportunist concessions to the Radical bourgeoisie. This was a reflection of the strengthening reformist tendencies within the working-class movement, which were having a corrosive effect. In the face of these difficulties, Jones finally attempted to form an alliance with the middle-class Radicals, essentially on their terms. This fateful move flew in the face of everything the Chartist

---

45 MECW, vol. 14, pp. 655-6.
46 MECW, vol. 14, p. 55.

movement, including Ernest Jones, had ever preached and fought against. At bottom it reflected an impatience with the working class, the isolation of the movement, and the general pressures of capitalist society, which had entered a period of upswing.

THE BREAK WITH JONES

In April 1857, Ernest Jones proposed a Chartist conference to which John Bright, Charles Gilpin and other bourgeois Radicals were invited. In doing so, Jones was grasping at straws. In drafting the platform for unity with these Radicals, he made important political concessions, removing all the original demands of the Charter apart from universal manhood suffrage. It was the same barren path that Harney had trodden. This caused deep disquiet in Chartist ranks and quite a number of them opposed the proposal. But after repeated postponements, a national conference was finally convened at St. Martin's Hall, London, on 8 February 1858. It was here that the Manhood Suffrage movement was formally launched with "registered, residential manhood suffrage" as its only object. This signalled Jones' political fall. Marx would criticise him for this class collaboration and was to publicly break with him over this question.

Jones, who had worked closely with Marx in combating such ideas of unity with bourgeois Radicals in 1851 and 1852 with a series of articles in the *People's Paper*, now travelled far in the opposite direction, moving rapidly away from Marxism. But in practice, he was like a fish out of water in attempting to patch together an unholy alliance. Despite this political somersault, Marx did not turn his back on Jones entirely, but continued to reach out to him, hoping correct his mistakes. Marx wrote to Engels in 1858:

> What do you think of our friend Jones? I still refuse to believe that the chap has sold himself. Perhaps his experience of 1848 lies heavily on his stomach. So great is his faith in himself that he may think himself capable of exploiting the MIDDLE CLASS or imagine that if only, ONE WAY OR THE OTHER, Ernest Jones could be got into Parliament, world history could not fail to take a NEW TURN.[47]

Jones, clearly demoralised, was eagerly looking for an easy route to success. But no easy route existed. Jones' unity with middle-class Radicals would lead nowhere, except for a break with the small group around Marx and Engels. Given the "few people" with potential, Marx strained every nerve to rehabilitate Jones. He was not prepared to give up without draining the last

---

47 MECW, vol. 40, pp. 249-250.

drop from the cup of hope. However, everything has its limits, including Marx's patience. These were reached in the autumn of 1858. As Marx wrote to Engels:

> Our friend Jones HAS DECIDEDLY SOLD HIMSELF AT THE LOWEST POSSIBLE PRICE TO THE BRIGHT COTERIE. The idiot has ruined himself politically without rescuing himself commercially... I'll cut out the articles relating to him in *Reynolds'* and send them to you.[48]

Some months later, Marx wrote to Weydemeyer:

> I have broken with Ernest Jones. Despite my repeated warnings, and although I had predicted exactly what would happen – namely that he would ruin himself and disorganise the Chartist Party – he took the course of trying to come to terms with the BOURGEOIS RADICALS. HE IS NOW A RUINED MAN, but the harm he has done to the English proletariat is incalculable. The fault will, of course, be rectified, but a most favourable moment for action has been missed. Imagine an army whose general goes over to the enemy camp on the eve of battle.[49]

Shortly afterwards Marx wrote to Lassalle in Berlin, reporting that:

> Here in England the class struggle is making most gratifying progress. Unfortunately, at the present moment no Chartist newspaper exists any longer, so that about two years ago I had to discontinue my literary participation in this movement.[50]

In July 1858, a high court case was heard, in which Ernest Jones brought a defamation suit against the proprietor of the *Reynolds'* Newspaper. Marx published a statement about Jones, which was published in a German political review. It summed up his views of Jones and is worth quoting at length:

> Ernest Jones, who was condemned to two years solitary confinement in 1848 for his revolutionary activities and, having served his sentence, reorganised the Chartist Party with much self-sacrifice and talent, as is known, conceived a plan in the autumn of 1857 to establish an alliance of the proletariat with the middle class. In order to put this idea into practice, he invited representatives of the bourgeoisie and of the workers to a joint conference, which took place nominally at the beginning of last year in St. Martin's Hall. But only nominally. From the Chartists no man of weight turned up, and as 'representatives of the bourgeoisie', instead

48 MECW, vol. 40, p. 342.
49 MECW, vol. 40, p. 375.
50 *Selected Correspondence*, p. 116.

of Messrs. Cobden, Bright, and so on, who had scornfully refused, a couple of ambiguous characters attended, like Mr. Coningham, the communist-Urquhartist Palmerstonian, and a certain Mr. Ingram, who has since been convinced [convicted – editor] of common fraud. The so-called conference drew up a 'Programme of Alliance' and preached a proletarian and bourgeois crusade against the aristocrats.

In vain. The proletariat protested, the bourgeois realised that there was nothing to be won, and Ernest Jones soon saw himself abandoned by his friends, old and new. The readership of *The People's Paper* and *The London News*, the two Chartist papers which he published, dwindled from day to day, and finally Jones decided to sell these newspapers to Mr. Baxter Langley, manager of Bright's *Star* – at best a case of excessive haste, which was all the less excusable since *The People's Paper* was at the time the only official organ of the Chartist Party.

As was to be expected, this step aroused great indignation among some of the Chartists. Ernest Jones was violently attacked, and *Reynolds's* newspaper, among others, carried a series of articles in which he was said to have sold himself to the Manchester School,[51] to have exploited the workers politically and financially, to be a corrupt traitor, and so on and so forth. Thereupon Jones brought a defamation suit against Mr. Reynolds. Owing to various circumstances the lawsuit was drawn out and did not come up for hearing before the Queen's Bench until last Saturday. The plaintiff demonstrated most convincingly that by fighting for the Charter principles he had ruined himself from the bourgeoisie's point of view, that he had never received money for himself from the Chartists and that he had not been bribed by the bourgeoisie, but on the contrary had been cheated by them in respect of the selling price of *The People's Paper*. Mr. Reynolds, who could furnish no proofs, solemnly retracted the accusations and was fined forty shillings for form's sake, but at the same time – and this is no trifling matter – was ordered to pay the costs of the proceedings, which amounted to several hundred pounds sterling.

Marx concluded the piece by saying:

> Ernest Jones has saved his personal honour, but he has not had his political honour restored to him by the verdict of the Queen's Bench. He has already paid dearly for his ill-advised attempt at mediation, but the proletariat can never forgive mistakes.[52]

While Jones won the lawsuit, and the charges against him were baseless, it had clearly damaged him and turned supporters away. With this, Chartism ceased its activities in 1858.

---

51 The Manchester School was an economic trend that argued for free trade.

52 MECW, vol. 16, pp. 410-11.

LACK OF CADRES

Marx was never one to blur matters when it came to political principles. This was one of his great strengths. Despite their political break, he and Engels always considered Ernest Jones to be an honest man who had made great personal sacrifices for the movement. They remained in contact with him sporadically, but did not meet face to face for several years. After 1859, Jones moved from London to Manchester, where he resumed employment as a lawyer until his death.

Having burned his fingers with the Radicals, Jones appeared to be slowly shifting back to his former position. Thus, on 17 May 1864, Marx wrote to his daughter Jenny: "I visited Ernest Jones yesterday and renewed my old friendship with him. He received me very cordially."[53] In the same year, Jones joined the International Working Men's Association, which was being led by Marx, and re-established his connections. Engels tried to get in touch with him in Manchester, but Jones was a difficult man to pin down. "It's impossible to get anywhere with Jones", wrote Engels to Marx. "Hardly are the *sessions* over when the Assizes begin. THE TRADE IN CRIME SEEMS HIGHLY FLOURISHING."[54] The correspondence between Marx and Jones became less and less frequent as Marx became more engrossed in the affairs of the International.

The minutes of the General Council meeting of the First International of 14 February 1865, some months after its founding, record a letter from Ernest Jones on the subject of manhood suffrage. Marx had informed the Council that a branch of the International Working Men's Association had been formed in Manchester. This information was based on a letter from Jones on 13 February, in which he wrote: "My dear Marx! I forgot to ask you in my last letter to enrol me as a member of the International Association; and if you send me a dozen cards, I dare say I could get a dozen members."[55]

Following the reconciliation, Ernest Jones visited Marx several times. During these visits, Marx came to suspect that Jones was only using the International for his own personal advancement. In this Marx was correct. In the years before his death, Jones strenuously attempted to get into Parliament, even on a Liberal ticket. This was particularly the case following the 1867 Reform Act, which had somewhat widened the working-class franchise. Engels wrote to Marx:

53 MECW, vol. 41, p. 526.
54 MECW, vol. 42, p. 127.
55 *Documents of the First International: 1864-1866*, pp. 72 and 385.

Jones is holding OPEN AIR MEETINGS here for the workers, but acts so tamely that he is already being attacked for it by his rival Henry. On Saturday evening he called Gladstone 'THAT GREAT LEADER OF THE WORKING CLASSES!' I heard this myself. He is being too clever once again.[56]

According to the historian Dorothy Thompson, in letters uncovered in the Moscow Archives, by November 1868 Jones was approaching Marx to ask if he could help secure him a nomination as an independent working-class candidate for Greenwich. But Marx apparently refused. Jones had once again gone off the rails.

A few days before his death, it was reported that Jones had argued:

"[T]here was a personal reason why he desired soon to get into the House of Commons, and that was that he could not afford to wait very long. What little work there was in him must be taken out speedily, or it would be lost altogether… when a man got to be fifty, he desired to make the best use of his time."[57]

Again, Jones was grasping at straws.

On the tragic news of Ernest Jones' death from pneumonia in Manchester in January 1869, Engels wrote to Marx that the event had "naturally caused deep dismay in our household, since he was one of our few old friends".[58] A few days later, Engels again wrote to Marx:

Tomorrow Jones will be buried with an enormous procession in the same churchyard where Lupus lies. It is a real pity about the man. After all, his bourgeois phrases were simply hypocrisy, and here in Manchester there is nobody who can replace him with the workers.

He added fondly that Ernest Jones "was the only *educated* Englishman who was, at bottom, completely on our side".[59] Jones passed away on 26 January, the day after his fiftieth birthday. "Labour should be lord of the earth, and we should be lords of our labour!" he once wrote. A fitting epitaph to one who sacrificed so much for the movement. His funeral was attended by more than 50,000 mourners.

In the end, both Harney and Jones turned out to be great disappointments for Marx and Engels, who had hoped they would become the kernel of a Marxist tendency in Britain. This failure to develop such a cadre was the real

---

56 MECW, vol. 43, p. 92.
57 K. Flett, *Chartism After 1848*, p. 17.
58 MECW, vol. 43, p. 207.
59 MECW, vol. 43, pp. 210-211.

tragedy. Marx and Engels had, after all, succeeded in building such a basis in Germany where the group around Wilhelm Liebknecht and August Bebel eventually gave rise to the mass Marxist party of German social democracy.

What this revealed was that the subjective factor in Britain was not up to the task, especially in this period of retreat. Perhaps it would be a little harsh to mention Marx's quotation of Heine, saying of certain disciples of his: "I have sown dragons and I have harvested fleas." But what was demanded at that time in Britain were precisely dragons: capable individuals able to swim against the stream, who could lay the foundation for a future mass revolutionary party.

Despite the decline of Chartism, Marx and Engels were convinced that the revolutionary wing of the movement would, in some form, be reborn and once again uphold the revolutionary traditions of socialism. While a small nucleus was created around Engels in the last years of his life – composed of Eleanor Marx and Edward Aveling – this also proved too weak, with tragic political consequences. It was precisely this failure in Britain that was to adversely affect the labour movement for decades to come. The British labour movement, rather than being directly influenced by Marxism, the ideas of scientific socialism, was exposed to the pernicious influences of reformism and Fabianism. The ideas of 'moral force' Chartism re-emerged in their most bastardised form.

Following 1848, the strengthening of reformist trends in the British movement was a reflection of the pressures on the working class from the objective situation, especially on its more privileged layers, and the influence of alien class ideas. Engels wrote to Marx in October 1858:

> The Jones business is most distasteful. He held a meeting here [Manchester] and the speech he made was entirely in the spirit of the new alliance [with the middle-class Radicals]. After that affair one might almost believe that the *English proletarian movement in its old traditional Chartist form must perish utterly before it can evolve in a new and viable form. And yet it is not possible to foresee what the new form will look like.* (Emphasis added)

This was a very perceptive point made by Engels. He then went on to expand it further, and provided, in a nutshell, the key to the whole demise of Chartism in this period:

> It seems to me, by the way, that there is in fact a connection between Jones' new move, seen in conjunction with previous more or less successful attempts at such an alliance, and the fact that the *English proletariat is actually becoming more and more bourgeois, so that the ultimate aim of this most bourgeois of all nations would appear to be the possession, alongside the **bourgeoisie**, of a bourgeois aristocracy and*

a bourgeois proletariat. In the case of a nation which exploits the entire world this is, of course, justified to some extent.[60]

This is a really striking statement. The development of an 'aristocracy of labour', a new phenomenon raised by Engels, was only just emerging in Britain, based on the development of its industrial and colonial monopoly. This advantageous position allowed the British ruling class to make super-profits, with which it was able to buy off a section of the working class, creating a more privileged aristocracy of labour. This process served to corrupt certain layers, especially the leaders of the movement, organised in the so-called Model Unions, who were flattered and groomed by the establishment, allowing them to 'rise above' their class. "You only have to compare them with the French," remarked Engels, "to see what the benefits of a revolution are."[61]

In a reference to England's vast colonies and monopoly profits mentioned by Engels, Lenin wrote:

> In both respects, England at that time was an exception among capitalist countries, and Engels and Marx, analysing this exception, quite clearly and definitely indicated its *connection* with the (temporary) victory of opportunism in the English labour movement.[62]

In 1850, however, this process was still in its early beginnings. As G.D.H. Cole stated:

> The labours of George Julian Harney and, later, Ernest Jones to keep it [Chartism] alive are interesting to scholars, and especially to Marxists, because it was only at this point that Marx's ideas began to influence the movement. Chartism became increasingly Socialist, and increasingly conscious of itself as a section of a growing international working-class movement. But this did not help it to regain its hold on the main body of the British working class, because Socialism and revolutionary internationalism were not the things in which the British workers were interested...

He concluded: "The reasons for this are simple. The main body of workers was coming to be less hungry, and a good deal less desperate."[63]

It was undoubtedly true that objective conditions were cutting across the prospects for the movement. In effect, the movement was paying for the past opportunities that had been lost. Unfortunately, revolutionary opportunities

---

60 MECW, vol. 40, p. 344, our emphasis.
61 MECW, vol. 48, p. 418.
62 V.I. Lenin, *Collected Works*, vol. 23, p. 112.
63 G.D.H. Cole, *Chartist Portraits*, p. 22.

between 1838 and 1848 had been squandered. A victory during that time would have completely transformed the situation. Primarily, this was down to a failure of leadership, the ever important subjective factor. This failure had definite consequences. As Engels explained:

> "[I]f the revolutionary party in a revolutionary period begins to let turning-points pass without raising its voice or if it does interfere without winning its point, you can fairly safely count it out of action for a considerable time."[64]

This certainly applies to Chartism. Clearly, when an opportunity is lost, the situation will not stand still indefinitely. The pendulum begins to swing in the other direction, which was the case after 1848.

Marxism, whilst basing itself on the working class as the motive force of history, does not idealise the masses. Under different conditions, the masses can act in different ways. We can see their strong sides as well as their weak sides. The strength of the working class lies in its self-sacrifice, resoluteness, solidarity and heroism, which are normally displayed in times of revolutionary upsurge. In periods of ebb in the class struggle, however, the workers' weak sides tend to come to the fore: heterogeneity, disunity, backwardness and narrowness of outlook. The working class can even turn to despair, fall into apathy and completely lose faith in itself. This was characteristic of the working-class movement after 1850, following the defeat of the European revolution. In Britain, this situation was to last some four decades, until the birth of New Unionism.

There was another element involved in this process: the British bourgeoisie had been forced to grant concessions to the working class in response to the revolutionary wave in Europe and the victory of the North in the American Civil War. They had little choice in the matter: either grant reforms from above or be faced with possible revolution from below. As a consequence, the Corn Laws were repealed, the Ten-Hour Bill was passed, and new factory legislation enacted. This was then followed by the Reform Act of 1867, then the Act of 1872, followed by the Reform Act of 1884, all of which either extended the franchise or introduced other democratic reforms. "It follows that even for passing reforms", explained Trotsky, "the principle of gradualness is insufficient and a real threat of revolution is necessary."[65]

All these measures were a by-product of the revolutionary struggles of the European masses, and those in America, from which the British working class

---

64 Quoted in G. Mayer, *Friedrich Engels*, p. 143.
65 L. Trotsky, *Writings on Britain*, vol. 2, p. 26.

benefited. However, it would be wrong to reduce such developments simply to foreign influence. The revolutionary fires of Chartism also had their effect. It was not scotched, but a dormant and ever-present threat. As Engels stated:

> The working class of Great Britain for years fought ardently and even violently for the People's Charter… it was defeated but the struggle had made such an impression upon the victorious middle class that this class, since then, was only too glad to buy prolonged armistice at the price of ever-repeated concessions to the working people.[66]

After 1850, capitalism began a long period of ascent. The productive forces developed at break-neck speed as markets were opened up and new areas of exploitation were discovered. Capitalism had brought into being a world market, the hallmark of 'globalisation', as the *Communist Manifesto* explained. This development produced a prolonged period of relative social stability, where the relations between the classes were softened. Even the trade unions, which had previously been persecuted, now benefited from legislation passed in 1875, which gave legal protection for carrying out their work. This included to a certain extent the calling of strikes, as well as picketing. This shows how the British bourgeoisie was able to adapt to the changing situation. The policy of Gladstone's Liberal government – attempting to crush the trade unions – was abandoned in favour of a policy of corrupting their leaders with all sorts of bribes. They were able to offer concessions due to the extraordinary advances of capitalism, which laid the groundwork for the increased confidence of the British bourgeoisie. This gave them a great ability to manoeuvre, which they used to their advantage. This is a far cry from the situation today, where the bourgeois strategists cannot see further than their own nose.

In the meantime, in 1863 Engels commented to Marx that "the English proletariat's revolutionary energy has all but completely evaporated…"[67] Three years later, commenting on the state of the English Labour movement, Marx lamented: "These fellows lack the METTLE of the old Chartists."[68] This was also the view of some of the survivors of the heroic period, like Thomas Cooper.

Cooper wrote his memoirs in 1872. In them, he compared the different times:

---

66 MECW, vol. 24, p. 386.
67 MECW, vol. 41, p. 465.
68 MECW, vol. 42, p. 253.

"In our old Chartist time, it is true, Lancashire workmen were in rags by thousands; and many of them often lacked food. But their intelligence was demonstrated wherever you went. You would see them in groups, discussing the great doctrine of political justice – that every grown up, sane man ought to have a vote in the election of the men who were to make the laws by which he was to be governed; or they were in earnest dispute respecting the teachings of socialism."

He went on to contrast that with 1872, some thirty years later:

"Now, you will see no groups in Lancashire. But you will hear well-dressed working men talk, with their hands in their pockets, of co-ops, and their shares in them, or in building societies."[69]

The revolutionary years had been exhausted, which coloured the outlook of the working class and strengthened opportunist tendencies within the movement. It would take time and big events before "the British workers will free themselves from their apparent bourgeois infection", noted Engels.

The breaking of England's industrial monopoly would be one such event. As Engels wrote:

It will do one great thing: it will break the last link which still binds the English working class to the English middle class. This link was their common working of a national monopoly. That monopoly once destroyed, the British working class will be compelled to take in hand its own interests, its own salvation, and to make an end of the wages system.[70]

Interestingly enough, Marx returned to the question of the potential of a British revolution in a revealing 1870 letter to Mayer and Vogt, where he linked its fate to the emancipation of Ireland:

England, as the metropolis of capital, as the power that has hitherto ruled the world market, is for the present the most important country for the workers' revolution and, in addition, the *only* country where the material conditions for this revolution have developed to a certain state of maturity. Thus, to hasten the social revolution in England is the most important object of the International Working Men's Association. The sole means of doing so is to make Ireland independent. It is, therefore, the task of the 'INTERNATIONAL' to bring the conflict between England and Ireland to the forefront everywhere, and to side with Ireland

---

69 Quoted in T. Rothstein, pp. 183-184.
70 *The Labour Standard*, 18 June 1881, MECW, vol. 24, p. 393.

publicly everywhere. The special task of the Central Council in London is to awaken the consciousness of the English working class that, *for them, the national emancipation of Ireland* is not a QUESTION OF ABSTRACT JUSTICE OR HUMANITARIAN SENTIMENT, but *THE FIRST CONDITION OF THEIR OWN SOCIAL EMANCIPATION.*[71]

Originally, as Marx admitted, he believed Ireland would achieve independence through the victory of the British proletariat. However, from the late 1860s he revised that view. It was now down to the Irish themselves to bring about their own emancipation, and in doing so they would stimulate class struggle in England.

However, the independence of Ireland was not achieved until 1921. Even then, it was only on the basis of a reactionary partition, with the creation of a sectarian Protestant state in the north and a Catholic-dominated state in the south. It was a classic case of British imperialism employing the tactic of 'divide and rule', which created a "carnival of reaction", to use the words of James Connolly.

Marx and Engels had originally envisaged that the bourgeois revolution of 1848 would be a prelude to the proletarian revolution, starting in Germany. But this perspective was falsified by events. This mistake had a factual, and not a methodological, character. Where Marx erred was to mistake the birth-pains of capitalism for its death agony. The productive forces under capitalism still had a long way to develop. The socialist revolution, despite all the upheavals, was therefore delayed for a period. In fact, it was not until 1871, and the glorious Paris Commune, that the proletarian revolution was once again placed squarely on the agenda in Europe. In many ways, what went before was only an anticipation.

FINAL END

Chartism as an organised movement did not formally come to an end until 1860, five years after Gammage finished his *History of Chartism*. However, even this is probably not quite accurate, as it faded away so gradually that it is impossible to be precise. As W.E. Adams explained:

"Our little band of propagandists kept the flag flying till the end of the fifties. Then, as the more active among them left London for the provinces, the Colonies or the United States, the movement quietly died out."[72]

---

71 MECW, vol. 43, p. 475.
72 K. Flett, *Chartism After 1848*, p. 128.

An old stalwart wrote to Ernest Jones in October 1859 from the former Chartist stronghold of Halifax:

> "I am sorry to inform you that there is no Chartist organisation in Halifax nor in any of the numerous villages surrounding it… Many of those that were once active Chartists have emigrated. And others, though residing here as usual, have become so thoroughly disgusted at the indifference and utter inattention of the multitude to their best interests that they are resolved to make no more sacrifices in a public cause."[73]

Conditions had changed and capitalism was on an upward trajectory, opening up the possibility of reforms, including an extension of the franchise. This change in the material conditions adversely affected the general outlook of British workers.

As Theodore Rothstein explained:

> Repudiation, not only of revolution, but of politics in general, and concentration on purely economic trade union action – this was the main background to the British labour movement of the post-Chartist period…[74]

People had been worn down by the period, the heat of the struggle, and then the protracted lull. "Revolution is a great devourer of men", wrote Trotsky after the defeat of the Left Opposition in Russia. The energies that are consumed in the struggle are colossal. This is especially the case after important defeats. After more than a decade of bitter struggle involving mass demonstrations, general strikes, and insurrection, the masses had become tired. Their enthusiasm for the cause had waned and their hopes for achieving the Charter were dashed. This was the psychological basis for the demise of Chartism. As dialectics teaches us, things turn into their opposites. Thus the revolutionary aspirations of the British working class gave way to demoralisation and inactivity. There was a turning away from politics to everyday matters. The pendulum had swung back in the other direction. Once again, the bourgeoisie could sleep more soundly in their beds. Nevertheless, although Chartism was exhausted, the movement had left its mark, not least in the memory of sections of the working class.

There are those historians – and there are many – who regarded Chartism as a lost cause from the very beginning, faced with hopeless odds and beset by violence. This was the clear view of the early twentieth century historian

---

73 A.L. Morton and G. Tate, *The British Labour Movement*, p. 104.
74 T. Rothstein, p. 202.

Mark Hovell. It chimed, in reality, with his own bourgeois prejudices. His conclusion following the first Chartist Petition is revealing in this regard: "The Petition was dead, slain by the violence of its own supporters, the tactlessness of its chief advocates, the inertia of conservatism, and its own inner contradictions."[75] Asa Briggs also saw things in similar terms:

> "In fact, it is very difficult to see how, given the nature of English society and government in the Chartist period, the Chartists could have succeeded in the way that O'Connor's critics claim that they might have done. The cards were too heavily stacked against them. Both Chartism and O'Connor in my view were doomed to failure…"[76]

Again, rather than reflecting the 'nature' of England, this reflects more the nature of Asa Briggs, who had no idea about the mechanics of revolution, the class struggle or the laws of social development.

For such historians, the Chartists were simply a childlike response to a set of unique circumstances. If there is any conclusion to be drawn from their writings, it is the futility of attempts by the working class to change society, seen by these historians as a utopian dream. Their conclusions add nothing to our understanding of this glorious period of class struggle in Britain.

With the demise of Chartism, individual Chartists went on to play roles in different movements. For instance, Jones and Harney, as we have seen, later became members of the First International founded in 1864, the cornerstone of working-class internationalism. Some became members of the General Council of the International Working Men's Association, such as John Leno and Robert Hartwell, who was one of the editors of *The Bee-Hive*, a weekly organ of the trade unions. Others were not so fortunate. Many spent their last years in the penal colonies of Tasmania, then known as Van Diemen's Land. Others emigrated to the United States and many of them played a role in building the American trade unions. Harney himself emigrated to the United States in May 1863, and for the next fourteen years worked as a clerk in the Massachusetts State House before returning to England.

Some played a less dignified role, such as the Glaswegian Chartist, Allan Pinkerton, who ended up establishing the notorious Pinkerton National Detective Agency, used to smash strikes and frame labour leaders. Another Chartist who emigrated from Fife to Pennsylvania was a poor hand-loom

---

75 M. Hovell, *The Chartist Movement*, p. 164, quoted by D. Thompson, *The Chartists*, p. 2.

76 Quoted in D. Thompson, p. 2.

worker from Dunfermline. His name was Carnegie, and his son Andrew became the famous steel magnate. But these are more the exceptions than the rule. The vast majority of emigrant workers from Britain achieved a more menial status. More importantly, Chartism remained lodged deep in the memory of the working class, a fact that could not be easily erased.

Interestingly, it was the followers of Bronterre O'Brien who kept the Chartist flame flickering in the 1860s. By this time, O'Brien had grown old and had been ground down by years of disappointment and defeat. Faced with the waning of the movement after 1850, he lost his original insights and developed illusions in co-operative banks and currency reform. His best years were behind him. He passed away on 3 December 1864, two months after the founding of the International Working Men's Association in London. While Marx had sharply criticised O'Brien's ideas on currency reform, O'Brien's supporters played a positive role in the General Council of the First International. As Marx explained:

"These O'Brienites, in spite of their follies, constitute an often-necessary counterweight to trade unionists in the Council. They are more revolutionary, firmer on the land question, less nationalistic, and not susceptible to bourgeois bribery in one form or another."[77]

This is certainly to their credit.

According to G.D.H. Cole:

For another ten years it lingered on, surviving to the eve of that revival of working-class political activity which we associate with the names of Karl Marx and the International Working Men's Association of 1864. Many links, indeed, serve to bind the two movements together. Many old Chartists played their part in the First International; and Chartist activity from 1848 onwards partly anticipated many features of Marx's International.[78]

The same point was stressed by A.L. Morton and George Tate:

All the same the Chartist tradition persisted, to serve as a vital link between the great struggles of the 1840s and the later development of socialism under the influence of Marxism. Without the heroic efforts of Ernest Jones and others during this decade it is very doubtful if the First International would have been possible in 1864.[79]

---

77 J. Charlton, p. 75.
78 G.D.H. Cole, *A Short History*, p. 118.
79 A.L. Morton and G. Tate, p. 103.

In later years, after his return from America, Marx contacted Harney and he would visit him as an old friend. The same was true of Engels, who maintained close contact with Harney until his death in 1895. In fact, just before he died, Edward Aveling, Marx's son-in-law, interviewed Harney. The interview was published in the *Social Democrat* in January 1897. Aveling wrote:

> "I am conscious that the two men, Engels and Harney, were cast in the same mould, soldiers in the same regiment. I know that long after the rest of us are forgotten the name of George Julian Harney will be remembered with thankfulness and with tears. A Straggler of 1848. But a straggler who cried then, and who will cry with his last breath that which shall be the motto helping us to remember him, 'The people want power, and by God they shall have it.'"[80]

Engels made a final attempt to stir the remnants of Chartism in the early 1880s with articles published in *The Labour Standard*, the weekly paper of the London Trades Council.

> "For five months I tried to link up with the old Chartist movement and spread our ideas through *The Labour Standard*, for which I used to write leading articles. I wanted to see if there would be any response. But there was absolutely none, and as the editor, a well-meaning but feeble milksop, became afraid in the end of the Continental heresies I wrote in the paper, I gave up."[81]

However, not long afterwards, in 1888, a strike of match girls in East London was to be the spark that would turn into a blaze and launch the mass movement of New Unionism.

By this time, British capitalism's world monopoly was being undermined, which laid the material basis for the rebirth of socialist ideas in Britain, the organisation of the great unskilled, and finally the foundation of the Labour Party. Engels hailed this new revival of the British working class, which Marx did not live to see, and which was led in many cases by Marxist socialists:

> A large class, like a great nation, never learns better or quicker than by undergoing the consequences of its own mistakes. And for all the faults committed in past, present and future, the revival of the East End of London remains one of the greatest and most fruitful facts of this *fin de siècle*, and glad and proud I am to have lived to see it.[82]

---

80 D. Black and C. Ford, pp. 232-233.
81 *Selected Correspondence*, p. 349.
82 MESW, vol. 3, p. 451.

Looking back, Engels drew on this historical experience in his work, *Socialism: Utopian and Scientific*, where he made the following point:

> In 1831, the first working-class rising took place in Lyon; between 1838 and 1842, the first national working-class movement, that of the Chartists, reached its height. The class struggle between proletariat and bourgeoisie came to the front in the history of the most advanced countries of Europe, in proportion to the development, upon the one hand, of modern industry, upon the other, of the newly-acquired political supremacy of the bourgeoisie. Facts more and more strenuously gave the lie to the teachings of bourgeois economy as to the identity of the interests of capital and labour, as to the consequence of unbridled competition. All these things could no longer be ignored, any more than the French and English socialism, which was their theoretical, though very imperfect, expression...
>
> From that time forward socialism was no longer an accidental discovery of this or that ingenious brain, but the necessary outcome of the struggle between two historically developed classes – the proletariat and the bourgeoisie.[83]

In the final years of his life, Engels witnessed the new stirrings within the British working class. In a February 1893 letter to Paul Lafargue he stated: "Among the workers here, things are going well. They begin to realise their strength more and more, and that there is only one way of using it, namely, by forming an independent party."[84] Within seven years, the Labour Representation Committee was formed, leading to the birth of the Labour Party, which was organically linked to the trade unions. "In recent years," Engels added, "socialism has made enormous headway among the masses in the industrial districts, and I look to those masses to keep the leaders properly in order."[85]

To the Chartists goes the honour of founding the first revolutionary proletarian party in the world. At this time, they had the honour of marching at the head of the European working class. Whatever their shortcomings, they nevertheless pioneered the way forward for the workers of the world. For that, we owe them a debt of gratitude. Because of them we can stand a head taller.

GREATER SIGNIFICANCE

With most of the demands of the Charter later conceded, was Engels wrong in regarding it as revolutionary? Clearly, 1890 was not 1844, when Engels first

---

83 MESW, vol. 3, pp. 131-2.
84 MECW, vol. 50, p. 115.
85 MECW, vol. 50, p. 84.

made that statement. The Charter, for him, had a much greater significance than its six points. This was what he was alluding to in its revolutionary content. In the formative struggles of the British working class, it was an anticipation of what was to come, a heroic chapter that is far from finished. The Charter was seen by Engels, as by the Chartists, as a means to an end, not an end in itself. That end was the emancipation of the working class.

Ultimately, the British ruling class proved confident enough to concede the programme, apart from annual parliaments. They had come to terms with a proletarian majority of the population long before any other country. But these democratic demands were never given freely and still had to be won through bitter struggle. The bourgeoisie were nevertheless able to contain the serious threat posed by revolutionary Chartism.

However, the demands of the Charter, at bottom, were not *simply* aimed at an extension of democracy. And this is the real essence of the question. Chartism was not simply an issue of constitutional tinkering, but very much linked to the economic and social emancipation of the working class. As Engels said, "the proletariat too needs democratic forms for the seizure of political power but to it they are, like all political forms, mere means."[86] In the hands of middle-class Radicals, however, these demands turned to dust and were simply a way to further their careerism and secure a greater share of the pie in political life.

Since the days of Chartism, even the word 'democracy' has changed from being a threat to the system to a description of the existing political setup. Five of the six demands were eventually met, but crucially, the demand for an annual parliament was firmly resisted. That was a step too far in accountability. The ruling class were able to concede the rest as they possessed other powerful instruments in which to mould 'public opinion'; through the schools, universities, the churches, the mass media and more besides, including the monarchy. "The ruling elite", *The Economist* admits, "forced to widen the voting franchise, decided that the country needed the monarchy as a symbol of stability and they needed it to help them retain control of the government."[87] They had bourgeois politicians in their pocket, better to represent their interests. In regards to the Labour Party, having failed to destroy it, they simply 'bought' or corrupted its leaders and representatives, who were wined and dined to ensure that it remained in safe hands.

---

86 *Selected Correspondence*, p. 371.
87 *The Economist*, 22-28/10/94.

Parliament is only a talking shop; the real decisions are taken in the boardrooms of the giant corporations, where all serious matters are decided. "Real class rule lay and still lies *outside* of Parliament", explained Lenin.[88] Bourgeois democracy, stated Marx, can simply be defined as allowing the workers to put a cross on a piece of paper every five years to choose someone to misrepresent their interests. This, put simply, is the reality of capitalist democracy.

Although democracy has been around for quite a while, and most people would regard it as a permanent fixture, in reality bourgeois democracy is a fragile plant. While capitalism was forging ahead, the system was relatively stable and could concede democratic rights: the right to vote and organise, freedom of speech and assembly, etc. However, we saw how these rights were undermined and even destroyed in periods of deep crisis, as in the 1930s with the rise of fascism. Sections of the British ruling class and monarchy openly admired Hitler and the fascists. The *Daily Mail* championed their cause with a front-page heading 'Hurrah for the Blackshirts!' Then, once the period of crisis had passed, these 'democrats' exchanged their blackshirts for posh business suits.[89]

The ruling class are quite prepared to switch to different forms of class rule, from democracy to dictatorship and back again, according to their interests. They prefer 'democracy' as it is a cheaper form of government, but whenever their property is in danger, they are quite prepared to revert to authoritarian rule. "If England is to remain free, private property and free enterprise must survive..." maintained Ian Gilmour, a former Conservative minister and author of a study of conservatism called *Inside Right*. An important Tory theoretician and strategist, he openly explained in his book that democracy was not a principle but a "device". And if this "device" was not working, then he outlined the case for ending it:

> Conservatives do not worship democracy. For them, majority rule is a device. Each individual no doubt *should* be the best judge of his own interests, and if he were, majority rule would be more than a device to Tories. But individuals do not always act in their own interest... Similarly, majorities do not always see where their best interests lie... For Conservatives, therefore, democracy is a means to an end not an end in itself. In Dr. Hayek's words, democracy "is not an ultimate or

---

88 *Lenin On Britain*, p. 199.

89 See R. Sewell, *Socialism or Barbarism: Germany 1918-1934*, appendix one, 'Hitler's British Connections', Wellred Books, 2018.

absolute value and must be judged by what it will achieve". And if it is leading to an end that is undesirable or is inconsistent with itself, then there is a theoretical case for ending it.[90]

He went on to quote Edmund Burke, a character we have met earlier, who said that "numbers in a state are always of consideration, but they are not the whole consideration". In other words, according to these individuals, majorities cannot be trusted. When a majority wants to change society, and capitalism is under threat, then the strategists of capital believe democracy should no longer be guaranteed. It should be shut down. They justified totalitarian rule as a defence of private property and a bulwark against communism. Gilmour laid the blame for ending democracy on the Left:

> There is no danger of a right-wing coup. Only if the constitution had already been destroyed by the Left, might the Right react and the Left find itself overthrown in its turn by a counter-coup from the Right.[91]

This was precisely the argument put forward by the ruling classes, including the British, to justify the murderous military coup of General Pinochet in Chile in 1973, who butchered 30,000 people to secure the rule of the capitalists.

We must therefore have no illusions in what the capitalists will do when faced with a real threat to their power and privileges. No ruling class in history has ever given up its power without a fight, with no holds barred. The British bourgeoisie is a cruel and ruthless class, which would take whatever measures were needed to safeguard its power. But if it were to move towards a dictatorship, given the strength of the working class, it would face civil war. While that in itself would not be of too much concern to the capitalists, what does concern them is that in a civil war, they could lose. They would therefore have to think long and hard before pursuing such a path.

Engels made a very interesting point about the use of universal franchise in changing society. He saw it very much as a gauge of support for the revolutionary party. He also understood that any attempt to legislate the abolition of capitalism through parliamentary means would provoke the ruling class to subvert democracy and block the will of the people. However, Engels believed that such an attack could be used to mobilise to break the capitalists' resistance and in so doing carry through the revolution. He wrote to Paul Lafargue:

90 I. Gilmour, *Inside Right*, p. 211.
91 *Inside Right*, p. 212.

Do you realise now what a splendid weapon you in France have in your hands for forty years in universal suffrage if only people had known how to use it! It's slower and more boring than the call to revolution, but it's ten times more sure, and *what is even better, it indicates with the most perfect accuracy the day when a call to armed revolution has to be made; it's even ten to one that universal suffrage, intelligently used by the workers, will drive the rulers to overthrow legality, that is, to put us in the most favourable position to make the revolution.*[92]

In August 1852, Marx wrote a review of the Chartist movement, which was published in *The People's Paper*, then in the *New York Daily Tribune*, in which he analysed the political situation in England. When it came to Chartism, he explained the importance of universal suffrage as a weapon, given the strength of the working class, in the struggle for socialism.

Universal Suffrage [with its adjuncts, added the editor] is the equivalent for political power for the working class of England, where the proletariat forms the large majority of the population, where, in a long, though underground civil war, it has gained a clear consciousness of its position as a class... Its inevitable result, here, is the political supremacy of the working class.[93]

Given its numerical strength, if granted the vote, the working class could come to power and carry through a revolution peacefully and 'legally'. Marx, however, never doubted for one minute the ferocious opposition of the ruling class. In dealing with Britain, he never forgot to add that the British ruling classes would never submit without a "pro-slavery rebellion".[94] In fact, he warned against illusions in parliamentary cretinism. To counteract this ruling class rebellion, the working class would need to mobilise its entire strength outside of Parliament and, in doing so, carry through the revolution and lay the basis for a new workers' state.

Clearly, Marx and Engels had no illusions about bourgeois democracy and how the ruling class would react to the threat of a real workers' government. The working class under those circumstances must react swiftly, using all its strength, to carry through its programme to a conclusion.

Could the Chartists have led a successful revolution? The potential certainly existed. In the 1842 general strike, for instance, Engels certainly thought so. "If it had been from the beginning an intentional, determined working

---

92 MECW, vol. 50, p. 29, our emphasis.

93 MECW, vol. 11, pp. 335-336.

94 See Engels' Preface to the English edition of volume one of Capital, 5 November 1886, p. 113.

men's insurrection, it would surely have carried its point", he explained.[95] In 1848, revolutions shook Europe. These were, however, bourgeois-democratic revolutions, which cleared the way for capitalist development. In Britain, the bourgeoisie were firmly established in the saddle. What was posed here was a revolution to overthrow capitalist rule, led by the emerging working class. Unfortunately, the Chartist leaders were in the dark as to what steps were needed to accomplish this outcome. They were deeply influenced by Owenism, while the ideas of scientific socialism were unfortunately not available to them. Their only real points of reference for revolution were the French Revolutions of 1789 and 1830 and the American Revolution of 1776. While they believed in the need to change society, they only had a very hazy idea of how to achieve it. This proved insufficient. Under such circumstances, the revolutionary potential was lost. By the time the Chartists adopted a socialist leadership and programme in 1851, the movement was already in steady decline.

In the first half of the nineteenth century, capitalism was suffering from acute birth pains along with the increasing immiseration of the working class. A successful revolution, which placed the working class in power, would have meant the reorganisation of society on the basis of co-operative and socialist planning, and would have provided the conditions for the harmonious development of industry, technique and science. This would have completely transformed the lives of the working class. But it was not to be.

The Charter was always regarded by the 'physical force' Chartists as a road to revolution. Bronterre O'Brien and the other leaders knew full well that the problems of the working class were rooted in capitalism and private ownership of the means of production. Today, this problem of 'Social Revolution' can only be solved with a bold socialist programme that abolishes private ownership in favour of the common ownership of the means of production, distribution and exchange. As Engels foretold, traditional Chartism needed to perish before a new form could arise. In that sense, the socialist programme has now superseded the Charter, although its revolutionary spirit lives on.

It is clear that the remnants of 'moral force' Chartism still dominate in the labour movement through the outlook of the reformists and the labour and trade union bureaucracy. They have no faith in socialism and seek to limit the working class to a struggle within the confines of capitalism. Rather than offer the vision of a socialist future, such leaders exude pessimism and submission. This is the school of class collaboration, subservience and the permanence of

---

95 MECW, vol. 4, p. 521.

private property. To them, as to William Lovett, communism is a "dreamy system". They instead prefer the road of pragmatism and 'social partnership'. But this road of class collaboration is a dead-end in this epoch of capitalist decay. Today, rather than reforms, there are vicious counter-reforms everywhere. The crisis of capitalism also means the crisis of reformism. As O'Connor correctly remarked: "Knowledge without power is useless". Today, only the abolition of capitalism can solve the problems faced by the working class.

OUR INHERITANCE

The stormy epoch of Chartism, and the revolutionary awakening of the British working class, had completely exhausted itself in the decade prior to the emergence of the First International, known as the International Working Men's Association. The legacy of proletarian Chartism, nevertheless, lived on in the revolutionary movement, and especially the Marxist tradition.

Inspired by the success of the German Social Democratic Party, which adhered to Marxism and in 1877 polled nearly half a million votes and took thirteen seats in the Reichstag, an old Chartist, John Sketchley of Birmingham, published a pamphlet called 'The Principles of Social Democracy'. In it, he argued for a similar party and programme to be established in Britain. Sketchley himself even attempted to organise a Midlands Social Democratic Association as a stepping stone to this vision. Furthermore, a few old Chartists still met in London under the guidance of two brothers, Charles and J.F. Murray, and were still active in the early 1880s. Benjamin Wilson recalled how on 7 July 1885, twenty-two Halifax Chartists sat down to a reunion dinner, and even wrote a book called *The Struggles of an Old Chartist*, published two years later. But it was not the old people, as such, but the new generation of workers who were inspired by Chartism. The older generation had nevertheless planted the seeds.

The 'old Chartist spirit' was still talked about in the North of England when the Independent Labour Party was founded in 1893. In fact, old Chartist comrades helped form the ILP as well as the Social Democratic Federation, which claimed allegiance to Marxism. In August 1903, *Justice*, the paper of the SDF, claimed its members as "the legitimate heirs and successors of the Chartists". The Chartist William Chadwick, who was imprisoned for sedition in 1848, spoke at meetings during the 1906 general election to support Will Thorne, a leading figure in the SDF.

Independent working-class politics is a key heritage of Chartism. As the historian Henry Pelling commented: "The Chartist tradition of independent labour politics was not entirely extinct."[96] In fact, it gave birth to the Labour Party. It was Engels and the small group around him, including Eleanor Marx, John Burns, Tom Mann and others, who vigorously promoted this idea.

When the British Communist Party was founded in 1920, they traced their revolutionary roots to Chartism and even earlier. They understood correctly that history did not begin with themselves. In 1925, Trotsky, in his book *Where is Britain Going?*, urged the young communists to seriously study revolutionary events in British history, especially the English Civil War and the Chartist movement. They should, he said, consider themselves the "Ironsides" and revolutionary Chartists of the modern epoch. We should therefore lay claim to these heroic struggles of the past, which are part of our revolutionary heritage, part of our political DNA. "Alongside the Britain of profit, violence, corruption and bloodthirstiness there exists the Britain of Labour, the intellectual might, and the great ideals of international solidarity", wrote Trotsky. "The era of Chartism is immortal."

Trotsky continued:

> In this sense the British working class can see and must see in Chartism not only its past but also its future. As the Chartists tossed the sentimental preachers of 'moral force' aside and gathered the masses behind the banner of revolution so the British proletariat is faced with ejecting reformists, democrats and pacifists from its midst and rallying to the banner of a revolutionary overturn. Chartism did not win a victory not because its methods were incorrect but because it appeared too soon. It was only an historical anticipation. The 1905 Revolution also suffered defeat. But its tradition lived on for twelve years and its methods were victorious in October 1917. Chartism is not at all liquidated. History is liquidating Liberalism and prepares to liquidate the pseudo-Labour pacifism precisely so as to give a second birth to Chartism on new, immeasurably broader historical foundations. That is where you have the real national tradition of the British labour movement![97]

---

96 H. Pelling, *Origins of the Labour Party*, p. 6.
97 L. Trotsky, *Writings on Britain*, vol. 2, p. 94.

10. MARXISM AND CHARTISM

"*History* does *nothing*, it 'possesses *no* immense wealth', it 'wages *no* battles'. It is *man*, real, living man who does all that, who possesses and fights; 'history' is not, as it were, a person apart, using man as a means to achieve *its own* aims; history is *nothing but* the activity of man pursuing his aims."
– Marx and Engels, (*The Holy Family*, MECW, vol. 4, p. 93.)

"People call him a dreamer. But dreams are only the light of a clear sky, too brilliant for our naked eye, and when we behold its radiance we turn aside and call it dreams. Ah, believe me, all thoughts which were ever born in majesty and expired in grief, which time has raised to maturity and glory, all of them were at first described as 'empty dreams'."
– Ernest Jones

DISCIPLES OF METHODISM

It has often been said, especially by those on the right of the Labour Party, that the British labour movement has been influenced more by Methodism than Marxism. For them, the movement has no need of or interest in foreign creeds, except perhaps religion. This view is part of the doctrine of British exceptionalism, the uniqueness of the British movement, its 'Britishness'. But what this really expresses is the backwardness of the labour movement, politically encapsulated in its reformist leadership. As Leon Trotsky explained in 'Where is Britain Going?':

"The outlook of the leaders of the British Labour Party is a sort of amalgam of Conservatism and Liberalism, partly adapted to the requirements of the trade unions, or rather their top layers. All of them are ridden with the religion of 'gradualness...'"[1]

---

1 L. Trotsky, *Writings on Britain*, vol. 2, p. 36.

This accurately sums up the outlook of the reformist Labour leaders, past and present, who are simply the loyal servants of capitalism. They lecture the working class, but in their dealings with the ruling class they bring to mind Dickens' character, Uriah Heep, noted for his obsequiousness and insincerity, with his constant references to his own "'umbleness".

This submissiveness arises from their attempt to ingratiate themselves with 'the powers that be'. It is a class question, but also a reflection of the subservient influences of the past. It is also a product of class collaboration, which is central to their existence. As the Hammonds, in dealing with the effect of Methodism on the origins of the labour movement, correctly explain:

> The spirit of its teaching was just the opposite of the spirit of the trade union movement of the time. It taught patience where the trade unions taught impatience. The trade union movement taught that men and women should use their powers to destroy the supremacy of wealth in a world made by men; the Methodist that they should learn resignation amid the painful chaos of a world so made, for good reasons of His own, by God. The trade unionist taught that men were not so helpless as they seemed, for combination could give them some control over the conditions of their lives. The Methodists taught that men were not so helpless as they seemed, for religion could make them independent of the conditions of their lives. Further, the trade union movement made loyalty to a class a virtue, teaching men and women to think of themselves as the citizens of a community struggling to be free. The Methodist movement had just the opposite effect.[2]

Therefore, whatever influence Methodism had on the British labour movement, it was a baneful one, reinforcing all the characteristics of reformism. One of the disciples of Methodism, among many, was Morgan Phillips, a right-wing general secretary of the Labour Party.

In 1951, he attacked Marxism at the International Socialist Conference in Copenhagen. A short report in the *News Chronicle*, entitled 'Marx Goes Out the Window', explained:

> Morgan Phillips made no attempt to disguise the fact that, so far as British Labour is concerned, it will have nothing whatever to do with materialism, and that if it comes to the choice Transport House [Labour's head office] will follow the Methodists and not the Marxists.

> He began by saying that British socialism owed little to Karl Marx either in theory or practice.

---

2   J.L. Hammond and B. Hammond, *The Town Labourer: 1760-1832*, pp. 283-284.

"British Socialism", he said, "pointed the way to the achievement of that most remarkable phenomenon in history, a revolution in political control, and class relations without physical conflict".[3]

This is the essence of reformism, namely the desire to work within the confines of the capitalist system. The results of this are evident today, as we face the deepest crisis in our history.

Fifteen years later, in September 1966, Harold Wilson, the Labour prime minister, repeated the attack on Marxism in his speech to Labour conference:

"We cannot afford to fight the problems of the sixties with the attitudes of the Social Democratic Federation, nor, in looking for a solution to those problems, seek vainly to find the answer in Highgate cemetery."[4]

How hollow these words sounded then, and how hollow they sound today! In Highgate cemetery you will find only bones, of no use to anyone. The reference, of course, is to the ideas of Marx, which have become extremely relevant. The role of the right wing of the British Labour movement is to continually peddle slanders against Marxism, which they equate with something alien and foreign. In its place, they are keen to propagate their own parochial slavish acceptance of capitalism. This was the foundation of British opportunism. Even G.D.H. Cole stated that the Independent Labour Party expressed the "soul" of the Labour Party, while the Fabians expressed its "brain", "far removed from that of Karl Marx".[5] The Fabian "brain" in fact was nothing more than the transmission belt for bourgeois and petty-bourgeois ideas into the Labour movement.

Writing before the war, Clement Attlee glorified this backward trait with the statement:

A further characteristic of the British movement has been its practicality. It has never consisted of a body of theorists or of revolutionaries who were so absorbed in Utopian dreams that they were unwilling to deal with the actualities of everyday life.

This is a reflection of the labour movement's aversion to theory, relying on bourgeois pragmatism instead. It is the 'common sense' of the Anglo-Saxon philistine, inspired by a utilitarian morality, which radiates submissiveness and the fear of revolutionary change. Attlee concluded that "the number of

---

3 *News Chronicle*, 3 June 1950.
4 http://www.britishpoliticalspeech.org/speech-archive.htm?speech=164
5 G.D.H. Cole, *A Short History of the British Working Class Movement*, p. 287.

those who accepted Marxism as a creed has always been small".[6] To begin with, Marxism is not a "creed", like some religious dogma, but first and foremost a method. As Engels explained, "Marx's whole way of viewing things is not a doctrine but a method. It does not provide ready-made dogmas."[7] This is something the reformists have never understood or wanted to understand. But Attlee was nevertheless forced to admit that, in the first half of the nineteenth century, including the Chartist period, revolution was a real possibility in Britain:

> Nevertheless the evils of Capitalism in the first half of the nineteenth century were so great that there seemed the possibility of a revolution by the workers... There was a period, indeed, in which there seemed the possibility of a violent revolution in Britain. But the moment passed. Revolutionary trade unionism died out. Revolutionary Chartism was, in effect, superseded by other movements, such as the agitation against the Corn Laws, which made a more immediate appeal... the impulse for the abolition of the system as a whole died away. Revolution gave place to reform...[8]

This reference to the campaign over Corn Laws has been dealt with and it was certainly not the reason for the demise of revolutionary Chartism. The problem of the British revolution was a problem of leadership, nothing more. Having failed to deliver revolution, the pendulum swung in the opposite direction, as we saw after 1850.

For a whole period prior to this, the revolutionary tendency was in the ascendency in the trade unions and in the Chartist movement, as Attlee recognised. However, the defeat of the revolutionary wave and the demise of Chartism resulted in all the worst features, the most backward tendencies, rising to the top. From then on, class collaboration and deference were on the order of the day, dressed up in the clothes of 'pragmatism'.

This reformist tendency, a reflection of bourgeois alien class ideas in the workers' organisations, held back the working-class movement, tying it firmly to the coat-tails of the Liberal Party for another fifty years. The reformists resisted tooth and nail the formation of an independent party of labour. It was the left wing, especially the Marxists, who championed this cause.

Between 1864 and 1871 – the time of the Paris Commune – Marx and Engels collaborated with leaders of the British trade unions on the General

---

6   C. Attlee, *The Labour Party in Perspective*, pp. 28 and 30.

7   Marx and Engels Selected Correspondence, p. 480.

8   C. Attlee, *The Labour Party in Perspective*, pp. 24-25.

Council of the International Workingmen's Association and tried to push them in the direction of class independence. Later, Marxists such as Eleanor Marx, Tom Mann and Will Thorne played a key role in building the mass trade unions in the 1890s. These trade unions developed into the ones we have today.

"On 31 March 1889 modern trade unionism was born in Britain", wrote John Edmunds, the then general secretary of the GMB.[9] That was the date of the founding of the National Union of General Workers and General Labourers of Great Britain, led by Will Thorne, and supported by Ben Tillett, Tom Mann, John Burn and Eleanor Marx, all of whom considered themselves Marxists.

What is true is that the history of the British working class contains two sides, a conservative side of deference and submission, and a revolutionary militant one. The conservative side, nurtured and promoted by the labour and trade union bureaucracy, constitutes an enormous barrier to the struggle of the working class in its fight for emancipation. The revolutionary side has been deliberately buried by the apologists of capitalism, inside and outside of the movement. Revolutionary Chartism is a prime example of this buried history. The Chartist movement provided a tremendous school for the working class, which was striving for its social emancipation, with different tendencies at play. As a result, revolutionary methods and slogans were born out of this experience, most notably the general strike and insurrection. These were, however, later discarded in favour of 'practicalities'.

The founders of scientific socialism learned a great deal from their relationship with Chartism, but they also gave a colossal amount in return. As the first independent political activity of the working class, it proved invaluable for Marx and Engels in developing their ideas. "A knowledge of proletarian conditions is absolutely necessary to provide solid ground for socialist theories", explained Engels. Above all, it provided them with fertile ground to test and verify their ideas, as well as a much wider audience. Just as they had earlier influenced the Communist League by convincing them of scientific socialism, so they hoped it would be possible to influence Chartism. As time went on, their close collaboration with the revolutionary wing bore fruit, and their ideas had a positive effect on the new socialist leadership that emerged after O'Connor's departure. Unfortunately, the height of this influence coincided with the sharp, and eventually terminal, decline of the Chartist movement, completely exhausted after ten years of bitter struggle.

---

9   Y. Kapp, *The Air of Freedom: The Birth of The New Unionism*, p. 11.

Having said that, it is truly remarkable how these two young men, who had recently arrived from the Continent, were able to have such an impact. It shows the extraordinary power of correct ideas whose time has come. After all, these two men lived in England, but were not of English birth. And yet, despite this, they managed to make considerable headway. That is because theirs were not just any ideas, but strikingly modern ones; ideas that would change the world, as they continue to do today.

It should be said at the outset that the ideas of scientific socialism are not and have never been an alien or 'sectarian' creed, without any connection with or bearing on the British working class. "Marxism, in fact, is as native to the soil of England as the class struggle out of which it grew", explained the historian Allen Hutt.[10] As we have already explained, many of these revolutionary ideas were part of an unbroken thread that stretches back far into our history. When the German revolutionary Weitling stated there was no English tradition of communism, Marx replied indignantly with a list: "Thomas More, the Levellers, Owen, Thompson, Watts, Holyoake, Harney, Morgan, Southwell, Goodwyn Barmby, Greaves, Edmonds, Hobson, Spence will be amazed, or turn in their graves, when they hear that they are no 'communists'..."[11]

Marx and Engels spent most of their adult years in Britain. Their ideas owe a great deal to the British 'experience', not least with the production of *Capital,* whose historical parts are based on English material and government Blue Books. Engels had also made a detailed study of the working class in his famous *Condition of the Working Class in England,* written in 1844. Marxism, however, is obviously far more than this. Its roots go far wider and extend much deeper, embracing a synthesis of the most advanced ideas of the time, namely German (Hegelian) philosophy, English classical economy, and French socialism, which Marx and Engels fused together to produce this all-embracing theory of scientific socialism. These are the three sources and component parts of Marxism that Lenin wrote about. As Marxism is a living theory, not a dogma, it is also further enriched by the generalised historical experience of the working class, including the British working class. As with all theory, it is precisely enriched by events. It was in this way, for instance, that Marx and Engels were able to enrich their ideas, especially about the state, from the heroic experience of the Paris Commune.

Scientific socialism is in reality the conscious expression of the unconscious historical process. This is reflected in the instinctive desire of the working

10 A. Hutt, p. 35.
11 MECW, vol. 5, p. 461.

class to transform society on socialist lines. This irresistible urge, deep in the psychology of the working class, springs to life precisely in periods of deep crisis and upheaval, symptoms of the revolutionary epoch.

Before Marx, it is true that the most advanced theories of classical political economy were evolved in Britain, where capitalism was most developed. The economic investigations into capitalism by Adam Smith and David Ricardo, in particular, laid the foundations for the labour theory of value. Marx continued their pioneering work, which he deepened, developed and extended, providing the actual proof of the theory. From this emerged the whole Marxist critique of the capitalist mode of production, where surplus value is derived from the exploitation of the working class, namely unpaid labour. "Scientific socialism," explained Engels, "dates from the discovery of this solution and has been built up around it."[12]

It is worth repeating the refutation here that Marx and Engels were not simply observers, 'academic Marxists', if you will, only interested in ideas. This false view of them chimes with the petty-bourgeois academic leftists who confine their struggles to the lecture room. As Allen Hutt correctly explained:

> It is necessary to emphasise this at the outset, for academic wiseacres and socialist writers alike have traditionally combined to initiate and perpetuate the myth that Marx and Engels were merely a couple of foreign fanatics, erudite after the German fashion, who spent their days pouring over musty tomes in the British Museum reading-room and never descending from their ivory tower to the hurly-burly of everyday life.

This is a "preposterous perversion of the facts", adds Hutt.[13] Marx and Engels were in fact intimately involved in the workers' movement, not only with the Chartists, but in the day-to-day work of the First International. For them, theory and practice were one and the same thing.

Marxism is certainly not foreign to the British Isles, as the right wing claim. Neither did it spring into existence ready-made out of the inspiration of a single genius. As the Communist International stated in its reply to the Independent Labour Party in 1920, Marxism "did not proceed from the imagination" of Marx and Engels, but was shaped by their experience. They had helped to define "the aims of the Labour movement by the study of capitalism and the experience of the first great revolutionary movement

---

12 F. Engels, *Anti-Dühring*, p. 243.
13 A. Hutt, *This Final Crisis*, p. 80.

of the working class, the Chartist movement of the British workers".[14] The experience of the British working class enriched this theory. Engels further explained that socialism is a product of the basic tendencies within capitalism:

> Modern socialism is, in its essence, the direct product of the recognition, on the one hand, of the class antagonisms existing in society of today between proprietors and non-proprietors, between capitalists and wage-workers; on the other hand, of the anarchy existing in production.[15]

These features were clearly visible in Britain in the epoch of Chartism.

COMMUNIST MANIFESTO

In 1948, on the occasion of the centenary of the *Communist Manifesto*, the British Labour Party republished this remarkable book with a foreword which stated:

> [T]he Labour Party acknowledges its indebtedness to Marx and Engels as two of the men who have been the inspiration of the whole working-class movement...
>
> Our own ideas have been different from those of continental socialism which stemmed more directly from Marx, but we, too, have been influenced in a hundred ways by European thinkers and fighters, and, above all, by the authors of the *Manifesto*.[16]

This is of course true. On the Continent, the ideas of Marxism won mass support in the workers' movement, while in Britain the ideas of reformism still prevailed. Before stating the reasons for this paradox, it is worth explaining that 'reformism', a term commonly used by Marxism, does not mean that Marxists are against reforms. On the contrary, Marxism is in favour of every meaningful advance under capitalism. However, reformism is the idea that you can gradually 'reform' capitalism and work within it to achieve real change, which is a fundamentally false idea. Capitalism cannot be changed into something that it is not, no more than a flesh-eating tiger can be transformed into a vegetarian. Reformism has been dominant in the British labour movement for more than a century. Several Labour governments have been in power, but we are no nearer socialism today. In fact it can be said, in one sense, that as a result of reformism, we are further away than before. In times of deep crisis, reformism exposes its limits. Today, capitalism can no

---

14 Quoted in A. Hutt, *The Post-war History of the British Working Class*, p. 52.
15 F. Engels, *Anti-Dühring*, p. 25.
16 *Communist Manifesto*, Socialist Landmark, London, 1948, p. 6.

longer afford lasting reforms, only counter-reforms. The crisis of capitalism is therefore also a crisis of reformist ideology. That is why we need socialism, a fundamental root and branch change in society that will do away with capitalism and private ownership of the means of production.

The dominance of reformism was reinforced by the sterile and dogmatic 'Marxism' that was espoused by Hyndman and the Social Democratic Federation, which Marx and Engels strongly criticised. It was easy to criticise this caricature, as Harold Wilson did in the 1960s, and others did after him.

It remains a mystery, nonetheless, that a country that gave so much to Marxism was so little influenced by it compared to other countries. This is part of the dialectic of historical development. In particular, the relatively long evolution of capitalism in Britain allowed for a greater accumulation of prejudices from past centuries, which weighed down on the movement. "All the ideological garbage of the ages can be discovered under MacDonald's skull", joked Trotsky in regard to Ramsay MacDonald in the 1920s.[17] But this contained a serious point. These prejudices formed an enormous conservative crust on the consciousness of the labour and trade union bureaucracy, and even of sections of the working class. The bourgeoisie, with all the resources at its disposal, also knew how to feed the top layers of the working class with such conservatism.

This peculiarity can also be partly explained as a result of the British labour movement's general aversion to theory and strong empirical tradition. This could have been successfully overcome by the development of a strong Marxist current in the workers' movement. But, unfortunately, this did not exist at that time.

Despite all the myths spread about Marxism, Marx certainly did not discover the class struggle and, furthermore, never made any such claims. Marx and Engels were nevertheless able to witness the class struggle at first hand in Britain. It was from such observations that they were able to develop and deepen their understanding, and draw certain conclusions in regard to a scientific theory of politics and the class basis of society. Chartism was invaluable in this regard. From this, as well as the experiences of the early trade unions, they were able to understand how the class moved into action and how class consciousness developed and was transformed. It was through such battles in a "long, though underground, civil war", to use Marx's words, that the English working class "gained a clear consciousness of its position as a class".

---

17 L. Trotsky, *Writings on Britain*, vol. 1, p. 17.

Engels described the early British trade unions as:

[T]he military school of the working men in which they prepare themselves for the great struggle which cannot be avoided... As schools of war the unions are unexcelled. In them is developed the peculiar courage of the English.[18]

This very idea was expressed ten years earlier in a letter in the *Poor Man's Guardian* (30 August 1834):

"The great advantage of a strike is that it increases the enmity between labourers and capitalists, and compels workmen to reflect and investigate the causes of their sufferings... The fruit of such reflections would be a violent hostility against the capitalist class; and the new converts would be prepared to second the efforts of emancipation made by labourers in other quarters of England."[19]

The labour theory of value, which in essence shows that value is produced, not by the capitalists, but by the working class, was accepted by the Chartists, especially its socialist wing, and later provided a scientific explanation for capitalist exploitation. Furthermore, the Chartists understood that the wealth of society, private property and capital all arise out of the unpaid labour of the working class. In other words, surplus value arises at the point of production, the point of exploitation by the capitalist class. The riches of the capitalists come directly from the poverty of the masses, from those who produce the wealth. As Bronterre O'Brien explained: "In our United Kingdom, which is attended with the most civilised country in the world, wage-slavery is attended with greater hardships, and subject to more privations and casualties, than anywhere else."[20]

All you need to do is to browse through the letters contained in the *Poor Man's Guardian* in the 1830s, more than a decade before the publication of the *Communist Manifesto*, to see the similarity of these ideas. One correspondent wrote a series of letters that were printed as a pamphlet. Let us listen to the worker's voice:

"When I hear master manufacturers and tradesmen say: 'We must get larger profits to enable us to pay you high wages,' my blood curdles within me, and I wish at once that I were a dog, or anything else rather than a man. Those large profits are the sole cause why wages are low... The profit is that which is retained and never paid back... There is no common interest between working men and profit makers."[21]

---

18 MECW, vol. 4, p. 512.
19 Quoted in A. Hutt, *This Final Crisis*, p. 34.
20 D. Jones, p. 37.
21 *Poor Man's Guardian*, 14 April 1832, quoted in A. Hutt, *This Final Crisis*, p. 36.

Can we not see a glimmer here of Marx's theory of surplus value in the phrase "profit is that which is retained and never paid back"? Is not profit here regarded as the unpaid labour of the working class?

Again, we have the same idea expressed in the same paper, on 7 January 1832:

"Wages should form the price of goods;
Yes, wages should be all,
Then we who work to make the goods
Should *justly have them all*;

"But if their price be made of rent,
Tithes, taxes, profits all,
Then we who work to make the goods
Shall have – *just none at all.*"[22]

It was the privilege of British workers to first rise up to challenge the capitalist system that helped shape the ideas of the founders of scientific socialism. The struggles of the British working class contained all the seeds, which Marx and Engels in a brilliant fashion were able to develop into the ideas of revolutionary socialism. Within the revolutionary struggles of the British working class can be discerned the ideas of Marxism in an embryonic and rudimentary form, as Lenin observed.

In the famous opening sentence of the International Working Men's Association's general rules, written by Marx, it is stated that "the emancipation of the working class must be conquered by the working class itself". Such an idea had been raised as far back as 1831, when trade unions and working men's clubs organised a body known as the National Union of the Working Classes. At its founding meeting, the following resolution was put forward:

"That as this Union is intended *to raise the working classes from their present degraded condition, it is necessary that it be done by themselves.* No person, therefore, shall be eligible to act on the committee unless he be a wealth-producer, that is, one who gets his living by labour."[23]

OPPRESSORS EVERYWHERE

Compare the statement of Marx and Engels in the *Manifesto* that "the executive of the modern state is but a committee for managing the common affairs of the entire bourgeoisie", to that made by Bronterre O'Brien:

---

22 Quoted in M. Beer, *History of Socialism*, vol. 1, p. 243.
23 Ibid., p. 237.

"Everyone seems to think that the government makes itself what it is, when the real fact is that the government is made by the profit-men to protect them in their exorbitant profits, rent, and impositions on the people who labour. It is the government who makes the laws, or is it not, on the contrary, the great profit-men who make them to enrich themselves and then have the government to execute them? It is the profit-men who are the *oppressors* everywhere. The government is the watchman and the people who labour are the *oppressed*."[24]

Here, possibly for the first time, the government is regarded as the executive committee and "watchman" of the interests of the ruling class. The state is the class organisation of the bourgeoisie used to suppress the working masses. Three years later, Bronterre O'Brien wrote:

"Up to this moment all the Governments of the world have been nothing but conspiracies of rich against poor, *allies* of the strong and cunning to rob and keep in subjection the weak and ignorant. The present Government of England is of this sort."[25]

When we consider Marx and Engels' conception of the state as armed bodies of men in defence of private property, and that the working class needs its own state as a transition to a classless society, we can compare this idea with the statement of a weaver to the *Poor Man's Guardian*. He said the taxes they paid were the "money given to the government to beat and torture you into submission" to obtain "rents, tithes, interest and profits." He explained the people should not be deceived with talk of capitalist democracy, but that "the people who make the goods" should be the *sole* ruling class:

"To talk of *representation*, in any shape, being of any use to the people, is sheer nonsense; unless the people have a House of working men, and represent themselves... The people should drop all contention, therefore, about electing a legislature in its present shape, and contend night and day, every moment of their lives, for a legislature of their own, or one made up of themselves... It is but common justice that the people who make the goods should have the sole privilege of making the laws."[26]

What is this if not a workers' democracy, or the dictatorship of the proletariat, to use Marx's expression?

---

24 *Poor Man's Guardian*, 14 January 1832, quoted in T. Rothstein, p. 107.

25 *Poor Man's Guardian*, March 1835, quoted in A.L. Morton, *Socialism in Britain*, p. 36.

26 *The Poor Man's Guardian*, 29 April, 26 November 1831, quoted in A. Hutt, *This Final Crisis*, p. 37.

A similar thought was expressed by James Morrison, a self-taught young operative builder, who edited *The Pioneer*, the paper of the Builders' Union. He wrote:

> "The growing power and growing intelligence of trade unions, when properly managed, will draw into its vortex all the commercial interests of the country, and, in doing so, it will become, by its own self-acquired importance, a most influential, we might almost say dictatorial part of the body politic."[27]

Without doubt, the Chartist leaders Ernest Jones and Julian Harney, under the influence of Marx and Engels, expressed the main conceptions of scientific socialism to a wide audience. Harney was forced to resign from *The Northern Star* following his breach with O'Connor and went on to establish another weekly, *The Red Republican*. In the first issue (July 1850), Harney announced its aim to the world:

> "As regards the working men swamping other classes, the answer is easy – other classes have no right even to exist. To prepare the way for the absolute supremacy of the working classes… preparatory to the abolition of the system of classes, is the mission of *The Red Republican*."[28]

In the same year, Harney had signed, on behalf of his English comrades, an agreement for the founding of a World League of Revolutionary Communists, the other signatories being Marx and Engels on behalf of the German Communists, as well as representatives of the French Blanquists. The opening article of this agreement stated:

> "The aim of the Association is the downfall of all the privileged classes and the subjection of these classes to the dictatorship of the proletariat by the maintenance of the revolution in permanence until the realisation of Communism, which is the final form of organisation of human society."[29]

Harney found it advantageous to translate the strange-sounding phrase "dictatorship of the proletariat" into the more comprehensible "absolute supremacy of the working class", but the meaning was the same.

In Marx's day the idea of 'dictatorship' did not have the negative connotations it has today, following the experiences of Stalinism and those of fascism in Germany, Italy and Spain. In fact, Marx's view was based

---

27 *The Pioneer*, 31 May 1834, quoted in A. Hutt, *This Final Crisis*, p. 37.

28 G.D.H. Cole, *Chartist Portraits*, p. 293.

29 Ibid., p. 293.

on the Roman Republic, where special powers would in times of crisis be bestowed on a dictator or 'magistrate' temporarily, for a six-month period. The proletarian 'dictatorship' was the organised power of the many over the few. In today's context, the term 'workers' democracy' conveys far better the meaning of what Marx was talking about.

The World League of Revolutionary Communists was not to last following the split within the Communist League in September 1850. Nevertheless, these remarkable ideas of the working class becoming the ruling class, as a step in the direction of a classless society, were already present in an embryonic form in the great trade union upsurge of 1833-34.

We have already quoted the rules of the Grand National Consolidated Trades Union which talked of "A DIFFERENT ORDER OF THINGS" and workers having "direction of its affairs". At Manchester, then London, a 'Builders' Parliament' was held, composed of 500 delegates. At this congress, the young building worker James Morrison stated, "the question to be decided is, Shall Labour or Capital be uppermost?" *The Poor Man's Guardian* of 19 October 1833 talked of the union congress as "a grand national organisation, which promises to embody the physical power of the country".[30]

This sense of working-class power was certainly present in the Chartist period. Near the village of Tolpuddle in Dorset in late 1838, at a large Chartist gathering of 6,000 in Blandford Forum, W.P. Roberts urged the workers to adopt the Charter and fight for "an immediate advance ... in the Wages paid to Agricultural Labourers". He then stated that the ultimate aim was "to elevate the labourer in the social scale. The time was come when some great moral blow would be struck to emancipate the working classes of England from the chains of oppression under which they laboured."[31]

The revolutionary trade unions of the 1830s also raised the idea of the representation of the working class on an industrial basis, a *class* basis: as producers, not as 'citizens'. In other words, they laid the basis for workers' councils. The Owenite *Crisis* wrote in 1834:

> "The only House of Commons is a House of Trades. We shall have a new set of boroughs when the unions are organised: every trade shall be a borough, and every trade shall have a council of representatives to conduct its affairs."

The editorial in Morrison's *Pioneer* expressed it more concretely:

30 A. Hutt, *British Trade Unionism: A Short History*, p. 17.
31 M. Chase, p. 37.

"Every trade has its internal government in every town; a certain number of towns comprise a district, and delegates from the trades in each town form a quarterly district government; delegates from the districts form the Annual Parliament; and the King of England becomes President of the Trade Unions!"

Morrison added his comment that:

"[T]he unions are of all the other means the only mode by which universal suffrage can safely be obtained, because it is obtained by practice, by serving an apprenticeship. Here they start to manage their own affairs on a small scale before they get management of larger affairs."[32]

This is a pointer to the future role of the trade unions in becoming the management of nationalised industry. This is the basis of workers' control and management that will involve workers, their unions and a workers' government in the democratic running of the economy. To make the unions equal to their future role they must be completely transformed and democratised, and freed from bureaucratic domination.

These were all important signposts to the future. All the elements were there, but they lacked an important ingredient, namely a fully worked-out theory that could draw all the threads together. This came some years later with the development of Marxism, or scientific socialism. It unfortunately came too late for the heyday of Chartism. When the *Communist Manifesto* was published in English in the *Red Republican*, Chartism was already in decline. It was not the fault of Chartism that it appeared on the scene not fully equipped, an immature response in many ways to the demands of the time. The workers were searching for a way out, as witnessed by the popular Chartist uprisings and mass movements of 1839, 1842 and 1848, but this also exposed the weakness of the movement, which was unable to give a conscious expression to the spontaneous yearnings of the masses to change society. In other words, it lacked a serious perspective for power despite all the striving in that direction.

OUR HERITAGE

History can be viewed as a double-edged sword. In the hands of apologists of capital, it can be used to show that revolutionary struggle leads nowhere, as is argued in the 'official' histories. However, it can also be used to explain the real lessons and as a consequence it can raise our sights and confidence. This very rich heritage is precious to us. We have a responsibility to uncover and explain it. We base ourselves not on its weak sides, on the backside of history,

---

32 A. Hutt, *This Final Crisis*, p. 39.

which is the vision of the reformists and apologists of capitalism, but on its strong positive sides, namely its revolutionary potential. Likewise, we do not idolise the working class, which is an oppressed and exploited class, but see it in its development, as it grows in class consciousness. The task of Marxism, as explained, is to make conscious the unconscious processes developing in the minds of the masses. This is where the importance of leadership and revolutionary theory comes in. "Those who do not learn from history will be doomed to repeat it", explained Santayana, an extremely wise statement. As Marx also said, "ignorance never did anyone any good". Therefore, the heroic pages of Chartism must not be lost to the new generation. That is the reason for the publication of this book.

We have to understand that there is no 'royal road' to socialism, like some grand continuous procession. Ultimately, the fight to change society comes down to the struggle of living forces. As John Bray, the Chartist, wrote:

> "There can be no doubt that they will ultimately succeed and the joys reserved for them in their futurity will amply repay them for whatever they suffer during their progress forwards; *but this progress will depend upon their activity*, stimulated by their sufferings under existing institutions."[33]

As Marxism explains, history is made by the activity of men and women, but coloured by the legacy of the past. The British working class, as Engels pointed out, was organisationally very advanced. It had solid, powerful organisations. However, its indifference to theory meant that it crawled along slowly on its belly.

But this was not always the case. The decade after 1825 was extremely rich in practical and theoretical developments. As we have seen, the working class was influenced by the ideas of Robert Owen, who made a massive impact on its leading layers. The same goes for William Thompson, Thomas Hodgskin, John Gray, John Francis Bray, and especially Bronterre O'Brien, the 'Schoolmaster'. This was a period of colossal theoretical advance in Britain. These people came close to discovering the secret of surplus value as the unpaid labour of the working class. They delved into the class nature of capitalist society. They fully understood the working class was an exploited class and that capitalist property relations were at the bottom of this. "The gain of the employer will never cease to be the loss of the employed", stated John Bray.[34] These early theoreticians made it possible for the working class

---

33 A.L. Morton, *Socialism in Britain*, p. 31, our emphasis.
34 A.L. Morton, p. 31.

to clearly identify its enemies, the bourgeoisie. In this way, the anger of the working class was redirected from 'Old Corruption' towards the money-grabbing exploiting capitalists.

These ideas pointed in the direction of Marxism and its conclusions. They arose in this epic period of revolutionary trade unions, revolutionary Chartism, and the independent class organisation of the British proletariat. This was truly the heroic period for the working class of these islands, when they stood on their own two feet. It was when they became fully class conscious.

This, however, was cut across for a whole historical period and undermined by the domination of reformism. Now is the time to put right this wrong. The working class needs once again to stand proud and re-establish the revolutionary theoretical basis of the movement.

Theory is a vital guide to action, for without it we are lost and blown hither and thither by events. This weakness of the British labour movement must be remedied, primarily by advancing the theory of Marxism, which provides us with clear tactics and strategy, free of opportunism or sectarianism. Marxism can be regarded as the memory of the working class, preserving its experiences. With this knowledge and understanding, we can successfully prepare the ground for the revolutionary events that impend, and intervene to bring things to a speedy conclusion.

"The Chartist tide may now seem to ebb low," wrote the Chartist John Watkins, "but the lower the ebb the higher will be the flood, and the next flood-tide will bear us to fortune."[35] Similarly today, after decades of setbacks, involving a prolonged ebb-tide, the tide has turned and we are swimming with the stream. The capitalist system is consumed by crisis and revolutionary events are on the order of the day, in which all political tendencies will be put to the test. Those that fail to offer a revolutionary way out will be found wanting. I certainly do not agree with the historian G.D.H. Cole when he says that Chartism speaks "to us across the years in a dead language".[36] The language, on the contrary, is a living one that speaks to us about fundamental change and revolution. These ideas resonate more with us today than at any time before. They are far from 'dead'. It is the attempt to patch up and rescue capitalism that is in a dead-end.

The revolutionary outlook of Marx and Engels is summed up in the *Communist Manifesto*, the most far-sighted document of the age. It is

---

35 *An Anthology of Chartist Literature*, p. 345.
36 G.D.H. Cole, *A Short History*, p. 147.

certainly not a "dead language". Despite the sneering and snarling of the bourgeois critics, Marx and Engels saw into the future much further than any of their contemporaries and possibly anyone since. Events have demonstrated the superiority of the method of Marxism in explaining phenomena. The *Manifesto* remains a profound piece of writing, which provides, in an amazingly short text, a brilliant understanding of the development of capitalism and the historic role of the working class.

At the present time, the knot of history is once again being re-tied as we head into a stormy period of intensified class struggle. The *Manifesto* is more relevant than when it first appeared in 1848. The representatives of capital look to the future with trepidation. Mark Carney, the former governor of the Bank of England, warned that conditions similar to the nineteenth century were preparing the re-emergence of Marxism internationally. Carney believed that the recent years of weak wage growth and falling living standards are fuelling such developments. He warned that:

> "If you substitute platforms for textile mills, machine learning for steam engines, Twitter for the telegraph, you have exactly the same dynamics as existed 150 years ago – when Karl Marx was scribbling the *Communist Manifesto*."[37]

Let these bourgeois representatives quake in their boots! Their system is doomed. The objective conditions for world socialist revolution are not only ripe, but rotten ripe. However, capitalism will not fall of its own volition. It will need to be overthrown and replaced with socialism. The *Manifesto* is not an abstract commentary, but a call to action; not a textbook but a programme for world socialist revolution. It replaced the slogan 'All Men are Brethren', prevalent at the time, with the slogan 'Proletarians of all lands unite'.

"You have nothing to lose but your chains; you have a world to win", were not the words of Bronterre O'Brien or Julian Harney, but the conclusions of the *Manifesto*. They nevertheless accurately capture the feelings and thoughts of revolutionary Chartism, and express today the message of millions who are fighting for a better life. This is no "empty dream", as Ernest Jones explained. It is for the here and now. The "spectre of communism", long pronounced dead, is actively "haunting" one country after another.

It can be said, with complete justification, that the revolutionaries of today are the real inheritors of Chartism and that the ideals of Chartism live on in the ideas of Marxism. "Chartism is not at all liquidated", wrote

---

37 *Daily Telegraph*, 13 April 2018.

Trotsky. "History is liquidating Liberalism and prepares to liquidate the pseudo-Labour pacifism precisely so as to give a second birth to Chartism on new, immeasurably broader historical foundations."[38] The working class will inevitably return to these ideas and methods, but on a higher level. They are ideas whose time has come as we enter into a prolonged epoch of revolution and counter-revolution.

We are today at a turning point, as was the case in 1838 and the birth of revolutionary Chartism, or in 1890 and the reawakening of the British working class. The mass strikes involving dockworkers and the unskilled workers represented the reawakening of the British working class, after a long hibernation, to use the expression of Engels. The massive May Day parade of 1890, instigated by Eleanor Marx and Edward Aveling, provoked Engels to write enthusiastically:

> There can be no doubt that on 4 May 1890 the English working class joined the great international army... Its long hibernation – the result, on the one hand, of the failure of the Chartist movement of 1836-50 and, on the other hand, of the colossal rise of industry between 1848 and 1880 – has finally come to an end. The grandchildren of the old Chartists are stepping into the front line.[39]

Once again, we, the descendants of Chartism, are called upon to step into the front line. The task still remains in Britain, as elsewhere, to rearm the workers' movement with the ideas and programme of scientific socialism, to root out any accommodation to crisis-ridden capitalism. It now falls to the working class to complete its task of abolishing capitalism and creating a world free of hunger, poverty and conflict. To do so, we must resolve the crisis of working class leadership. To accomplish this we need to build a new revolutionary leadership, based on the audacity of revolutionary Chartism but grounded in the ideas of Marxism, that is prepared to go to the end. On the outcome of this struggle depends the future prosperity of the working class of these islands, and indeed the entire fate of humanity. We are confident that in this period the proletariat, imbued with a new consciousness, will play its revolutionary part and bring about a new society that is crying out to be born. If we proceed boldly and confidently, on the basis of a revolutionary programme, the working class can succeed.

Not only will we read about our history, but more importantly we can start making history. In the words of Abraham Lincoln: "The best way to predict

---

38 L. Trotsky, *Writings on Britain*, vol. 2, p. 94.

39 MECW, vol. 27, p. 66.

your future is to create it." In this way we can pay honour to the legacy of the Chartists.

The final word of this book should go to Friedrich Engels, who had a great affinity with the workers of Britain:

> The working class remains what it was, and what our Chartist forefathers were not afraid to call it, a class of wage slaves. Is this to be the final result of all this labour, self-sacrifice, and suffering? Is this to remain forever the highest aim of British workmen? Or is the working class of this country at last to attempt breaking through this vicious circle, and to find an issue out of it in the movement for the ABOLITION OF THE WAGES SYSTEM ALTOGETHER?"

> And the sooner this is done the better. There is no power in the world which could for a day resist the British working class organised as a body.[40]

---

40 MECW, vol. 24, pp. 385 and 388.

APPENDIX: INTERNATIONALISM

"On the other hand – as in the case of America – once the workers over here know what they want, the state, the land, industry and everything else will be theirs."

– F. Engels, January 1895

"But it is not the French, nor the Germans, nor the British who, by themselves, will win the glory of having crushed capitalism; if France – PERHAPS – gives the signal, it will be in Germany, the country most profoundly influenced by socialism and where the theory has the most deeply penetrated the masses – where the fight will be settled, and even then neither France nor Germany will ensure final victory so long as England remains in the hands of the bourgeoisie. Proletarian emancipation can be only an international deed."

– F. Engels, June 1893

An important aspect of the labour movement in Britain, especially of Chartism, was its internationalism. This refutes the view that the labour movement at this time was insular, which is very far from the truth. The British working class was greatly influenced by the French and American Revolutions, both of which had rekindled the thirst for democratic rights. The British workers saw their struggle as part of this wider international struggle.

This international tradition was present in the Corresponding Societies, in the trade unions, the Owenite movement and in Chartism. There was not a hint of nationalism.

With the developing international character of capitalism, and with it the class struggle, the interests of the working class took on an internationalist nature. The class struggle cut across national barriers, uniting workers from different countries and different continents. The interests of the working class are the same for workers in all countries. The need for an international organisation flows from this fact.

As Theodore Rothstein explained:

> The International was born in England, and it is on English soil that we have to look for its preceding history. It was no mere accident that the movement originated in England and drew its nourishment chiefly from the English soil... England witnessed the first political movement of the proletariat as a class. It was in England that the working class first organised itself into trade unions. It was the consciousness of the English proletariat which arrived at the first clear understanding of the class struggle both as a historical factor and as a tactical principle. And, last but not least, it was in England that the proletariat first acquired a deep sense not only of its solidarity with the workers of other countries, but also of the imperative need for concerted action in the fight against capitalist society, based upon this solidarity.[1]

In the 1830s, the National Union of the Working Classes, in the words of the historian Max Beer, "fostered international solidarity with particular ardour. It celebrated the anniversaries of the French Revolution and of the Polish insurrection, and opposed Palmerston's foreign policy, which it severely stigmatised as dictated by the Tsar."[2]

Internationalism permeated the powerful working-class press of the time. John Doherty's weekly, *The Voice of the People*, which in 1830-31 reached a mass circulation of 30,000 copies, campaigned for the repeal of the Irish Union and carried news of revolutionary events in Europe. Chartism was imbued with a strong internationalist spirit. The London Working Men's Association expressed its solidarity with the oppressed everywhere, including the struggling Polish people, but also those of the colonies. The Manifesto of the LWMA stated that "fellow producers of wealth have in reality but one great interest... The interests of working men of all countries of the world are identical" (13 November 1836). The same view was expressed in *The London Dispatch*: "What care we in what language our cherished principles are expressed – they are still our principles, whether uttered in Canadian, French, or Belgian, Dutch, or Polish, or modern Greek."[3]

The Chartists had links to the Fraternal Democrats, established in London in 1845 by German, Polish and Italian refugees. Harney, Jones and others

---

1   T. Rothstein, p. 125.
2   M. Beer, *A History of British Socialism*, vol. 1, p. 244.
3   *The London Dispatch*, 9 April 1837.

became prominent members of the society, and their activities were widely reported in *The Northern Star*. The organisation's programme was outlined in a speech by Harney on its first anniversary:

> "We renounce, repudiate, and condemn all political hereditary inequalities and distinctions of caste; we declare that the earth with all its natural productions is the common property of all; we declare that the present state of society which permits idlers and schemers to monopolise the fruits of the earth, and the productions of industry, and compels the working class to labour for inadequate rewards, and even condemns them to social slavery, destitution and degradation, is essentially unjust."

And in regard to internationalism, the organisation denounced any national prejudices which served to cause contention among peoples:

> "Convinced too, that national prejudices have been, in all ages, taken advantage of by people's oppressors to set them tearing the throats of each other when they should have been working together for their common good, this society repudiates the term 'foreigner,' no matter to whom applied. Our moral creed is to receive our fellow men without regard to 'country,' as members of one family, the human race; and the citizens of one commonwealth, the world."[4]

In 1846, Julian Harney delivered a speech which also echoed the concluding slogan of the *Communist Manifesto*, "Workers of the world, unite! You have nothing to lose but your chains", when he stated:

> "The cause of the people in all countries is the same – the cause of labour, enslaved and plundered labour... The men who create every necessity, comfort, and luxury, are steeped in misery. Working men of all nations, are not your grievances, your wrongs, the same? Is not your good cause, then, one and the same also? We may differ as to the means, or different circumstances may render different means necessary, but the great end – the veritable emancipation of the human race – must be the aim and end of all."[5]

When the capitalists talked about the national interest, Peter McDouall reminded his readers that the "capitalist belongs to no nation".[6] This is very close to Marx's aphorism that 'the workers have no country', and therefore need to unite internationally.

---

4   T. Rothstein, pp. 131-132.

5   *The Northern Star*, 14 February 1846, quoted in *Spokesmen for Liberty*, p. 320.

6   D. Jones, p. 124.

As we have already mentioned, when Marx and Engels came to London to attend the Second Congress of the Communist League in the winter of 1847, they addressed an international public meeting along with other Chartist leaders. It was a Chartist theme that a nation that oppressed another could not be free. A defeat for the ruling class in any country was a victory for workers everywhere. In the middle of 1847, the Fraternal Democrats held a meeting to support the revolutionary events in Portugal, at which Harney spoke:

> "The people are beginning to understand that foreign as well as domestic questions do affect them; that a blow struck at Liberty on the Tagus is an injury to the friends of Freedom on the Thames; that the success of Republicanism in France would be the doom of Tyranny in every other land; and the triumph of England's democratic Charter would be the salvation of millions throughout Europe."[7]

The 1848 Revolutions had a massive impact in Britain, as we saw, with mass meetings in many towns pledging their support.

The Fraternal Democrats laid the basis, through its successor in the International Association, for the future foundation of the First International, which was established in London in 1864. It arose out of a meeting held in St Martin's Hall in connection with the Polish anniversary. There were French workers present who came forward with "a plan for the promotion of a better understanding among peoples", and a resolution was enthusiastically accepted to establish an International Working Men's Association. This was a vital milestone in the international collaboration of the working class, at least of its advanced layers, in which Marx and Engels played a leading role. It was the bridge between the old Chartism and the socialism of the 1880s and laid the basis for the labour movement in Europe, Britain and America. In fact, it is the organic link between this formative period of the British working class and the struggle to overthrow capitalism today.

---

7   *The Northern Star*, 19 June 1847.

CHRONOLOGY

1789

July   The Storming of the Bastille

1811-12

The Luddite unrest

1815

June   Napoleon defeated at Waterloo

1819

November   Peterloo Massacre

1820

February   The Cato Street Conspiracy

1824

Repeal of the Combination Acts

1829

December   The Birmingham Political Union founded

1830

September   Whig government formed

August-   The Swing Riots
September

1831

May	The National Union of the Working Classes and National Political Union founded

1832

June	Passing of the Great Reform Bill
December	First general election under the new system

1833

May	Calthorpe Street Affair
June	Factory Act limiting child labour

1834

February	The Grand National Consolidated Trades Union founded
March	Prosecution of the "Tolpuddle Martyrs"
July	Passing of the New Poor Amendment Act
August	The Grand National Consolidated Trades Union dissolved
December	General Election, Peel becomes Prime Minister

1835

April	Melbourne becomes Prime Minister

1836

March	Newspaper Act passed, reducing stamp duty to one penny per issue
June	London Working Men's Association founded
August	National Radical Association of Scotland founded

1837

January	East London Democratic Association founded
February	The LWMA held first public meeting at Crown and Anchor tavern
April	Strike of the Glasgow Cotton Spinners
May	The Birmingham Union revived
July	General Election; defeat of many Radical MPs
November	First issue of *The Northern Star* in Leeds

| December | Prosecution of leaders of Glasgow Cotton Spinners; sentenced to transportation for seven years |

1838

May	East London Democratic Association changes name to London Democratic Association
	People's Charter published in London
	National Petition published in Birmingham
	150,000 at mass meeting in Glasgow
June	The Great Northern Union founded in Leeds
	Northern Political Union founded in Newcastle
	Mass meeting in Newcastle-Upon-Tyne
August	Mass meeting in Nottingham
September	Manchester Anti-Corn Law Association founded
	250,000 at Kersal Moor Meeting, Manchester
	30,000 attend meeting in London to elect delegates

1839

January	Stephens committed for trial
February	The General Convention of the Industrious Classes met in London
March	The Anti-Corn Law League set up as national organisation
April	Harney launches *London Democrat*
April/May	Riots in Llanidloes
May	The Convention moved to Birmingham
	Beginning of the Rebecca Riots in Wales
	Mass demonstrations over Whitsun
June	Petition presented to parliament by Attwood and Fielden
July	The Bull Ring Riots in Birmingham
	The Convention returns to London
	House of Commons rejected the first National Petition (235 votes to 46)
	Chartists discuss "ulterior measures"
	Convention calls for Sacred Month for 12 August
	Scottish Patriot launched
	'Battle of Spittal' (Newcastle)

Summer	May Chartists arrested
August	"Sacred Month" called off followed by demonstrations
	Rural Police Bill passed
September	Convention disbanded
	Chartist Circular founded in Glasgow
November	The Newport Rising
December	Trial of John Frost on charge of high treason begins

1840

January	Verdict of 'guilty' on Frost; Death sentence passed on Frost, Williams and Jones
	Abortive Sheffield and Bradford risings. Imprisonment of Samuel Holberry
February	Sentences on Welsh Chartists commuted
	Chartist trials at Liverpool begin
March	Chartist trials at York
	Convention in Manchester
April	Convention in Nottingham
Winter and Spring	Widespread Chartist arrests
July	Chartist conference in Manchester
	The National Chartist Association founded

1841

February	National delegate meeting in Manchester
April	Lovett founds the National Association of the United Kingdom for Promoting the Political and Social Improvement of the People
	O'Connor takes up the land question
August	General Election. Tory victory. Sir Robert Peel becomes Prime Minister
November	Joseph Surge takes up Suffrage question

1842

April	Complete Suffrage Union Conference at Birmingham
	Chartist Convention in London
May	The Commons rejects the second Chartist Petition (287 votes to 49)

July	Trough of trade cycle. Wage cuts. Unemployment
5 August	Strike begins at Stalybridge
12 August	Conference of trade delegates in Manchester pledge to strike for Charter
15 August	Great Delegate conference in Manchester
August-September	The Plug Plot general strike
December	Conference of Chartists and Complete Suffrage representatives in Birmingham
	Collapse of the Complete Suffrage Union

1843

March	Trial of O'Connor and others. Acquittal on main points
September	Chartist Convention in Birmingham
	Land Reform accepted
	Chartist Executive moves to London
October	Harney becomes sub-editor of *The Northern Star*

1844

April	Chartist Convention in Manchester
November	*The Northern Star* changed to *Northern Star and National Trades Journal*. Headquarters moved from Leeds to London

1845

April	Chartist Convention in London
	The Chartist Land Cooperative Society launched
September	Society of Fraternal Democrats founded
December	Manchester conference on Land Plan

1846

June	Repeal of the Corn Laws; Peel replaced by Lord John Russell as Prime Minster

1847

April	Financial Crisis
May	Ten-Hours Factory Act passed

	O'Connorville opened
July	General Election. Whig victory. Lord John Russell becomes Prime Minister. O'Connor elected for Nottingham.
November–December	Communist League conference in London

1848

February	Revolution in France
	Publication of the *Communist Manifesto*
April	Chartist Convention in London
	Kennington Common demonstration
	National Petition ridiculed in Parliament
	Joseph Hume's "Little Charter" put forward
May	Chartist National Assembly meets
May-July	Chartist disturbances. Large-scale arrests. Imprisonment of Jones.

1849

June	Harney launches *Democratic Review*
August	Karl Marx arrives in London
November	Engels arrives in London
December	Chartist delegate conference in London

1850

January	O'Brien launches National Reform League
	O'Connor defeated by Harney and the Fraternal Democrats on Chartist Executive. Chartism reorganised
March	Defeated O'Connorites launch National Charter League
June	Harney launches *Red Republican* and announces socialist objectives
July	Ernest Jones released from prison
November	Resignation of Chartist Executive at O'Connor's tactics

1851

January	O'Connorite Chartist Conference in Manchester a failure
February	Bill to dissolve the National Land Company
March	London Chartist conference adopts socialist programme

May	Jones launches his *Notes to the People*
	The Great Exhibition

1852

January	O'Connorite Chartist Conference in Manchester a failure
February	Bill to dissolve the National Land Company
March	London Chartist conference adopt socialist programme
May	Jones launches his *Notes to the People*
	The Great Exhibition

1852

January	*The Northern Star* changes hands and discards label "Chartist"
April	Harney buys *The Northern Star* and changes name to *Star of Freedom*
May	Jones launches the *People's Paper*. Open breach between Harney and Jones
	Chartist Convention in Manchester
June	O'Connor declared insane

1854

March	Jones establishes The Mass Movement and Labour Parliament in Manchester

1855

August	O'Connor dies

1858

February	The last National Chartist Convention

BIBLIOGRAPHY

Attlee, Clement, *The Labour Party in Perspective*, Gollancz, 1937.

Bagehot, Walter, *The English Constitution*, Oxford University Press, 1945.

Beer, Max, *A History of British Socialism*.

— vol. 1, London, 1920.

— vol. 2, Spokesman, 1984.

Black, David and Chris Ford, *1839: The Chartist Insurrection*, London, 2011.

Bray, John Francis, *Labour's Wrongs and Labour's Remedy: Or the Age of Might and the Age of Right*, 1931.

Briggs, Asa, *Chartist Studies*, Macmillan, 1972.

Brown, Richard, *Before Chartism: Exclusion and Resistance*, London, 2014.

Brown, Richard and Daniels, Christopher (Ed.), *The Chartists: Documents and Debates*, MacMillan, 1986.

Carlton, John, *The Chartists*, Pluto Press, 1997.

Carlyle, Thomas, *Chartism*, London, 1840.

Challinor, Raymond and Brian Ripley, *The Miners' Association: A Trade Union in the Age of the Chartists*, London, 1968.

Chase, Malcolm, *Chartism: A New History*, Manchester University Press, 2007.

Charlton, John, *The Chartists: The First National Workers Movement*, Pluto Press, 1997.

Cole, G.D.H., *Chartist Portraits*, London, 1941.

— *A Short History of the British Working Class Movement: 1789-1947*, London, 1966.

Cole, G.D.H., and Postgate, Raymond, *The Common People*, London, 1938.

Cole, G.D.H. and Filson, A.W., *British Working Class Movements: Selected Documents 1789-1875*, MacMillan, 1967.

Cole, Margaret, *Makers of the Labour Movement*, London, 1948.

Cordell, Alexander, *Rape of the Fair Country*, 1959.

— *Hosts of Rebecca*, 1960.

— *Song of the Earth*, 1969.

CPSU, (Ed.) Institute of Marxism-Leninism, *Documents of the First International: 1864-1866*, vol. 1, Lawrence & Wishart, 1974.

Davies, John, *A History of Wales*, Penguin, 1994.

Deane, Phyllis, *The First Industrial Revolution*, Cambridge University Press, 1969.

Deutcher, I. (Ed.), *The Age of Permanent Revolution: A Trotsky Anthology*, New York, 1964.

Dickens, Charles, *Hard Times*, Penguin, 1969.

— *A Christmas Carol*, in *Christmas Books*, London, 1876.

Disraeli, Benjamin, *Sybil*, Wordsworth Classics, 1995.

Edwards, Ness, *History of the South Wales Miners' Federation*, Lawrence & Wishart, 1938.

Engels, F, *Anti-Dühring*, Lawrence & Wishart, 1969.

Fegan, Melissa, *Literature and the Irish Famine 1845-1919*, Oxford University Press, 2005.

Flett, Keith, *Chartism After 1848*, Merlin, 2006.

Frost, Thomas, *Forty Years' Recollections*, London, 1880.

Gammage, R.C., *History of the Chartist Movement*, London, 1976.

Gilmore, Ian, *Inside Right*, London, 1978.

Hammond, J. L. and Hammond, B., *The Town Labourer: 1760-1832*, Longmans, 1995

— *The Village Labourer: 1760-1832*, Longmans, 1995.

— *The Skilled Labourer: 1760-1832*, Longmans, 1995.

— *The Rise of Modern Industry*, London, 1925.

— *Lord Shaftesbury*, Pelican, 1939.

— *The Bleak Age*, Pelican, 1947.

— *The Age of Chartism*, London, 1930.

— *The Rise of Modern Industry*, London, 1925.

— *The Town Labourer: 1760-1832*, Longmans, 1995.

Harrison, Stanley, *Poor Men's Guardians*, Lawrence & Wishart, 1974.

Hegel, G.W.F, *The Phenomenology of Mind*, in J. Loewenberg (Ed.), *Hegel Selections*, New York, 1929.

Hill, Christopher, *Reformation to Industrial Revolution*, London, 1968.
Hollis, Patricia (Ed.), *Class and Class Conflict in Nineteenth Century England: 1815-1850*, London, 1973.
Hobsbawn, Eric, *Industry and Empire*, Pelican, 1969.
— *Labouring Men*, London, 1968.
— *Revolutionaries*, London, 1973.
Huberman, Leo, *Man's Worldly Goods*, London, 1936.
Hunt, Tristram, *The Frock-coated Communist*, London, 2009.
Hutt, Allen, *This Final Crisis*, London, 1936.
— *British Trade Unionism: A Short History*, 1975.
Jackman, Sidney (Ed.), *The English Reform Tradition: 1790-1910*, New Jersey, 1965.
Jackson, T.A., *Ireland Her Own*, London, 1971.
Jenkins, M, *The General Strike of 1842*, Lawrence & Wishart, 1980.
Jenkins, Simon, *A Short History of England*, London, 2012.
Jones, David, *Chartism and the Chartists*, London, 1975.
Kapp, Yvonne, *The Air of Freedom: The Birth of The New Unionism*, Lawrence & Wishart, 1989.
Lenin, V. I., Collected Works, 45 volumes, Moscow.
Lindsay, Jack and Rickword, Edgell (Ed.), *Spokesmen for Liberty*, Lawrence & Wishart 1941.
Marlow, Joyce, *The Peterloo Massacre*, London, 1969.
Marx, Karl, *Capital*, vol. 1, Penguin, 1990.
Marx, Karl and Friedrich Engels, Collected Works, 50 volumes, Lawrence & Wishart.
— *Selected Correspondence.*
— *Selected Works*, 3 volumes.
— *Communist Manifesto*, Socialist Landmark, London, 1948.
Mather, F.C., *Public Order in the Age of the Chartist*, London, 1959.
Mayer, Gustav, *Friedrich Engels: A Biography*, New York, 1936.
Meek, R.L., *Studies in the Labour Theory of Value.*
Morton, A.L., *A People's History of England*, Gollancz, 1938.
— *Socialism in Britain*, Lawrence & Wishart, 1963.
Morton, A.L. and Tate, George, *The British Labour Movement*, Lawrence & Wishart, 1979.
Murphy, J.T., *Preparing for Power*, Pluto Press, 1972.
O'Brien, Mark, *Perish the Privileged Orders*, Redwords, 1995.
Paine, Thomas, *The Thomas Paine Reader*, Penguin Classics, 1987.

Palme Dutt, R., *The Internationale*, London, 1964.

Pelling, Henry, *Origins of the Labour Party*, Oxford University Press, 1976.

— *A History of British Trade Unionism*, Pelican, 1969.

Ponomarev, B.N. (Ed.), *The International Working Class Movement*, vol. 1, Progress Publishers, Moscow, 1980.

Porter, G.R., *The Progress of the Nation*, London, 1847.

Postgate, Raymond, *A Pocket History of the British Working Class*, NCLC, 1947.

— *A Short History of the British Working Class*, Plebs League, 1926.

— *Revolution From 1789 to 1906*, New York, 1962.

Ramelson, Marion, *Petticoat Rebellion*, Lawrence & Wishart, 1972.

Rothstein, Theodore, *From Chartism to Labourism*, Lawrence & Wishart, 1983.

Rudé, George, *Ideology and Popular Protest*, Lawrence & Wishart, 1980.

— *Paris and London in the 18th Century*, London, 1970.

Saville, John, *1848: The British State and the Chartist Movement*, Cambridge University Press, 1990.

Schneierson, Vic (Ed.), *Engels: A Short Biography*, Progress Publishers, 1988.

Sewell, Rob, *In the Cause of Labour: History of British Trade Unionism*, Wellred Books, 2003.

Shelley, P.B., *The Works of P.B. Shelley*, Wordsworth, 1994.

Simon, Brian, *History of Education: 1780-1870*, Lawrence & Wishart, 1966.

Schwarzkopf, Jutta, *Women in the Chartist Movement*, London, 1991.

Tawney, R.H., *The Radical Tradition*, Penguin, 1964.

Trotsky, Leon, *Writings on Britain* (3 volumes), New Park, 1974.

— *The Revolution Betrayed*, New Park, 1967.

— *History of the Russian Revolution*, vol. 1, Sphere, 1967.

Thompson, E.P., *The Making of the English Working Class*, Penguin, 1968.

Thompson, Dorothy, *The Chartists*, London, 1984.

— *The Early Chartists*, London, 1971.

Webb, Sidney and Webb, Beatrice, *The History of Trade Unionism*, London, 1911.

Wheen, Frances, *Karl Marx*, London, 1999.

Woodhouse, A.S.P. (Ed.), *Puritanism and Liberty: Being the Army Debates (1647-49) From the Clarke Manuscripts*, London, 1992.

Woodham-Smith, Cecil: *The Great Hunger*, London, 1968.

Zeigler, Philip, *The Black Death*, Penguin, 1969.
An Anthology of Chartist Literature, Moscow, 1956.
Notes to The People: 1851-1852, vol. 1, Merlin, 1967.

INDEX

A

Abinger, Lord 254
Acts of Enclosure 6
Adams, W.E. 110, 337, 349
    Rural life 21
Althorp, Lord 76
American Revolution XXXVII–XXX-
    VIII, 39, 41, 47, 159, 359, 383
    Declaration of Independence
    XXXVI
Andrew, Alfred 304
Annual Register, The XXVIII, 39
Anti-Corn Law League (formerly As-
    sociation) 129, 130, 131, 132,
    201, 209, 237
Arnott, John 268, 273
Ashley, Lord 216, 259, 260
Atkinson, Richard 24
Attlee, Clement 365–366
Attwood, Thomas, MP 99–100, 104,
    116, 123, 124, 132, 133, 160,
    164–165
    Moral force argument 100
Aveling, Edward 344, 353, 381
Ayr, James 80

B

Bakunin, Mikhail 150
Bald, Thomas 247
Ball, John XXXIV
Bamford, Samuel 58

Barbes, Armand 329
Barmby, John Goodwyn 368
Barnard, Joshua 117
Bebel, August 344
Bee-Hive, The 351
Beer, Max 114–115, 224, 245, 254,
    257, 271, 296, 306, 384
Beesley, William 223, 246
Benbow, William 74–76, 147, 194,
    198, 233
    'Grand National Holiday and Con-
    gress of the Productive Classes'
    74, 156
Beniowski, Major 143, 151, 183
Berkeley, Bishop 274
Bible, The 5, 26, 114, 138, 233
Birmingham Political Union, The 76,
    99, 108, 117, 120, 125, 148
Black Dwarf 57, 64, 82, 84
Blake, William 26, 42, 192
Blanc, Louis 320, 329
Blanketeers, The 56, 74
Blanqui, Louis Auguste 329
Blewitt, Reginald, MP 175
Bolshevik Party, The XVI, 141
Bolton handloom weaver 11
    Lifespan of 14
    Wages of 12
Braxfield, Lord 44–45
Bray, John Francis 68, 70, 92, 113,
    378–379
    Labour's Wrongs and Labour's Rem-
    edy (1839) 70, 113

On women 71
Briggs, Asa 351
Bright, John 131, 209, 259, 332, 339,
   341
British Constitution, The XXV, 36, 44
British General Strike (1842) 76
   Committees of Action 230–232
   Delegates meeting in Manchester
      223, 227
   End of the strike 245–246
   General strike call 233
   'Plug Plot' 217, 219, 220
British General Strike (1926) XLIII,
   220, 231
Brougham, Lord 11, 78, 244
Broughton, Lord 172, 191
Brown, George 43, 172
Bull Ring Riots, The 162
Buonarroti, Philippe 93
Burke, Edmund XXIII, XXXV–XXX-
   VI, XXXVIII, 37, 51, 247, 357
   Reflections on the Revolution in
      France 47
Burns, John 162–163, 167, 173, 182,
   198, 361
Burns, Robert 42–43, 44, 124
Bussey, Peter 121, 136, 142, 162, 173,
   182, 184, 195
Byron, Lord 53, 61, 123
   Speech on frame-breaking 54

C

Campbell, John 237
Cardo, William 136, 173, 182
   Arrest of 183
Carlile, Richard 35, 56, 82–83, 92
Carlyle, Thomas XXVI–XXVII, 55,
   120, 280
Carnegie, Andrew 352
Carney, Mark 380
Carpenter, William 136, 167, 173
Carrier, William 172
Cartwright, Major John 39, 55
Castlereagh, Lord 52, 55, 56, 57,

   59–60
Cato Street Conspiracy XI, 60
Cazenove, John 74
Chadwick, Edwin 29
Chadwick, William 360
Champion, The 196
Charter, The 97–98, 184, 186
Chartism
   and the middle classes 170
   Arrests (1848) 306–307
   Arrests of leaders 193–195, 254, 255
   Chartist Co-operative Land Society,
      The 264
   Convention 133–134, 140, 193
   Birmingham Convention 148–
      150
   Calling of a general strike 166
   Convention (1848) 285
   Convention (1851) 314
   'Manifesto of the General Conven-
      tion of the Industrious Classes'
      152
   Move to Birmingham 148
   Return to London 164
   The First Convention (1839)
      140–145
   Discuss insurrection (1848) 302
   Dispute over signatures 300–301
   Electoral tactics 203–207
   Links with trade unions 223, 257
   Moral force 126
   National Assembly 288, 300, 302
   National Petition (1839) 155
      Rejected by Parliament 164–165
   National Petition (1842) 210
      Rejected by Parliament 215–216
   National Petition (1848) 270, 283,
      284, 286, 287, 291, 294
      Rejected by Parliament 309
   National petitions 120, 126,
      133–134, 140
   Physical force 43
   'Programme of the Charter and
      Something More' 314
   Women's Charter Associations 31,

247–254
Chartist Circular 43, 203
Child labour 15–17
  Children's Employment Commis-
    sion of 1842 15
  Commission's Report on Children's
    Employment of 1833 16
Clarendon, Lord 277, 289, 293
Clarke, Thomas 16, 310
Class consciousness 36
Cleave, John 108
Close, Reverend Francis 253–254
Cobbett, James Paul 141
  Resignation of 149
Cobbett, William 31, 36, 57, 61–62,
    77, 85, 104, 200, 223
  Death 92
  Flees to America 62
  On the French Revolution 62
  Political Register 55, 59, 62–63, 82,
    92
  Rural Rides 62
Cobden, Richard 130–132, 332, 341
Cockburn, Lord XXXVII
Collins, John 198, 209
  Arrested 122, 163, 172, 194
  Release 201–202
Combination Acts repealed 86
Communist International (Third) 369
Communist Manifesto XVIII–XIX,
    XXXIII, XLII, 93, 280, 291,
    314–315, 317, 319, 321, 324,
    326, 327, 347, 370, 372, 377,
    379, 385
Complete Suffrage Union 101, 209
Connolly, James 191, 349
Co-operative Magazine, The XXXVIII
Cooper, Thomas 211, 213, 233,
    237–239, 239, 244, 246, 255,
    266, 269–270, 347
Corah, William 235
Cordell, Alexander 177
  Rape of the Fair Country 15
  Song of the Earth 175
Cornish, James 304

Corn Laws (1815) 55–58, 69,
    129–132, 366
  Chartist disruption 129–130
  Food riots 55
  Repeal of XX, 80, 208, 258, 346
'Correspondence with Enemies Act'
    119
Corresponding Society Act of 1799
    200
Cotton Spinners Association (1843)
    257
Country Police Bill 147
Craig, Bailie Hugh 122, 167
Crisis, The 88, 92
Crown and Government Security Bill
    301
Cuffay, Mary Ann 308
Cuffay, William 296–297, 301,
    308–309

D

Daily Mail, The
  "Hurrah for the Blackshirts!" 356
Darby, Abraham 15
Darwin, Charles 242
  On the Origin of the Species 243
Davies, David 184
Debs, Eugene V. 51
Deegan, John 136, 172
Democratic Review 315, 325
Depressions 7
Desmond, Adrian 243
Destructive and Poor Man's Conserva-
    tive, The 92
Devyr, Thomas Ainge 143
Dickens, Charles 364
  A Christmas Carol XIII–XIV
  Hard Times 18–19, 22
  Oliver Twist 30
  The Old Curiosity Shop 19
Diggers XXXIV, 263
Dispatch, The 266
Disraeli, Benjamin 134, 216, 258
  Sybil XIII, 11–13, 136–137,

156–158, 222–223
Dixon, William 13
Doherty, John 86, 259
Voice of the People, The 384
Downing, John 308
Doyle, Christopher 212
Duffy, James 136
Duke of Wellington XXV, 61, 79, 197, 230, 244, 293
Dulcken, H.W.
A Picture History of England... Written for the Use of the Young (1866) 196
Duncombe, Thomas 205

E

Economist, The 28
Edinburgh Magazine 208
Edmunds, John 367
Edwards, Ness 176
Eldon, Lord 46, 52, 55, 59
Elliott, Ebenezer 82
Encyclopaedia Britannica (1854) XXIV
Engels, Friedrich 72–73, 131, 135, 192, 270, 319, 323, 324, 325, 344, 346, 382, 386
Break with Harney 332
Condition of the Working Class in England, The IX, XXXIX, 7, 103
Conflict with Jones 337–338
Hails revival of workers 381
On Chartism X, XVIII–XIX, XX, XXIV, XXVIII, 106, 209, 326–327, 327, 329, 330, 335, 344, 353, 354
On England's industrial monopoly 348
On English ruling class 8–9
On Ernest Jones 342–343, 344
On history XXX
On Ireland 275–276, 279
On Malthus 27–28
On Marxism 366
On party building 318
On Robert Owen 63
On Ten Hour Act 260
On the general strike 159
On the labour aristocracy 345, 347–348
On trade unions 366, 372
On universal suffrage 357–358
On women 16–17
Socialism: Utopian and Scientific 354
English Chartist Circular, The 196, 252
Examiner, The 283
Extinguisher, The 84

F

Factory conditions 36
Factory Act of 1833 62
Fairplay, J. 194
Fay, Thomas 308
Felkin, William 20
Ferguson, Adam 22
Fielden, John, MP 160, 205
Fife, John, Mayor of Newcastle 155
Fletcher, Matthew 162, 166
Fourier, Charles 63, 254
Fox, Charles 40
Fraternal Democrats 103, 281, 323–324, 325, 328, 386
Aims 384
French Revolution (1789) XVI, XXV, 3, 26, 40, 41–43, 45, 47, 51, 65, 102, 140, 151, 238, 247, 278, 384
Jacobins 51, 134, 142, 273
Jacobin Terror XXXVII
Louis XVI 43
French Revolution (1830) 92
Friend of the People 84, 312, 329, 332
Frost, John 136, 157, 167, 173, 181, 182, 184, 185–186, 188, 189, 190, 192, 193

Transported 192
Frost, Thomas 219, 281
    Forty Years Recollections: Literary
        and Political (1880) 298
    On Kennington rally 295
Fussell, John 306

G

Gammage, R.C. 30–31, 96, 98–99,
        100–101, 104, 111, 122, 135,
        180, 201, 204, 206, 252, 267,
        269, 303, 310, 314, 330, 349
    On Kennington rally 292–293
    Torchlit meetings 137
Gast, John 95
Gauntlet, The 92
General strike ('Holy Month') 143,
        155–159, 233
    12 August 165–168, 182
General Union of Operative Spinners
        86
German Social Democratic Party 360
Gerrald, Joseph 44
Gigot, Phillipe 270
Gill, William 136
Gilmour, Ian 356–357
Gladstone, William 13, 191, 216,
        343, 347
Glasgow cotton-spinners strike (1837)
        88, 120
'Glorious' Revolution XXV, 3, 76
Godwin, William XXXVII, 26–27, 42
Gomm, Major-General Sir William
        160
Gordon Riots 40
Graham, Sir James 228–229, 231,
        246–247, 255, 256
Grand National Consolidated Trades
        Union 67, 86
    Rules 87
Grant, Ted XLII
Gray, John 68, 70, 92, 378
    Lecture on Human Happiness
        (1825) 68

Great Northern Union 111–112
Great Reform Act (Betrayal) of 1832
        XXV–XXVI, 31, 36, 80, 91,
        96, 120, 191, 208
Great Reform Act of 1867 342, 346
Great Reform Act of 1872 346
Great Reform Act of 1884 346
Greaves, James 368
Grenville, Lord 76
Grey, Lord 76, 77–78, 284, 289,
        293–294, 300
Grocott, William 330

H

Habeas Corpus 45, 52, 57–58, 301,
        304, 307
Halliday 136
Hamer, Edward 178
Hammond, J.L. and B. XXVI, 21, 32,
        90, 281
    On Methodism 364
Hanson, Abraham XXIX
Hardy, Thomas 43, 45–46, 104
    Charged with treason 46
Harney, Julian XIX, XX, 1, 50, 67,
        84, 91, 97, 102–103, 107,
        109, 111, 129, 139, 142–143,
        145, 149–150, 151, 153, 155,
        163, 164, 182, 192, 195, 197,
        205, 212, 238, 250, 255, 262,
        266, 271, 282, 283, 291, 296,
        310–311, 312, 313, 314–315,
        319–321, 324–325, 326,
        327–329, 330, 338, 343, 345,
        351–352, 368, 375–376, 380,
        384–385
    Challenging Lord Palmerston 270
    Launch of National Party 332
    Looking for shortcuts 329
    Meeting Engels 103
    Montagnards 142, 160
    On Ernest Jones 310
    Relationship with Marx and Engels
        313

Threat of expulsion 151
Hartwell, Robert 351
Heath, Thomas 17
Hegel, G.W.F. XII, 5, 318
Heine, Heinrich 344
Hepburn, Thomas 113, 155
Hetherington, Henry 35, 77, 80, 83, 84, 85–86, 92, 93, 95, 96, 98–99, 102, 108, 112, 119, 122, 165, 178, 181
Hill, Reverend William 238–239, 239, 245, 255, 262
Hobson, Joshua 113, 368
Hodgskin, Thomas 68–70, 72, 92, 378
Holberry, Samuel 190, 194
    Death 254
Holcroft, Thomas 37
Holmes, John 194
Holyoake, G.J. 162, 368
Hone, William 82
Hovell, Mark 136, 351
Hume, Joseph 309
Hunt, Henry 56, 58–59, 61, 77, 83, 104, 200, 236
    Death 92
Hutchinson, Alexander 232–233, 246
Hutt, Allen 368–369
Hyndman, Henry 371
Hyslop, James 250

I

Illustrated London News, The 290
Industrial Revolution XXVI, XXX-VIII, 1–2, 5, 18, 21–22, 36, 38, 64
International Working Men's Association (First International) 103, 324, 342, 348, 351–352, 360, 369, 373, 386, 396
    Jones and Harney join 342
Ireland
    Coercion Act 276
    Emigration 14, 277
    Famine 274, 276, 277
    Penal Codes, The 274
    Radicalism 15
Irish Confederation 274, 277
Irish Tribune, The 307

J

Jackson, T.A. 278
Jewett, Benjamin 10
Johnson, Dr. Samuel 2, 59, 82, 164, 205
Jones, Edmund 286
Jones, Ernest XVII–XVIII, 32, 66, 84, 103, 108, 135, 269, 270, 282–283, 288, 289, 296, 306–307, 310, 310–312, 313–314, 317–319, 321, 324–325, 331, 332–335, 335–337, 342–346, 351–352, 363, 375, 380, 384–385
    Arrest 306
    Death 342
    Imprisonment 310–311
    Rebuilding Chartism 326–331
    Relationship with Marx and Engels 313, 339–342
    'The Song of the Low' XVII–XVIII, 321–322
    Wins court case against Reynold's 340
Jones (Welsh Chartist), William 185, 189–191, 212
Justice 360

K

Keats, John 42
Kersal Moor XXXII, 135, 161
King (Manchester Chartist), Mrs 264–265
Kingsley, Charles 297–298
Kydd, Samuel 309

L

Labour Representation Committee 354
Labour Standard, The 353
Lacey, William 308
Lafargue, Paul 354, 357
Laissez-faire economics 10, 13
Lamartine, Alphonse de 282–283
La Mont, John 252
Land Plan 109, 112, 263–265, 268, 302, 328
  O'Connorville 265–268
Langley, Baxter 341
Lassalle, Ferdinand 318, 340
Leach, James 201, 237, 239, 246, 279
  The Charter as a means to an end XXVII
Leach, John 212
Leeds Intelligencer, The 19
Leeds Working Men's Association 111–112
Lee, R.E. 92
Lenin, V.I. XXV, 225
  On Chartism XXXI, XLI, 160
  On English labour movement 345
  On parliament 356
  On the Webbs XXXI
Leno, John 351
Lewis, Lewis 77
Liebknecht, Wilhelm 344
Lilburne, John 106
Lincoln, Abraham 381
Linney, Joseph 213
Liverpool, Lord 52, 55, 58, 61
Llanidloes Riots 154, 178, 181, 189
Lloyd, George 194
Lloyd's Newspaper 266
London Corresponding Society XI, 43–46, 59, 104
London Democrat 84, 112, 143, 150–151
London Democratic Association (East) 50, 101–102, 107–108, 109, 112, 183, 247

  Contrast with LWMA 101
  Founded 102
Londonderry, Lord 249
London Dispatch, The 384–385
London News, The 341
London Working Men's Association XXXI, 96, 98, 100, 101–102, 112, 123, 180, 384
  Crown and Anchor meeting 104
  Founded 95
  On women 108
  Relations with ELDA 107
Lovett, William XXXI, 95, 96–98, 99, 100, 104–105, 107–108, 108, 111, 119–120, 121–122, 127, 142–143, 145, 148, 164–165, 183, 185, 198, 201, 208, 208–209, 360
  Arrest 122, 162, 172, 194
  Moral and physical force 97
  'National Association for Promoting the Political and Social Improvement of the People' 98
  On Bull Ring Riots 162
  On O'Connor 185
  Pacifism 96
  Resigns from the Chartists 207
Lowery, Robert 117, 124, 136, 142–143, 159–160, 165, 167, 182
Lucas, Elizabeth 178
Luddites XXVI, XXXVIII, 54

M

Macaulay, Thomas 2, 214, 274
  Defence of property 214–215
Macfarlane, Helen 321
Malthus, Thomas 11, 26–29
  An Essay on the Principles of Population 26
Manchester and Salford Advertiser 131, 134, 186
Manchester Examiner 266, 300
Manchester Guardian 188, 221,

251–252
Manchester Times 11
Mann, Tom 361, 367
Man, The 85, 92
Marat, Jean-Paul 102, 142, 151, 238
Margarot, Maurice 44
Marsden, Richard 136, 142, 151–152,
    165
Marseillaise 271
Martin, John 307
Marx, Eleanor 344, 361, 367, 381
Marxism defined 366
Marx, K. and Engels, F. XXVIII, XLII,
    3, 68, 72, 94, 102, 271, 280,
    313, 315, 319, 323–325, 326,
    328–329, 330, 331–332, 335,
    337, 339, 343, 358, 366–369,
    371, 373, 373–374, 379, 386
  1848 prelude to socialist revolution
    349
  Attend Congress of the Communist
    League 386
  Break with the Communist League
    330
  Holy Family, The 363
  On Robert Owen 63
Marx, Karl XXIV, XXV, XXVIII, 9,
    72–74, 91, 94, 103, 105, 254,
    270, 273, 280, 318–321, 323,
    324, 329, 332–335, 336–337,
    337, 342–344, 347, 352, 356,
    358, 368, 370, 371, 378, 385
  Break with Jones 339–342
  Capital 6, 25, 68, 72, 274, 368
  Collaboration with Jones 331
  On dictatorship of the proletariat
    373–375
  On exploitation 25–26
  On insurrection 245
  On Irish independence 348–349
  On Robert Owen 67
  On the origins of capitalism 5
  On theory of surplus value 369
  Strained relations with Harney
    329–331

Theory of surplus value 373
The Poverty of Philosophy (1847)
    72
Mason, John 130, 213
Match girls strike (1888) 353
Mather, F.C. 154
Mayer, Joseph 348
Mazzini, Giuseppe 320, 329
McDouall, Pete Murray XXVII, 136,
    137, 154, 162, 168, 194, 198,
    201–202, 205, 219, 224, 237,
    239, 246, 262, 303, 385
  Arrest 172, 194, 308
  Escape to France 255
McGrath, Philip 282, 285, 296
Meagher, T.F. 302
Melbourne, Lord 76, 87, 145, 179,
    191, 203
  Bans torchlit meetings 139
Meredith, Amy 189
Meredith, Margaret 178
Merrick, Daniel 224
Merthyr Guardian 179
Merthyr riots 55, 77, 176
Mill, John Stuart 9, 225
  Principles of Political Economy 6
Miners' Association of Great Britain
    88, 257
Mitchel, John 277–278, 289, 307
  Arrested 302
Moir, James 166
Moore, James 243
Moore, Thomas 125
More, Thomas 368
  Utopia XXXIV
Morgan, Jenkin 184
Morrison, James XLIII, 375–377
Moss, John 16
Muir, Thomas 44–45
Murphy, Thomas 123
Murray, Charles and J.F. 360

N

Napier, Colonel William 101

Napier, General Sir Charles James
    XXVI, 101, 146–147, 153–
    154, 160, 188, 191, 196, 222
Napoleon I XXV, 51, 234
Napoleonic Wars 28, 51, 76
Napoleon II 294
National Association of United Trades
    for the Protection of Labour
    253
National Charter Association 201,
    207, 210, 211, 236, 240, 281,
    314, 337
  Founding 199
National Reformer, The 93
National Typographical Association
    (1845) 257
National Union of the Working Classes
    (1831) 74, 77, 93, 96, 102,
    373, 384
Neesom, Charles 165–166
  Arrest 172
Neeson, Elizabeth 251
Neue Rheinische Zeitung 280–281,
    326
Newcastle Journal 89
Newcastle Weekly Chronicle 84
New Moral World 113
Newport rising 186, 187–191,
    192–193, 195–196
News Chronicle 364–365
New York Daily Tribune 335, 358
Noakes, John 263
Nonconformist 297
Nore and Spithead mutinies XXVI, 46
Northern Liberator 84, 89, 117, 196
Northern Star, The 139, 161, 165,
    168–169, 170, 172, 189, 194,
    195, 198, 203, 205, 207, 209–
    210, 214, 216, 219, 221, 223,
    224, 238, 245, 252, 263–264,
    265–267, 269–270, 273, 276,
    279, 280, 283, 284, 306, 310,
    312, 320, 323, 325–326,
    328–329, 375, 385
  Changed to The Northern Star and

National Trades Journal 262
  "Hurrah for the masses" 202–203
  O'Connor gives up ownership 313
  On Neue Rheinische Zeitung 280
Notes to the People 328–329,
    331–335
Nottingham Journal, The 266
Nottingham Mercury 252, 266

O

Oastler, Richard XXVIII, 18, 31,
    112–113, 116, 142, 223, 259
  'Factory King' 115
O'Brien, James Bronterre XXXIII,
    67, 72–73, 79, 81, 84, 86,
    92–95, 98, 102, 105, 112,
    116, 117–118, 121, 129, 131,
    142–143, 148, 165, 167–168,
    173, 186, 194, 198, 203–204,
    205, 209, 262, 266, 269, 313,
    317, 328, 352–353, 359, 372,
    373, 378, 380
  Against Anti-Corn Law-ers 132
  Arrest 172
  Attacks land plan 266
  Chartist aims 107
  Crown and Anchor report 105
  Life of Robespierre 93
  On history XXX
  On Poor Law 31
  Release 206
  'The Schoolmaster' 92
O'Brien, Mark 262
O'Brien, Smith 282, 302
O'Connell MP, Daniel 77, 88, 95,
    107, 109, 164, 274–275, 277,
    278
  Death 276
O'Connor, Arthur 109
O'Connor, Feargus XXIV–XXV, 77,
    84, 88, 97, 99, 100, 103, 108,
    108–110, 112, 113, 116, 117,
    119, 121, 124–125, 125–126,
    131, 134, 136, 137, 139, 142–

143, 148, 161–162, 167–168,
172–173, 185–186, 190,
194–195, 198–200, 204–207,
209–210, 216, 221, 223, 237,
240, 245, 255, 257, 261–262,
263, 264, 265, 266–268, 269,
271, 276, 282, 284–285, 288–
289, 295–296, 297, 300–301,
302, 309, 312–313, 313–314,
315, 325–329, 351–352, 360,
367, 375
Address to Irish people 279
Arrest 172
Attack on Harney and Jones 312
Death and funeral 313, 337
Election in Nottingham 270
'One party, one programme' 210
On Ten-Hour Bill 259
On the Anti-Corn Law League 132
Relations with Lovett 111
Release 206
Threat of assassination 288
Trial of 229
On the general strike 244
Operative, The 84
Orange Tree conspiracy 307
Otley, Richard 233
Owen, Robert XXXVIII, 63–65,
66–67, 69, 77, 85, 88, 92, 99,
113, 116, 263, 306, 368, 378
A New View of Society 64
Communist colony 65–67
Criticism of private property 64
'Harmony Hall' bankrupt 268
New Harmony 65–66

P

Paine, Thomas XXXV–XXXVI, XXX-
VII, 36, 41–42, 43, 45, 46–50,
61–63, 80, 102, 104
Age of Reason 83
Attack on monarchy 47
Common Sense 47
Escape to France 50

Mob attacks on him 50
Outlawed 50
Rights of Man XXXV, 40, 47, 49
Statue 51
Palmer, Fyshe 44
Palmerston, Lord 258, 270, 282, 293,
301, 384
Paris Commune XLIII, 349, 368
Partington, James 154
Peddie, Robert 190, 195
Peel, Robert 51, 65, 197, 203,
243–244, 255–256, 258, 282
Pelling, Henry 225, 360
Penderyn, Dic 77
Pentrich rising (1817) 42
People's Paper XXIV, 329, 333, 335,
337, 341–342, 358
Marx speaks at Anniversary meet-
ing 337–338
Peterloo massacre XXVI, XXXVIII,
42, 58–61, 102, 122, 135, 138,
140, 162, 188, 209, 223, 243
Phillips, Morgan 364–365
Phillips, Thomas 195
Phipps, Colonel C.B. 293
Pilling, Richard 221, 223, 232, 254,
256–257
Pinkerton, Allan 351
Pioneer or Trade Union Magazine 1
Pitkeithly, Lawrence 205
Pitt the Younger, William 45, 50, 94
Death of 52
Place, Francis 28, 78, 95, 96, 104,
111, 119, 121, 130
Plain Speaker 84
Plekhanov, Georgi 239
Poor Law, New XXVI, 27–28, 29–32,
36, 63, 91, 102, 104, 109, 112,
113–115, 117–118, 120, 123,
126, 132, 134, 157, 178, 204,
211, 221, 234, 251, 257
Guardians 15
Poor Rate 28
The Commissioners 29–31, 123
Workhouse 29, 30

Poor Man's Advocate 84
Poor Man's Guardian XXXVIII, 25,
    29, 35, 66, 72, 76, 77, 80–81,
    83–86, 92, 93, 98, 117–118,
    262, 372–374, 376
Potters' Union (1843) 257
Powell, 'Lying Tom' 308
Price, William 183, 184
Proudhon, Pierre-Joseph 72, 150
Punch 307
Putney Debates XXXV, 39, 141, 231

R

Radcliffe, T. 194
Radicalism 41, 43, 55, 77, 105, 112,
    116
  American 47
  Definition 41
Rainsborough, Colonel XXXV
Rebecca Riots 178–179
Red Republican, The 310, 312, 315,
    317, 320–321, 327, 375, 377
Reeve, Henry 281
Republican 82
Reynolds, G.W.M. 287–288, 312
Reynolds Political Instructor 84
Ricardo, David 10, 68, 72, 369
Richards, John 234
Richardson, R.J. 126
  Arrest 172
  Rights of Women 248–249
Ridley, Ruffy 213
Riley, Edward 194
Riot Act 58, 155, 170, 187, 222, 228,
    235, 236, 282–283
River Aire 19
Roebuck MP, John 95, 119, 205
Rothstein, Theodore 92, 350
Rotten boroughs 36–37, 78
'Rule, Britannia' 3
Rural life 20–22
Russell, Lord John 76, 101, 111, 119,
    154, 160, 164, 181, 192, 258,
    278, 294

Speech against universal suffrage
    214–215
Russian Revolution XXV, 49
Ruthwell, Miss 253
Ryder, William 151, 152

S

Sadler MP, Michael 258
Sankey, William 147
Scotch Cattle XXVI, 176–177,
    181–182
Scottish Chartist Circular, The 196
Scottish Convention 44–45
Seditious Meetings Act (1795) 46
Seditious Meetings Act (1817) 57, 140
Senior, Nassau 9, 13, 259
  Last hour theory 10
  On Ireland 10
Sexby, Colonel Edward XXXV
Shakespeare, William XXXIV
Sharpe, Alexander 306
Shelley, Frances Lady XXXVII
Shelley, Percy XXVIII, 42, 321
  The Masque of Anarchy 59–60
  'To the Men of England' 32–33
Shell, George XL, 186–187, 193
Sheridan, Richard 51–52
Sidmouth, Lord 52, 55, 57–58, 60
  Introduces Six Acts 59
Six Acts (1819) 59, 82
Six points of the Charter, The XL, 106
Sketchley, John 360
Skevington, John 166
Skirving, William 44
Slave trade 1, 4–5, 57, 191
Smith, Adam 6, 10, 68, 369
Social Democrat 353
Southern Star 196
Southwell, Charles 368
Spa Fields riots (1816) 42
Spectator, The 216
Speenhamland system 28
Spencer, Herbert 209
Spence, Thomas XXXVII, 43, 368

Stamford Mercury 50
Stanhope, Lady Hester 50
Stanley, Lord XXXI, 80
Star of Freedom, The 329
Stephens, Reverend R.J. XXVIII, XL,
  31, 112–113, 114–116, 117,
  121, 123, 125–127, 134, 136,
  137, 139, 172, 182, 248
  Arrest 139, 194
  Knife and fork question XXXII
Sturge, Joseph 208–209, 262, 283
Suffield, Lord 77
'Swing Riots' 77, 139
Szonakowski 282

T

Taunton, William XXVII
Tawney, R.H. XXXI
Taylor, Alexander 213
Taylor, Cooke 2, 255
Taylor, John 91, 108, 117, 142, 147,
  155, 161–162, 164, 167–168,
  181, 182, 195
  Arrest 172
Taylor, Lt. Colonel Pringle 190
Ten-Hour Bill 132, 259–260, 260,
  346
  Movement 257
Thackeray, William 4, 48
Thelwall, John 35
Thomas, Dylan 85
Thompson, Dorothy 190
Thompson, E.P. 5, 84
Thompson, William 68–70, 368, 378
Thorne, William 360, 367
Times, The 33, 49, 59, 189, 253, 274,
  296, 321
  On socialism and communism 290
  "Scotched not dead" 305
Tocqueville, Alexis de 273, 279
Tolpuddle Martyrs 85, 87, 89
Tone, Wolfe 40–41, 42, 51, 277
Towns
  Growth of 18–20

Trades Journal 232
Trade unionism 52–53, 91, 257,
  366–367
  Oath taking 52
Treason Act (1817) 57
Trevelyan, Sir Charles 277, 290
Tribune of the People 84
Trotsky, Leon 346, 350, 371, 381
  On British power 2
  On Chartism XXVII, XLIII–XLIV,
  361
  Where is Britain Going? 361–362,
  363–364
True Scotsman 93, 196
Tyler, Wat XXXIV, 303

U

Unfettered Thinker and Plain Speaker
  for Truth, Freedom and Prog-
  ress 84
United Irishman, The 277–278
  Irish Felon 289, 307–308
United Irishmen 40, 44, 51, 146, 162,
  183, 274
Unstamped press XXVI, 59, 82–86,
  102
Ure, Dr Andrew 9–10

V

Vale, Reverend Dr. 244
Vernon, W.J. 306
Victoria, Queen 49, 195, 229, 243,
  293
Vincent, Henry 100–101, 119, 136,
  141, 143, 148, 163, 164, 176,
  180–182, 184–186, 189, 205,
  209, 264
  Arrest 172
  Closure of paper 196
  Teetotal plan 199–200
Vogt, Karl 348

W

Wade, Reverend Arthur 123, 141
Walker, Thomas 45
Warden, John 136
Waterloo, Battle of XXV, 51, 184, 293
Watkins, John 207, 379
    Address to the Women of England
        250
Watson, James 56, 92, 96
Watts, John 368
Webb, Richard 264–265
Webb, Sidney and Beatrice XLIII
    Disdain for Chartism XXXI
Weerth, George 110
Weitling, Wilhelm 368
Welshman, The 177
Wemyss, Colonel 160, 222
Western Vindicator, The 101, 140,
        141, 189, 196
West, James 212
Westminster Review 67
Weydemeyer 340
Wheeler, T. 213
Whiteboys, The 109, 112
White, George 202, 213, 219, 253
Whitlam, Gough 47
Wilberforce, William 57
Wilkes, John 37–40, 104
    Expelled from the Commons 37
    Lord mayor 38
    Political rights 38
    Popular agitation 38
    Support for America colonists 39
Williams, Ann 178
Williams, Caroline Maria 108
Williams, Chris 196
Williams, Joseph 306
Williams, Zephaniah 184, 185,
        188–190, 192, 212
Wilson, Benjamin 242, 284
    The Struggles of an Old Chartist
        360
Wilson, Harold 365, 371
Winstanley, Gerrard XXXIV, 263

Wollstonecraft, Mary XXXVII, 42
    Vindication of the Rights of Men, in
        a letter to the Right Honour-
        able Edmund Burke 247
    Vindication of the Rights of Women
        247
Women workers 247–253
Wordsworth, William 41–42
Working Man's Friend, The 92
Wyvill, Reverend Christopher XXXVI,
        46

Y

Young Ireland 274, 277

LIST OF TITLES BY WELLRED BOOKS

Wellred Books is a UK-based international publishing house and bookshop, specialising in works of Marxist theory. A sister publisher and bookseller is based in the USA.

Among the titles published by Wellred Books are:

Anti-Dühring, Friedrich Engels

Bolshevism: The Road to Revolution, Alan Woods

Chartist Revolution, Rob Sewell

China: From Permanent Revolution to Counter-Revolution, John Roberts

Dialectics of Nature, Frederick Engels

Germany: From Revolution to Counter-Revolution, Rob Sewell

Germany 1918-1933: Socialism or Barbarism, Rob Sewell

History of British Trotskyism, Ted Grant

Imperialism: The Highest Stage of Capitalism, V.I. Lenin

In Defence of Marxism, Leon Trotsky

In the Cause of Labour, Rob Sewell

Lenin and Trotsky: What They Really Stood For, Alan Woods and Ted Grant

Lenin, Trotsky and the Theory of the Permanent Revolution, John Roberts

Marxism and Anarchism, Various authors

Marxism and the USA, Alan Woods

My Life, Leon Trotsky

Not Guilty, Dewey Commission Report

Permanent Revolution & Results and Prospects Leon Trotsky

Permanent Revolution in Latin America, John Roberts and Jorge Martin

Reason in Revolt, Alan Woods and Ted Grant

Reformism or Revolution, Alan Woods

Revolution and Counter-Revolution in Spain, Felix Morrow

Russia: From Revolution to Counter-Revolution, Ted Grant

Spain's Revolution Against Franco, Alan Woods

Stalin, Leon Trotsky

Ted Grant: The Permanent Revolutionary, Alan Woods

Ted Grant Writings: Volumes One and Two, Ted Grant

Thawra hatta'l nasr! - Revolution until Victory! Alan Woods and others

The Classics of Marxism: Volume One and Two, by various authors

The First Five Years of the Communist International, Leon Trotsky

The First World War: A Marxist Analysis of the Great Slaughter, Alan Woods

The History of the Russian Revolution: Volumes One to Three, Leon Trotsky

The History of the Russian Revolution to Brest-Litovsk, Leon Trotsky

The Ideas of Karl Marx, Alan Woods

The Permanent Revolution and Results & Prospects, Leon Trotsky

The Revolution Betrayed, Leon Trotsky

The Revolutionary Philosophy of Marxism, John Peterson [Ed.]

The State and Revolution, V.I. Lenin

What Is Marxism?, Rob Sewell and Alan Woods

What is to be done?, Vladimir Lenin

To order any of these titles or for more information about Wellred Books, visit wellredbooks.net, email books@wellredbooks.net or write to Wellred Books, PO Box 50525, London E14 6WG, United Kingdom.